D0876999

NEW DIRECTIONS IN PORTFOLIO ASSESSMENT

NEW DIRECTIONS IN PORTFOLIO ASSESSMENT

REFLECTIVE PRACTICE, CRITICAL THEORY, AND LARGE-SCALE SCORING

Edited by

Laurel Black
Saint John Fisher College

Donald A. Daiker
Miami University

Jeffrey Sommers
Miami University-Middletown

Gail Stygall
University of Washington

Boynton/Cook Publishers
HEINEMANN
Portsmouth, NH

Boynton/Cook Publishers, Inc.
A subsidiary of Reed Elsevier Inc.
361 Hanover Street
Portsmouth, NH 03801
Offices and agents throughout the world

© 1994 by Boynton/Cook Publishers, Inc.
All rights reserved. No part of this book may be reproduced in any form or by any electronic or mechanical means, including information storage and retrieval systems, without permission in writing from the publisher, except by a reviewer, who may quote brief passages in a review.

Editor: Peter Stillman
Production: Nancy Sheridan
Cover design: Phillip Augusta

Every effort has been made to contact the copyright holders for permission to reprint borrowed material where necessary. We regret any oversights that may have occurred and would be happy to rectify them in future printings of this work.

Library of Congress Cataloging-in-Publication Data

New directions in portfolio assessment / edited by Donald A. Daiker . . . [et al.].
    p.   cm.
    Includes bibliographical references.
    ISBN 0–86709–338–2
    1. English language—Composition and exercises—Study and teaching (Secondary)—Ability testing.   2. English language—Rhetoric—Ability testing.   3. Portfolios in education.   I. Daiker, Donald A., 1938–
    LB1631.5.N48   1994
    808'.042'071—dc20
                                                                    93–43350
                                                                    CIP

Printed in the United States of America on acid-free paper.
98   97   96   95   94   EB   1   2   3   4   5   6   7   8   9

Contents

Acknowledgments

We thank the colleagues and friends who helped to make this book and to organize the Miami University conference on "New Directions in Portfolio Assessment" from which these essays come.

We are especially grateful to the following:

Max Morenberg—a conference director without peer;

Conference coordinators Debbie Bertsch, Bob Broad, Kathy Burton, Meaghan Hanrahan Dobson, Edwina Helton, Cindy Lewiecki-Wilson, Erica Scott, and Shannon Wilson—who made it all happen;

Program committee members Paul Anderson, Bob Broad, Kathy Burton, Jennie Dautermann, Meaghan Hanrahan Dobson, Edwina Helton, John Heyda, Bob R. Johnson, Cindy Lewiecki-Wilson, LuMing Mao, Max Morenberg, Diana Royer, Erica Scott, and Janet Ziegler—who selected the presentations that became the essays here;

Miami University Department of English Chair C. Barry Chabot—whose support has been enthusiastic, substantial, and constant;

Erica Scott—who helped in many, many ways with manuscript preparation;

Peter Stillman—a good friend, fine poet, and wonderful editor;

The Fund for the Improvement of Postsecondary Education (FIPSE) of the U.S. Department of Education—which made possible the establishment of Miami University's Portfolio Writing Program and which supported both the conference and this publication.

Thank you all.

Laurel Black
Don Daiker
Jeff Sommers
Gail Stygall

NEW DIRECTIONS IN PORTFOLIO ASSESSMENT

Introduction

Gail Stygall
Laurel Black
Donald A. Daiker
Jeffrey Sommers

Portfolios have dominated discussion about writing assessment and classroom evaluation over the past five years. In 1989, as the four of us began work on our proposal to the Fund for the Improvement of Postsecondary Education, several portfolio assessment projects were already under way, including Pat Belanoff's and Marcia Dickson's collection *Portfolios: Process and Product*. As we write this introduction, we know of large-scale portfolio assessment projects or classroom evaluation programs in an increasing number of sites. The American Association of Higher Education now publishes a pamphlet listing institutions where portfolios are used, the ERIC system Clearinghouse for High Education Assessment Instruments recognizes portfolios as an independent assessment tool, and it now also publishes a pamphlet listing articles and contacts for those exploring portfolios. Portfolio use exploded as those concerned with writing assessment and classroom evaluation of writing saw the portfolio as the natural extension of our prior demands for direct-writing assessment and our perceived need to evaluate writing in the process-driven classroom.

While the move away from indirect writing assessment through multiple-choice grammar and style instruments and the concomitant move to direct assessment through holistic scoring of single-sitting, impromptu essay exams answered questions of "face" validity, issues of content and construct validity continued to loom. While many teachers who used a process approach to teach writing no longer faced the problem of a multiple-choice grammar and style test in their own classrooms, they often found themselves and their students facing a single-sitting, impromptu writing exam at the end of the term or at the beginning of the next level of instruction. Thus, the discipline's first move toward "face validity," assessment of an actual piece of writing, was only a partial solution. It did assess actual writing, but only one piece of it, generated in a short period of time, under test conditions. Moreover, it did not reflect how students had been taught or what they had learned from that teaching. Surely, a single piece of writing could not and did not represent the range of students' abilities; consequently, content validity—the range of abilities being measured—was still an issue. Perhaps more importantly, and to some observers more ominously, the questions of construct ability remained unanswered. What is good writing? What are its elements and how widely does the community share those elements? Portfolios seemed to us and to many others a reasonable answer to questions of content validity and at least a partial answer to questions of construct ability, insofar as the wider community of English teachers could agree on the definition of good writing. As Peter Elbow stresses in his introduction to the Belanoff and Dickson volume, "it's a matter of improved *validity*. That is, portfolios give a *better picture of students' writing abilities*" (xi).

It is evident from these essays that practitioners and researchers in portfolio assessment embrace the often messy, usually ambiguous package that portfolios represent. The essays in this volume represent a range of approaches found in serious discussion of composition issues, but they focus most heavily on reflective practice. We believe that the essays in this volume describing classroom practice have moved beyond "show and tell," and into well-theorized reflective practice. Portfolios, as they are presented in this volume, seem to crystalize two rather different constructs of writing ability. One construct presupposes a general competence in writing. This general competence is abstract, but measurable, and separable from any specific context. The other construct is based in the writing classroom and is specific, local, and assumes there is no student writing separable from the context of the classroom. Not surprisingly, there is considerable tension demonstrated in this volume between the competing and conflicting demands of these two constructs.

The felt knowledge of writing teachers, the one that says portfolios adequately address the connection between classroom and writing, is tenacious. In spite of a number of calls for experimental and positivistic research to "prove" that portfolios do a better job of teaching or assessing writing, the discipline has resisted this specific call. Instead, the research on portfolios has been more classroom-based, more reflective, and more qualitative in nature. Even when the traditional educational research paradigm is invoked and presented, the researcher can still "feel" that somehow such research couldn't capture what portfolios were about. The recent *RTE* article by Nancy Westrich Baker, "The Effect of Portfolio-Based Instruction on Composition Students' Final Examination Scores, Course Grades, and Attitudes Toward Writing," is a case in point. Though she could not demonstrate that portfolios worked better in classrooms using a traditional research design, Baker nonetheless concludes that

> despite a lack of significant results, this study still shows portfolios to be a feasible instructional and evaluative tool in college composition courses. Instructors in the portfolio-based classrooms noted that students responded positively to the use of portfolios and that a relaxed atmosphere developed, possibly as a result of delayed evaluation and the shift in the teacher's role from judge to mentor. (171)

Why the tenacious belief in portfolios? We suggest at least two reasons: as above, we believe Baker's felt sense of the classroom was telling her that portfolios made a difference. Additionally, we have come to believe that the research paradigm she used to capture the effectiveness of portfolios was inadequate for this particular purpose.

In order to reflect teachers' felt experience, we present essays that closely examine individual classrooms, problematize particular practices, and isolate sites rich for portfolio evaluation. But we also present essays that begin to sketch a research perspective on portfolios, research emerging from the aggregate data available in large-scale portfolio projects. Portfolio scoring sessions, gender issues, and writing program administration problems are presented and a variety of research methodologies are evident: the case study, quantitative analysis, discourse analysis, and reflective administrative practice. This is not, of course, the single methodology that some educational researchers, Bereiter and Scardamalia, for example, have argued is necessary to validate research in composition. We believe, as does Gesa Kirsch, in methodological pluralism. Kirsch argues that research itself is socially constructed and suggests that composition, like feminism, must embrace methodological pluralism. She says,

> For composition studies, this kind of research means opening up the research agenda to subjects, listening to their stories, and allowing them to actively participate, as much as possible in the design, development, and reporting of such research. (257)

We believe that the essays in this volume begin the effort to theorize our practice and begin to construct new research agendas in writing assessment.

The Structure of the Volume

Our own FIPSE-funded project tested the possibility of improving that picture of students' writing abilities by examining the efficacy, fairness, and validity of using portfolios for large-scale assessment. One of the by-products of that research carried out from 1990 to 1992 was the Miami University Conference on Portfolios held October 1-4, 1992. Through that conference we attempted to bring together some of the diverse strands, weaving portfolios into different material conditions, "new directions" in both teaching and assessment. This volume represents the conference papers that we thought best represented these new directions.

We have divided this volume of twenty-six essays into three parts. In Part One, we highlight the perspectives of the four keynote speakers for the conference—Pat Belanoff, Edward M. White, Peter Elbow, and James Berlin. In Part Two, we take up the issues and directions of portfolios in the classroom. Thirteen essays constitute this classroom section, and we have further divided them into subsections on *Students' Voices, Teachers' Voices,* and *Teacher Training.* In Part Three, we present discussion on issues of large-scale portfolio assessment, in nine essays, divided into two sections on scoring and administration. We believe that these perspectives identify the major themes in contemporary discussions of portfolios. Accordingly, there is no repetitive, cheerful note here; instead we find extensive problematization of portfolios and full recognition of the ambiguities of school-sponsored writing and portfolio assessment.

In Part One, the tension between teaching and testing is at issue in Pat Belanoff's essay "Portfolios and Literacy: Why?" as she asks us to examine why portfolios have become relevant in the current educational climate and what cautions are needed to prevent portfolios from becoming opportunities for conventional testing rather than full literacy events. Following the Belanoff essay, the debate between Peter Elbow and Edward M. White identifies a new tension between those who see portfolios as a source of discussion and disagreement within the community of writing teachers, and those who see portfolios' potential reliability and validity as the English composition community's best defense against quantitative testing proponents. Thus, on the one hand, Peter Elbow in "Will the Virtues of Portfolios Blind Us to Their Potential Dangers?" argues that reducing portfolios to a single score, as is necessary in most portfolio assessment schemes, represents a very real problem, perhaps undermining our own teaching with portfolios. Edward M. White, on the other hand, in "Portfolios as an Assessment Concept," reminds us that portfolios represent the best possibility we have in writing assessment to prevent a return to indirect measures of writing. The final essay in this initial grouping, by James Berlin, "The Subversions of the Portfolio," suggests that we reconsider the meanings of portfolios through the framework of postmodern theories of subjectivity and texts, cautioning against the commodification of our students—via their rich portfolios—into just another product on the market, packaged, dressed-up, and presented to prospective employers.

For Part Two's first section, *Students' Voices,* we have selected five essays in which student voices are heard most clearly. Two of the five articles present perspectives on the portfolio cover letter, often the first piece of writing readers of portfolios experience. Tom Romano's piece, "Removing the Blindfold: Portfolios in Fiction Writing Classes," points to the portfolio cover letter as a site for self-evaluation where writers must demonstrate their understanding of the change and success in their writing. Romano emphasizes the difference between fiction writing and the exposition and explanation that student portfolio cover letters demand. Glenda Conway's "Portfolio Cover Letters, Students' Self-Presentation, and Teachers' Ethics" examines the port-folio cover letter quite differently by interrogating our desire as teachers to have students take a positive rhetorical stance toward their work and their writing classes. Conway asks us to reflect on our own motivations for portfolio cover letters and reminds us that we must provide opportunities for students to practice what we are requiring in the letters, and perhaps even to consider not requiring the letters at all. John Beall and Cheryl Forbes write the two follow-ing essays from different points—hearing students' voices from our perspec-tive of portfolio audience. In his essay "Portfolios, Research, and Writing about Science," John Beall argues that students can become teachers of their teachers when the students make more specialized science topics accessible to the lay reader. Beall's essay points out that this is possible even in the high school classroom and that portfolios allow the student to develop the topic over time while he (Beall's school is all-male) becomes comfortable in the role of expert. In "Reading Portfolios Conversationally," Cheryl Forbes scrutinizes the developing and interacting relationships between students in the portfolio classroom, a classroom in which those relationships can have considerable impact. Forbes reads two female students' portfolios, one from a Korean immigrant, one from a conventional white middle-class student, collabora-tively, listening for both voices in each portfolio. Finally, we close the section with a research essay by William H. Thelin, "The Connection Between Response Styles and Portfolio Assessment: Three Case Studies of Student Revision." In this essay, Thelin carefully examines a teacher's commentary on portfolios, students' revision, and the teacher's original goals for the course. In this case, students' voices indicate that the course goals and the portfolio assessment were in considerable conflict. Collectively, these five essays ask us to hear student voices differently, to ask the fiction writer to become analytic, to consider the impact of teachers' desires on students' portfolio letters, to ask the high school science writer to step into the expert's role, to allow students' voices to be read interactively, and to envision how students hear and act on their perceptions of our goals.

The second subsection, *Teachers' Voices,* suggests a wide range of teacher responses to portfolios. Two of the four essays discuss the authors' decisions *not* to use portfolios in their classrooms, considered within the context of the profession's increasing use of portfolios. In the first essay, "Collabora-tion, Collages, and Portfolios: A Workshop" by Agnes Cardoni, Rebecca Fraser, and Janet Wright Starner, we read a collage of voices drawn from a collaborative workshop as teachers try, doubt, explore, and assess portfolios. Sandra Murphy, in "Writing Portfolios in K-12 Schools: Implications for Linguistically Diverse Students," argues that portfolios are particularly potent for such students. Using California's public school population composed of 52 percent ethnically diverse students as an example, Murphy emphasizes that we can demonstrate through portfolios what our students know and what cultural and rhetorical approaches work in diverse classrooms. In "Portfolio Pedagogy: Is a Theoretical Construct Enough?" Sharon Hamilton affirms that while portfolios may encompass a theoretically sound approach to pedagogy and assessment, portfolios are not *necessarily* connected to process-based classrooms and consequently not every writing class is a portfolio classroom. James A. Reither and Russell A. Hunt take this idea a step further when they discuss their program's early experience with portfolios, which led them to reject portfolio use for assessment. Their solution, based on the Bakhtinian definition of utterance as always being a response, is to create a classroom where all the documents always have consequences.

In the final section of Part Two, *Teacher Training,* we present four essays focused on how portfolios can be used in teacher training. Chris M. Anson, in the first essay in this section, "Portfolios for Teachers: Writing Our Way to Reflective Practice," presents an argument for developing teaching portfolios to provide a deep representation of our teaching practice. Anson suggests a variety of ways in which teaching portfolios can be serious, professional documents of how and why we teach writing as we do. He closes with vignettes on how those teaching portfolios would vary among institutions. Nedra Reynolds' essay, "Graduate Writers and Portfolios: Issues of Professionalism, Authority, and Resistance," shows us the possibilities available to graduate students in rhetoric and composition when we structure graduate coursework around the portfolio. Reynolds uses the portfolio to assist graduate students in writing professionally, by preparing proposals, conference papers, and reflections on that work. Here, too, portfolio cover letters become an important vehicle for examining how our own teaching practice is received, by examining cover letters that suggest the writer's burgeoning authority or the writer's resistance. The next two essays, Kathleen Blake Yancey's "Make Haste Slowly: Graduate Teaching Assistants and Portfolios," and Irwin Weiser's "Portfolios and the New Teacher of Writing," speak directly to each other. Yancey's essay cautions against overloading with portfolios the new graduate teacher of writing when such teachers may be overwhelmed with the process of teaching and evaluating itself. She suggests that many programs make no allowance for the conflicting demands faced by graduate teachers and that requiring portfolios—in addition to all other requirements—may push new teachers away from long-term portfolio use in the classroom. Weiser suggests otherwise. He argues that the new teacher of writing can be supported by institutional training and subtle schedule adjustments so that these teachers' obligations are spread more evenly. He fears that not using portfolios—even with new and inexperienced teachers of writing—perpetuates a conflicting message about the process classroom: single paper grades count more than the revision process.

Part Three, the final section, takes up the questions of large-scale portfolio assessment. We have divided this section into two subsections, one focused on portfolio scoring, the other on administration of portfolio assessment. The essays in these two sections take up important questions of research and reflective practice in the larger scale.

In *Issues in Portfolio Scoring* we have selected five essays in which examinations of portfolio scoring, rater training, and scoring sessions are foregrounded. One category meriting special scrutiny is gender as our own Miami University Portfolio Assessment Project provided the data for the first two articles. Laurel Black, Donald Daiker, Jeffrey Sommers, and Gail Stygall's "Writing Like a Woman and Being Rewarded for It? Gender, Assessment, and Reflective Letters from Miami University's Student Portfolios," clearly indicates that women students fare more successfully on portfolio assessment than they had on single-sitting, impromptu exams in the past. Black, Daiker, Sommers, and Stygall review the research on women and writing and examine a stratified sample of the 1991 Miami portfolios and especially their reflective letters for gendered rhetorical stance. Men and women students typically, but not always, enacted gender role expectations. However, women's indication of the importance of writing in their private lives as well as school lives was probably an asset in their portfolios' assessment. Stygall, Black, Daiker, and Sommers in "Gendered Textuality: Assigning Gender to Portfolios" make the argument that because portfolios provide a more complete range of students' writing, raters will inevitably "construct" a student writer when reading portfolios. In doing so, raters are also attaching gender to writing samples as the results of a session in which raters assigned gender after reading portions of portfolios would indicate. The authors also suggest that calibration, training, and scoring must explicitly address constructions of the student writer's gender and other categories so as not to reenact hierarchical patterns. Robert L. Broad, in " 'Portfolio Scoring': A Contradiction in Terms," argues for a fundamental rethinking of scoring portfolios. Drawing on theoretical work in reading—including the principle that there is no single fixed value for any text—Broad asks how it is that we have come to award a single score to a body of a student's work. In "Maintaining a Portfolio-Based Writing Assessment: Research That Informs Program Development," William Condon and Liz Hamp-Lyons demonstrate that changing how readers are trained can lead to more fairness in portfolio readings. Drawing from their earlier work in which the students' reflective letters appeared to have a powerful impact on readers' judgments, Condon and Hamp-Lyons adjusted the training and reading process and traced readers' responses to portfolio readings. They find that it is possible to change the process so that no one piece has any greater impact than any other on readers, suggesting that training and scoring sessions may be modified toward better practice. Finally, in the last essay in this section, Russel K. Durst, Marjorie

Roemer, and Lucille M. Schultz examine the conversations of teachers evaluating portfolios. The authors suggest that these conversations—of extraordinary importance in the effect they have on students—deserve serious and ongoing scrutiny for their markers of program effectiveness, teacher understanding of program goals, and negotiation of programmatic standards.

The second section of essays on large-scale portfolio assessment takes up the question of portfolio administration, and we offer four essays providing perspectives on this aspect of the uses of portfolios. Two of the essays examine portfolios from a writing program administrator's perspective. In the first of these, David W. Smit, in "A WPA's Nightmare: Reflections on Using Portfolios as a Course Exit Exam," looks carefully at how administrators use portfolios as assessments of students' performance in writing courses. Smit poses the problem as an opposition between locally-generated criterion referencing versus general writing competence. He argues that we have the former when we might want to pay more attention to the latter. In a close examination of borderline portfolios at his institution, he finds that the percentage of surprise cases—those portfolios that the instructor expected to pass and didn't or that the instructor expected to fail and passed instead—were quite small. However, the percentage of "surprise" cases disputed was very high. He closes with a plea that we rethink the tension between the local site and general competence. In the second essay examining portfolio administration, Charles W. Schuster emphasizes the tension between the portfolio as a pedagogical device and means of assessment and the demands of large-scale institution assessment. His essay, "Climbing the Slippery Slope of Assessment: The Programmatic Use of Writing Portfolios," sets out four scenarios in which conflict between these two aspects of portfolios is most visible. He suggests that institutional uses may undercut the pedagogical value of portfolios. This concern is echoed in the third essay in this section, Brian Huot's "Beyond the Classroom: Using Portfolios to Assess Writing." Huot argues that actual knowledge about portfolios is sparse and that in our zeal to shift assessment to reflect our teaching practice, we may be using portfolios in inappropriate instances. He suggests that portfolios should be considered as a part of a range of assessment options rather than an all-encompassing assessment instrument. In the final essay, "Portfolios in the Disciplines: Sharing Knowledge in the Contact Zone," Carl R. Lovitt and Art Young present a case study of alien cultures in the "contact zone," Mary Louise Pratt's term for the moment of meeting between the colonizer and the indigenous population. In this study, Lovitt and Young examine what happens when a Department of Finance works with English Department faculty on developing Writing-in-the-Disciplines (WID) perspectives through the use of portfolios. Study and acceptance of one another's culture is necessary for collaborative work on curriculum.

We believe that we present here a snapshot of the discipline's current perception of portfolios. It is a photograph in which some patches have faded and others have become more completely focused. Reflective practice, critical theory, and methodological pluralism combine here in a rich diversity. We hope, like Pat Belanoff and Marcia Dickson in their introduction to *Portfolios*, that our enthusiasm for this kind of thoughtful practice with portfolios will inspire and suggest other new directions.

Part One:
Perspectives

1

Portfolios and Literacy: Why?

Pat Belanoff

The burgeoning—perhaps even exploding—use of portfolios continues to startle me. Equally startling are the wide-ranging sites of portfolio use: school districts (inner city and suburban), state education departments (voluntary and mandated), colleges and universities (public and private, small and large), professional programs (teaching certification, nursing supervision), and departments in almost all disciplines from developmental writing to doctoral programs in quantum physics. This essay grows out of my struggle to come to grips with what is motivating this pervasive development. Behind my desire to understand lies a concern for the status of literacy in the writing classroom and the potential that portfolio use offers to nourish that literacy.

Literacy, a protean concept, can only be defined within the social context in which it is discussed. For my purposes, I adopt the three-part approach set forth by Scribner that she bases on the inevitable connection between literacy and society (8). She sees three metaphors at work in our understanding of literacy: first, "literacy as adaptation," which stresses functional aspects of the ability to read and write; second, "literacy as power," which stresses ways in which reading and writing can advance group and community status; and third, "literacy as grace," which stresses "intellectual, aesthetic, and spiritual participation in the accumulated creations and knowledge of humankind, made available through the written word" (14). Scribner concludes that "ideal literacy is simultaneously adaptive, socially empowering, and self-enhancing" (18). My argument here is that separation of these necessarily intertwined literacies weakens all of them.

When Peter Elbow and I introduced our portfolio system at Stony Brook, we never could have predicted either the conference that produced this collection of essays or the ensuing varieties of portfolio use across all levels of schooling. Why have so many teachers of such a variety of subjects and so many administrators in a variety of settings turned to portfolio use within classrooms and for purposes beyond the classroom? And, finally, echoing a question asked by Witte, Trachsel, and Walters, "What assumptions about the nature of literacy are made by those who create and administer writing assessment [specifically portfolio assessments in this case] and by those who judge writing performance?" (14).

In her 1986 article documenting the history of the testing of writing, Andrea Lunsford suggests several stages. The first, beginning in ancient Greece, was an oral stage. All education aimed to prepare upper class males to be literate, to be able to use language to bring about personally desired action within a particular environment at a particular time. The three literacies Scribner describes were inseparable. The primacy of oratory and its purposes in education survived through the Roman Empire and into the medieval universities of Europe. This primacy was particularly evident in the testing of students by oral examinations, which continue to be part of most doctoral programs.

Even in the early years of American universities, based as they were on English models, oratory maintained its primacy. Universities such as Harvard prepared young men to become masters of an oral literacy through which they could influence the public. Oral forms of testing maintained the interactive nature of literacy, and the exclusiveness of a system that barred women and males of non-elite classes from this education attests to the connection between literacy and power. Disregarding for the moment this elitist stance, one can applaud the symbiotic connections of oral testing, literacy, and the practice of literacy beyond the walls of educational institutions.

When institutions began to value the written word over the spoken word, these symbiotic connections started to fragment. Elizabeth Larsen traces this demise through an examination of the life and works of William Ellery Channing. She concludes:

> Channing finally places composing and rhetoric not within the arena of active truth seeking for purposes of political persuasion and explication—an arena where the boundaries are public and the audience composed of immediately reactive human beings—but within a private room with activity he thinks of as passive. (163)

Oratory became its own enemy as it often slipped into mere performance where the only outcome was applause. Debates on public issues tended to focus not on whether debaters could motivate listeners to action but on formal features of oratory. As print became the focus of schooling, testing changed from speaking in a public forum to reading aloud in the classroom. Harvey J. Graff quotes an eighteenth-century Boston school superintendent's "list of the characteristics of a good oral reader: 'a just enunciation of sounds as well as words; a careful regard to distinctness of pronunciation, and a proper fullness and modulation of voice' " (289). Graff describes an oral testing situation in which 150 students were tested in reading fluency during a one-and-a-half-hour period: thirty-six seconds per student! Small wonder that Horace Mann criticized oral testing and argued for written tests (Witte 18-21). This travesty and the growing reliance on print, as well as the "increasingly influential voice of empiricism" (Lunsford 5), led Mann and other educators to be suspicious of the subjective quality of oral examinations and convinced of the objectivity and impartiality of written tests (Witte 18-21). Such a belief in objectivity grew from the assumption that writing reproduced reality and could be judged by how accurately and clearly it did so. Accuracy and clarity were matters of form, independent of content or reality that by definition was accurate if not always clear.

This developing dichotomy had disastrous consequences for the teaching of writing, coming as it did at almost the same historical moment as the move toward departmentalization. Form became the province of English departments, and content the province of other departments. English departments were in charge of literacy-as-grace; other departments were in charge of disseminating knowledge, or literacy-as-adaptation.[1] This resulted in the separation of these two kinds of literacy, and literacy-as-power went underground. The literate person became defined as one who was "well-educated, having or showing extensive knowledge, learning, or culture."[2] This definition assumes that reading, writing, knowledge, learning, and culture, i.e., literacy, exist independent of power.

Graff concludes that our century began with two concepts of literacy: utilitarian and spiritual. The utilitarian concept viewed literacy "as a functional medium for the spread of practical information which could lead to individual and social progress"; the spiritual concept viewed literacy as salvaging "the drooping spirit of Western man from the death of religion and the ravages of progress" (6). The first view dismissed the role of language; the second view dismissed the role of the economic, political, and social realities of the world outside the academy. These two dismissals resulted in a dismissal by the academy of direct consideration of literacy as power.

Nonetheless, power stayed where it always stays: in the hands of those who can embed knowledge in language that moves others to think and act. English studies, including writing instruction, largely ignored nourishing the development of such language. Faculty in English departments dissociated themselves from instruction in oratory and tended to see functional literacy as comprised of a set of discrete skills, which could be taught and measured separately with no regard for the aims of discourse. This functional literacy was viewed as something different from the higher levels of literacy that grew out of reading and interpreting canonical literature. This is the period during which indirect assessment of writing became the norm: testing writing through multiple-choice tests that did not require students to write.

As long as the numbers and diversity of new students were limited, language educators could continue to believe they were imparting literacy to students by correcting their slips from standard language and their deviations from accepted forms and modes.[3] In truth, my parents profited from this schooling. And I—as a member of a white, upwardly mobile, lower class surrounded by many who spoke the language of power—profited too. My parents and I wanted to be part of a class of people whose language differed from ours; our outside-of-school motivation to learn that new language ensured that we would absorb inside-of-school lessons. But eventually this academic system of language inculcation could not counteract the pressures of changing demographic, economic, and political structures; the old methods became less and less effective.[4] After World War II, the nature of the American professoriat and student body changed. With the influx of nontraditional students, largely spawned by the GI Bill, colleges saw the need for general education courses, and with them came a renewed interest in the role of effective writing in reaching a general audience. At the same time faculty realized they could no longer ignore the painful truth that traditional teaching methods were not helping these "new" students become literate.

The search to improve writing instruction culminated during the 1970s in the process movement, which shifted classroom focus from *written products* to *writing processes*. With its strategy of intervention in a student's writing *as* she writes, process teaching emphasizes the role of purpose, situation, audience, and feedback—emphasizes, that is, context. In terms of testing, process pedagogy led to the rediscovery that a piece of writing is always more than the sum of its parts and that literacy needs to be evaluated holistically. Thus, process pedagogy was instrumental in ushering in a third stage of assessment: holistic evaluation of actual pieces of writing—though indirect testing of writing is far from obsolete.[5]

After the first flush of enthusiasm for direct assessment, doubts began to complicate our complacency. Most mass testing situations, even though they ask for actual writing, do not allow for genuine literacy; what ends up being evaluated has been generated under conditions where context—the testing situation itself—downplays content. Students are often given a serious subject and asked to write something about it with no opportunity to read about it, talk it over with others, or give it some thinking space. Realizations like these were our chief motivation for instituting our portfolio system at Stony Brook. We knew—and still know—that in a two-hour testing situation, students are hardly likely to take ideas seriously. Furthermore, researchers discovered that a given student's scores on such tests varied significantly and seemed to depend on the topic, the writer's state of mind, the particular situation, and other factors. In other words, whether one could generate an effective piece of writing was contextual even in situations that worked toward decontextualization.

Thus, our initial portfolio use at Stony Brook grew from the need to meet objections raised by timed, self-contained assessments of writing, recognition that process pedagogy is undermined by such testing, and a growing awareness of the contextuality of all language use.[6] As our system settled in, however, we began to see ramifications that produced unforeseen benefits. It was these ramifications that prodded me to examine more closely the connections between portfolio use and the varieties of literacy posited by Scribner: functional, social/political, and personal. I came to realize that portfolios are far more powerful instruments for change than we had first thought. One of the outcomes of introducing portfolios into a classroom or an assessment system—as almost everyone who uses them discovers happily or unhappily—is that they restructure everything. I have written elsewhere about these changes (Belanoff, "Addendum"); here I want to examine my growing awareness that the reasons we originally gave for using portfolios can explain neither their power to create change nor their omnipresence in today's academic world. The second part of my essay looks at this complexity.

Lunsford notes that one of the reasons for the movement from oral to written testing was the greater objectivity and impartiality seemingly attached to the latter. Now it is just that sort of scientism and its claim to empiricism that we are suspicious of. And so we move back to accepting the validity of the "inexact and imprecise" (Lunsford 5). Increasingly, scholars in all fields recognize that knowledge is the product of a particular stance in a particular situation: all knowledge is subjective and contextual. If that is the case, how can we defend assessing an individual student on the basis of a situation in which she may never again be?

Another factor Lunsford identified as contributing to the change from oral to written testing was the proliferating body of knowledge in our world and the growing specialization developed to cope with that proliferation. This specialization led to the development of diverse discourses within academia and eventually to the realization that academic language is not one thing but many. Now at least some of us (I wish it were more) have begun to realize that even though the discourses of specific fields have a purpose and need to be mastered by students, rigid styles of academic discourse do not facilitate communication between disciplines nor between a particular discipline and the public. I think this, in turn, has made us generally suspicious of the potential of one kind of writing to indicate over-all writing skill. As Patricia Bizzell notes in "Arguing About Literacy," too often literacy, as assessed by educational institutions, is academic literacy that recognizes no literacy other than its own. Portfolios seem to be a way of validating more than one kind of literacy.

But the collecting of multivoiced and multigenred pieces of writing into portfolios for evaluation has occurred for more reasons than the questioning of objective standards or the explosion of information into alienating professional language or jargon. College populations are continuing to diversify, cutting across ethnic, class, and racial lines more and more and, with the increasing numbers of English-as-a-second-language students in our classes, college populations are cutting across language lines also. The multicultural makeup of our classrooms inevitably alters our perceptions.

Alan Purves' survey of standards across national lines reveals that ideal rhetorics vary from country to country (see also Connor and Kaplan). Thus, both our experience and our research force us to realize that our literacy is just that: *our* literacy.

But then, of course (begins an often-repeated argument), if students are being educated in our schools, they ought to be educated to our standards. Certainly that was the accepted argument for many years and for many immigrant groups. However, perhaps because of sheer numbers, perhaps because of changes already underway as a result of our increased sensitivity to racial, gender, and class discrimination and increased awareness of the molding power of culture, standards and canons are coming under unrelenting attack and defense. Witness, for example, the debate about how much leeway to allow ESL students. Four years ago when we surveyed Stony Brook faculty, 80 percent of those who responded said they did not penalize ESL students for the sorts of errors that did not interfere with communication. Change is occurring. Feminist issues, often entangled with the place of the personal in pedagogy, and doubts about the primacy of expository discourse in the composition classroom further muddle our once secure confidence in academic monolingualism.

Economics (as usual) plays a role also since the number of college-age students is declining and institutions of higher education, needing to insure their income, have begun developing special programs to attract nontraditional students—some of them foreign, many of them older, but most of them United States citizens of a traditional age who have to work so much to pay for college that it takes them five or more years to acquire a diploma. These students often differ among themselves just as greatly as they differ from traditional students. Many of us have learned to respect what these students bring to the classroom and have consequently altered our teaching strategies. And so context begins to alter standards here, too, instead of standards always being in the driver's seat and distorting context.

In prior years, we were teaching the language of the academy, the kind of literacy that almost everyone agreed was the language needed for social, economic, and political success. Now we are not so sure we know what that language is. In some contexts, it is not wise to speak the traditional language of the white, educated male; it makes one suspect. Richard Rodriguez may have been happy that formal literacy in English gave him the tools to express certain ideas he thinks he could not have expressed otherwise, but if he was so happy, why the nostalgia, why the poignant sense of loss, why the title, *Hunger for Memory?* The question becomes whether or not we need to destroy native ways of using language in order to teach the prestige language. Keith Gilyard asks "if such cultural loss is a desirable aim of public education." He answers with a resounding "No! . . . the eradication of one tongue is not prerequisite to the learning of a second. Rodriguez participated in such self-annihilation *for as long as he did* because he thought it benefited him personally. It would be tragic, however, to translate his own appraisal of his pain into pedagogy" (143). And, of himself, Gilyard says: "Contrary to what some might have anticipated, mastery of the standard dialect did not in and of itself lead to outstanding formal academic progress, and, as the narrative indicates, I foundered badly" (159).

Multiculturalism, language and dialect diversity, and feminist awakenings have made many of us realize that we all have multiple languages—though, of course, Martin Joos told us that years ago. The diversity of my own students has spoken to—even nourished—the diversity contained in my own individuality. Modern critical theory posits a self that is a multiplicity of selves. It follows that these selves are not likely to speak the same language. Like us, all our students come into our classes literate in languages other than classroom language—a recent article in *Smithsonian* magazine discusses the language deaf students use among themselves as being different from that which they use in class with their teachers, although both are American Sign (Wolkomir). There is always a way of using language that the classroom asks students to set aside, with little attention to the value of such language in the students' world.

Then there are the psychologists who tell us that there is no such thing as a single IQ—that there are all varieties of IQs relevant to particular abilities: music, physical movement, art, composition, and so forth, as well as the purely intellectual ability that the old IQs supposedly measured. Most school systems have discontinued use of traditional IQ tests because they recognize the multiplicity of students' abilities and the single gaze of the IQ test. Is it not interesting that investors too do not want to put all their eggs in one basket, that where money is concerned—that thing our world revolves around—people want to diversify: they want stock *portfolios*, not just stocks. The best over-all gymnast or diver is not decided on the basis of one routine or one kind of dive, but on a variety. The baseball World Series is not just one game. Why is it that we do not unquestioningly give our students the same treatment and recognize that we cannot adequately decide their value on one event either—or even on a series of events viewed in isolation?

If Susan Miller is right, "composition, defined as the field around a freshman course, began in a political moment that was embedded in ambivalence about how to assimilate unentitled, newly admitted students in the late nineteenth-century 'new university,' which was in turn formed to address its era's social, economic, and political changes" (79). Is it possible that portfolio assessment is developing because we are not so sure about how to assess another influx of "different" students? And even those who are sure usually run chock-a-block up against others who are just as sure—but about directly opposing ideas. Before us sit students whose first language is not English, nontraditional students, students with widely differing cultural backgrounds and skin colors, students of widely varying ages, students far more interested in securing a job than in getting a liberal education, women who have new and different senses of themselves as learners. Mass testing can become a way, as Miller suggests, of keeping interlopers out while at the same time instilling in them the dream to get in. Are we doing that again?

But just as that earlier wave of students changed our colleges and universities, so this new wave—along with altered theoretical perspectives—is influencing what we do and think at the same time we are trying to influence how they write. When you do not know what to test for, it is best to spread what is tested over a wide field—a net spread widely is bound to catch something. I certainly do not mean to suggest by this that portfolio assessment is invalid. Just as that earlier wave of students eventually made us better teachers, so this new wave can force us to do what it would benefit us to do anyway. Bizzell "identifies the academy as 'an agent of cultural hegemony,'" which, by overlooking differences in discourse communities, represents certain world views and values as universals" ("Cognition" 22). Portfolios enable us to recognize and validate the multiple literacies that define genres as well as individuals.

Multiculturalism, nontraditional students, and new ways of approaching the world of texts can bring about a reaction opposite and opposed to what I have just set forth. While some seek ways to acknowledge and validate these trends, others seek ways to bring them in line with traditional educational values. These others often push for nationally standardized tests to ensure uniformity in educational goals throughout the country—a kind of re-homogenizing of society. Thus, we have one group pushing for portfolio assessment because it allows for diversity and another group pushing for standardized testing because it creates homogeneity. We can expect these two impulses to clash roughly in the next few years. My emphasis here on portfolio testing exists within my awareness of powerful forces pushing for something quite different. Indeed, I believe that part of the reason for the proliferating interest in portfolios may well be a recognition by many of us that we need to meet the demand for mandated testing at all levels with systems that do not undercut our teaching. Without that fear, many of us would have little interest in mass testing at all.

So this is the climate in which portfolio assessment has taken root and taken off. It has brought us to a fourth stage of language testing, chronologically subsequent to the earlier three stages: oral, indirect, direct. Everywhere I turn there is portfolio talk. It often frightens me. In truth, portfolios are not a cure-all; they are not going to magically make students better writers. What they are is enough: a way of integrating testing, teaching, and curriculum; a way of reintroducing a piece of the most laudable feature of oral testing, the awareness that literacy of all kinds exists within a social setting. I do not claim that portfolio testing can bring back a fully literate context. Since a good piece of writing is one that does what its author wants it to do in a particular situation, the only valid way to test writing is to follow its author to some context appropriate to what she wants to write and assess how well what she writes does what she wants it to do. I remember Neal Postman talking about this once and saying that in one of his early teaching jobs he did try to do this ideal testing. He asked students to write their parents a letter asking for $50.00. If they got it, they got an A. He asked them to write instructions for him to get to a particular place. If he got there with no false turns, they got an A. Interesting approach—like a performative portfolio of some kind. I like it. Perhaps some day that will be feasible; it is not now. So we have to see what we can do to get as close as possible to the ideal.

Brandt's definition of literacy as "one's involvement with other people—rather than with texts" (*Literacy as Involvement,* 32) helps me understand in other ways how and why portfolio assessment brings a degree of literacy back into the picture, even if the result is a less inclusive literate environment than prevailed in oral testing. It cannot be the same environment any of us write in outside school walls, but it does reproduce some of the complexity of this other environment: a variety of writers, readers, audiences, standards, purposes—a complex environment in which language exerts power at both functional and aesthetic levels. That is, portfolios engender the literacy within which they are created and evaluated; like language, portfolios both reflect and create the culture within which they communicate. As students produce the contents of a portfolio, the portfolio becomes an ever richer context for each of its elements. The teacher who reads and grades a classroom portfolio is forced to recognize the complexity of the author who produced the pieces, the way that author's skill developed over time and through genres, and her own varied ways of reading the variety of pieces before her. If this teacher shares portfolio reading with another teacher or other teachers, the environment defined by the portfolio doubles and triples. Teachers begin to discuss assignments, goals, methods of responding, classroom management, and standards. These discussions become part of who the teacher is when she closes her door and returns to her own now-not-so-isolated classroom. Through her, students participate in this enlarged context. If teachers grade portfolios collaboratively, standards become a part of the whole discussion. Eventually students are writing for a larger audience, partly known, partly unknown. If administrators recognize the validity of portfolio evaluation for bureaucratic purposes, they too become part of the literate environment in which they all work. Literacy, to repeat Brandt's words, is "one's involvement with other people—rather than with texts." Portfolio assessment brings people together to create a literate environment.

Potential power resides in the literate person. She knows how to use language and knowledge to make things happen: to change people's minds, to prod them to act, to encourage them to listen and weigh new, perhaps contrary, ideas—and she knows how to do that in all settings important to her goals in school and outside school. We cannot pretend to be educating students to be literate outside the school if we do not recognize that power functions within schools too. As Susan Miller says, "language *learning* [her emphasis] is the crucial locus for power, or for disenfranchisement, in any culture" (7); assessments of that learning are how power and disenfranchisement are wielded in school settings. The inherent connections between literacy, power, and language learning become increasingly complex in the contexts created by portfolio use. Mass assessment takes power away from teachers; it says that they cannot be trusted to evaluate their own students. Some portfolio systems maintain this distrust, but since portfolios represent more fully the complexity of an individual writer, they also represent the classroom teacher more. And if teachers design portfolios, as I think they should, some of the power once in the hands of administrators and test-producing corporations comes into the hands of teachers.

Portfolio assessment allows teacher authority and power to be distributed in a number of ways. For example, a particular teacher values argument above all other genres. In her classroom she stresses the writing of argument to the exclusion of other genres. Another teacher sees the writing course as a service to other disciplines and seeks to develop those skills which these other disciplines value. Another teacher places greater value on narrative and on writing from personal experience. Still another teacher weighs grammatical correctness heavily while the teacher in the room next to him accepts deviations from standard English with equanimity and rarely penalizes students for them. Our students have always known how widely the standards of their English teachers vary. We and they need to see this multiplicity as strength, not weakness. Portfolios can help here by enacting and rewarding diversity: they can require both arguments and narratives for completeness and insist that at least one or two papers be totally free of errors in standard English. They can include some pieces of writing assigned deliberately to prepare students for the writing required in other courses as well as pieces that have little to do with academic writing—fiction, letters to the editor, poetry, and such. Individual teachers' power shifts: they exert less over their own students and more over others' students.

Am I saying that portfolios are a way of keeping everyone happy? No, not exactly, but not *not* exactly either. What I *am* suggesting is that there was once a time when we saw, rightly or wrongly, our students and our own aims and those of our institutions as fairly homogeneous; thus we could assess writing on single pieces that exemplified our standards. Now, students and faculty are becoming heterogeneous and we are not so sure what our standards are and what our courses should be doing. Portfolios allow us to make our complexity—or confusion—manifest. The downside of this is that it may perplex our students and free us from making any commitment to what it means to write in a school setting and outside of it. The portfolio could be a way of being all things to all people and present such a mishmash to students that they end up with no way of structuring for themselves what it means to write. Worst of all, as teachers, we can look as though we are incompetent.

But there is a way in which teachers' power and authority are weakened even more definitively by portfolio use. Most of us teachers want univocality from our students; we want to believe that one piece of writing represents them well—simply because that implies a world that can be controlled. But different texts in a portfolio may actually conflict in some way, and then what do we do with that when we judge quality? In the one-to-one confrontation with an individual paper, we can feel in control; we can feel powerful, but we cannot feel quite so powerful in front of a portfolio. We are forced to face the writer, not just the writing. Perhaps this is one reason why I see people in some places turning or trying to turn portfolios into single statements of a student's ability rather than a polyvoiced statement whose voices are not necessarily harmonious. In addition, portfolios that incorporate student self-evaluation and allow them to choose contents lessen the authority and power of the teacher a bit more, and systems that require teachers to grade collaboratively dilute that power still a bit more. In sum, though teachers may gain power from administrators and from increased input into program standards and goals, they lose some of that power to students and other teachers.

In truth, portfolio assessment systems—when designed by those teaching the students to be assessed—redistribute power, draining some of it from the top and redistributing it along the bottom. Such redistributions of power can be threatening, particularly to those who now hold most of the power to determine what kinds of writing tests to administer and by what standards to assess the resultant writing. Were this sort of system adopted in institutions at all levels throughout the country, we would see power residing in groups of individual teachers and students. Since this power would be inextricably bound up with decisions about writing quality, we could see a literacy functioning within school walls that mimicked fairly well how literacy functions outside school walls. Unfortunately, decentralized authority is scary; to many it smacks of anarchy.

Perhaps those with power over assessment recognize these possibilities; those who stand to lose power are not likely to cede it willingly. I presume that they will attempt to bring portfolio grading into line with older forms of assessment by demanding that it be empirically demonstrated as valid and reliable. But attempts to squeeze portfolios into these traditional molds will cut into their lifeblood, for the literacy that they have created cannot exist within the artificial climate created by empiricist notions of assessment. Portfolios are valid and reliable within the contexts in which they are created. Outside those environments they are likely to become just another education gimmick to be discarded because they have not fulfilled their early promise.

Good teachers in all disciplines have always created environments in their classrooms that represent literacy in its fullest sense: literacy as adaptation, power, and grace within a social setting. Unfortunately, institutional requirements have a way of making it very difficult for individual teachers to create fully literate environments. I see portfolios as possessing certain inherent characteristics that introduce a fuller sort of literacy into assessment than that which existed in multiple-choice tests and one-shot essay tests of writing. This richer concept of literacy is one that contextualizes all writing to some degree. It is this sense of the shaping role of context that our students need to carry with them out of our institutions. In the end, the only genuine test of our students' writing and literacy occurs *after* they move away from us and our institutions.

Notes

1. My assumption here is that "knowledge," the facts imparted in departments such as history, mathematics, and chemistry, represents a high level of functional literacy since it enables its possessors to function within specific environments both in and outside of school. Lower levels of functional literacy—reading signs, instructions, and so forth—are looked upon as the responsibility of elementary and secondary institutions.

2. David B. Guralnik, ed. *Webster's New World Dictionary*. New York: Simon and Schuster, 1980.

3. For a full discussion of the social, political, and educational roles of language correctness at the end of the nineteenth century, see Boyd.

4. History is necessarily reductive and tends to ignore trends counter to those it is highlighting. I recognize that my history is far more complex than I have thus far stated. Even in the 1950s and 1960s when objective tests were at their zenith, there had been those who believed they undercut true literacy. J. M. Stalnake, for instance, advocated a notion of literacy as "an active, or interactive, one, a notion that stands in direct contrast to the utilitarian point of view, which sees literacy as enabling students to extract factual information from a text or to produce mechanically correct prose" (Witte 30).

5. Huot's "A Survey of University Writing Placement Practices" looks at questionnaires returned by eleven hundred postsecondary institutions; approximately 50 percent of these schools continue to use indirect testing for placement in levels of college composition. The CCCC Committee on Assessment recently distributed a questionnaire to elicit information about all purposes and forms of testing writing in colleges and universities; preliminary conclusions will soon be available.

6. At the Miami conference, I asked my audience to write briefly about why they or the academic systems in which they worked were interested in portfolios. Over two-thirds of those responding mentioned a lack of compatibility between teaching and testing methods as primary.

2

Portfolios as an
Assessment Concept

Edward M. White

In November 1991, I found myself in a suburb of Washington, D.C., participating in, what seemed to me, an ominous conference sponsored by the United States Department of Education called "National Assessment of College Student Learning (NACSL): Issues and Concerns." It seemed ominous because the conference was designed to gain the support of the assessment community specifically and higher education in general for a new educational idea, a bold stroke that would never have occurred to lesser politicians of previous generations. The government proposed to require a single national assessment for all American college graduates, a test whose results would be used to compare the effectiveness of different colleges and universities.

The information provided by this test, we were told, would lead directly to improvement in higher education at little cost to the government, since institutions whose graduates performed poorly on the test would be forced to shape up to look better in the ensuing glare of publicity. Thus, if the graduates of Harvard had better scores on this new national assessment than those of Cal State, San Bernardino (a not unlikely prospect), my university would be shamed into doing a more effective job in the future. (Indeed, as a longtime interviewer for the Harvard schools committee, I would bet on the scores of the *entering* Harvard class against ordinary state university *graduates;* such is the "outcome" of even a prospective Harvard degree, when we enter the world of naive political measurement.) Meanwhile those students and their parents who might be perplexed about which is the better institution, Harvard or Cal State, would have those doubts at last resolved by the test scores.

I hope you are duly astounded at the insensitivity of this enterprise, which is pressing forward despite many educational, social, technical, and financial difficulties that have surfaced. (The illusion that government can improve

25

education at low cost by naive measurement is so politically attractive that it will remain potent no matter who may be in power.) I also hope that you are shocked about hearing so little about a plan that would affect us all profoundly. Keep the acronym NACSL in mind, for it will not go away. No doubt it will change shape as it develops, perhaps gaining some wisdom as it goes. We, however, were told at the outset of the conference that the issue was not *whether* such an assessment should proceed but *how* it should be conducted.

In some ways, I found it hard to take the 1991 conference on NACSL seriously. For example, the conferees were supposed to develop ways to give a national test for college graduates in three skills defined by the presidential Goals Panel. The organizers of the conference imagined these skills as distinct: critical thinking, problem solving, and communication. In my irreverent way, I commented that only in Washington, D.C., could anyone imagine that critical thinking and problem solving have nothing to do with effective communication. Or, turning it around in response to the political campaigning then under way, only in Washington could anyone imagine that effective communication could occur without any kind of thinking at all.

But it would be a mistake to take the whole business as if it were a joke. Numbers of those at the conference registered alarm at the concept of a national assessment in critical thinking, problem solving, and communication. Many of us hoped that such an assessment, if it must happen, would be more than one more multiple-choice test and that it might be useful in the national debate about educational goals. The officials running the conference, however, and many of the conferees, spoke regularly of "the test" as if a national exam was a foregone conclusion and the only serious way to improve the skills of college graduates. There was more agreement than I imagined possible among the eighty educational and governmental leaders present that this kind of assessment—apparently massive in scope, cheap in cost, manipulative, and illiberal in purpose—would have to be multiple choice or otherwise machine-gradable. We must hope that new position papers and new conferences (for we may take comfort in the fact that nothing is likely to happen rapidly in Washington) will continue to argue against this scheme and continue to seek to moderate its simple-minded measurement assumptions.

I took it as my task at the 1991 conference to argue for portfolio assessment. I was one of the very few faculty in composition invited and the only one in composition asked to prepare one of the fifteen position papers that formed the working agenda of that conference. Half a dozen of those papers, including mine, were published in the January and June 1993 issues of the *Journal of General Education;* all of them are also in ERIC, under the general number of ED 340 (mine is ED 340-767). My paper argued as forcefully as possible that any national assessment of the effects of college upon students, if one had to take place, should happen by means of a portfolio assessment system. Instead of test development, I argued, the funding for the assessment should support the creation of a wide variety of sample portfolios for different kinds of students in different kinds of programs at different kinds of institutions. Assessment data could emerge from local comparisons to these sample portfolios.

Following the advice of that great sage of our time, Ann Landers, who says that when offered a lemon we should make lemonade, I was trying to take a bad situation and turn it into a funding source for portfolio assessment. Instead, I found myself entirely isolated in arguing for portfolios; I was treated as if I were calling for the rattling of bones and the examination of the entrails of birds. The elaborate summary of the conference that was later distributed to those who attended virtually ignored my proposal. The only mention of my argument is buried on page fifty-nine of the official conference report: "The portfolio idea, strongly advocated, won little support, as people felt they [portfolios] were uneven, unwieldy, and perhaps not relevant to NACSL as presently conceived." It seems clear that portfolio assessment is not yet perceived as ready for the major leagues, in part because of the special nature of these leagues, in part because of the immaturity of portfolio assessment itself.

As a public advocate of portfolio assessment, a partisan of an idea whose time has surely come, I am accustomed to recite the usual litany of portfolio virtues for teaching. But I write here as one who would like to see the portfolio concept move beyond the comfortable boundaries of the classroom, where portfolios have been in use for many years, into the larger arena where assessment affects policies, budgets, personnel decisions, and institutional goals. I come forward as one who has been a lone defender of portfolios in this arena, where the assumptions and practices with which we in the writing community so easily work are taken with great skepticism. The "new direction" I would most like to see is one that will allow portfolios to enter this world and change it. Portfolios offer to the world of assessment a view of student learning that is active, engaged, and dynamic, as opposed to the overwhelmingly passive concept that still dominates the assessment movement. Portfolios can bring to assessment a rich complexity to combat its overwhelming reductionism. Furthermore, portfolios bring teaching, learning, and assessment together as mutually supportive activities, as opposed to the artificiality of conventional tests. If we can make the case for portfolio assessment beyond the classroom, we can have a profound impact on the nature of American education.

We need not debate here the great benefits of portfolios for student learning or for course evaluation. As a writing teacher, I have been using portfolios with my own students for two decades; most of my colleagues also need no convincing on that score. However, if we are to see portfolios and all they imply about the writing process and about assessment of active learning enter into educational policy, educational funding, and the national debate about educational outcomes, then we have substantial work to do. If our colleagues judge (as the 1991 conference group did) that portfolios are "not relevant" measures of student learning "as presently conceived," then we are *not* writing in this book about a new and exciting assessment concept as we think we are, but merely about one more neat teaching tool.

This problem became clear to me during a casual conversation I had some time ago with a high education official from the state of Washington. He was a great supporter of portfolio assessment, he told me, and he knew I was as well. His "support," however, made me uncomfortable, with its easy enthusiasm so reminiscent of what I hear from many writing teachers. He was so supportive, he told me, that he was dead set against using portfolio assessment at the state level. Portfolio assessment, he maintained, should not produce data, but only feedback to students on their writing process. Very well, I responded, but then where do you get your information for setting budgets, curriculum goals, and proficiency standards? Oh, for that, he replied, we use our old assessments, the multiple choice ones that yield numbers. I left the conversation with a heavy heart: this great supporter of portfolios had defined them as only a teaching device, without institutional value or measurement meaning. The assessments that inform and shape funding and policy, that are used to determine whether teachers and schools are doing their jobs, and that actually define what the educational enterprise should accomplish would come from the usual standardized tests and other simple traditional measures. Like those attending the 1991 conference outside Washington, he saw portfolios not as an assessment device but as one more attractive pedagogical fad.

Many teachers who use portfolios as part of their teaching also resist the expanded use of portfolio assessment. Part of the resistance to portfolios comes from a well-justified suspicion that the expansion of portfolios beyond the classroom will mean some loss of instructor autonomy and local control. As soon as portfolio assessment becomes meaningful outside the classroom, there are inevitable pressures for consistency, for agreement on goals and even on some assignments, and for departmental, institutional, or even national rather than personal standards. Note the irony. We have complained for decades about writing assessments that ignore what we *do* in our teaching and have not noticed that these tests give us freedom to do what we choose in class. Assessments that *reflect* our teaching, however, also *affect* our teaching. I happen to think that, on the whole, this is a good thing, but I know that many sincere and thoughtful teachers prefer to keep portfolios in the classroom rather than risk the intrusion and exposure that expanded assessment will bring into our teaching. However, I argue that, even at its worst, intrusion is a small price to pay for the benefits that large-scale portfolio assessment can bring to us, our students, and American education.

Assessment, public policy, and instructional budgets connect, and we ignore this connection at our peril. Here, for example, is a paragraph from the editorial in the July/August 1993 issue of *Change, The Magazine of Higher Learning:*

The public perception is that higher education is unable to manage its own affairs. American higher education is facing more than a poor economy—it is undergoing a test of public trust. All of our publics are asking hard questions about the cost, pricing, productivity, access, outcomes, and effectiveness of college. For the most part, we arrogantly ignore these questions—acting as if they were an insult to our integrity. Reduced financial support is one way in which the public is expressing its dissatisfaction—and our responses to date support their greatest fears. (4)

I argue that portfolios provide an answer to these profound and substantial problems. Even at this point, however, it is not clear if portfolios are in fact part of the solution or actually part of the problem.

Portfolio assessment is a pedagogically useful *collection* procedure that in some ways resembles an *assessment* procedure. Most of the efforts that have gone into portfolios have focused upon their value for pedagogy; minor theoretical and systematic attention has been paid to assessment of the material after we collect it. The most dramatic example of this imbalance occurred a few years ago in a large midwestern state, whose flagship university collected thousands of incoming freshman portfolios for placement purposes. Unhappily, for a series of embarrassing reasons, the portfolios were never evaluated at all.

If we want portfolio assessment viewed as genuine *assessment,* we must produce evidence beyond personal testimony of its unique value. Even in our classroom use of portfolios, we have thought little about assessment after the writing has been collected. Can we demonstrate as well as assert that teacher grades given for portfolios are more fair, more credible, more useful to students, more informative to graduate schools or employers, and more able to show that students have benefited from instruction? Has anyone sought to determine if teacher response to writing, one of our most notorious inadequacies as a profession, is more valuable when we collect lots of writing in one folder? Does student self-assessment, one of the key goals of every composition course and one of the most frequently asserted benefits of portfolios, actually improve as a result of portfolio assessment? I very much hope that some evidence will become available—beyond assertion and lore—that students gain and maintain improved habits of self-assessment as a result of their work with portfolios, as opposed to their detachment from more conventional assessment methods.

I know that some scholars have been working on these problems, and I look forward to seeing in the near future the fruits of research about portfolio assessment. But, in general, portfolio assessment gained popularity in our profession because it looks like assessment but allows us to avoid many of the hard issues of assessment. One leader in the field recently told me that she liked portfolio assessment because it represented a "deconstruction" of assessment. The usual reductionism of testing, with its oversimplifications and misleading labeling, becomes very difficult with portfolios, since measurement itself is so difficult. Many of our colleagues praise portfolios as a means of avoiding assessment altogether. We can, they argue, abandon the judgmental comparing of people and the negative business of grades; portfolios let us appreciate each student as an individual. All students who complete, write about, and admire their portfolios can feel good about themselves. We, too, can feel good about ourselves even when forced to make judgments, since our judgments are now based on the individual student's writing process and on real writing rather than on tests. We can indulge our hostility to tests and the abuses of testing, even as we undertake assessment, or, perhaps, only pretend to do so.

Unless we can show that our judgments of portfolios can stand up to outside scrutiny, we buy that good feeling about portfolios at the cost of irrelevance to the assessment community and of self-deception that we assess student work merely by collecting and appreciating it. That deconstruction of assessment—when it becomes a pretense at assessment—weakens portfolio assessment from a potential education reform to one more supportive teaching device. I also suspect that it does not lead to very good teaching. I am surely old-fashioned in my view about this, but I continue to believe that serious and honest assessment of student work, using more than merely personal standards, is not only an essential part of a teacher's job but absolutely essential for student learning.

Let me focus for a minute on what many of us consider to be the least pleasant aspect of assessment: evaluation and grading of our students' writing. Some well-known compositionists have argued that we should not be involved in such a demeaning activity, or that we should do it only because our jobs depend on our filing grades. To be sure, there is much wrong with the ways grades work in American education and we have all experienced some of its evils, such as overmarking, substitution of means for ends, and abuse of the system. We should certainly do what we can to improve the sensitivity and fairness of grading in our courses and on our campuses. But abuse of a symbol system does not invalidate the importance of the differences those symbols represent. Making distinctions between levels of performance is not only something that we must be able to do if we are professional but something that is necessary for the good of our students who, like all learners, want to know how well they are doing.

The ability to make judgments is a defining characteristic of a professional, a necessary if not sufficient condition. We want physicians who can tell bacterial from viral infections and judge how sick we are; we want building inspectors who turn down unsafe or shabby construction; we want literary critics who can distinguish between Batman and Hamlet. A recent issue of *The New York Review of Books* (September 24, 1992) has a fine article on Shelley by Richard Holmes, based on six recent books on the poet. At the end of his introduction, Holmes sums up the questions he considers important: "How do we remember him, how do we read him, how do we *rate* him?" (19) Why should we even try to "rate" a romantic poet, to rank Shelley above or below Wordsworth or Southey? Just as judging without appreciation is harsh and empty, appreciating without judging is sentimental. It is professional to ask just how good a poet Shelley is, or just how good a senior thesis or a freshman theme is.

I don't mean to belabor the obvious, but I do need to assert in the face of modern romantic resistance to making judgements that a professional is one who knows how to make significant distinctions, one who can *rate* performance, one who can assess, one who can convince others that the assessment is fair. We do need to point out the complexity and difficulty of making judgements, and we ought to emphasize that not every writing need be judged, but if we argue that we cannot make judgments and defend them on more than merely personal grounds, we disqualify ourselves as professionals; if we argue that no judgments should be made, we simply look foolish. In both cases, we are sent out of the room and others are brought in to make the judgments we will not make.

That is as it should be, for we cannot teach writing well if we will not assess. I mentioned that a major purpose of assessment in a writing class should be to help students become self-assessors. One crucial difference between novices and professional writers is that experienced writers know how to revise; that is, they have learned how to assess their drafts so that they can improve them. Most students do not revise their writing unless compelled to do so, not because they are lazy or perverse (though some are), but because they don't see anything wrong with their first drafts. Surely, one goal of any writing course is to help students learn how to revise. Without teacher assessment that leads to self-assessment there is no revision. For me, the great strength of portfolios is that they allow a richer, fuller, and more meaningful assessment of student work than do other methods of assessment.

I reject the view that portfolios let us avoid assessment or the symbols of assessment. I think that view, which is one basis for resisting the expansion of portfolios outside of the classroom, diminishes portfolios and the teaching of writing itself. Surely, one of the great strengths of portfolio assessment is its hospitality to revision, which can only emerge from assessment. And portfolios, for the first time, allow us to assess revision as part of the assessment of writing. Portfolios should not "deconstruct" assessment but should make it work more effectively for us and our students; we should not use portfolios to become even more private and mysterious in our response to writing than we now are, but rather more public and accountable, more helpful to students, more responsive to the complexity of students and the way writing helps them envision their worlds. Indeed, since portfolios offer such enriched assessment possibilities, we come together in conferences and publish this book to explore the "new directions" they open.

My argument so far has been that we have an obligation to bring portfolio assessment out of our classrooms into the assessment community, since portfolios have so much to offer to American education. That community does not take portfolio assessment seriously at this point because we, like the artistic community before us, have failed to bring assessment concepts to bear upon portfolios. If we can meet the challenge to portfolio assessment posed by the assessment community, we can alter assessment itself.

Some of the most creative minds in the assessment community are interested in what they call "performative assessment," but they see no successful way to make fair and feasible the idiosyncratic and expensive performance measures now available—including portfolios. The "new direction" I hope portfolios will follow is one that will bring credibility and practicality into portfolio assessment so it will no longer seem "uneven, unwieldy, and perhaps not relevant" to important assessment of student learning. But to do that we must meet three specific problems. For an assessment to be useful beyond the classroom, it must be (1) demonstrably valid, (2) demonstrably reliable, and (3) cost effective.

Validity

Validity means honesty, that we are measuring what we say we are measuring and that we know and can show what it is we are measuring. For the last twenty years, much of the debate about the measurement of writing ability has turned on issues of validity. The new popularity of portfolios has made the debate even more heated, since portfolios claim greater validity than any other assessment method. These claims, however, sound familiar to those of us who participated in the last round of this continuing conflict.

In the 1970s, those of us who were promoting holistically scored essay tests fought the predominant multiple-choice tests on the grounds of validity. Such fill-in-the-bubble tests as the Test of Standard Written English (TSWE) or the College-Level Examination Program (CLEP) general examination in English composition were invalid, we argued, since they did not measure directly either reading (aside from the reading of test questions) or writing. When those responsible for these and similar tests argued that the measure was indirect, we developed and publicized evidence showing that the correlation between those indirect measures and more direct writing measures was weak while the correlation with race and class was strong (for example, White and Thomas). Our victory in the debate was not total by any means, but in general we were persuasive that the "real writing" by students on a writing test was an essential performance measure. The result of that debate is obvious: as opposed to the situation twenty years ago, most writing tests today demand at least some writing. Unless an assessment can show that it is honestly measuring the construct it claims to measure, it loses credibility and will eventually die—as the TSWE is now slated to do.

Yet, twenty years later, our arguments for the validity of essay tests look pretty shaky themselves. To be sure, in contrast to the fill-in-the-bubble tests, essay tests seemed obviously valid since they contained real writing. But with multiple-choice writing tests in retreat, or in hiding, the claim that an essay test represents real writing now seems questionable. What does an essay test measure? Some would argue that it measures a quick memory, fluency, ability to turn out reasonably clean and organized first draft work to someone else's topic under time pressure. I am no longer prepared to argue that this is "real writing," since it is so specialized a form of writing, though it has some relation to real writing. My point is that the correlation of essay test writing to the construct "writing ability" cannot just be assumed; it must be defined, established, and defended. What seemed too obvious to discuss two decades ago now is not obvious at all. Claims and counterclaims about essay tests demand some systematic evidence of validity. Some essay test programs produce such evidence by comparing student performance on the test with independent teacher evaluations of student writing in class, for example. But it is now clear that those of us promoting essay testing gave insufficient attention to the problem of essay test validity, in the heat of combat with multiple-choice tests.

I see portfolio assessment following exactly the same pattern of response to validity in the 1990s. Just as twenty years ago we saw the obvious invalidity in multiple-choice testing but were blind to the validity problems of essay testing, so many portfolio advocates today see clearly the validity problems of essay testing—a certain amount of abuse of essay testing seems necessary to establish portfolio credentials these days—but ignore the problems with their own claims that portfolios represent "real writing." Let me illustrate with two examples some of the problems that need attention.

A few years ago I served as a consultant to a portfolio program that was assessing the curriculum of an excellent small liberal arts college. We were reading with care a randomly selected series of portfolios produced by college seniors representing all major fields of study. In order for our assessments to be original, all grades and comments on the student papers had been removed, though the assignment given by the teacher was attached to each paper. (In passing, let me say that the assignment variable really complicates the validity of portfolio assessment: some assignments are so creative and supportive that most students write very well on them, while other assignments are so vague and boring that very few students will produce good writing.) As we scored the portfolios, I had strong reactions to two particular papers, one on the War of the Spanish Succession, which I thought was witty and wise, and the other on Faulkner's novel *The Sound and the Fury*, which, though written fluently, reflected serious misunderstanding of the book and included foolish statements about the author. As it turned out, I stood alone on the assessment team in my scoring of both papers and of both portfolios. My ignorance of European history had misled me on the Spanish Succession paper, which placed the war in the wrong century and had distorted most of its facts and interpretations. And I was the only one in the room who knew the Faulkner novel, which I occasionally teach, so that paper's superficial fluency impressed the other readers, who had no way of knowing how uninformed the paper was.

This experience is not unusual when portfolios move beyond the individual classroom. Our assessment team had a well-developed scoring guide, so we thought we knew our scoring criteria. The issue became quite muddled, however, as soon as we read papers outside our fields of expertise. We did agree on such matters as mechanical competence, organizational ability, and style, but we all brought much more than those matters to our response to student papers. We were also concerned with issues of critical thinking, demonstration of ideas with informed evidence, sensitivity to complexity, and other substantial issues, about which agreement was much more difficult. Essay testing handles this problem by requiring all students to reply to the same question and by developing consensus among the readers on the range of responses to that question. Thus the scores on an essay test define the writing ability being assessed as the ability to write well to a particular question; the sample papers at different score levels and the scoring guide locate and define the meaning of "writing well" for that test. On the other hand, portfolios cannot standardize topics or levels of response very well, so the validity problem becomes exceedingly complex.

Without question, portfolios can claim greater validity than essay tests on the clear ground that portfolios give several writing samples, and multiple measurement is always more valid than single measurement—it is bound to be more representative. But with that greater inclusiveness comes much greater difficulty in scoring, which diminishes the validity of the measure. So nobody should be content with mere assertions that portfolios are necessarily more valid than essay tests, at least until we have some careful studies to demonstrate the case.

A second problem with validity comes from the relationship between portfolios and the process/product issue in writing. Process theory argues that first-draft writing is only the beginning of a process, that revision is the heart of writing, and that portfolios offer the opportunity to measure what really matters—the writing process. Thus some portfolios require students to include all stages of the development of a paper from notes to presentation-level finished copy. Such portfolios can claim to assess the process of writing instead of focusing only on products. This is an attractive argument, particularly for those of us committed to process theory and process pedagogy.

But we must examine such claims for validity closely. In the first place, portfolios are traditionally collections of products, indeed, products selected to be the very best that have been made. Some make the assumption that since a fine product is clearly the result of a process, that process need not be exposed to view. The evaluator can intuit the process from examining the product. The same assumption, incidentally, is normally made on an essay test, that students who can turn out a fine impromptu paper have learned a process that enables them to do so quickly on demand; the product is of value in large part because it reveals the quality of the process that produced it. In assessment, as in teaching, we need to be aware that the product/process division is neither neat nor even logical in practice.

We need to be careful when we talk about process and product measurement, since we tend to find what we look for. For example, writing teachers often respond to student essays as if they were part of an ongoing process, as if the student were going to revise even final drafts; but students often see those same papers as products, finished, merely awaiting a grade. So our process comments are perceived by the students as product judgments and what we imagine to be supportive advice can appear to the student as negative evaluation. Student papers are normally both product and process, with an unclear line between the two. We ought to reconsider our too-easy depreciation of writing products, even if we are committed to process teaching.

Further, a recent study (Hamp-Lyons and Condon 1993) shows that well-trained and professional portfolio readers at the University of Michigan have some trouble dealing with the writing process as revealed in a series of drafts. Many readers see the first draft as the most dependable production and distrust the authenticity of the revisions. For these readers, the improvements shown in subsequent drafts may reflect the advice of the teacher or of the Writing Center rather than the writing ability of the student, and so they discount those improvements. Despite the argument that the construct "writing ability" should include the ability to improve writing through revision, and despite their careful training, these readers actually define what they are measuring differently—as something best shown through first draft work.

This validity problem is difficult to deal with at every level. I confess that I promise my students that I will give their portfolios a process grade at the end of the term, to go along with grades on their written products. I do indeed look for a student's ability to improve from draft to draft and I do give some credit for improvement. But I cannot get myself to value highly a diligent writing process that nonetheless yields bad writing. Besides, how can I judge among the infinitely various processes, many of them not evident even in the portfolio, that lead to writing products?

When we find ourselves asking over and over again what and how we evaluate—and I hope that most of us continue to ask such questions—we are showing perplexity over the validity of our measurement. And we must confess that the claims of validity made by portfolio advocates, including me, remain on thin ice. As we tell our students, repeated assertions do not in themselves demonstrate an idea. We need to buttress these claims with some clear evidence, and I hope that research into the validity of portfolio assessment becomes an important new direction to follow.

Reliability

If you agree with me that the strong suit of portfolio assessment is validity, and that nonetheless this validity has yet to be demonstrated, you will be uncomfortable indeed when we turn to reliability, because reliability means fairness and consistency, the weakness of all performance measures. Some portfolio defenders, despairing at ever achieving reliable scoring of portfolios, argue that we should rest our claims on validity and ignore reliability as a mere technicality. In his introduction to *Portfolios: Process and Product* (Belanoff and Dickson) Peter Elbow goes so far as to assert that reliability of measurement is not only unimportant but actually in conflict with validity: "Given the tension between validity and reliability—the trade-off between getting good pictures of what we are trying to test and good agreement among interpreters of those pictures—it makes most sense to put our chips on validity and allow reliability to suffer" (xiii). But this is a false dichotomy, like choosing between jobs and environmental protection. We need both and they are functions of each other. The fact is that no measure—this is a cliche of measurement—can be more valid than it is reliable, that reliability is the upper limit of validity. If our results are inconsistent and depend more on chance than on the criteria of measurement, the appearance of validity is deceptive. It is illogical to say that we have to throw away fairness in order to be honest in our measurement, and we make ourselves irrelevant to serious assessment if we assert that we must. Unreliable measures are merely subjective impressions by disparate individuals and we have more than enough of that already; unreliable grading is one reason why many students do not learn self-assessment and will not revise, since they are convinced that good writing is wholly a matter of the teacher's disposition, which is beyond student control and will not be affected by revision.

At the same time that we need to attend to reliability of measurement, we need to learn from the experience of essay testing, which has become almost obsessed with scoring reliability over the last two decades. Just as in the past we made the mistake of assuming the validity of essay test writing, we made another mistake by trying to compete with the computer in our quest for scoring reliability—a frustrating and impossible dream. We might as well admit that the consensus scores we can obtain from assessment of essays or portfolios will never be absolutely reliable and that it is the nature of performance evaluation to accommodate differing opinions.

Statisticians have developed something called "generalizability theory" to describe this situation, since some difference of opinion on the value of complex performances is to be expected, even desired. Nonetheless, after we grant that our scoring reliabilities will never match the computer's, we should do all we can to develop consistency in our judgments, not only so that our measures will be reasonably reliable (and hence support our claims for validity) but so that our students will be able to develop self-assessment by internalizing consistent criteria.

How can we approach reliability in our assessment of portfolios? The obvious answer is to adapt the measures that have led to high reliabilities for essay test scoring: develop a collegial discourse community for assessment, use a scoring guide to describe the measurement criteria, and agree on sample portfolios at different score levels to illustrate the scoring guide. This is the procedure Miami University of Ohio has been using, and that program's reliability is quite satisfactory.

We have learned from holistic essay scoring that some sacrifices are necessary to reach high reliabilities. For example, individual readers need to put aside their idiosyncrasies and agree with group judgments; a reader who scores differently than everyone else does is by definition wrong. Some romantic teachers see such conformity as an outrage, a violation of the way one would naturally read, a version of groupthink. To be sure, some unprofessional holistic scoring sessions are oppressive and uncollegial, enforcing scoring criteria that seem artificial and meaningless; such readings are hateful and I have no excuses to offer for them. But the more usual essay reading elicits a genuine consensus on the criteria for scoring from the readers and enforces that consensus, to everyone's benefit. I have no interest in protecting the right of my more eccentric colleagues to fail brilliant essays with two spelling errors, or to rate every essay at the top of the scale because the students mean well. I have a cantankerous colleague who declares with some regularity that for him to be forced to hear how his colleagues evaluate student work violates his "academic freedom" and his integrity. Such teachers, not to speak of their students, benefit from a certain amount of social coercion to use evaluation criteria their colleagues share.

Other sacrifices of more substance may be necessary to gain the reliability needed for valid assessment. Many portfolio programs will mandate the kinds of writing to be included, and that may limit the possibilities for teaching and learning. Other programs will require one or more common writing assignments for every portfolio, perhaps a self-assessment or an in-class essay. Portfolios that require numbers of drafts of a single assignment are in fact mandating a process pedagogy, which to many of us seems reasonable; but there are surely some teachers who will see such a mandate as unwarranted interference with their own teaching approach. Even more problematic is portfolio scoring done by an interdisciplinary team such as the one I mentioned earlier, coming from different discourse communities with different ways of posing and dealing with questions. Consistent and reliable scoring of portfolios is bound to be more difficult than is holistic essay scoring, perhaps by a factor of three or four, for we have barely begun to uncover the reliability problems peculiar to portfolios.

So I urge a search for ways of conducting reliable portfolio scoring as another new direction for portfolio assessment. I have seen draft reports of two research projects on this matter submitted to journals and surely more such work is under way. Until we have a literature documenting the reliability of portfolio scoring, we cannot expect to be taken seriously by the assessment movement. Remember, reliability matters profoundly: it is the upper limit of validity, and without reliability portfolios remain localized in the classroom as one more example of how subjective and unpredictable teacher grading can be.

Cost

I do not need to say much about cost, since one principle is obvious to everyone: if an educational activity costs too much money it just won't happen. In assessment, time is another form of money. So portfolios need to demonstrate that they can be assembled and scored at reasonable cost in time and money before they can command the respect of the assessment community or of higher education generally.

One of the achievements of the Miami University program has been to demonstrate the financial possibility of portfolio assessment. Miami can score student portfolios reliably and at reasonable cost; by setting a benchmark in these two areas, Miami has made an important contribution to higher education portfolio assessment. But we need to accumulate much more experience on how to manage portfolios economically and efficiently. Essay testing had the example of the Educational Testing Service Advanced Placement essay readings to show the feasibility of holistic scoring; without such a prominent model, portfolio assessment has a more difficult task in becoming accepted.

Essay testing made one advance in assessment cost that portfolios should build on: we argued that the term to use was "cost-effectiveness" rather than simply cost. We showed that an essay test did more than deliver a score. For example, test development and test scoring were also important faculty development activities and could draw on faculty development funding. Portfolio assessment has even stronger arguments for use of funds beyond testing budgets, since student portfolios have so many uses and advantages beyond generating measurement: student self-assessment, student investment in the curriculum, advisement support, career counseling, and job interview presentation, for example. The first objection to portfolio assessment is always cost, either in money or time; but I think a case is waiting to be made that portfolios can represent the most cost-effective assessment available.

Throughout this article I have assumed the value of portfolios in the classroom and I have only alluded to other obvious campus uses of them. Some teachers will be content to keep portfolios in those comfortable roles, where they serve student learning and student assessment very nicely. My concern, however, has been to explore the new direction I hope portfolios will take: beyond the classroom and into the assessment movement. Large-scale assessment will go on, with us or without us. The metaphor I heard repeatedly at the Washington conference described at the beginning of this paper was as outdated as the measurements anticipated, but powerful nonetheless: the train has already left the station; are you on it or are you left behind?

I hope that, ten years from now, higher education no longer takes portfolio assessment to be "irrelevant" to college student learning. Indeed, I hope that portfolios will have become accepted as a reliable, valid, and cost-effective way to assess student performance in college as well as in the writing course. I hope that passive multiple-choice tests will be replaced increasingly by active performance measures that support the teaching of writing and writing across the curriculum. Ten years from now, the federal government will no doubt still be trying to get its NACSL off the ground and will be commissioning yet another round of position papers for yet another planning conference. I would like to believe that some of those position papers will argue that the development of portfolio assessment has progressed to the point that national multiple-choice tests and other passive measures of student learning, to quote and redirect the proceedings of the long-ago 1991 conference, now deserve "little support, as people felt they were uneven, unwieldy, and perhaps not relevant to NACSL as presently conceived." If such a day dawns, it will reflect not only a change in assessment but also a change in education itself. But all of us interested in portfolio assessment have a great deal of work to do before such words can be spoken.

3

Will the Virtues of Portfolios Blind Us to Their Potential Dangers?

Peter Elbow

A portfolio is nothing but a folder, a pouch—an emptiness: a collection device and not a form of assessment. But portfolios lend themselves to assessment, and for assessment they have enormous virtues and dangers. I have been a voice in the chorus of praise for portfolio assessment (Elbow and Belanoff, "Foreword"; Belanoff and Elbow) and remain so, but am now more aware of some dangers.

Virtues

I'll put my praise into a new conceptual framework by noting how portfolios introduce the dimension of *time*. A portfolio gives us an all-at-once picture of writing that was produced over time. For this reason portfolios rescue us from the contradiction in many of the paradoxes or binary oppositions that lie at the heart of good learning and teaching. That is, many of these paradoxes are contradictory in pure logic because logic exists outside of time. But when we add the dimension of time, the contradiction or conflict often disappears. (For more on this issue in general, see my "Binary Thinking.")

Teacher as Ally/Adversary

Portfolio evaluation helps us deal better with what is perhaps the central difficulty of teaching: it's inherent in a teacher's job to try to accept and welcome all students, yet also to try to reject those who are not worthy.

Teachers must try to be open, noncritical welcomers, but also hawkeyed, critical, vigilant "bouncers." Portfolio assessment that occurs at the end of the semester helps us be ally to students for virtually all of the semester: students don't need to fight us as the enemy, because the more help they get from us, the better their portfolios will be and the higher their grades. Our critical feedback is something they can welcome and use to their own pragmatic advantage rather than (as so often now happens) something they need to fight because it justifies the low grade we gave. However, at the moment of portfolio assessment, we can turn around and be as toughminded as we want. We don't have to hold back on critical standards since we've already given students so many opportunities to improve their work and benefit from our help.

Process/Product

Perhaps everyone is rushing to embrace portfolios because they mediate so well between this binary opposition that has bedeviled us for so long. On one hand, portfolios serve our need for a product. They help us demand the high quality that we want or some other constituency wants: the hard texts themselves, "the real thing," the bottom line. We don't have to accept ineffective writing and justify it to ourselves or to colleagues with defensive talk about the lovely process that lies behind it. On the other hand, portfolios help us with our justifiable preoccupation with process—they help us pay better attention to the writing process. Portfolios emphasize process in two ways. First, unlike conventional writing exams, portfolios reward students for using a good writerly process: to explore a topic in discussion and exploratory writing; to complicate their thinking; to allow for perplexity and getting lost; to get feedback; to revise; and to collaborate.

Second, portfolios permit evaluators to look at and perhaps even assess the process itself, for example a student's strengths or weaknesses at generating copiously or revising or giving and using feedback. If a portfolio contains *only* final drafts, it might *seem* to show us nothing about process, but that's not true. If we see four or five papers, we can make a somewhat justifiable inference about a student's ability to generate lots of ideas or to organize—which we cannot do if we see only one paper. Most portfolio systems ask for some early drafts and journal writing, however, not just final drafts. Indeed, one of the most important and useful documents in most portfolios is the cover letter or self-analysis. The student must explain and reflect on what is in the portfolio and talk about processes used in writing the pieces and putting the portfolio together. The cover letter helps students become more thoughtful and aware about their writing processes—helping them with metathinking and metadiscourse. It also helps portfolio readers make better sense of the other pieces in the portfolio. (See the various papers in this volume about cover letters, in particular that by Nedra Reynolds).[1]

Review of Neglected Processes

Portfolios have been instrumental in helping teachers and programs look at processes that are often ignored in writing pedagogy or assessment, e.g., the ability to see other points of view, to use different genres, to use exploratory or journal writing productively, or to use different kinds of voice in writing. Indeed I believe that one of the most important benefits of portfolios is in helping us break out of the "assessment mind-set" that has so long whispered in our ear, "You can only measure what is easily measurable." (Thus the preoccupation with grammar and mechanics.) When people use portfolios, they are likely to turn to each other one day and say, "Hey, we can evaluate *anything*—not just what traditional writing exams have focused on." In short, portfolio assessment invites us to ask ourselves the *real* assessment questions: "What do we really want in successful students? What are we trying to produce? We can name it and look for it."

Thus, faculty from other disciplines in general education programs have used writing portfolios produced over a student's first two years to look for particular skills or abilities we don't talk about in composition assessment, but which are seen as central to general education. Skills such as critical thinking and problem solving surface in writing portfolios. Awareness of other cultures and the ability to see things from points of view different from that of mainstream culture reveal themselves in portfolios. The ability to question, to wonder, to invite perplexity; the ability to have dialogue with others and to connect one's discourse with that of others; the ability to reflect on one's own performance or have dialogue with oneself—all of these abilities can emerge in portfolio writing and assist instructors in general education programs.

The Paradox About Audience Awareness

If writing is to be effective with readers, it must reflect awareness of those readers. The writer must realize (even if unconsciously) how different from her own views other readers' points of view are liable to be. The writer must, sometimes, even think about hostile readers who will try to shoot her down at every point. The writer needs to make a host of large and small adjustments to accommodate readers' needs. Yet the traditional rhetorical advice *always and from the beginning* to think about readers is simply wrong—unhelpful, even disastrous—for many students and even professional writers (certainly for me). Many writers find it crucial to spend a good deal of their writing process not worrying at all about the audience, not even thinking about them. Here too, portfolio assessment, in contrast to all other structured or formal assessment procedures, rescues us from the contradiction: students can do lots of writing without worrying about audience, but then revise for the portfolio and think hard and carefully about audience.

The Paradox About Mechanics: Grammar, Spelling, Usage, Typing

The paradox here is that mechanics are both the most important and the least important thing about writing. They are most important because they tend to preoccupy unskilled writers more than anything else and because mistakes are the first thing that most readers notice. When most ordinary readers find a mistake, they become distracted from the message and often decide that the writer is a dumbbell. (Despite all the criticism we get on this score, we English teachers tend to be the only people in the world who can notice surface mistakes and still pay full attention to the meaning.) Yet of course mechanics are the least important parts of writing because they are totally superficial—completely surface code and not substance. Virtually all of us, from expert to novice, succeed better at any writing task when we can ignore mechanics while we are working out our thinking, and perhaps even while working on matters of style.

Students get understandably confused here. When teachers stress spelling and grammar as important, students often lose track of their thinking, produce tangled prose, or resort to wooden writing that contains only simple words and simple sentences. They squander their attention on the goal of simply *avoiding* mistakes. But when teachers say, "Oh, don't worry, mechanics don't matter," they are misleading students: mistakes *do* matter because they take such a large toll on the reactions of most readers.

Portfolios come to the rescue here. They invite students to function in the way most of us would like them to function and also to *understand* the paradox better. Portfolio assessment permits us to say to students, "Don't worry about spelling and grammar during your drafting. But final drafts must be well copyedited or they are not acceptable; they must be free of mistakes or you cannot pass." This implied message is surely the one we want to give: "You do not have to *know* spelling and grammar, but you must be able to do whatever it takes to get rid of mistakes in your final drafts." This message is the one that best reflects how the world works. That is, plenty of people in many fields function successfully as good writers without being good at spelling and grammar. But often they must get certain pieces successfully copyedited if they want those pieces to be judged fairly and accepted. Conventional writing exams are particularly flawed on this score. They must have a *single* answer to the question of whether mechanics are important, and a single answer is always wrong. There has been too little attention paid to the skewing of holistic scoring by surface features.

The Conflict Between Teaching and Testing

This is the conflict that currently does most damage in education, and the rush to portfolios reflects how much they help. An emphasis on testing almost invariably reflects a distrust of teachers. Teachers and school districts are often directly rewarded or punished on the basis of test scores, so this puts great pressure on "teaching to the test." Thus testing not only drives teaching, it often drives it down the wrong road. If the test asks only for recall of information, teachers are sucked into stressing that. If the test asks students to write an impromptu essay on a question they've never seen, they do best to use a superficial five-paragraph format and not think too deeply.

When portfolios are used for testing, they drive teaching down the right roads. They reward students and teachers for the kinds of behavior we want: exploring and revising and getting feedback in their writing—that is, for a good "real world" writing process rather than just a "test taking," "playing it safe" approach to writing. Most other forms of evaluation tend to disrupt the context for learning and teaching by tempting students to care more about the grade or the test than about learning. And they tempt teachers to teach to the test instead of teaching for deep transformative learning—which almost always involves confusion and disruption. Portfolio evaluation could be called "a test that's good to teach to."

A Potential Danger: Holistic Scoring of Portfolios

Because of the genius of portfolios as collection devices that hold many pieces of writing, they give us much better validity than other structured or formal assessment procedures. That is, they give us a better picture of what we are trying to evaluate: a student's skill or ability in writing.

What a relief. Direct measures of writing (exams where students actually write) may have been a big advance over indirect measures (multiple-choice tests) in getting at what we're actually trying to assess, but nevertheless the shortcomings of writing exams have been painfully obvious for a long time. No one can make a trustworthy judgment about a student's skill or ability in writing without seeing multiple pieces of writing, written on multiple occasions, in multiple genres, directed to different audiences, written in more or less realistic writing conditions. Conventional writing exam conditions automatically prevent us from getting a picture of the very thing we are trying to evaluate and thus destroy any possibility of trusting the results.

But because of the relief at finally assessing what we want to assess, people have tended to be lulled into complacency about the other half of the assessment package: interreader reliability on holistic scoring. Thirty or forty years ago testers couldn't get reliability in scoring actual writing samples, but enormous efforts in the intervening years have produced truly impressive-sounding numbers for reliability. So now the feeling goes like this: "It's been a long struggle but we've finally learned how to achieve reliability in scoring actual writing samples. Now that portfolios have come along, we can finally achieve validity too. By Jove, we've done it!"

But we can't just take reliability for granted as something we've already achieved. Validity and inter-reader reliability work against each other. In fact, they present us with yet another conflict or opposition. Only this time portfolios can't pull off the kind of happy, win-win outcome described in the first section. When portfolios *enhance* validity, they *undermine* reliability.

Look at it this way. Because portfolios finally give us a better picture of what we are trying to evaluate—a student's skill or ability in writing—they finally seem to give us a good answer to the real question: "How good a writer is this student?" But do they really? Yes and no.

The crux is in the phrase, *how good a writer is this student?* (a phrase in which validity and reliability intersect). If it means "What are the student's strengths and weaknesses?" we are on fairly solid ground. Portfolios give us a much more accurate and trustworthy picture of strengths and weaknesses than we can get by looking at single papers from a classroom or an exam. Portfolios give us a good indication of what kinds or genres of writing someone is better and worse at (e.g., narration vs. persuasion vs. explanation of complex data vs. memo vs. lyric poem), and what skills or abilities someone is better and worse at (e.g., boundless invention vs. clear organization vs. good revising vs. clear syntax vs. lively and characteristic voice).

Unfortunately, when most people ask, "How good a writer is this student?" what they have in mind is a number: a single grade or holistic score such that all students are ranked along a single dimension. (At least this is true in most academic and legislative settings. Actual writers and literary critics tend, in fact, to mean something much more complex than a number when they talk about how good a writer someone is. This in itself ought to make us wary of single numbers.)

The point is that portfolios do *not* give us a better picture of "how good" a writer someone is, if what we have in mind is a number. In a sense they give a worse picture than we get from single essays. That is, if we look only at single pieces of writing—all answering the same question and written under the same conditions, all in the same genre to the same audience—we are much more likely to agree with each other in our holistic numerical rankings than if we look at portfolios containing five to a dozen pieces by each student—different kinds of writing produced under different conditions. (But even though readers agree on a score for a single piece, does that score represent a fair assessment of the student's actual ability?) When all the writing is alike, it's easier to agree on a single number. When a portfolio gives us a pile of diverse pieces by each writer, and one writer's selection of pieces is different from that of another writer, it is vain to think we can trust a single holistic score that pretends to sum up this diversity of performances by each writer and compare all writers along a single quantitative scale. If the story and the personal writing were strong and the expository and argumentative and analytic pieces were weak, what score does this add up to? Readers will differ according to their values.

LaRene Despain and Tom Hilgers give us carefully gathered empirical evidence to support the conclusion that common sense and experience have long been showing many of us: that there is far more disagreement among readers of portfolios than readers of single papers. They conducted an elaborate study of seven experienced holistic scorers working over ten sessions and keeping reading logs. Each session began with a full training period and then proceeded to portfolio rating. Despain and Hilgers were trying to see how far they could get toward agreement or reliability among readers in the holistic scoring of portfolios. First they let readers work toward consensus without criteria imposed by the leaders, but this produced very little reliability. They found they had to give "a more prescriptive, criterion-referenced scoring guide . . . to describe the grades from A to F" (30). Over the course of their ten sessions, they kept giving more specificity to the criteria and putting more emphasis on the importance of using the scoring guide. At a certain point Despain and Hilgers stopped using actual portfolios for training sessions, since the portfolios contained mixtures of strong and weak features in this and that genre. Real portfolios didn't give enough help in getting readers to agree. "Thus, the training packets became 'model' portfolios [with pieces chosen to conform better to each other] rather than 'representative' portfolios" (30). Readers were then asked not to score whole portfolios, just score individual papers, and get "portfolio scores" by adding up these individual scores. "The standardizing scoring guide achieved a better "fit' with characteristics of individual essays than with the more varying characteristics of nonuniform portfolios" (32).

Yet after *all* of these stratagems (can it really be said that they were still "scoring portfolios"?), they still couldn't get interreader reliability better than the .60 level—"far from the .80 that is frequently used as the standard for minimally acceptable level of agreement in circumstances where a score has significant consequences" (30). In the end, the researchers talk about "tradeoffs between validity and reliability," and wonder, "how we can achieve the control necessary for satisfactory levels of reliability without sacrificing the validity sought through use of portfolios" (34). "The reading itself tends to be more unruly than the readings of single pieces of writing produced under controlled circumstances in response to identical prompts" (33). See Hamp-Lyons for further evidence of how portfolios undermine holistic scoring. (For others who testify to how reliability and validity undermine each other, see Wiseman [178] writing in 1956, and Greenberg writing now and citing yet others on this point.)

Until the recent publication of the impressive research by Despain and Hilgers, I was more worried that the success of portfolios might lull people into further complacency about interreader reliability. In fact portfolios may now finally give us the leverage we have needed to dislodge our overreliance on holistic scoring in general: our habit of using single numbers to rank complex performances along a single dimension. The diversity of pieces in a portfolio simply makes more obvious what is just as true of single pieces: there are always a diversity of features or qualities in any complex performance, and readers who are not scoring in conformity to a scoring guide simply don't agree on a single score—even for single pieces. A number of us have been arguing that the high reliability results in the scoring of single pieces of writing are really epiphenomenal. They are a product of the training that gets readers to agree in ways they would never agree in normal reading. "[T]he reliability in holistic scoring is not a measure of how texts are valued by real readers in natural settings, but only of how they are valued in artificial settings with imposed agreements" (Elbow "Ranking" 189). Despain and Hilgers also acknowledge that they had to try for "a structured approach to reading that differs from the flexible reading one ordinarily finds in a real-world community of writing teachers" (32). See Brian Huot ("Reliability") and Davida Charney for strong critiques of the pervasive reliance on holistic scoring. See Bob Broad's strong argument in this volume for the same point. See Barbara Herrnstein Smith (*Contingencies*) for an extended and powerful philosophical critique. Ed White argued in 1990 that it doesn't make sense to look for one "true score" for a piece of writing:

> But when we evaluate student writing . . . we sometimes find differences of opinion that cannot be resolved and where the concept of the true score makes no sense. . . . Some disagreements (within limits) should not be called error, since, as with the arts, we do not really have a true score, even in theory. ("Language and Reality" 192)

Ed White now argues *for* holistic scoring of portfolios (in this volume and in his review of Belanoff and Dickson), though the basis of his argument seems to be an *a priori* claim that reliability and validity can't get out of whack: "Reliability means consistency and fairness, and no measure—this is a cliche of measurement—can be more valid than it is reliable" (review 538). But his argument is also pragmatic: if we don't ally ourselves with the practices of the professional and government testing establishments—using holistic scoring of portfolios and nationwide assessments instruments—they will proceed onwards and ignore the composition community and do regressive things like returning to multiple-choice testing.

I acknowledge that there is some real danger here. Having been a writing program director for quite a few years, I know how to make strategic retreats when necessary in the face of institutional exigencies, and accept the lesser of two evils when a fight will necessarily lead to the greater of the evils. I'm fighting now against holistic grading of portfolios and I acknowledge that this is a lesser evil than multiple-choice exams.

But we mustn't assume we'll lose. The composition community is more powerful than Ed White implies. In only twenty years or so, we have twice changed the world of assessment, and we did it by *resisting* conventional practices of the testing community and setting an example of sound practices. First, we've seriously discredited multiple-choice tests of writing (not that we've gotten rid of them all). Second, we have convinced educational institutions, the public, and significant portions of the professional testing community to take portfolios very seriously. So instead of prematurely capitulating, let's argue well and engage in sound practice, and we stand a good chance of being as persuasive here as before.

What is crucial for this strategy is clear thinking. We mustn't let a pragmatic political danger cloud our analysis of trustworthiness in assessment. In particular, we mustn't let political pressures stampede us into accepting the idea that assessment means holistic scoring or single-number verdicts—that we haven't *got* evaluation unless we rank performances along a single quantitative dimension. To accept this idea is to surrender to the cultural hunger for simple numbers and the feeling of students when they look at an evaluative comment on their writing and cry, "But you didn't evaluate my paper. What's my grade?" I insist that we don't have real evaluation of any complex performance unless we avoid the distortion of a simpleminded, single-number holistic score and develop something more descriptive or analytic—something that does some justice to the conflicting standards of real readers.

Exploring a Strategic Retreat on Holistic Scoring

But that's a very pure position: that we should avoid all holistic scoring—all bottom-line, single-number evaluation. I suspect we are wiser on both theoretical and practical grounds if we avoid absolutely pure positions and instead find ways to make our thinking complex and answerable to pragmatic institutional and cultural needs. Anyway, the thinking that follows is nothing if not impure, and no one will be able to accuse me of being unable to make strategic retreats.

The central issue is number—quantification. We are bombarded by scores. Galileo used a traditional figure of thought when he called the universe a book or a text, but he made a radical departure when he declared that the book was written in the language of *number*. In 1918, E. L. Thorndike articulated the central premise behind modern assessment when he said, "Whatever exists at all exists in some amount. To know it involves knowing its quantity as well as its quality" (16, cited in Calfee 5). I resist our culture's obsession with quantifying everything and the premise that assessment *means* scores and grades. But what if *some* quantification were both pragmatically necessary and theoretically justified?

It may be that portfolio assessment can come to the rescue here and have a paradoxical influence on our thinking about quantification. On the one hand, portfolios show us the absurdity of holistic scoring as it is currently practiced, with scales from one to six. Yet I think portfolios also suggest the virtue of a peculiarly crude, simple, minimal kind of holistic scoring.

Let me explain. The way in which portfolios undermine conventional holistic scoring is through their capaciousness as containers: Portfolios give us "mixed bags," not single pieces of writing, and the bags are too mixed for a single number. Human performance varies from occasion to occasion and single pieces of writing shield us from that variability. But what if the portfolio bag is not so mixed? What about a full and rich portfolio about which readers agree that most of the pieces are excellent? Are we not then more than usually justified in calling the writer very strong? Similarly, what if most readers agree that most of the pieces are very poor or unsatisfactory? Are we not more than usually justified in calling the writer weak?

I'm suggesting, then, that portfolios might justify giving *two* holistic scores: EXCELLENT and POOR/UNSATISFACTORY. What a theoretical scandal I am playing with: to give holistic scores to a few portfolios at the margins and no scores to the rest. Yet it could also be described as theoretical wisdom to give holistic scores only to those portfolios where a single number verdict has any justification, and to refuse to give indefensible scores to that whole range of portfolios about which readers cannot agree. The data from Despain and Hilgers showed that readers had the most disagreement about middle-range papers (30), and also that their middle scores were often an averaging of higher and lower ones on different papers. Middle rankings depend on a concatenation of accidents: the weightings of different genres and features as specified by the test leaders, or random compromises between readers' conflicting standards and weightings.[2]

Such a practice of minimal or marginal holistic scoring can be bolstered on pragmatic grounds. That is, sometimes we really do need a single "bottom line" verdict, namely a holistic score. In certain circumstances, we need to decide which students should be denied a place if we have limited resources, or denied credit, or required to repeat a course, or take a preparatory course. Sometimes we also need to decide which students should get an award or scholarship. If enough readers agree that certain work is good, that work will probably serve as a helpful example to others. These decisions about excellence or weakness can never be wholly fair, but they are much fairer and much more secure and justified than most of the holistic scores we now give, especially all those fine-grained rankings in the middle range.

Speaking of pragmatism, this minimal holistic scoring cuts testing time and costs at least in half. It is the procedure used at Stony Brook, and we discovered that most portfolios can be read very quickly. Readers are looking only for strikingly good or bad portfolios. Many portfolios soon disqualify themselves by having too much weakness to be excellent or too much strength to be terrible. What a pleasure to save all the money we normally spend on giving indefensible and misleading scores.[3]

It makes me nervous to defend *any* holistic scoring on pragmatic grounds since so many people now frantically assert that the world would come to an end if we didn't have all the tests and scores and grades and GPAs that we currently have. This is the view of naive students and anxious parents who feel they can't go on unless they know whether someone's ability is B or B-. Still, those few holistic scores might be justified on both theoretical and pragmatic grounds. And our best hope of ending the injustice of most holistic scoring might be to keep a little bit of it.

I have been experimenting with this curious system in my individual courses by giving students a holistic or quantitative mark when their papers or portfolios seem to me particularly strong or particularly weak and giving other students nothing but my comment. (Of course I also give a comment on the strong and weak ones.) It feels like a promising approach. The main benefit is this: when I give those few holistic scores for which there is the greatest need, it takes away most of the pressure and anxiety to have a holistic score for *everything*. Students know that if the news is particularly bad or particularly good, they will hear. If they don't hear, they can listen to my mixed comments and pay attention with less anxiety about "What is my grade? What is my grade?" (For more, see my "Ranking.")

Another Potential Danger of Portfolios

A number of years ago every window in our car was labelled "window," the radio "radio," the mirror "mirror," and so on. Our children had gotten a DYMO labelling machine, and it was so wonderful and effective to use, especially on car trips, that they went around labelling everything in sight. If we start with what I would call a correct claim, namely that portfolio assessment is a good thing because it's so much better than other assessment procedures we have— and if we live in a culture that is crazed for assessment—it is hard not to slide into a frightening and dangerous claim: portfolio assessment is a good thing so let's use it on everything. The government seems to think that it can improve education simply by giving more tests. The danger then is this: portfolios have the potential for *reinforcing* rather than questioning the cultural juggernaut of testing. When doctors have a good procedure, they want to use it: in cities with more eye surgeons, there is more eye surgery. When defense departments have a good weapon, they want to use it.

Even worse, portfolio evaluation, in a horribly perverse manifestation of its very virtues, opens the door to the ultimate assessment dystopia: where students feel that *everything* they write—the tiniest scrap of exploratory writing, private journal writing, or feedback to a buddy—might find its way into their portfolio and be fodder for assessment. Thus every occasion for engaging in writing of any sort is an occasion for being assessed. Put it this way: in "the bad old days," students did lots of exercises and other work, and on a few occasions each semester they "had an exam" so that their work could be assessed; now everything they do hovers over the wide maw of the portfolio, liable to be sucked in with the least effort. Portfolios permit the smell and the feel of evaluation to permeate every crevice of a course. I credit this insight to a good teacher and poet at Stony Brook, Ron Overton. He made exactly this point to me over and over again, but in my enthusiasm for the virtues of portfolio evaluation, I couldn't get it. Finally I get it.

The danger wouldn't be so bad except for the outside pressures to evaluate, which students have internalized as a hunger always to know "how they are doing" in quantitative terms. Great sums of money are available for testing but not for teaching. Parents and legislators and school committees want ever more scores in order to see how everyone is doing. In such a context, it is frightening to see people, in their enthusiasm for portfolios, proposing to put evaluation where it didn't before exist, effectively suggesting more occasions and ways to subject student work to evaluation.

Here is a concrete example. Most writing assessment in higher education is for placement. (This is the finding of three important surveys: CCCC Committee on Assessment; Greenberg, Wiener, and Donovan; Lederman, Ryzewic, and Ribaudo. Cited in Greenberg 17.) Is it really useful to spend such extraordinary amounts of time and money in order to move some students either into a remedial course or to exemption? Does it take all that time and money to produce such a small effect, especially since the results are highly dubious? Are there not quicker and easier ways to identify those students? Do we really want to send the symbolic message that is sent when every student's first encounter with a university is to undergo assessment?—when the first act by the university is to sort the students into sheep and goats? Do we really want to exempt some students from the first-year writing course thereby sending the message that the course is a punishment for incompetence, instead of the message that a writing course is what everyone does as part of the liberal arts? Is segregating weaker students into courses by themselves away from contact with all other students the only way to give them the extra help they need? Can't we explore ways to give weaker students *supplemental* help rather than help-through-quarantine? If we gave supplemental help, we could skip placement testing, since the need for help would simply emerge as the course gets under way. We already have many models for supplementary help: supplementary tutorials, workshops, visits to a center.[4]

Also, weak students could simply be required to stay in a course longer until they attain the desired level of skill. Why are we trying harder and harder to achieve more and more sophisticated segregations of students into different classrooms at the very time when the schools are trying harder and harder— and more and more successfully—to learn to teach heterogeneous classrooms? The money used for placement testing and developmental courses would be better used for these purposes: to give poor writers weekly help in individual or small group tutorials (and to pay for a certain number of them to stay longer in the class); to fund exempted students to take a writing class; and to provide workshops to help teachers learn to teach in heterogeneous classrooms. All this placement testing rests on the pervasive assumption that more testing and segregation of students into different levels will create better learning. The assumption needs questioning.

If we did less evaluation, then we could do it better. We could make evaluation descriptive and instructive rather than just a sorting device that spits out numbers with no diagnostic information at all.

A common objection suggests itself at this point:

> There's no such thing as too much evaluation. We are always involved in evaluation of some sort every moment that we teach. How else will students improve if they don't get constant evaluative feedback of one sort or another about strengths and weaknesses of their writing. Perhaps they don't need formal testing or holistic scoring or even numbers at all, but they need constant evaluative responses as to strengths and weaknesses. In short, you should cheer rather than complain about the potential for portfolios to make evaluation pervasive.

It's important to question this common sense doctrine. Of course students need *some* evaluation or assessment of their writing. But I strongly doubt that this is what leads to improvement. I sense more and more that the vital factor for improvement is the experience of having serious readers genuinely engage with their writing. The longer I teach and have chances to observe the teaching of others, the more I sense that the comments that lead to real growth in writing are the ones where we manage to make a real and felt response to what the student is actually saying: where we tell our feelings and reactions, the thoughts on our mind about the topic, or the bearing of the student's thinking on our own experiences. In trying to explain or justify this conviction I would contrast two different student experiences in writing classes: an experience where what a student cares about is how the words are evaluated; and an experience where what a student cares about is whether the words actually communicate to someone, that is, the student has something on his mind and it matters to him that it get across.

In short, I suspect students don't improve much until they experience writing as an effort to communicate and that what holds so many students back is that they experience writing as an exercise only in being evaluated. I suspect that it is only when students experience a serious reader *engaged* with their text that they finally benefit from a bit of assessment. Of course it's not so easy always to have this kind of response to student writing, especially when students are young and naive and when we are reading so many papers. (Peer readers help here, not that it's so easy to get all of them to engage seriously with each others' papers.) I recommend trying out the following hypothesis in your teaching: assessment of strengths and weaknesses is really of limited value and what helps more is to coax the students into genuine dialogue with us and each other about the meaning or content of their writing.

Let me make the same claim in a more general way: the least interesting and useful question to ask about any piece of writing is how good it is. Yet our emphasis on evaluation keeps everyone stuck on this question. Is it not more interesting and useful to ask: What is it actually saying? What does it imply?

What are the consequences for us and others of what it is saying? How do we feel about what it is saying? What can we learn from it? How would we reply to it? How does it relate to other messages from our culture about this matter? (If we want to function more like literary critics, I'd still argue that questions of quality are less interesting and useful than those above and others like these: How is it shaped? How do its parts function? What is its relation to its historical and cultural context, and to ours? Notice that the interminable debates about the canon pretty much disappear when people stop obsessing about quality. When we decide what texts to teach on the basis of questions like those above, it's obvious that we need to read both "dead white men" and also a multitude of noncanonical works.)

Of course I acknowledge that there usually is an evaluative element in any response to anything. But that is no reason to foreground or celebrate it. The most intellectually primitive response is always the binary "I like it/I don't like it," and our obsession with evaluation simply reinforces that knee-jerk level of response. We need assessment procedures that encourage people not just to make statements of holistic approval or disapproval but to try to understand and describe. When students experience writing only as fodder for evaluation, they don't take risks or engage in the other kinds of behavior that make the biggest difference in learning.

Conclusion

Perhaps I can sum up this essay by pointing out that portfolios are inherently more personal than other forms of assessment. When we read only one text per student, we can easily forget the complexity of the person behind the paper and thus be more comfortable scoring it with a single number. But when we read a portfolio we get a much stronger sense of contact with the person behind the texts: an author with a life history, a diversity of facets, a combination of strengths and weaknesses, someone who had good days and bad days. For example, when we read portfolios we sometimes find ourselves making inferences like this: "In this essay the student doesn't seem to mean what she is saying as much as she did in that other piece. She seems to be on her best behavior, to be tiptoeing around in her Sunday dress-up persona. She somehow lost the complexity of feeling, the richness of point of view, the flexibility of persona that she had in that other paper." How do we score this kind of thing, especially when we see this paper as more coherent and successful by most measures, but feel more attracted and touched by the other paper?

Seeing the person in the portfolio complicates the hunger for that holistic bottom line. Imagine the absurdity of trying to score a *person* with a single number. For one thing, people are too mixed and complicated; for another, "raters" don't seem to agree on a single scale for persons. So too with a person's writing: a full portfolio is too mixed and complicated; and raters don't agree on a single scale. Surely most of us have learned that we don't so much help people improve as persons by giving them constant diagnosis of strengths and weakness. We help them improve by engaging with them in serious and felt relationship.

Let me sum up my essay. We have two major problems in evaluation. The first problem is that most current evaluation practices are pretty terrible. Portfolio evaluation is the best evaluation we have and so it's a big help here. But bad evaluation turns out to be the lesser problem. The greater problem is too much evaluation. Portfolios could help here too, but they run some danger of exacerbating this problem.[5]

Notes

1. At what point, however, does an emphasis on process become stupidly doctrinaire? Should we penalize students who can turn out good writing, but who are unskilled or uninterested in processes we love, such as freewriting, revising, or getting peer feedback? I remember noticing that the first violinist for the Juilliard String Quartet had what my teachers called terrible bowing arm technique—but he seemed to get by pretty well.

2. This kind of approach that insists on honestly communicating the complexity of how readers actually read instead of hiding behind arithmetical simplification suggests another new practice that might be fruitful to pursue for those people who want to emphasize numbers and scores: to refrain from doing *any* averaging and simply giving students whatever scores the readers actually give, even if three scores are at great variance with each other. With this approach a few students would get consistent scores, but many or most would get a mix of conflicting scores. Our present practice of always giving one score to a portfolio or paper reflects the premise that there is a "true score," and I quoted Ed White's argument against that premise. What stops us from being honest enough to admit to students and other readers that there is no "true score," just the conflicting responses of skilled, thoughtful readers?

3. At Stony Brook the "minimal holism" is somewhat different. Instead of the three piles I'm suggesting here ("excellent," "poor," and unclassified), Stony Brook portfolios are sorted into two piles: "better than C or satisfactory" and "worse than C." This procedure is less defensible on theoretical grounds, since it is exactly the middle-range portfolios that are most arguable. But still it is better than the available alternatives. Given our obligation (mandated by the faculty senate) to make this judgment, we figured out the most defensible way to do it. The judgment is more trustworthy than an exam. And we figured out how to waste a lot less money trying to sort out students into unneeded piles. (We left that to the students' own teachers.) For more on this procedure, see Elbow and Belanoff "State," Belanoff and Elbow "Using."

4. In 1992 the Writing Program at the University of South Carolina made a remarkable program-wide change of this sort. They dropped the placement test and all sections of the remedial or developmental course (but not the ESL course). Entering students bring a portfolio of precollege writing to the opening class of their first-year writing course. When a teacher judges (with possible consultation) that students need extra help, they are placed in "Writing Studio," a weekly tutorial in groups of four—using a very promising approach. At the end of the first semester's trial with all

freshmen, only a half dozen (6%) of the Writing Studio students failed the course, and they tended to fail lots of courses—thus it wasn't the writing that was holding them back. Many Writing Studio students got very strong grades. The program is even more successful in its second year. For more about it, see Grego and Thompson and my "Assessment."

5. This is to acknowledge help and feedback from Pat Belanoff, David Laurence, and Brian Lavendel, without implicating them in any of the weaknesses here.

4

The Subversions of the Portfolio

James A. Berlin

The use of the portfolio method as a device for program evaluation and as a teaching instrument in the writing classroom represents one of the most progressive developments in composition studies since the introduction of the process model of composing. It is in fact subversive of "business as usual" in schools and colleges as they have been defined during the last twelve years. The portfolio method addresses contradictions in the educational system that dominate the teaching of writing—the conflicts between considering students as ends or means, their activities as personal or professional goods, and the teacher-student relation as human encounter or business transaction. It offers teachers and students an opportunity to unveil the university's efforts to reproduce the conditions of profit-making corporations as well as a device to resist these conditions. Indeed, at the heart of the dispute between the learning and teaching devices encouraged by the portfolio is a challenge to the very economic and political relations that mark the contemporary school setting.

I want to consider the subversions of the portfolio and the way they function in a postmodern school setting. My analysis involves two efforts. First I will look at the ways the most commonly encouraged system of student evaluation in the high school and college setting is designed to deflect any challenges to existing meritocratic structures and interests. This means looking at the role education plays as cultural capital in the economic circuit of power and privilege. The challenges to this circuit posed by the use of portfolio evaluation on a programmatic scale will be central here. Next I consider how placing the portfolio at the center of the writing class introduces practices that offer a corrective to the inadequacies of the unreflective liberal humanism commonly found in composition studies, inadequacies revealed by the theoretical speculations of postmodernism.

Let me begin by describing the freshman English program at the University of Cincinnati during my six years as head of the program, from 1981 to

1987. As I learned in reading Pat Belanoff and Marcia Dickson's *Portfolios: Process and Product,* this program was not at all unusual. Students were required to write a one-hour placement exam during the time they were on campus for their summer orientation. This exam was then ranked on a scale of one to four by two raters, with four the highest score. As motivation, students were told that if they received two fours on the exam, they could waive the first course in their sequence. The most crucial score was between one and two: a score of one meant the student was placed in English 100, Developmental Composition. (In the event of a tie, a third reader made the final decision.) Most students dreaded English 100 because it usually does not count toward graduation. In certain programs with many required courses—most notably engineering—it places a student out of "sync" with her format of studies, which means she might have to go to summer school or take an extra year to graduate.

After the initial exam the placement procedure was still not over. My associate director and I commonly received so many calls and visits from parents, teachers, and the occasional lawyer complaining that a mistake had been made in placing a student in English 100, that we introduced the policy of giving another placement test in all sections on the first day of class. This only seemed fair since we discovered that some students were so distracted by the excitement of the three-day summer orientation that they just could not focus on the business at hand. Teachers who thought a student was misplaced were asked to give me a copy of the essay for confirmation, and together, we made a decision.

After completing the second placement exam, all students in freshman composition classes were told about the exit exam. At the University of Cincinnati students were expected to take this exam at the end of their required course sequence—three quarterly terms for all students (except engineers, who needed only the first two). This exam, students were told, was given during a two-hour period on the Saturday morning before final-exam week, and the student was asked to write a persuasive essay in response to a rhetorical situation. One week before this exam, students were given five or six short essays that provided materials for use in the test essay. The product was rated by two teachers using a four-point scale with a third reader available if a dispute arose over a score between one and two. Students who did not pass the exam could not receive credit for the final course in their sequence until they did pass, preferably at the next make-up session offered at the start of each term. We even set up a one-credit-hour course in exam-writing for those who suffered from disabling test anxiety.

Having been made thoroughly familiar with the placement and evaluation procedures, the students were ready to write. But why, we almost invariably asked ourselves, did they now display so little enthusiasm for the course? Why did they not see that their writing classes enabled them to cultivate their highest potential for living a full and rich life, exploring their own value system (in 101), their public voice in political discourse (in 102), and their delicately nuanced aesthetic responses to some of the best that had been thought and said in English and American literature (in 103)? Why did so many students regard composition as just another required hurdle to be scaled before moving on to the real world of work and community and family life? Why were they so damn anti-intellectual?

One does not have to be a cynic to conclude that these students quickly detected the deadly commodification of the educational experience that lay beneath this entire evaluation process. What President Reagan, Secretary of Education William Bennett, and so many corporate heads told them about the real purpose of education had just been dramatically demonstrated (see Blitz and Hurlbert): schools and colleges were places where one learned skills that could then be sold in the open market; the value of a college education was determined by the amount of money it enabled a person to make in the world of work. The use value of education, like the use value of writing ability in the freshman English program, was determined by its exchange value in the marketplace. A grade point average of 3.5 could be exchanged for a job that paid more than a grade point average of 2.5, just as a higher numerical score on the placement test could be exchanged for a better course than could a lower score. Education, like work—indeed, like life—was finally reducible to a matter of numbers. As for the supposed joy of learning in the writing course— the thrill of self development, the exhilaration of political engagement, the sublime satisfactions of literature—these were extraneous. The real business at hand was to learn enough about writing to get through the exit exam and figure out a way to get grades that would enhance one's attractiveness in the job market.

I am not, I hasten to add, arguing that we in composition studies alone create such attitudes. We most certainly do not. Most of the students at Cincinnati (as well as those I presently see at Purdue) bring with them from high school this impulse to transform into commodities all features of their experience. After all, they have been the victims of one of the most test-crazed eras in the history of our country. For example, in the 1980s all students in Ohio were ranked by the California Achievement Test (CAT) each year, subjected to a number of other internal measuring devices for placing them within school programs, and then required to take a number of tests during their junior year, some mandated by the state of Ohio and others required for college entrance. At the same time, there was constant pressure from business leaders and politicians for additional yearly accountability tests for students (Indiana now has its own) and for teachers (as in Texas, for example). Our students had been thoroughly and bluntly educated in the ways of the meritocracy.

As Evan Watkins has pointed out in his recent *Work Time: English Departments and the Circulation of Value,* since at least the turn of the century schools and colleges have been organized to evaluate and rank students on an ascending scale of accomplishment. The purpose is to provide products who can then be placed in the hierarchical slots within the work force. There the analysis of all tasks into their component parts to be managed for more efficient performance—what is called "Taylorization," after its inventor F. W. Taylor, —has been installed to create a sliding wage scale. The best trained and most able workers are given the most difficult, best paid, and, usually, most engaging jobs, while those with less training are given work less rewarding on all counts—difficulty, pay, and interest. This system requires that all jobs be given a fixed place in a hierarchy so that workers and jobs can be easily managed. However, differences in jobs are not always easily determined, so educational attainments rather than the actual nature of the work performed often determines position in the stratification network. In this case, the educational hierarchy is used to support the work hierarchy, and the entire system is meant, of course, to control the costs of wages by creating differential compensation scales even when there are no genuine differences in the work performed.

As we have seen, the placement and evaluation procedures of freshman composition are ideally suited to validate this meritocracy. In addition, these procedures undermine the best intentions of the process model of composing, the commitment to teaching all stages of text production in the classroom. Systems that emphasize results at the expense of the procedures that went into the product's construction mystify the production process. In our society, this mystification is part of a larger economic mode of operation, and I would like briefly to explore the relation of this mode to composing.

At the most obvious level, the activities that go into the production of nearly all commodities we buy are largely invisible to most consumers. For example, as Ira Shor has demonstrated, students do not know where the fast-food hamburgers they eat almost daily come from. Not that any person or group has dictated that this information be kept from consumers, but it is simply considered unnecessary for most people. Thus, the complex economic, social, and political operations that make possible the fast-food hamburger, the place of students as consumers, and the workers who are part of these operations are simply not discussed. The result of this process is the kind of atomized and disconnected thinking that is incapable of grasping complex systems of relationships that help shape our daily activities.

Most students have no inkling of the intricate web of social networks that contribute to the production of food they eat, clothes they wear, or homes in which they live. In fact, advertising often designedly discourages such reflection. Marketing campaigns do not relate commodities to the conditions of their production, but instead aim to create longing, consumption, and enjoyment with regard only for personal pleasure. Furthermore, this entire process of consumption is so managed by advertisers that it can quickly be restimulated to begin anew. The effects of the production process on the environment, worker health, the stability of international relations, world peace, and the future are simply not considered and, indeed, are not meant to be considered.

The methods of teaching composition that emphasized product over process were designed to reinforce this "bottom-line" thinking. As I have tried to indicate in my two histories of college-writing instruction, it is no coincidence that current-traditional rhetoric arose at the very moment when the university turned its attention to serving the profit objectives of newly emerging national and multinational corporations. A central element of this rhetoric is that it does not matter how or where you find the content of discourse or what your motive for writing happens to be. The important consideration is presenting your message in a manner that renders it effective with your audience. Unlike most of the rhetorics of the past, political and ethical questions are simply not part of the rhetorical act.

We can see how revolutionary (and, considering the larger concerns of older rhetorics, also reactionary) the process model of composing can become. It refuses to ignore the components that are part of text production. It sees writing as an act that creates and discovers knowledge instead of simply recording it. The process model asks questions about the sources of knowledge in the psychological and social processes of our daily thinking and acting. It acknowledges that this process cannot be reduced to a simple matter of arranging established truths and polishing them. The process model encourages the interrogation of accepted wisdom as it takes the very formation of meaning as its province.

My description of the progressive purposes and effects of the process model of composition instruction may be a bit exaggerated, but the model's potential for realizing these purposes and effects is difficult to deny. It likewise requires little imagination to see how use of the portfolio for evaluation works to realize this potential. First of all, portfolio use reclaims the student text from the worst effects of the instrumental thinking encouraged by the university's typical testing procedures. Rather than surrendering the activity of the course to its use value in getting a high score on the placement test or exit exam, students can turn the course to their own uses. Since students can select the work they will submit for final evaluation rather than being subjected to a timed and pressure-packed exam, they can re-appropriate the purposes for writing. Students need no longer complain that, while creative writing or expressive writing or political writing may be helpful to their development as individuals and citizens, these genres finally do not prepare them for the exam or for the work world.

Instead, students can feel more free to explore diverse forms of writing to discover the complex relations of these forms to the comprehensive development of a writer, of someone who can address the constraints of a variety of discourse situations. Writing then becomes more than training for work and profit: it returns composing to the liberal arts and becomes a concern for students as an end of learning. The portfolio then promises to recover students from the realm of commodities, to which even the NCTE recently unwittingly relegated them, referring to students as "human capital" ("Standards for

English" 1). This brings me to a consideration of the actual uses of the portfolio in the writing class.

I agree with Catherine Lucas and Kathleen Blake Yancey that making the portfolio a central feature of teaching the process model of composing is part of a larger project for reclaiming the classroom for student-centered learning. In other words, to rid students of the worst consequences of the product model of composing—encouraged by placement and exit exams—and to adopt portfolio use in the classroom will encourage liberatory practices for teachers and students. As Yancey indicates, the portfolio method used correctly is "first, longitudinal in nature; second, diverse in content; and third, almost always collaborative in ownership and composition" (102).

Portfolio practices thus place the students' development as individuals and members of a community at the center of the classroom. Teachers are encouraged, Yancey explains, to "design their own portfolio projects relative to their own curricular demands and concerns" (107). This connects the portfolio to the teacher-as-researcher model as the professional instructor responds to her learner's unique conditions. Teachers also begin to read student work differently, placing it within a process of development and growth and not simply evaluation. This involves sharing the selection of learning objectives with students, including the use of grades and what they indicate. As Elbow and Belanoff argue, portfolio projects get teachers as well as students to work collaboratively, collectively examining their activities and purposes. The portfolio gives teachers and students greater control over the learning process in a manner that encourages personal growth and the democratization of school and society. In short, everyone stands to gain.

There are, however, certain retrograde features of the literature extolling the portfolio project. Most important, it seems to have completely ignored how portfolio pedagogy might offer a credible response to the critique of composition studies posed by postmodern theoretical speculation. Instructional methods encouraged in the portfolio classroom can serve to demystify not only the composing process but also the related economic, political, and cultural processes that go into consciousness formation as revealed by postmodern theory. In short, as I hope to demonstrate, the portfolio is a postmodern development. First, let me briefly examine the major postmodern conceptions that must be taken into account: the primacy of signifying practices in the formation of subject and society; the loss of the unified, autonomous, self-present subject of liberal humanism; and the end of foundational master narratives.

Signifying practices are radically reconceived in postmodernist speculation. Language is no longer taken to be a transparent conduit of an externally independent thing-in-itself. Instead, language is regarded as a complex system of signifying activities that construct realities rather than simply presenting or re-presenting them. Our conception of the material and social are the productions of language, the fabrications of culturally coded signs. Invoking structuralism, postmodern speculation presents signifiers not as the derivatives of signifieds, external referents, but as the effects of a relation to other signifiers, the semiotic systems in which they are functioning. Just as the sound of *b* is significant in English because it contrasts with *p*—making for a difference in meaning between *bat* and *pat*—a term such as *boy* has significance in a given discourse because it contrasts with another term, such as *girl* or *man* or *chimpanzee*. Just as the sounds of a language are culturally variable, so are its terms and their structural relations. Thus, a sign has meaning as a function of its position relative to another sign or signs within a given system, not as a function of its relation to an externally verifiable reality. These signs, further-more, are arranged hierarchically so that one is "privileged" and considered more important than its related term. For example, in many works of Ameri-can literature the individual is defined in contrast to the group and is consid-ered superior to it. Such hierarchies, it should be recalled, are not universal but are culturally specific. Thus, in Japanese literature group interests are usually forwarded against concerns for the individual.

This conception of signification throws into question the unified, autonomous, self-present subject of liberal humanism. The subject can no longer be regarded as a free and rational agent who adjudicates competing claims for action. She is no longer the author of all of her actions, moving in complete freedom to decide how she will live. Instead the subject is consid-ered the historical product of social and material conditions as mediated by language. Thus, the subject is the construction of the various signifying practices, the uses of language, of a given historical moment. This means that each person is formed by the various sign systems, the discourses that sur-round her. These factors account for everyday uses of language in the home, school, media, and other institutions, as well as the material conditions that are culturally arranged in the manner of sign systems—such as the clothes we wear, the way our school and home environments are organized and the way we carry our bodies. These signifying practices, then, are languages that tell us who we are and how we should behave in terms of such culturally coded categories as gender, sexual orientation, race, class, age, ethnicity, and the like. Each of us then is heterogeneously made up of competing discourses—of conflicted and contradictory scripts—that make our consciousness anything but unified, coherent, and autonomous.

These anti-foundational assertions about the subjects and objects of expe-rience are extended to totalistic conceptions of the past or of the present. Discourses such as Hegelianism or Marxism or the theories of scientific progress or the natural laws of economics are all declared illusions and attempts to impose foundational master narratives that are, in fact, human and social constructions. They are regarded as language games that are inherently partial and interested, intended to endorse particular relations of power and to favor certain groups over others in historical struggles. The alternative is the limited and contingent narrative that is always conditionally offered, an account remaining open to revision and change.

I should quickly add that these postmodern formulations do not mean that we live in a radically indeterminate realm of free-floating signifiers, that the subject is incapable of agency, or that no larger narratives can ever be invoked in understanding individual events. While I cannot rehearse my case here, I have elsewhere argued against this extreme version of postmodernism (see "Postmodernism, Politics, and Histories of Rhetoric" and "Poststructuralism, Cultural Studies, and the Composition Classroom: Postmodern Theory in Practice"). Thus, while signifying practices mediate all experience of the material and the social, this does not mean that certain mediations are not better than others in accounting for these conditions.

For example, the ability of certain economic decisions to redistribute wealth more evenly than certain other decisions can be verified over time. However, there is no guarantee that these decisions will provide the same results always and everywhere. As historical conditions change, other decisions may need to be made. Similarly, the social construction of the subject does not mean that agency is out of the question. Since we all occupy a unique position in relation to the discourses around us, we all bring a slightly different perspective to our common experience. Thus, while we are not totally autonomous subjects, a certain measure of originality in human action is possible as we engage in the interchange of conflicting perspectives on experience. And finally, as I suggested earlier, the absence of foundational master narratives does not mean that contingent, historicised accounts are not useful. Indeed, without some larger conception of our historical context we would be doomed to a radically atomistic response to experience that would result in chaos and destruction.

But what does this have to do with the practices of the portfolio in the composition class? As I said before, the use of the process model of composing in a portfolio setting enables us to consider the elements and activities that make up text production. It works against the idea that writing is a product-centered activity concerned only with economic exchange value. More to the point, considering postmodern conceptions of signification, subjectivity, and contingent narratives encourages us to examine the process of composing that includes formation of the subject producing the text, the audience interpreting it, the cultural codes involved in the mediation of the content of the discourse, and the signifying practices involved in each.

Let us first consider the subject of composing. As Yancey has indicated, the portfolio nurtures "self-reflexiveness about writing" as well as "the identity of writer in the student" (104). Through the portfolio, the student begins to grasp the distinction between the subject who composes the text and the subject who is presented in the text. In other words, students can learn that the subject—sometimes called the voice but including much more—who appears to the reader in the text is constructed by the subject who is constructing the text.

For example, the subject who appears in the text to which you now listen is a version of Jim Berlin as created by the Jim Berlin who has written the text. The speaking subject—the author of the text—possesses features not presented in the text he is composing. Jim Berlin, the speaking subject, has created Jim Berlin, the spoken subject who appears in this text. To understand this distinction one need only recall how many features of Jim Berlin/the speaking subject are not included in Jim Berlin/the spoken subject of this text. None of us would like to be condemned to assume the personae we construct in academic discourse in all our relations with others, even though at times there may be the temptation to do so. When I try to play college professor with my wife or sons by creating in my discourse with them the academic spoken subject I am creating here, they usually respond with laughter or anger or both: "Lighten up, Dad. I'm not one of your students." Or, more regrettably, "Drop it, Jim. I'm your wife, not an undergraduate." Sociologists refer to this creation of a subject in discourse as role playing, of course, and this is a useful way to think of the spoken subject, the subject created in a discourse by the speaking subject, the multiple split subject behind the scenes.

The important matter to recall here is that this argues against telling the student in a writing class to "be yourself" in composing, or even to "find yourself" in composing. The subject that appears in the text may represent some element of the speaking subject, but the two are never identical. Self-reflexiveness about writing then involves discovering the difference between the speaking subject—the writer who is writing—and the subject spoken—the subject who appears in the text. I am not in any way suggesting that students should create spoken subjects that conflict with speaking subjects. In other words, I am not suggesting that students be insincere or dishonest—say, in the manner of advertisers who, in all seriousness, cynically create speakers in texts who they know are entirely fabrications, without any imaginable sane referent. We must, however, teach students that the subject presented in their texts is only one set of characteristics in their complex web of subject formations. Doing so, indeed, serves two purposes simultaneously.

First, the student discovers that the subject of a text can only be created through language. Thus, discursive devices must be learned to understand the textual construction of a subject in a text. For example, to create the persona of the college professor in a professional text, certain lexical items, certain syntactic structures, and certain patterns of organization must be used. These indicate a specific way of mediating external experience and certain invention strategies and attitudes. All of these together create a spoken subject in discourse who is likely to hold the attention of the academic audience. The student learns that this subject position is only one of many she can assume in written discourse, just one of the subject formations that writing enables her to construct. She also learns that changing the conventions that go into the creation of these subjects is not an easy task, indeed, virtually impossible for students and often beyond the reach of even senior members of a discourse community (as Peter Elbow has recently noted in "Reflections on Academic Discourse"). More to the point, this activity places this subject in relation to other subjects, other voices in the dialogue that operates in the formation of the student. Each of us is the site of a number of conflicting and contradictory subjectivities, all constructed by language. The portfolio enables the writer to explore these formations as they interact in our daily lives.

Second, this examination of conflicting subjectivities is enhanced by the variety of writing encouraged in the portfolio class. Engaging in creative writing, academic discourse, and political discourse, for example, enables the student to locate the different subject positions possible for her. This in turn leads to examining the rhetorical features of each—the patterns of invention, arrangement, and style that discourse makes possible for each. Once again, the differences in genre encourage an understanding of the different kinds of reality that texts construct. Just as important, multi-genre writing leads the student to examine the contradictions in her own subjectivity uncovered by these different genres. For example, the student who, in writing poetry, portrays the subject as the totally free and unique center of human activity—a kind of unmoved mover—may discover that the subject of political discourse or academic discourse offers a contradictory formation, not nearly as powerful as we might like to believe. The absolute autonomy of the subject of creative writing is accordingly cast in doubt.

This sort of contradiction occurs to students when they have the means to analyze the cultural codes, the signifying practices, that construct subjects along the lines of race, class, gender, sexual orientation, and the like. Indeed, it is only after students begin to uncover the coded character of their subject formations that they are ready to explore what it means to be different, to resist dominant codes. As many freshman writing teachers quickly realize, beginning writers commonly regard themselves as being totally unique, but, significantly, unique in exactly the same way as their peers, each establishing singular identities in strikingly similar ways. To be different for most of our students means to "personally choose" patterns of behavior that, upon inspection, are virtually identical to most of their classmates' choices. This is a gesture that surely deserves to be labeled as personal mystification. The stance offered here, on the other hand, is that difference exists only in relation to what is not different. Before I can depart from dominant patterns I must be able to identify these dominant patterns.

Thus, the portfolio in a postmodern context enables the exploration of subject formation. As students begin to understand through writing the cultural codes that shaped their development, they are prepared to occupy different subject positions, different perspectives on the person and society. The narratives of their developments as writers recommended by the portfolio become accounts of their larger intellectual, personal, and social growth.

Looking at the process of producing texts for a variety of discourse communities in a collaborative setting makes for discoveries about the process of producing subjectivities for and by students. They can examine the ways institutional and other relationships are continually interpellating them, inviting them to assume certain subject positions and to behave accordingly. This leads to a consideration of the audience and of the relation between the writer and readers.

Audiences, as Victor Vitanza has lately been reminding us, are tyrants. In their insistence on particular discursive strategies and rhetorical patterns, they are positioning us as certain kinds of subjects who, because of this positioning, can experience events only in particular ways. When Maxine Hairston, for example, insists that I must use only language that is familiar and accessible to her, she is trying to "subject" me to her ideology and her vision of things as they are and ought to be. The postmodern stance that I offer requires that in my writing I use different terms, different syntax and different patterns of arrangement in order to explore a representation of events I find more persuasive. As David Bartholomae has pointed out, we college writing teachers routinely ask entering students to do what Professor Hairston refuses to do, knowing that their compliance with new modes of discourse makes for limitations as well as gains in their experience. Unfortunately, any genre always excludes more than it includes, but this is the nature of signification: a way of seeing is a way of not seeing, as Kenneth Burke reminds us. The point of education in a democracy is to discover as many ways of seeing as possible, not to rest secure in the perspective we find the easiest and most comfortable or the perspective of those currently in power.

In the portfolio class students will examine and, most importantly, challenge the conditions of this subjection (but not by refusing to consider unfamiliar formations, as does the anti-intellectual Professor Hairston, an expedient simply not available to them if they are to succeed in college). As we have seen, when students are asked to assume different subject positions in different genres, they are being asked to inhabit certain race, class, gender, sexual orientation, age, ethnic, and other roles. These in turn are related to power relations involving economic, social, and political arrangements. This places us in the realm of the larger narratives necessary to understand particular experiences. These narratives are, of course, historically contingent, but they are necessary for locating and responding to the complex power relations of our moment.

For example, certain women asked to assume agonistic discourse strategies in word, syntax, and organization may find themselves uncomfortable because they have learned that women of a particular class simply do not write or think agonistically: it is just not womanly. This commonly prevents them from even considering certain professions that require this sort of writing—for example, law or scientific research. Thus, even after law schools and graduate schools cease to discriminate against women in admission procedures, a large percentage of college-educated women may exclude themselves from application because they have been hailed as subjects, "subjected," in a manner that prevents them from thinking of themselves as lawyers or scientists. This sort of cultural coding of subjects obviously serves the economic and political interests of certain groups at the expense of others. It encourages what is called a "self-selection" process in which women "freely choose" the careers that insure their continued exclusion from positions of power and privilege and men "freely choose" positions of dominance. The portfolio can encourage students to explore in an unthreatening situation the intersections of private behavior and larger economic and social categories in a way that enables both women and men to construct and, in the same moment, critique the spoken subject that is appropriate to discourses of power. Creating the subject position, the voice, of the powerful can be fruitfully studied from the perspective of rhetoric, of the textual devices that construct this voice. In its insistence on the creation of diverse texts and extensive reflection on the differences in these texts as they unfold over time, the portfolio is well suited to this effort. Such activities simultaneously demystify discourses of power and enable writers typically excluded to enter their circle, a position from which the discourses can be effectively resisted and reformed.

It will be the duty of the postmodern portfolio writing class to explore these larger economic and political narratives as well as the more localized directives of race, class, gender, sexual orientation, and the like. In its concern with subject formation, signification, and provisional narratives, and in its creation of a context where the student writes in a variety of genres, reflects on this writing, and works within a collaborative framework for text production and evaluation, the portfolio writing class addresses the needs of students as workers, citizens, and individual sites of desire. The portfolio method can enable the re-appropriation of the use value of education, seeking benefits for the personal lives of the students and the operation of a democratic society. Finally, this repossession will serve the best interests of those who deserve to be considered first by school, work, and related institutions—our young people—now regarded not as "human capital" that can enhance corporate profits but as human beings who deserve to be the beneficiaries of history.

Part Two:
Portfolios in the Classroom

Students' Voices

5

Removing the Blindfold: Portfolios in Fiction Writing Classes

Tom Romano

As much as I value excellent writing, I have come to value the developmental nature of learning just as much. I measure success not simply by where learners end their journey but also by where they began, how and where they traveled, what they encountered along the way, and what they did in the face of it. To understand their development as fiction writers, I look at more than my graduate and undergraduate students' final products. I try to get inside their learning. I want to know what concepts, strategies, and skills matter most to them.

Portfolios offer a way for me to find out such information. Portfolios that let me get inside students' learning must be more than collections of their best stories—even revised ones—which I grade, bringing to bear my history as a reader and writer of fiction, my course goals, my relationship with each student, my prejudices about various genres and styles of fiction, my tastes, and my moods. I'm not interested merely in grading papers. I can do that without lugging around a briefcase full of portfolios.

I am, however, interested in becoming one with students' understanding. I want to see what fiction-writing values students are developing and what they are doing or paying attention to that makes them better writers. I want to get so close to students' learning—become so informed and surprised by their knowledge—that I become embarrassed to think I might presume to evaluate them without the information they reveal in their portfolios.

Dan Ling Fu states my position precisely in her article that appears in Bonnie Sunstein and Donald Graves' *Portfolio Portraits*. Fu reports on research she did with her seven-year-old son, Xiao-di, who spoke only a smattering of

English. Fu compared adults' perceptions of Xiao-di's literacy learning to his own notions of it as revealed through an interview about his portfolio. Near the end of the article, Fu writes, "Xiao-di's talk about his own work not only convinced me that learners can have more control of their own learning if they can be included in the evaluation of their learning, but also taught me that we, teachers and parents, will understand our children better if we are willing to listen to what they say about themselves instead of judging them by our own standards of what we wanted them to be" (182-183).

Listening is the key. That was the skill on which I had worked hard during the last eight years. Hold off judgment, throttle preconceived ideas. Listen well to students and try to understand better than I expect to; listen to what they tell me in class discussion, in conferences, and most often, in their writing.

The Courses

My students maintained learning portfolios in Beginning Fiction Writing and Advanced Fiction Writing. In each course they wrote four to seven pages of fiction weekly in addition to one-page metacognitive commentaries about that writing. Students also met with me each week in conference to discuss their writing.

Fifty-five percent of their grade was based on good faith participation, which included doing all homework assignments suitably, completing their fiction and commentaries each week, and attending class and conference. Twenty percent of their grade was based on my judgment of the quality of their fiction—one grade for a story they deemed their best work of the quarter. Twenty-five percent of their grade, then, was left to the learning portfolio that they compiled and presented at midterm and quarter's end. The learning portfolio was the students' chance to teach me the details and complexities of their learning, information I might miss by merely listening to their writing each week and grading a final story.

Midquarter Learning Portfolios

To ease students' anxiety about compiling a portfolio, I shared mine with them before midterm. Although not confined to the one topic of fiction writing as theirs would be, my portfolio was, nevertheless, a demonstration of someone who reflected on his learning, gathered together the significant bits of it, and explained their meaning in a cover letter.

A week after my presentation, students presented part of their learning portfolios to the class; they also photocopied their cover letters for one another. This midquarter trial run was instructive to all of us. From each presentation and cover letter students learned about areas they might explore and concepts they might have forgotten. Probably the most important thing I learned was where some students had gone askew, usually with poor organization or inadequate explanation in the cover letters about the meaning of the portfolio's contents.

Jason's portfolio, for example, was a jumbled mass of papers and photocopied pages, some labeled, some not. It was often unclear to me if I connected the correct artifact with the correct part of his cover letter.

Heather provided a typed draft of a story she had revised in longhand. In her cover letter she wrote, "I learned a lot as I really tore into the piece."

Angela, too, left all the work to me when she included in her portfolio a long article by Bruno Bettelheim, mentioning in her letter that it should shed light on her process of writing fiction.

Such portfolios left me adrift, trying to guess what students had learned.

An Expository Act

Compiling and presenting a portfolio is an expository act. In fiction writing we prize dramatizing scenes, revealing character through dialogue, action, and thoughts. I pushed students to create uninterrupted fictional dreams with little or no exposition, thus creating a paradox. We did not write about ideas; we wrote about the "experience of ideas" (Burroway 297). We came to value leaving unsaid what was shown.

Amid work in this implicit genre of fiction writing, however, I asked students to be explicit when they put together their portfolios. I was after a transactional act of communication.

Organization of the portfolio is critical. I must know where I am at every moment I am reading a portfolio. The portfolio keeper must direct me precisely to what he or she wants to show me. Otherwise I become lost, frustrated, and short-tempered—not a state of mind for an evaluator. After one midterm portfolio gathering, I wrote a letter to the students giving them more detailed instructions for putting together their final portfolios. To one class I wrote in part:

> Isolate what you are illustrating in your portfolio. Let a paragraph appear on a page by itself if what you are showing is contained in it. If you are showing how you've revised something, highlight the illustrative part.
>
> Don't make your portfolio reviewer go through pages of manuscript before finding what you are talking about. Mark off the pertinent material, designate it, nail it down. Make it a breeze to look through your portfolio and discover your meaning.

In both classes the final portfolios were, indeed, better organized. Jeri, for example, gathered her portfolio in a three-ring binder with sections and subsections marked in labeled, colored tabs. She reprinted the appropriate paragraph from her cover letter at the heading of each section. Leaunda, a technical writer in her nonstudent life, organized her portfolio in a bound folder with a textured cover. In a week-by-week analysis she meticulously catalogued her learning. In contrast, Laurie, who compiled an equally accessible portfolio, ordered hers in an "event" approach. "My learning experience," she explained, "came more in terms of specific insights that were not necessarily directed by course chronology."

As exquisite as such portfolios were, I also valued plain ones tucked into manila folders with separate artifacts neatly clipped together and a clear correspondence between each artifact and the germane part of the cover letter.

Although my students were avoiding exposition in their fiction writing, I hungered for persuasive, expository prose in their portfolios. The moment of assessment was not a time for me to rummage around trying to figure out what students had learned. Before I read the portfolios, students were to have assessed their learning and explained it in cover letters. I wanted Heather to articulate exactly what she had learned about craft or her subject matter when she "tore into" her story. I wanted Angela to explain exactly how the Bettelheim article had shed light on her writing process.

I wrote to one class:

> In your letter amplify the meaning of the artifact. Use your best expository skills. Explain and persuade. Your facility with language will help you here. One of you said you learned about *continental revision* (as opposed to *global revision*). Another said that you wanted your writing to be "dry," not "wet." Those are wonderful. But don't neglect to explain the concepts well. Use specific detail to illustrate generalities and assertions.
>
> If you say "I learned from doing my story about baseball catchers and transsexuals," that is nice, but I am not hip to exactly what you learned. I'm adrift. If you say that you learned about using indirect characterization, however, and then refer me to the artifact in the portfolio that has your use of indirect characterization highlighted, then the clarity and truth of your assertion comes swiftly home to me.

Learning About Learning

Most students took pains to organize well their final portfolios and to write explicit explanations in their cover letters. Consequently, I pointedly learned about their learning. Part of all students' portfolios was devoted to skills they attained. Many of them learned to use dialogue for the first time. And many of them stubbed their toes—gloriously. Laurie, for example, tried hard to capture the particular speech of a character from a specific part of the country. She explained her struggle with dialogue in her cover letter:

> In my commentary . . . I wrote about creating dialogue that included the actual sound of the old man's English. In this particular case the comments from Dr. Romano helped me sort out how much phonetic spelling to use in the piece. I learned that some phonetic spelling helped, but spelling most of the dialogue phonetically was distracting from the story.
>
> I also realized that the old man's grammar added to his cultural distinctiveness. In the first draft when I combined his grammar with phonetic

spelling, it placed the reader in a cultural presence the size of an elephant rather than in the presence of an elderly western gentleman. So the learning outcome of my efforts to write "authentic sounding" dialogue is "don't use too much phonetic spelling."

Laurie included these examples of dialogue from her story (The scene involves an elderly man from Idaho who plows his grocery cart into that of a young woman):

From the original:
"Oh fer hell sakes honey. Are you ok? I didn't mean ta do that."

Revised:
"Oh for hell sakes honey. Are you ok? I didn't mean to do that."

First draft—authentic grammar with phonetic spelling:
"Ah never wuz no good at this groc'ry store drivin'."

Second draft:
"I never was no good at this groc'ry store drivin'."

Dawn, an undergraduate, indicated that She, too, grappled with dialogue:

> Dialogue is the area in which I had the most problems, as well as the most improvement. My writing this quarter illustrated the fact that I had never tried to write dialogue until I had this class. I experienced several problems in this area. Comma-splice hell is one way to describe some of my dialogue passages. Dialogue tags present several problems. Not only was I describing how something was said through adverbs, but I had forgotten the utility of "said." I also over used dialogue tags, often including them when they weren't needed. . . .
>
> The combination of these problems produced some very scary dialogue passages. I have included samples of some of my worst dialogue mistakes and what I did to correct the problems.
>
> Before: "I was an island then," she stated, "things were rough, but you were always kind to me. Thanks," she added.
>
> After: "I was an island then," she said. "Things were rough, but you were always kind to me. Thanks."

Dawn included twelve such examples to illustrate the elimination of adverbs, overuse of dialogue tags, the utility of *said*, and—as I've often experienced when reading students' papers—"comma-splice hell."

On a different front, Anna discussed her battle with adjectives. She began with a shameless confession:

> I love adjectives! I've always assumed that the more description there is, the better. . . . Dr. Romano commented to me "Anna, go easy on the adjectives." Before this epiphany, I thought that I could somehow make the story more believable to the readers if I could just describe it thoroughly, without any loopholes. I didn't want to make readers labor through my story

and force them to figure it out for themselves. I guess I was trying too hard to please the readers. In essence, I underestimated readers' sensitivity and cleverness."

Anna included some pages from her stories with the indulgence in adjectives underlined and highlighted in yellow. Here are two examples she caught:

> The sparse silver-colored bikini that clung to Ashley's tan sleek body didn't leave anything to the imagination.

> Ashley's long shiny and full blond hair and her luscious deep-sea blue eyes seemed angelic.

We worked hard on creating and sustaining what John Gardner calls "the fictional dream," "a rich and vivid play in the mind" (30). So critical is the novelist's responsibility in this respect that "one of the chief mistakes a writer can make," Gardner believes, "is to allow or force the reader's mind to be distracted, even momentarily, from the fictional dream" (31–32).

Matt was eloquent when describing his relationship to this concept and in revealing the optimal psychological experience that weaving a fictional dream can have on a writer. For an artifact in his portfolio Matt included the page-and-a-half climactic scene from his first story when the point-of-view character, lost in the mountains, stumbles and is knocked unconscious. In his cover letter Matt wrote:

> For me the term "fictional dream" has double meaning. First there is the dream that . . . a writer creates for the reader. I think the term also applies really well to the experience the writer experiences as he/she is writing. They are actually tied together. If the writer lives well enough his fictional dream and is talented enough to write down all he experiences then the reader will also experience the dream.
>
> Whether or not I succeeded in transmitting it to the page or not I experienced quite vividly a fictional dream from the writer's point of view while writing "Frozen." My whole body was shaking, I felt dizzy at times, and without a doubt, lost. . . .

Surprises

Portfolio artifacts about specific skills were related to in-class craft lessons, textbook advice, and individual conferences. Students dutifully attended to my skills agenda. I was smug about that until I learned that the part of portfolio assessment I found most gratifying as a teacher was students' understanding and ways of working that took me totally offguard. When students surprised me, my knowledge and respect for them deepened most.

Les, for example, nearing completion of his master's degree in English and contracted to teach at a nearby junior college the following year, had been dissatisfied with our large group workshops. Instead of just complaining, though, he wrote an essay setting forth the benefits of peer-response sessions and explained how they could be run most effectively. Along with the essay, he included a two-page form he developed for students to use when responding to their peers' creative writing. Les, I learned, was taking his education seriously, already determining how his own experience as a writer would affect his teaching style.

Elizabeth, one of the struggling students in Beginning Fiction Writing, chagrined me by demonstrating that she had been working harder to become a better fiction writer than I'd thought. She included a handwritten draft of an exercise she had performed without any prompting from me or our textbook. In her cover letter she wrote:

> I'm putting in a copy of the exercise I did one day in my ongoing endeavor to improve on writing fictional dream. I decided to choose a scene from a movie that would be very descriptive on paper, so I chose the scene from "Mr. Mom" where Michael Keaton is changing his daughter's diaper after she ate some chili. While writing the scene, some descriptive phrases like "I thought about waiting until my wife came home so she could have the honor, but compassion for my daughter overrode my rising nausea" just seemed to pop into my head. Others didn't come so easy.

Even though I would have liked expansion of her explanation—some discussion, perhaps—of what it was like trying to recreate on paper using language the images just seen on a video screen, or how the exercise affected her fiction writing, I was still grateful to learn of Elizabeth's efforts. Her reflective look at her struggle to write a fictional dream and her reporting that struggle to me complicated my easy assessment of her efforts during the quarter. I was glad to see it.

Another undergraduate, Karla, coined a phrase that captured the imaginations of most students in Advanced Fiction Writing. In her midterm portfolio, Karla's most important learning revelation was titled, "IF IT'S WET, WORRY." She explained in her cover letter:

> This is a saying that I learned when I was a nurse's aide. Someone asked the supervisor when rubber gloves were necessary in dealing with patients (you can't wear gloves all the time, because it affects the patients' morale): "If anything is ever wet, consider it germ-infested and get those gloves before you soil your hands."
>
> It applies to my writing because mentally, I always classify overly rich writing as "WET." I have a tendency to look for rhythm and overwrite things, losing a decent story under a barrage of complicated sentences. (I used to read a lot of Toni Morrison. I tried to copy her and did a lousy job.) So—if it's wet, it's probably germ-ridden, and it needs to be CUT. Because I worry about WETNESS so much, I changed my writing style and adopted the short-sentence, first-person narrative, which became the story I'm handing in today. . . .

Introduced in her midterm portfolio, Karla's medically charged dictum to avoid producing overly written prose became a repetend among the students. The phrase frequently came up in class and worked its way into a number of the students' weekly commentaries and final portfolios, including Karla's. But in her final portfolio she put unexpected spin on her learning:

> Item one is all about wetness and worry. Again. We've all been through its possible meanings. I have heard several comments on it, and I really don't know what to say about any of them, except that I'm flattered you even bothered to stop and talk to me about it.
>
> More importantly, the wetness/worry thing has taken several shades of embarrassment in my writing this quarter. . . . Some good things came out of that "overwriting" for which I razed myself so harshly. The very example of dry vs. wet writing that I used in my commentary . . . I decided to leave in the final draft. I accept it as part of my own system of writing, and know that if it's too much, there is always revision.

I was surprised and initially sorry to see Karla discard her "wet/worry" theory, but then I looked past my own agenda and realized that Karla's rethinking showed me she wasn't hidebound. This young woman was interested in expressing herself well, not merely in abiding by cliches and dicta about good writing, whether from Strunk and White or Romano. Karla valued her experience and respected her intellect. She took a close look at how she worked as a writer and what strategies helped her get writing done. She honored her perceptions by revising and deepening her theory: If it's wet, worry, but not right away.

Commitment

In his discussion of portfolios that art students submit to colleges, Harlan Hoffa, Associate Dean in the college of Art and Architecture at Pennsylvania State University, says

> A portfolio tells the college faculty more than simply whether the student can draw or not—important though that is. It also speaks volumes about attitude, about work habits, and about those most necessary qualities of drive, inner discipline, commitment to art and the compulsion to succeed (17).

What I learned about some of my students' commitment to fiction writing were the most startling surprises I got from their portfolios.

Leaunda, for example, who was writing a historical novel based upon early Mormon settlement of Utah, titled a section in her portfolio "Influences on my Writing From Sources Outside Class." Under this heading she included poems she'd collected that captured the mood and setting of the West she was after, two articles about writing historical fiction (which she briefly annotated), and a map of the principal wagon-freighting routes into Utah during the mid-nineteenth century to remind her of her fictional wagon train's location.

Joe, a senior, included two articles from a popular writing magazine, one a piece about fiction openings accompanied with an analysis of the young adult novel opening he'd written in the fall; he added a revision of that opening incorporating the new strategies he'd learned. The other article was about writing crime fiction and included author tips about police and forensic work. Joe highlighted an excerpt about lifting fingerprints from cigarette lighters. Coupled with this artifact, he included a page from his murder mystery to show how he'd used that information.

Bert illustrated how the campus' efforts to enliven the intellectual atmosphere in the arts had paid off. During spring quarter our campus was visited by novelist Tony Hillerman and writer Donald Murray. In his portfolio letter Bert wrote, "Tony Hillerman said to write every day. Don Murray states 'Nulles dies sine linea' (Never a day without a line) . . . So, I tried a little during the twilight between sleep and being awake."

With this, Bert included in his portfolio more than a dozen quick writings he'd produced in the early morning, just trying to let go and write with velocity, as Murray advised.

Bert went on to vividly describe how one morning his writing about the Los Angeles riots led to further thinking about the plight of inner city youth. That thinking, he explained, sparked a story idea he mentally rehearsed while mountain biking one afternoon. He then completed a drafting session with great velocity, keeping a specific person in mind as audience (more Murray advice), discovered a theme that dawned on him during the writing, and made a hopeful promise to finish the story by quarter's end, which he kept.

Conclusion

Portfolio assessment is perfectly synchronized with a personal growth model of language learning, a philosophy of teaching I've come to embrace in recent years. The use of learning portfolios in my fiction writing classes has put me closer to students' learning and enabled me to move some of the weight for class grades from my arbitrary grading of their papers to my assessment of their portfolios. Although I still determine grades for portfolios, my grading is informed considerably by the students, who show and explain what they have learned and come to value. They remove the blindfold from my eyes, and I am a much more efficient, confident, and trustworthy evaluator when I see clearly.

My students wrote thousands of words of fiction over a quarter term. They read a textbook and articles. They listened to their classmates' stories and talked about them. They talked to me each week about their writing. The learning portfolios enabled them to step back, reflect upon their experiences with language, and explicitly say what they had learned and how they had grown.

Although some students resented keeping the learning portfolios because of the time it took to compile them and because their notions differed about what should be done in a creative writing class, many more students saw the benefits of portfolios. One student wrote, "I don't know that I learned anything *per se* from the portfolio, but I thought it was encouraging to see that my writing had improved and that there were areas where I had made progress."

Another student, a portfolio enthusiast, wrote, "Compiling my portfolio gave me a chance to organize and summarize the most valuable things I've learned in this class. It gave me the opportunity to *briefly* yet specifically locate/pinpoint my greatest learning experiences as a fiction writer. Without this portfolio project, I truly believe that I would've let a lot of things slip from my mind. . . . [The portfolio] is a productive way to end a whole quarter worth of writing."

In *Seeking Diversity,* Linda Rief makes the case that the real value in evaluation is for the learner (135), not the teacher, or the board of trustees, or a national standards data bank. Portfolio evaluation is eminently suited for students to discover what they have learned. As a side benefit, I, too, learn about their education—crucial information if I presume to grade students.

Not long ago I heard Delfeayo Marsalis tell an interviewer what he was about as a jazz musician. He said he sought to enhance the human experience. As a teacher that's what I'm about, too. Compiling learning portfolios enables students to see what they've learned and to monitor and communicate their growth. Their confidence increases because of that seeing and saying. Their human experience is enhanced. And as their teacher, so is mine.

Note

I wish to thank the good faith participation of my fiction writing students at Utah State University and the helpful response and editorial advice of Bonnie Sunstein of the University of Iowa.

6

Portfolio Cover Letters, Students' Self-Presentation, and Teachers' Ethics

Glenda Conway

The cover letter is probably the most consistently required document appearing in students' writing portfolios. Regardless of whether portfolios are prepared at the elementary or the college level; whether they are used in courses with expository, research, or creative goals; whether their purpose is to determine a proficiency level or a course grade—invariably the final packages submitted to teachers are expected not only to show the documents students have written, but also to tell something about the people who wrote them.

Self-reflection is the inclusive term used in composition literature for this kind of telling. The documents of self-reflection are known by a variety of names; nevertheless, they share a singular rhetorical function. Whether teachers ask their students to submit a cover letter, an introduction, a writer's memo, an attachment, a self-analysis, a rationale, a completed questionnaire, or some other form of metadiscourse with their portfolios, the reality is that teachers want to read first-person accounts of their students' writing processes. Teachers who assign these reflective documents generally consider them to be at least as valuable and meaningful as the other written materials submitted in portfolios.

Given our field's high regard for the processes as well as the products of writers, it seems entirely appropriate and honorable for us to want our students to reflect on their ways of writing. However, when we require a self-reflective document to be included in a package of materials that we will be evaluating, there are serious ethical questions that arise, or that should arise. The reason for this has much to do with the privileged position cover letters hold in the minds of their readers, something that shows blatantly in the reverence in portfolio literature for high quality cover letters. Not insignificantly, it also has to do with the cover letter's featured position as the front document in the portfolio package. It is the cover letter that gets to speak the portfolio's first words, that portrays the character and the commitment of the writer, that conveys or appears to convey assumptions about the reader. It is the cover letter that has the most potential of all the portfolio documents to engage or alienate an audience.

When I taught my first portfolio-centered course, an honors composition class at the University of Louisville during fall 1991, I did not begin to realize the crucial role of cover letters until the last few weeks of the semester. As I wrote out final instructions for portfolio preparation, and as I discussed these instructions in class, I found myself beginning to look forward to the letters. I wondered what my students would say in them, what kinds of insights I might gain about my students' values, whether they would feel comfortable being direct with me, and if I would learn anything about myself as a teacher. In spite of my curiosity, I was not at all prepared for the overwhelming effects the letters actually had on me as I began evaluating portfolios to determine my students' semester grades. Some of the letters were engaging introspections on grand-scale changes (including shifts in writing practices and attitudes). Some analyzed the nature of our class structure and its influence on the ways students viewed themselves as writers. Some quite consciously factored me into their positive results. Some simply continued pleasant conversations about their papers begun during conferences or in exchanges on earlier drafts. These letters, I openly admit, pushed just the right "buttons," especially given the particular audience—a teacher ending a semester during which she had tried something new.

Following are some brief excerpts from a few of my most pleasurably impressive letters. (Note: The names of writers in these letter excerpts, along with those of others quoted in this essay, are pseudonyms.)

> . . . I would like to thank you for your time and effort necessary for the extensive comments on each of the essays. They highlighted the strong areas of the essays and my strengths as a writer. Your comments also pointed out the weaknesses in the paper and how I could improve those areas. The conferences we had also helped me an enormous amount. On the outset of this class, I did not enjoy writing at all. Amazingly, through this class, I actually enjoyed writing the essays. I remember in an in-class essay I told you that I found my own writing dull, but now I think its pretty interesting.
> Thanks for an interesting semester!
> Manny Mashni

> . . . The second paper that I have included is *The Origins of Slavery in the United States*. I spent . . . more research time on this paper than I ever have doing any research. It has also been through more revisions and changes than any other paper I have written. It is my most improved paper from what I

initially submitted in class. It has the best mechanics of any paper that I have written. I am also quite proud of its content. . . .
Paul Dan Harper

. . . I've revised the heck out of this one, and I'm still doing it. I've cut out a lot of unnecessary phrases, and I am currently trying to integrate the concept of "deep play" earlier in the paper without destroying its flow. Hopefully I've succeeded. I've tried to introduce the Bentham concept between the description of old-time politics and modern politics without completely explaining it. I still prefer to keep the full explanation of "deep play" later in the paper after all of my historical introduction is complete. While I would have much preferred to have it all in one pretty section, I couldn't find any way to do it without destroying the natural flow of the paper.
Kenneth Sudduth

Dear Glenda,

Before I begin discussing my essays, I'd like to first take the time to tell you how much I appreciate your class. I realize it was really loose and wild at times, but I believe that that coincides with the way creative writing should be. So, I'd just like to thank you for not being the stern professor that you could have been . . .

Carlos Jones

Obviously, Carlos' letter and the others excerpted above might have been deliberate attempts on the part of those students to write what they thought would be in their best grade-point interests. Notwithstanding, a deliberate effort is not necessarily a false effort, at least to some extent. What can be said about Carlos, Kenneth, Paul, and Manny—according to the values they espoused explicitly and implicitly in their cover letter language—is that they knew some of what it means to think like academic writers. It may well be that such knowledge is really only a mask adopted for the purposes of writing a strong cover letter. But that's not to imply there's something wrong with such a mask; indeed, there's nothing really false about it either. One of the most established ways for a newcomer to work her way into a field is to learn and use the language valued by that field (Bartholomae 135). It is in the light of this premise that I quote the following paragraph from Reagan Sanders' cover letter:

The revisions I made along the lines of your suggestions have improved the quality of the content in each essay. Writing, however, has not been the most important skill I improved this semester; the art of "re-writing" and revising has acquired a much higher priority than has formerly been the case.

Even though I know that Reagan could have written this paragraph merely out of a desire to insure a positive response (and thus a positive grade) from me, what I believe is what is more important than what I know. And what I believe is that Reagan chose to assign a high status to revision in her cover letter out of her knowledge that revision is necessary and expected in college writing. Whether Reagan really believed in the benefits of revision does not matter in the end; what is important is that she *knew* it was an important matter to discuss in her cover letter. And yes, this knowledge did elicit a favorable response from me.

Perhaps the best way of emphasizing the positive rhetorical power of the "good" cover letters I received is to contrast them with two letters that disappointed me and, on a certain level, even insulted me. These letters, for the most part, appeared to have been written merely to fulfill an obligation, to get a job finished and out of the way as effortlessly as possible. As mirrors of their writers' course experience, the disappointing letters did not offer a very pretty reflection. Unlike the pleasurable letters, the disappointing letters were brief, general, and disengaging. On the surface they conveyed little or no sense of student self-reflection, while what seemed to be between the lines often spoke louder to me than what was present. These letters, in short, pushed the wrong "buttons."

> Dear Mrs. Conway,
>
> The greatest strengths of my essays are that they deal with areas of interest to me. The University of Louisville interests me for obvious reasons. Family strength is also very important to me. Family is one of those institutions which has made it through the ages and could be the institution that brings about world peace. Biosphere II interests me because technological advancements are cool.
>
> I have revised these essays to be more precise and clear. They are also directed at the correct audiences.
>
> Thanx,
>
> Jonathan T. Raleigh

> Ms. Conway,
>
> I chose three essays: Essay 3—"God in Songs," Essay 5—"What Is The Deal With The Ozone Layer," and Essay 6—"Mr. Steinem's Story."
>
> I chose essay three because I think that the message it delivers good, and needs to be shared with other people.
>
> I chose essay five because you suggested it, and said that it proved that the more educated you become, the more questions you ask.
>
> I chose essay six because I really enjoyed writing this essay, because it is the only creative writing that we did all semester.
>
> Susan Carter

The negative effects that Jonathan's and Susan's cover letters had on me may or may not have been related to their brevity and to the fact that they were handwritten on loose-leaf notebook paper. Jonathan's letter was not particularly surprising to me; it pretty much matched the below-average quality of his work during the semester. Susan's letter, however, cast a distinctly negative shadow on her frequently mentioned desire to receive an A in the course. I clearly recall experiencing an immediate disappointment upon reading Susan's letter—beginning, of course, with the virtual absence of any reflection on either the content or the processes involved in her essays. Further, she gave no indication of changes in her writing practices or values resulting from the course structure in general or from the portfolio process in particular. In other words, Susan's letter did not include the kind of open, personal, or—I must admit—positive reflection that seemed to me a natural expectation for the cover letter. Her letter confirmed what in hindsight seemed evident: the course had little effect on her; in fact, it was probably even disappointing (as indicated by her lightly veiled complaint about the lack of "creative writing" opportunities). Moreover, she wanted me to know that I was directly responsible for at least one-third of her final evaluation, since the primary reason she submitted one of the three essays in her portfolio was "because [I had] suggested it." I resented this explanation, not because I questioned its truth, but because it suggested that Susan was resisting part of her assignment—to take responsibility for her choices.

A reading of the composition field's existing literature on portfolios clearly indicates that I was not alone in being deeply affected—negatively and positively—by what was and what was not in my students' cover letters. Students' self-reflective pieces have been called the most "significant entries" that appear in writing portfolios (Camp and Levine 203) and even the "most important aspect of the portfolio process" (Weinbaum 214). The reason they are so significant, it appears, is that they rhetorically position students to take responsibility for their writing choices (Herter 90). In other words, self-reflection calls on students to portray a conscious awareness of what they have and have not done in their papers (Camp and Levine 197). Further, self-reflection calls on students not only to sound mature, but also to make claims indicating that some identifiable part of their present maturity is directly connected to the portfolio process (Paulson, Paulson, Meyer 62). Implicit in all these expectations from self-reflection, i.e., taking responsibility for choices, portraying conscious self-awareness, describing one's self as a fully definable before-and-after being, is undeniable evidence that we look for portfolios to present not just our students' writing, but also their selves.

As many of our field's conference presentations and published articles on portfolios have stated unequivocally, we want our students to demonstrate in their cover letters that they think like writers, indeed that they see themselves as writers. That means, of course, that the ways students construct themselves and their writing in their cover letters inevitably have a crucial bearing on how we will evaluate their portfolios. In fact, it may very well be that more than in any other writing evaluation we have done in the past, in portfolios we evaluate not only students' writing, but also students' selves, based in large part on the ways they construct themselves in their cover letters. For that reason, I believe it is vital that cover letters occupy a major part of any discussion of writing portfolios, and that this discussion needs to take place not only in our journals and at our conferences, but also in our classrooms. Given the cover letter's prominent position in the portfolio and in the evaluator's judgment, we must unveil and then openly deconstruct its often hidden agenda.

While I read my students' cover letters at the end of the fall 1991 semester, I realized that my responses to each had much to do with my own teacher values. As in any assignment I give, I wanted the portfolio letters to state claims and then to support those claims with specific evidence. In addition, I realized I wanted my students to convey positive attitudes toward their writing, as well as a clear sense of the rhetorical choices they had made. Further, I wanted them to show confidence about their choices. Of course, I also wanted my students to show respect for their audience (i.e., me). I recognized without a doubt, in other words, that whatever my good intentions with the cover letter, I also had a definite hidden agenda in assigning it.

I fear that some of my students may not have perceived the cover letter as much more than a formality, in the sense that it may not have seemed very important—or at least not as important as the actual papers in the portfolio. And why shouldn't they have thought this? Why would any student assume that the most important writing in the portfolio is something other than the papers that the cover letters introduce? In most cases, their papers have been the major topic of discussion and evaluation during the entire school term. These papers have often received hours of attention, not only from the students themselves, but also from their teachers. Understandably, the self-reflective piece could seem secondary.

Compounding matters, teachers may exacerbate this impression innocently through the language they use in handouts and in discussions. I note in retrospect that my instructions emphatically specified that the papers in the portfolio should be "revised for the best of clarity, correctness, and purposeful communication." My description of what the cover letter should be, on the other hand, did not say anything about either revision or quality expectations. In much the same way, the student handout "State University of New York at Stony Brook Portfolio-based Evaluation Program," quoted in Belanoff and Dickson's widely read *Portfolios: Process and Product,* that explains the requirements for English 101 portfolios at the State University of New York at Stony Brook, gives these instructions:

> Each paper must have an informal but typed introductory sheet that explains what you were trying to accomplish and describes some of your writing process, e.g., what feedback you got and what changes you made in revising. (Elbow and Belanoff 6)

In these instructions, Elbow and Belanoff clearly emphasize to students that the introductory sheets are not evaluated (8). That and the adjective "informal," could have the effect of limiting students' concern about the content or quality of their letters. Besides the potential of underemphasizing the importance of the cover letter, there are several crucial factors that neither my instructions nor the Stony Brook instructions make explicitly known to students. First, there is the very significant fact that the cover letter may be the only document in the entire portfolio that the teacher has not read some version of in the past. Second, the cover letter will often be our only example of what our students can do on their own. And third, the cover letter will probably be the only document in the portfolio that is addressed exclusively to the teacher. Collectively, these three factors indicate an audience that will simultaneously have an active academic agenda and a very personal stake in the letters. In other words, the cover letter is, more than any of the portfolio's other documents, the piece for which students need to most consciously know—and impress—their audiences.

This is not to say that knowing and impressing an audience is an inherently unfair achievement to expect from composition students. What's difficult to overlook, however, is that most composition teachers are much better trained to read the cover letters than most students are to write them. Teachers know, for instance, that a lot more goes on between writers and readers than a straightforward delivery of meaning. This can be especially obvious in the drama that takes place between readers and writers of portfolio cover letters, where communication takes place on levels of which students may not be aware. It is certainly unlikely that students will see their letters as social representatives of themselves.

However, the cover letter is, as previously stated, essentially a mask, a performance piece such as Erving Goffman describes in *The Presentation of Self in Everyday Life*. An individual's mask, according to Goffman, serves for better or worse to "define the situation" (1) between presenter and audience. Under Goffman's theory, the cover letter would clearly qualify as a particularized example of a consciously assumed mask functioning as a representation of an individual self. Goffman argues that every human performance "makes an implicit or explicit claim [that the presenter is] a person of a particular kind" (13), motivated by a desire to be treated in an appropriate way. Importantly, however, Goffman emphasizes that an individual's skill as a performer in an established role (such as the role of student writer in this case) is directly connected to that person's access to the role's institutional context (27). Composition students, typically first-year freshmen, often spend their first terms in college beginning to develop the kind of authority that enables them to "perform" comfortably in front of established members of the academic community. Given Bartholomae's conclusion in "Inventing the University" that students must reach an advanced stage before they can "establish their authority as writers" (158), it does seem problematic for teachers to scrutinize students' cover letters for evidence of the kind of sophistication and self-awareness expected of experienced writers. On the other hand, it is not wholly unfair for composition teachers to expect students to demonstrate some level of progress towards developing confidence and authority as writers. After all, Bartholomae's judgment is based on analysis of holistically evaluated, timed essays written by incoming students; portfolio cover letters, by contrast, are written by students who have been through at least one semester of college writing instruction and who have quite a bit of revision opportunity. Improvement and growth resulting from a college course are by no means unreasonable or unethical expectations.

I had tried in my own way to encourage strong cover letter performances from my students. In class I discussed with them several principles from business writing that seemed to apply equally to the portfolio cover letter. The cover letter, I told my students, should be aimed at persuasion, much like the cover letter a job applicant might attach to a resume. In a very real sense their cover letters would be presenting their portfolios, indeed their full semester's accomplishments, to me. As such, their letters—just like any other persuasive documents—should be simultaneously specific, positive, and personal. I suggested that they think of their cover letters as their chance to guide the way I read their papers. It was probably in the light of my experience teaching business writing that I chose to omit a request that my students use their cover letters as an outlet for recording any weaknesses in their portfolios or in their writing processes. To me, asking students to list their weaknesses in the semester's only context that I would be evaluating with a grade just didn't seem fair. Like Winfield Cooper and B. J. Brown, who explain their notion of the goal of self-reflection in the portfolio in an *English Journal* article, I believe cover letters are best used by students to "invite us to look at what they can do, not what they can't; at what they have instead of what they haven't" (40).

This does not imply that I discourage students from recognizing and admitting their writing weaknesses. But within the particular rhetorical circumstances in which I would read their cover letters—that is, as a person getting ready to assign them a grade for their semester's work—I felt that my students should be given every opportunity to make a positive impression. This goal of making a positive impression leads me to a second theoretical challenge to our dependence on cover letters for knowledge about our students. Quite frankly, the whole concept of the cover letter is entangled with a questionable belief that students can lay claim to the selves they are becoming. Ever since Lester Faigley published his observations about teachers' apparent tendency to evaluate autobiographical writing according to the kind of self portrayed by the writer, we have had an embarrassing awareness that our assessment practices may not be in line with our theories. Based on analysis of samples of highly evaluated student writing and of teachers' comments about that writing, Faigley argues that the most highly-regarded "truths" in student papers are the kinds of truths that mean something to English teachers (408). In addition, he provides evidence that writing teachers judge successful first-person writers on the basis of their ability to "create . . . the illusion of a unified and knowing self that overviews the world around it" (408). Finally, he concludes that the most frequently occurring way of demonstrating the kind of rational knowledge of selves favored by English teachers is "by characterizing former selves as objects for analysis" (411). Faigley's description of successful student writing, interestingly, is nearly identical to Bartholomae's description of the typical nature of successful entrance essays, which portray students' current selves "against earlier, more naive versions of themselves" (153). By valuing the self that is not only developing but consciously aware of its development, Faigley warns, teachers essentially construct their jobs as no more than "making a student aware of the desired subject position she will occupy" (411). Unfortunately, however, many students do not realize that whatever subject positions they adopt will be judged by "teachers' unstated cultural definitions of the self" (410).

Beyond being seen as manifestations of students' selves, cover letters are also seen as indicators of other vital information. For example, one essay on writing portfolios makes the point that in addition to serving as an introduction, a self-reflective document can also be employed by teachers as "an internal check on the authenticity of the student's writing" (Holt and Baker 41). Another essay expresses a belief that students' reflective pieces can serve to convey knowledge that might otherwise be invisible. "Reflection," this essay argues, "makes visible much in learning that is otherwise hidden, even from the student writers themselves" (Camp and Levine 197). This claim recalls my earlier statement that teachers may be better at reading cover letters than students are at writing them; but I do not wish to imply that the meanings teachers construct are more "correct" than the meanings students might have thought they were conveying.

Still another essay extolling the cover letter's merits clearly implies that the cover letter functions as the richest piece of written evidence in the student portfolio. Reflecting on her own process of evaluating portfolios, the writer of this essay states without reservation, "The quality of the writing and the sophistication evidenced in the cover letters alone told me what I needed to know, so much that the pieces themselves became almost secondary" (Weinbaum 213).

In cases such as mine, when portfolios are being used as the sole object of course evaluation, I believe teachers need to be especially aware of their motives in assigning self-reflective pieces. Looking back, I believe that it wasn't so much the presence of the cover letters in my students' portfolios that caused my evaluation crisis, but the absence of other similar kinds of self-reflection attached to their papers in the past. If I had required cover pieces on earlier drafts, I could have let my students know how I was "reading" them; I also could have gotten past the initial excitement of being personally validated by what the pleasurable letters said. I know now that when I use the portfolio approach in a composition course again, I will give my students frequent opportunities throughout the semester to assess their progress through self-reflective writing. And such reflection will not be limited to the times when drafts are turned in, but throughout the timespan allotted for their preparation, as Mary Beaven suggests in a "pre-portfolio era" article on self-evaluation in writing classes (144).

Following Jeffrey Sommers' description of "The Writer's Memo" to engage students in taking responsibility for their development (174–176), I see a clear benefit in initiating self-reflection by first assigning and later suggesting questions that will lead to the kinds of metacognitive writing I (like most other writing teachers) clearly value. And using Pamela Gay's ideas for generating purposeful reflection in basic writing courses, I plan to make efforts to create reflective writing assignments that encourage students to compose explicit before-and-after comparisons of selected pieces that have been prepared in multiple drafts. Like Gay, I know there is a need—a need that is both reasonable and ethical—to teach them ways to "scrutinize" their own work (191). What there will also be a need for is my honest responses to what my students write in their self-reflective pieces. Because of the enormous impact this kind of writing can have on its audience, students need to be aware that self-reflection, like any other writing they do, will itself benefit from reflective consideration.

In conclusion, the point I mean to make is that I don't believe it is necessary to throw out reflective writing assignments simply because one is skeptical about them. I still think cover letters and other forms of written self-reflection can function not only to encourage, but also to enable, students to think substantively about their writing processes. And, admittedly, I also think these writings can offer a good deal of valuable information to teachers about students' writing behaviors and attitudes. But I most emphatically do not believe that it is either fair or appropriate for an end-of-semester cover letter to be given the burden of conveying the only reflection on a whole semester's work. Required reflection is ethical only if it exists as an ongoing component of a course and if the teacher of that course openly discusses his or her reactions to the reflections with students.

Most of us who have used the portfolio approach have done so with hopes that students would be allowed maximum writing development with maximum grade potential. In order to do this with full integrity, I believe we need to be aware of the cover letter assignment's potential to be the trump that defeats this ideal process. Instead of withholding assignments that ask for reflection until final portfolios are due, we need to institutionalize self-reflection throughout the course term as a valid—and valued—component of students' writing development.

7

Portfolios, Research, and Writing about Science

John Beall

A decade ago, when I taught English at King's School, Canterbury, fifteen-year-old students received one grade in each subject at the end of the year—a grade based solely upon their performance on a national examination (the "O" or "Ordinary Level" exam). Now fifteen-year-olds in England are evaluated by the GCSE (General Certification of Secondary Education), one option of which enables each student to select her or his best work from an English course to present for assessment. The examiners set criteria for various types of work that must be submitted and then give students and teachers the responsibility for presenting the portfolio as part of a national examination.

A similar shift has taken place in my own "Writing for Science" course, one I first taught to students at Cornell University by assigning separate essays and giving essay tests. Students gained the experience of writing about science but did not see their work evolve as a whole. I first tried portfolio assessment in a trimester-long elective called the "Craft of Poetry." There the creation of a portfolio was a natural development for the course. Young poets wrote a poem or so a week over several weeks. They frequently revised those poems and finally selected their best work to present as a self-designed book. Along with that book students included in their portfolio their best revision of several analytical essays about poetry, as well as a review that they had written about a book of poems each student read independently. The final grade depended significantly on my assessment of this portfolio, an assessment process that matched my evaluation with the virtues I sought to instill—revising and selecting poems for a chapbook, evaluating and rewriting analytical essays, and writing a review for readers about a book of poems.

After success with portfolios in the poetry course, I shifted my means of assessment in "Writing for Science," an expository essay course whose students write about scientific subjects for a reader like me who is less informed than they are about the material. The "Writing for Science" course begins with the assumption that students can learn to write more clearly by writing to educate "lay" readers about scientific theories and discoveries. Whereas most teachers give assignments so that students can demonstrate what they have learned about topics that teachers presumably know well, "Writing for Science" places students in the position of writing to a less-informed teacher. Writing for teachers who have more knowledge of the subject implicitly places the students in a role of relative powerlessness; they write on a test for a teacher with a preconceived model of perfection—the correct process of calculations, the richest explication of a poem—that may freeze the student's willingness to risk a divergent answer under the pressures of an examination. Oddly, such a relationship of master-teacher and apprentice-student is not characteristic of the relationship between adult writers and their readers.

Most adult writers compose over a period of time, with room for fits and starts, from a standpoint of knowing as much about their subject as do their readers. Moreover, their writing—be it a legal brief, a book of sermons, a play, a cookbook, an ad campaign, a cartoon series, or a scientific paper on "Spin-Label Electron Spin Resonance Study"—often gathers together disparate thoughts, random jottings, false starts, or separate chapters into one text. Writing often comes at the end of a process wherein notes are stored, drafts are shared for enlightened criticism, and the final product emerges at the end of a long struggle to communicate what one sees. Frequently, that communication is from a position of knowledge greater than that of the readers'. As one of my former students wrote me when he was a couple of years into college, "I believe that later in life the majority of my efforts to communicate will be done from a position of superior knowledge. Whether I will be a lawyer pleading to a jury, a doctor rendering a diagnosis to a patient, or a stock broker selling an idea to a client, I will be compelled to succinctly explain material that I understand better than my listener" (Beall 43). There are virtues in inverting the traditional relationship between teacher and student in order to teach skills of expository writing: when a writer is, in effect, teaching his teacher, he learns better the importance of clear and dynamic prose. In order to invert that traditional relationship, I have found in portfolios a way to make my evaluation of students' writing complement my emphasis on writing as a complex process that leads to a finished body of work.

At the end of my current syllabus outlining the course "Writing for Science" is this statement: "Your final grade will be an assessment of your complete portfolio, in addition to an assessment of your final exam." That simple sentence has strikingly altered the nature of the course. Instead of handing in separate essays that might or might not be kept together in a folder, all students now hand me a bulging portfolio a week before the end of the course. On one side of their folder, students place all pieces of work completed in the course—every draft of an essay, all the installments of the research paper, and corrections sheets for grammar and spelling mistakes made in the original compositions. Thus, one side of the folder is what Catherine D'Aoust has called a "process portfolio," containing notes, drafts, corrections, and so on (40–41). On the left-hand side is a collection of the student's best work as judged largely by the student. This "exemplary portfolio" (D'Aoust's phrase) must include the final and clean copy of a research essay, a personal or argumentative essay about science, and an expository essay about a scientific discovery or experiment.

The last week of the course is devoted to an individualized review of past work. On top of that collection on the left-hand side of the folder is a page of my final comment to the student developing my assessment of the term's work. That comment focuses on the entire body of work, and on what lies ahead for the writer. In response to the portfolio of one student, a gifted violinist now studying at Juilliard, I wrote:

> The portfolio is a testament both to what you have accomplished this term and to what work lies ahead. The essay on "Musical Understanding" is the most satisfying whole. Its liveliness of expression is matched by a sense of wholeness, of completion. In contrast, the environment essay remains ragged. During our conference we should focus on page 3, where I lose the drift of your argument and where your writing becomes less fluid.

Such a comment illustrates how the portfolio encourages an assessment that compares different essays and offers a relatively complete picture of the student's accomplishments—a weaker argumentative essay about the environment judged alongside a stronger personal essay about science and music. In the remainder of the comment, I discussed at some length the research essay about the physics of atonal music, an essay that explained "home ground" and "tonal center" of harmonic compositions in a way that enabled me to comment on an essay's central theme as its "home ground." In sum, portfolio assessment, ideally including an individual conference with each student, results in more satisfying judgments about students. As Peter Elbow has argued in "Ranking, Evaluating, and Liking," final grades with portfolios "are more trustworthy and less damaging because they are based on so many diverse performances over many weeks" (Elbow 193). They help us see a whole, rather than the parts, of a student's achievement.

Portfolio assessment has been particularly fruitful in this course in part because it centers on a research essay. Students select their own topics for exploration; as a result, each year brings a collection of research essays about widely various subjects—the best way for a teacher to stay somewhat educated about science during an era of information explosion. In the past couple of years, students have written about the physics of bubbles, the biology of tissue cultures as a tool for brain research, fractals, the theory of relativity, the historical significance of calculus, the biochemistry of venomous frogs, and so on.

Crucial to the success of these research essays is a step-by-step process of writing the paper in "installments." Since both peer editors and I comment on each installment of the essay, students receive significant response well before the final draft is due. For many students this process of breaking down the construction of a research essay into smaller parts is crucial for successful learning. As one student explained, "The installments brought a culmination of thorough ideas and research together that would be unlikely to occur if there was only one draft. The installments galvanized our desire to learn more on a particular subject so as to be sure to explain our concepts clearly." During the weeks that students are writing their research essays, we spend many classes as a group discussing individuals' installments as "works in progress." As one student wrote me, "I am dyslexic and have always struggled in English. I remember going to a tutor and working so hard to only get a C+. But thanks in large part to Writing for Sci., I got a lot of confidence and gained a lot of skills especially in revision and in learning to write as if someone were actually going to read my work."

Portfolio assessment enhances the "installment" structure (which could be used in courses with different means of assessment) because students receive the message that the most important factor in their grade is the final version of the essay, not the graded pieces completed during the process. Thus, portfolios encourage students to break down the process of writing a longer essay into smaller steps, and give students meaningful context of writing for an audience who has discussed the work even before its completion.

One major university granting academic credit on the basis of reading high school students' portfolios specifically excludes "a research essay that merely assembles information from other sources" (Black, Daiker, Sommers, Stygall). The research essays in "Writing for Science" demonstrate how students can achieve much more in such compositions than merely a regurgitation of information gleaned from secondary sources. Indeed, the Miami University exclusion of research essays should only be continued after a reconsideration of what students can learn by composing such an essay.

One virtue of completing research essays is that students can learn to employ imaginative language to "translate" complex concepts for lay readers. In his essay about brain slicers used to excise tissue cultures, one student began with a lovely picture of the prenatal brain:

> Like a peninsula jutting out of a non-existent continent, long, branching fibers interweave in a thin, protective border. Inside the enclosed area, small circular dots grow into island-like masses, and at the same time some of the stringy fibers extend away from the greater mass, like arms of a jellyfish reaching out for food.

In sentences like these, the writer showed how much he had learned about metaphorical language as a vehicle for transforming abstract information into a clear visual image. Similarly, another student found—in the middle of an

Figure 7–1

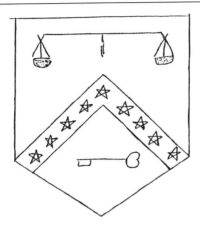

essay about bubbles—that explaining the physics of refraction led him to compose a prose poem: "Soap bubbles are golden just before they die. Bubbles begin their brief lives clad in an assortment of bright colors that shimmer in the sunlight. . . . Finally, even the gold disappears, and the bubble is transparent right before it bursts." With such images, the writer can convert the reader to his conviction that "the science behind the bubble does not detract from its beauty, but rather stretches one's imagination to encompass beauty and order on the molecular level." The research essay can be a means to write about science beautifully.

Furthermore, students can learn from writing a research essay about the expository skills of explaining processes clearly. For their first essay in the course I ask students to describe an abstract design, such as that illustrated in Figure 7–1. The writer's job is to describe the design so clearly that a classmate, after reading the essay, can reproduce the drawing exactly. This assignment introduces students to the notion that they are writing for an audience that cannot see what the writer sees and for an audience that depends upon the writer's precise and clear phrases. During the first half of a class, the students describe one of three designs that I distribute. During the second half of the class, after I collect the essays, each student tries to draw, on the basis of a peer's essay, a design never before seen. At the next class we discuss what types of writing produced reasonable facsimiles of the original design and what types produced comical distortions. Since the students know that this essay is only a step in a process that culminates in the portfolio, they learn to transfer skills of exposition learned in shorter essays onto longer projects. Remembering this exercise years after the course had ended, one student connected the initial essay to his research paper about an environmental disaster in Alaska: "Although the first assignment nearly erupted a few of my arteries, as I was strikingly unable to describe an abstract drawing, I achieved a distinguished level of fluency in the final paper when I had to explain the significance of the single-lined hull of the Valdez."

I suspect the reason why many research essays seem mere regurgitation of secondary sources is because they are assigned without enough preliminary preparation to help students become ready to write them. Again, the portfolio system, by structuring this course into an interconnected whole, introduces students to ways of treating secondary sources as springboards for independent and creative writing. Such skills are not learned overnight and are not attained without opportunities for writers to fall on their faces. One such failure came when a student tried early in the term to translate the concept of "naive precipitation hypothesis," about which he had read in a scientific journal. Reflecting on his discombobulating essay, the writer later commented:

> What often happened was that I used a great number of scientific terms which I strove nobly to define for the reader; however, once I had stated my makeshift "definition," I used the words relentlessly in the paper. Concepts such as "naive precipitation hypothesis," which even the scientists didn't really understand and left me baffled, took on an almost religious significance shrouded in mysticism. They seemed undefinable. Thus, all I was left with in the end was vague and confusing language.

By imitating the abstract language that had baffled him, this writer had learned how to write poorly. However, because the portfolio encouraged such self-reflection, he also learned from his mistakes without going to pieces over the penalties summative grades can impose.

There is no reason, I suggest, why writing research essays about science need impede students' discovering their own voices by teaching their teacher. The same student who stumbled in writing about precipitation found the research essay a catalyst for inventing, in effect, a new language. His comment, written months after he completed the course, remarks upon a new language, one different from either the technical jargon of his scientific sources or the slang of common speech. This student thought the research project improved his writing by encouraging him to write for a reader who was not a scientist:

> My actual task as a writer about science was to translate the scientific language, and the language in which my own thought processes and understanding lay, into a language readily understandable to *any* reader. What I did not realize until the very end was that, since the system of scientific understanding was so different from lay language, I actually had to create my own terminology. Scientific terms were precise, but lacked the flavor inherent in natural speech. In translating them I had to recreate this "flavor": otherwise, the scientific language, which is based on reason, would be totally incompatible with everyday language, which contains a broad range of emotions. In

this way I was able to breach the division between the way I understood ideas, and the way I explained them to people. Writing was clearly a job of translation between my own inner language and the "vernacular" of writing. This was an important revelation both for my last project in "Writing for Science" and for all the papers I have written since. It was not a revelation that came in a flash, but a process of incremental learning that occurred through the course.

Such revelations that writing about science involves much more than a mere assemblage of information from secondary sources have come often in this course, particularly in the final paragraphs of essays that strive to answer the skeptic's "So what?" question. After ten pages full of clear explanations, imaginative analogies, and computer-generated diagrams of space-time vectors, one student concluded the essay titled "It is Absolutely Relative," with a touching appeal to readers:

> Think how often you have traveled to a new place, feeling that the journey was interminable. Think again about how short and easy the return trip home felt. Perhaps this is because once we have tried a new path, it no longer seems as forbidding. One could hypothesize that the experience had a relative effect on perception. Having had your first experience in pondering Einstein's theory of general relativity, it may no longer seem as ominous any more, and it may be a journey into scientific thought that you choose to make again.

Perhaps because this writer was discussing a topic that he understood much better than his teacher, he wrote with confidence, with clarity, and often with a warm and human voice. As another student wrote, the research essay "took scientific learning away from simple biology and physics to the most complicated state-of-the-art science where we realize how much science has to do with imaginative thought and not with triple beam balances and Bunsen burners."

Granted, some outstanding research essays appeared from my students before I ever used the word "portfolio" in presenting the course. However, portfolio assessment has improved the course by providing a format wherein students could see that their work belonged to a whole. They could write about fields of personal interest from the position of authority. They could pursue inquiry from an interdisciplinary approach because portfolio assessment allowed the time for more complex and multifaceted approaches to questions. Without delaying final assessment unto kingdom come, the teacher using portfolio assessment can place within the structure of a course's syllabus incentives *and* time for self-reflection and self-improvement. Receiving comments both from their teacher and from a peer editor, students can engage in what Catherine Lucas has called " 'reflective evaluation,' a kind of formative feedback the learners give themselves" (2). Since the final grade derives so much from the portfolio, the incentives for additional revision often spur students to make further progress in composing their best work.

There are pitfalls into which students can stumble while compiling their portfolios, and into which teachers can fall while worrying about the politics of school reform. One student might select her best previous work and revise little if at all, instead of selecting her most promising work for rewriting. Another, knowing that he can always revise work at the eleventh hour, might be haphazard about his assignments during most of the course. Portfolios might be seen as allowing too much opportunity for intervention by tutors and parents. Or, at the other extreme, weaker students might be left too much on their own with too little feedback from peers or from the teacher who delays judging the student's work until the end of the term. Portfolios might increase the opportunities for plagiarism and dishonesty. Further, teachers facing a high stack of portfolios may find themselves with too much to grade at the stressful end of term. Students and adults, concerned about how well students will be prepared for a new SAT with a twenty-minute writing sample, might clamor against the devaluation of timed tests and exams that take less time to grade and offer more opportunities for producing "valid" data about how well students and schools are performing.

It is beyond the scope of this essay to offer a comprehensive response to each of these by no means trivial concerns. However, a few suggestions and observations—not terribly original or profound—might be better than silence. In order to adapt portfolios to energize the complacent or haphazard student, teachers can make clear from the outset that the evaluation of the portfolio will include an assessment of revision, self-reflection, and growth. Part of the evaluation for course work can include one's judgments about interim stages of work, like an essay or an initial installment of a research essay. Providing class time for writing, peer editing, conferencing, and revising also enables the teacher to monitor students' progress. Bad teaching, not the portfolio system, is to blame if students do not receive frequent feedback during the process of writing. And can't one accept that sometimes eleventh-hour work can be fantastic, while also keeping tabs on the weaker student who may need more active intervention and guidance?

Since portfolio assessment depends greatly on revision outside of class, there are indeed opportunities for excessive tutoring or dishonesty. At the same time, there is no reason why in-class essays cannot be the starting point for most compositions. Working with students on essays begun in class, teachers can gain a picture of how the students' work evolves. Since the portfolio may give students a greater sense of ownership over the finished body of work, as opposed to a constant sense of the evaluation process as adversarial, there may be less incentive for relying on tutors. In contrast, when students complete work outside of class during a process whose stages are invisible to teachers, is there not more likelihood that the ideas are not original with the student?

If a research essay is part of the portfolio, teachers can build a source check into the evaluation process in order to instill a firm sense of integrity. For instance, one might collect a full draft of an essay with footnotes and bibliography well before the final portfolio must be completed. If students know that one or more of their sources will be requested and reviewed, in comparison with what they wrote, then they will understand that among the lessons emphasized are principles of academic honesty. Just as important as deterring dishonesty is explaining clearly how to be honest. The portfolio process can include exercises in paraphrasing, footnoting, and responding to secondary sources. Unfortunately, with any process of evaluation, there are no guarantees that students will not be dishonest. However, if dishonesty is detected, in addition to assessing the failure of the writer's honor, one can ask a student to include in his portfolio a reflective statement explaining the principles of honesty that were violated. Thus, the portfolio might become a means towards education in ethics.

My guess is that the largest resistance to employing portfolios will come from students, administrators, and parents concerned about how well students will be prepared for college exams and the time-pressured facts of adult life, and how well schools and school systems can be evaluated during an age of accountability. First, there is no reason why timed tests need be more or less valued in a portfolio system of evaluation, so the teacher need compromise neither the value of the portfolio nor the value of practice with timed writing. Furthermore, one of the most forceful expositors of the potential for portfolio assessment has been Roberta Camp, a development scientist at the Educational Testing Service. One may not wish ETS to co-opt portfolio assessment, nor may ETS be prepared to do so. However, portfolios are not necessarily irreconcilable with uniform, national tools of assessment. In effect, whatever their flaws, the Advanced Placement Exams share with portfolio assessors the practice of basing a grade on combining evaluations of different types of work. Finally, some adult professions, like trading on the Commodities Market and running a high-stakes auction, may favor workers adept at coping with enormous time pressures, but many more depend on the imaginative performance of professionals skilled in a variety of tasks completed over a period of time.

The greatest resistance to portfolios from teachers may come because of the grading load. However, if the teacher is working closely with the students regularly during the term, then the final assessment of the portfolio can be relatively less time consuming. One can read the portfolio with relative speed in order to react to the work as a whole by writing a comment at the top of the portfolio and forsaking marginal notations on the final copy. If necessary, instead of narrative comments that are more time-consuming to compose, one can use gridded evaluation forms to check areas of strength and weakness about the students' portfolios. A due date for the final portfolio can be set early enough for teachers to have time to assess the work. Finally, peer evaluation can be a vital part of the process in compiling a portfolio. Ellen Geisler heads a large English department at one of the biggest high schools in Ohio, a department that both employs portfolio assessment and requires that all students complete a research essay in order to graduate. As she wrote in a letter to the families of Mentor High School, "As students look at a piece of peer writing and tell the writers specifically what is good, what works and why, they are actively engaged in the process of learning what makes one piece of writing better than another" (1992).

Portfolio assessment has helped me structure the evaluation process in order to give credit when students learn to edit each others' work, to edit and revise their own work, and to write about complex ideas with sufficient clarity that a less-informed teacher could understand what they were trying to explain. Assessing students' work by means of portfolios has been a beneficial step away from the traditional grading practices of averaging (let us say) three papers of C, B-, and B+, two tests of B and C-, and an exam of C+, and finding a formula to turn those results into a final grade of C+. Let me concede that my assessment of a student's portfolio might result in the same grade of C+. Even if one were to acknowledge that the grade might not be any different or be any more fair, I would still argue that the process of assessment offers students a more valuable lesson about their education—that their work is a cumulative process culminating in a final body of work that they have selected, arranged, and preserved for reflection, remembrance, and (one hopes) for self-respect. Students and teachers gain a vision of work completed as a whole, rather than as a string of more or less discrete exercises. If nothing else, the portfolio provides students with incentives to view their work as a part of themselves—a tangible monument to their studies and struggles—rather than as scatterings of scribblings to be disposed in the dustbins moments after the teacher's evaluation has been scanned in a nanosecond's glance at a single number or letter. As one student wrote me on his anonymous course evaluation last year, "The idea of a portfolio for the final exam is a *terrific* one because it gives you a chance to see all you have accomplished and how much you've improved."

8

Reading Portfolios Conversationally

Cheryl Forbes

Michael Apple of the University of Wisconsin has said, "Thinking is social. It's a dialogue, both with the past and with others at the same time. If you teach it as an individual thing, you miss the whole point. A higher literacy would be one that was eminently social" (Brown 33). What he says about literacy sounds comfortably familiar to those of us who teach writing in a workshop setting and use portfolios for assessment. We believe that writing is a social "thing," not an individual "thing," what Apple claims for thinking. We believe that portfolios, as Pat Belanoff persuasively argues elsewhere in this volume, contribute to "higher literacy." She emphasizes the complexity of the portfolio process that only now, after several years of praxis, are we coming to realize. Part of this complexity, I would claim, comes from the reading demands portfolios make. Yet despite our talk about collaboration and cooperation—and all the collaborating in our classes—we continue to read students much as we always have. By doing so, we simplify and deny the complexity Belanoff emphasizes and the richness that portfolios bring to the writing process.

What do I mean? After our students' collaborations end, we open a portfolio, what I have come to call a student's canon, and read it as the work of one person writing in isolation and without regard for the suggestions of others. We revert to what Apple is criticizing, teaching as an individual thing. Even worse, we ask for assessment from readers who don't know the writer or the social context of her particular classroom and colleagues. In other words, we tend to read each writer's canon the way new critics used to read the canon of Shakespeare or each of his plays. We tend to read noncontextually, nonsituationally, nonsocially, as if the text before us had emerged like Botticelli's *Venus*. We fail to hear the implicit, sometimes explicit, conversations between a writer and her own texts, or how a writer and her portfolio answer questions of another writer and portfolio and in turn raise questions to be answered. This back-and-forth writing, what in some contexts we might term *call and response,* results in students becoming co-authors of each other's texts, true collaborators. And if we have been involved in the process, as we usually are, then we, too, must share the credit line.

Composition researchers have finally begun to investigate how we read. In *Writing and Response: Theory, Practice, and Research,* Chris Anson has edited one volume and Bruce Lawson, Susan Sterr Ryan, and W. Ross Winterowd another. The appendix to the latter volume could well serve as a description of this essay's objectives: "to present [a teacher's] rigorous, personal descriptions of and reflections on how [she] *reads* student writing. . . . What does it mean and feel like to read student texts?" (235). The editors conclude with the hope that such reflection will "open new areas for all of us to explore." It is within this framework that I offer what follows.

There has been much recent discussion about the advantages and disadvantages of blind portfolio reading, which ignores the social processes of the collaborative classroom. I argue that to fully assess students' work we need to read as contextually as possible. In fact, I don't know how reading is possible without context. Even when I read an author I've never before encountered, I have numerous contextual clues that help me interpret what I'm about to read. In a magazine or journal I have an author's biography, the kind of periodical I'm holding, perhaps the editor's introduction. The typeface, the layout, even the kind of paper provide a social context. If I am reading an article in a book, particularly a scholarly article, the editors make sure in an introductory chapter that I understand the context: they tell me who is writing about what and how and why it fits with the other articles, just as this book has done. When I read a non-academic book, I have the information the publisher supplies me, either on the back of the book or on the flap copy; the title page; a list of previous publications; and even who else has read the book and found it fascinating. I am never left without a context for anything I read. Experts in how children learn to read have taught us that children need a context for print. We do students a disservice when we ask for a less than complete contextual reading. In fact, we contradict our theories about the writing process itself.

Therefore, I suggest that we read as *conversations* the portfolios of our students who have worked and written together. To demonstrate such reading and the written responses appropriate after such reading, I would like us to listen for the voices of two women students, Grace and Joy, two members of a four-member writing team who worked together for the last half of a semester. We will hear Grace's voice in Joy's portfolio, and Joy's voice in Grace's portfolio. Their intermingling voices thus become a paradigm of the way writers in collaborative classrooms speak to each other across time and space through their portfolios. Occasionally I hear my own voice entering the conversation, because both women sought my friendship and advice throughout the semester, and I came to know them well. I recognize, too, that their voices meld with my own, for after I read them they become part of me. However, the focus here is not on how much Grace and Joy have influenced me, or on how much I have influenced them, but on how much they have influenced and written each other.

I am convinced that only when we begin to perceive the multiple voices within any given portfolio—voices that, yes, may include our own—can we begin to assess fairly what our students have written. Unless we read portfolios intertextually and critically, what I have called conversationally, we cannot really understand what our students have written. But before moving to Grace's and Joy's portfolios, let me give some background about each woman. Then I will read, trying to convey the sense of reading as it occurred: present tense reading, not past tense. My comments exemplify the responses I give to students as part of my final written evaluation of their portfolios. In addition, both women have read and talked with me about this essay and so influenced its final form. Grace and I talked for several hours, her comments driving me to reread through her eyes what I had written, as well as through my own and Joy's.

Grace, a Korean, came to this country six years ago from Egypt where her mother is a missionary. Her father was killed in a car accident in Egypt when she was six. Grace did not want to attend the school her mother had chosen for her, but she had no choice, because she needed to take care of her sisters who are still in high school. So Grace lives with her sisters and commutes to a small, private, religious, liberal arts college. Grace wanted a large, public institution and she wanted atheists for professors and non-Christians for friends. A feminist uncomfortable in a mostly patriarchal institution, she expected her classes to conform to her view of the institution. Because of her expectations, Grace at first refused to participate in the community. Things began to change when she realized that our particular community was not in sympathy with patriarchy.

Although Grace is Korean, she speaks fluent English. She conceded her original language to English, which she thinks of as her mother tongue. This is significant in understanding her work, for she speaks Korean with her mother, and her mother's voice, in translation, is loud in Grace's thirty-five-page portfolio, comprising two essays, a journal, and a brief piece of in-class writing. She kept the journal voluntarily; unlike most journals it was typed, and she rewrote parts of it. Of the more than fifty pages she wrote during the semester, these four texts are the only ones she considered worth presenting as her portfolio—thirty-five pages constituting her canon. Only a few themes dominate her work: mother-daughter relationships as seen by Asian-American immigrants and writers; the need for educational reform and multiculturalism; the role of reading and writing in the creation of identity; and, finally, the interplay of race and gender. She chose these themes, large issues for a first-year student who had been labeled by the institution as "developmental," hardly justifiable in light of her curiosity and intellect.

Joy could not have been more of a contrast. She wanted to attend the institution and already had numerous friends there. She is white, blonde, and blue-eyed, from an upper-middle-class, traditional family. Her father works; her mother stays home and cares for the house. Her family takes vacations to places like Edinburgh and offers Joy frequent multicultural experiences. She spent last summer in China, where she taught English, and traveled to Greece in January. Like most students at the school, Joy is Dutch, not an ethnic minority like Grace. Because there are so few ethnic minorities, Grace's background is obvious; Joy's is not. At the beginning of class Joy wrote that she didn't think much of feminist ideas and didn't have much need of them; this was an indirect response to what she considered my "feminist" use of the pronoun "she." (At least she noticed it; many students don't.) Whereas Grace had no idea about her plans for the future, Joy had decided on medicine, though that changed during the semester. Joy was as outwardly conventional as Grace was unconventional. Joy was bright, an achiever, and a good student; Grace, too, was bright, but because she frequently missed deadlines she had been given developmental status, which she interpreted as "bad student." Joy turned in a fifty-five-page portfolio, almost everything she had written during the semester. Despite the obvious differences between Grace and Joy, I found similar themes as I read their portfolios.

Joy, like Grace, explained how writing and reading work together to achieve identity. Instead of focusing on Asian-American women writers, Joy focused on the feminist work of Margaret Atwood. Joy's own feminist interests and concerns began to surface, and they grew into a wish to major in women's studies—not possible at her institution. Joy talked about being publicly discredited by a former teacher who had asked her to return to the class and talk about her first college writing course. The reason? Her views on writing did not validate his own. Grace wrote about being verbally attacked about her ethnicity and ridiculed because those who assaulted her assumed she couldn't speak English. Joy found herself wondering about mother-daughter relationships, identity, and social roles—themes that also formed the core of Grace's portfolio. Although I took a risk with both students when I put them in the same writing group, I think that neither student would have explored their issues in quite the same way without the conversations they shared. We will hear them raise issues that reach the heart of our concerns about education today, problems that relate to identity, learning styles, development, student-centered versus teacher-centered classrooms, and competition versus cooperation.

Now to the reading. I first read Grace, then Joy, then reread them together. Here is Grace.

> I have lived a multicultural life because of my parents. My writing reflects
> the summary of cultures I have seen and participated in over the years. But

I have not learned to use this experience effectively. All because I was unintentionally programmed to learn passively. I didn't know how to dig for information and write about it. To question the information and come up with my own conclusions and opinions. To integrate my life into my papers even when I do apply it to my life in my head.

Grace then shifts to a new paragraph, one sentence long: "I was introduced to feminist literature."

In her first paragraph, Grace claims she was "unintentionally programmed to learn passively." Programmed? My mind trips over that metaphor, and I pause to consider it. Someone turned Grace into a machine, or so she thinks. An unthinking, unfeeling machine. She rejects the image, though, because implicitly she compares the passive machine to the active, questioning, self-authentic, and self-aware writer she wants to be. It is no accident that her next paragraph consists of only one sentence: "I was introduced to feminist literature"—feminism and multiculturalism in contrast to passivity, as reflected in the passive voice.

As I read this, I begin to shuffle the pages of Grace's portfolio. "Where have I heard something like this before, especially this business of multicultural writing?" I asked myself. "Hasn't she written about this elsewhere?"

My desk is getting messy. Grace's portfolio is out of order.

Something in Grace's essay, "Tan's Mothers," catches my eye. I stop my search to read it: "the idiosyncrasy of the conflict between mothers and daughters arises when the two divergent generations—one whose life has been soaked purely in Chinese dye and the other, frosted in American dye—strive to form a connection (an intimate and delicate relationship). So I tell my mother. . . ."

Grace is trying to integrate her voice into the voice of research. I stop reading silently to read aloud, trying to reproduce her voice in my own. Grace almost chokes herself off at the beginning, but "the idiosyncrasy of the conflict" and "divergent generations" yields to "So I tell my mother." The passive constructions—"I was programmed," "I was introduced"—resolve into: "So I tell my mother." I note her laundry image, soaking in dye, and recall all the other domestic images in her portfolio: dirty shirts and sorting socks, washing whites and colored clothes separately. I also note her mixed metaphor, "frosted in American dye." "Frosted" makes me think of cakes, another domestic image; Grace does use food metaphors, I've noticed. But "frosted" also makes me think of hair, hair dye, and cosmetics; not quite domestic images, but certainly female, at least in her social context. The ordinariness and the femaleness of her images contradict her claims to resist traditional roles, just as they undercut her claims that she does not know how to put herself in her writing. I remember that her mother has sent her to this country, to college, so that Grace will have a future other than traditional Korean housewife. But Grace's domestic metaphors tell me that a big part of her is

Korean housewife, though she may not know it or want to admit it. (In her writing, Amy Tan, one of the writers Grace chose to study, makes domesticity a big part of many women characters. Isn't domesticity a reason why women writers have been heretofore excluded from the canon?)

Still, because of my distraction, I have not found what I have been looking for. It must not have been in Grace's writing. Could it have been Joy who wrote it?

Now the pages of Grace's canon are completely out of order. Why didn't she provide page numbers for easy reassembly? But how could she know the kind of reading I would do?

I turn to Joy's folder and find what I am looking for, on page two of her final essay:

> A misconception of many professors is that a class needs to be monocultural, "her culture"—the professor's enclave. Instead, Cheryl believes, a class-room is a circle of multicultural views. So Grace is Korean and interested in Asian-American voices in writing and art. So what does culture have to do with voices? If multiculture is many cultures and many cultures involves many people than is a culture a person? Is Grace a culture? Is her voice a culture?

Now I go back to Grace and reread once more what I found there. "I have lived a multicultural life because of my parents. My writing reflects the summary of cultures I have seen and participated in over the years." Isn't Grace say-ing what Joy is saying? Grace is like a simile, Joy a metaphor. Grace says that her life and voice reflect—or are like—multiculturalism. Joy puts it stronger, in a rhetorical question. Metaphorically, "Is her voice a culture?" I translate: Grace's voice is a culture. Joy tells me that Grace wants her voice to sound clearly in what she writes but that she fears her voice is not accept-able because many professors want monoculture. As Grace intuits, if *they* are unwilling to accept the culture of a white student, then surely *they* will not welcome the culture of a woman of color and holder of a green card. Here my voice enters, as an advocate for circles and multiple cultures—many voices, many cultures, going round and round together, in a dance, in intimate conversation.

Joy is helping me read Grace. Surely Grace will help me read Joy, if I am alert to her prose.

Grace senses that her voice is culture, or at least conveys a culture to others, and not always a welcome culture. What she hears doesn't always please her, even as she struggles to give voice to her writing. From her journal I learn about her first days as a high school student in the United States:

> I was not proud anymore for being Korean. To everyone I was a Chink. I tried so hard to cover up my embarrassment. I refused to go out to restaurants with my family and relatives because everything they did was so Korean that it embarrassed me. I did not like who I was. The way I looked. My small eyes

and blunt nose and straight black hair. . . . I feel as if I had betrayed my own kind.

Straight black hair? Frosted dye?

When her white friends mock her speech, Grace becomes angry. Those friends who don't see her as Asian but simply as herself also disturb her: "I wondered if I had betrayed my heritage so much that people could not see the Korean in me." Or hear the Korean in her. Johnnella E. Butler puts it this way:

> Students of all racial backgrounds come with an acute ignorance about American history and culture. They therefore possess a false sense of self, based on ignorance of ethnicity and the intricate role it can play in not only dividing whites from people of color, but also in dividing whites from each other—indeed, people of color from one another.(234)

This is exactly Grace's struggle, and Joy struggles *with* her as together they read an essay by Marilyn Cooper, "The Unhappy Consciousness in First-Year English" (in *Writing as Social Action*). Joy writes:

> After reading Marilyn Cooper aloud with Grace, we came to the conclusion that not all learning was up to the professor, but rather that students need to take initiative. . . . Then we moved to talking about her paper, not her final but a research paper on Amy Tan. (And now we're still talking about getting to know each other and helping each other become better writers by asking questions and responding critically and appreciatively.)
>
> Grace told me she didn't really like her writing and she read to me what Cheryl had said about her first research paper—Grace's that is. Cheryl said that Grace had removed herself from her paper, that Grace was angry about her topic but it didn't show. Grace read what she had written in her r.a. [rhetorical analysis] about not being able to hear her own voice. With that in mind—like reading Margaret Atwood's autobiography before reading her short stories—I read her paper aloud to her. (Lately reading someone's paper aloud to them has been really effective. We can both construct meaning, individually and together.) So, after reading her paper to her, I started asking questions. Why did you use the word "tragedy" in this sentence? Why did you call attention to the mother-daughter conflict? Why does the American culture mean endless opportunity? Does your mother hold to Korean values like obedience that Amy Tan calls attention to in Chinese culture? . . . I like to ask questions of Grace; I think she is a wonderful example of how [our school] could be multicultural.

Grace is helping me understand why Joy writes about multiculturalism and classroom community. But what does Joy do here? Now Joy's pages and Grace's pages are all mixed up on my desk.

Joy reads aloud. Grace can't hear her own voice in her writing, and so she despises what she's written. Earlier in class she had told her colleagues, "I think this one *sucks!* You can't even hear *me* in it. This is *not* my paper." So to allow Grace to hear the voice she thinks is absent, Joy takes on, embodies, becomes Grace's Korean voice in an oral reading. She compares it to her own approach to Margaret Atwood, reading Atwood's autobiography before her short stories. Joy listened hard for Atwood's voice; she wants to help Grace listen hard for Grace's own voice. Joy also understands that together they can construct meaning, which they might not have done separately. When they construct meaning together, it becomes collaborative writing. Without Joy's experience with Grace, Joy could not have written the essay I have just quoted. Without Grace's experience with Joy, Grace could not have written "Tan's Mothers." She could not have said:

> The book dealt with mother and daughter relationships. It narrates—mostly in broken English dialogue—the conflict between four first generation Chinese immigrant mothers and their second generation—definitely Americanized—daughters. . . . The clash occurs when the overly ambitious mothers, who seek to prepare a better life for their daughters, push Chinese values, stories, superstitions, and admonitions. This description is a replicate of my mother's interruptions in my life. She sometimes tries so hard to make my life a 'success' that she does not realize or hear what I want out of life. . . . "Mom, you're so Korean." I'd finally say. Then she would say, "you're so Americanized."

The conversation between Grace and her mother occurs in Korean. It is reminiscent of one of Tan's mothers who says, "I want my children to have the best combination: American circumstances and Chinese character. How could I know these two things do not mix?" Grace comments: "The 'American circumstances' refers to the endless opportunities that the daughters may pursue." I hear Joy ask, "Why does the American culture mean endless opportunity? Does your mother hold to Korean values—like obedience—that Amy Tan calls attention to in Chinese culture?" I hear Grace answer, "[My mother] said that as a Korean female I had a responsibility to my family and obedience to parents." I hear Grace answer Joy again, when she gives this dialogue about wearing eyeliner:

> "Don't talk back at me. I'm your mother. No other Korean children I know are like you. They never talk back and wear eyeliner." "Well, then I guess you haven't seen the other kids in my school?" "They are American. You are Korean. Why must you disobey me and try all those things that are so American? *Eun-Hae*, do as I say . . . someday you'll thank me for it."

Eyeliner? What was that about frosted dye, black hair, and small eyes? Eyeliner to make her eyes look bigger? Wider? Not so Korean? "I feel as if I had betrayed my own kind." Maxine Hong Kingston's *The Woman Warrior*, which Grace had read, enters the discussion.

I stop to find my copy, to look for the places where Kingston talks about Asian women who seek operations to get rid of their slanty-eyed look. But had Joy read Kingston? No, but Lisa had—and Lisa worked with Grace, too.

So Joy has the answer to her question "Does your mother hold to Korean values?": "Yes Grace's mother does hold some of the same values." Joy makes explicit what is implicit in Grace's portfolio by asking, "Can we go so far as to say that a person is a community of voices? . . . A person with many voices, then? Give me that much." Grace answers through another question, "Am I Korean or an American? . . . I do not want to betray the Korean in me or the western influence in me. I'm a product of both. A mixture of this and that. As Koreans would say, a "*jan-pbong* (a kind of stew)." Here is another domestic image, a Korean food image, for me to place next to her word, "frosted."

OK, so that's one side of the conversation, Joy's side. But I also want Grace's side. It must be in Grace's portfolio somewhere.

I find this:

My first version, I had written over two weeks ago, displeased me so much I did not hand it in. I had Joy read it to me out loud and asked for criticism. She read it and said that I should use intertextuality—my life. She pointed out that I use words like "choked" and "overprotective" to describe the mothers. Why did Grace use these words? Is it something she can relate to or situations which she identifies with? Let your personal life interact with the parallelism Grace sees with Tan's characters. Joy helped me make this paper my own. She said she wanted to hear my voice. I tried and the paper turned out a lot more personal than what I started off with.

Grace writes for herself, in her own voice, but then switches to third person in referring to herself, thus in effect becoming Joy. "Why did Grace use these words? Is it something she can relate to or situations which she identifies with?" The questions are those Joy would write, just as she wrote about a character in Atwood's short story, "Bluebeard's Egg": "So why does Mary-lynn have everything that her heart desires?" Joy develops a style of asking questions in her work that Grace helps me hear and understand. Where Joy relies on questions Grace relies on a distinctive set of metaphors. Yet here *Grace appropriates Joy's voice as her own, in order* to bring out her own voice. "I tried and the paper turned out a lot more personal."

Grace's words return me to Joy's portfolio, where I read about identity and women's voices, in particular that of Joy's mother. Here I also read that Joy thinks of herself as many voices in one. Grace helps Joy ask the question, "So what does culture have to do with voices?" Grace helps Joy write about her own culture in a paper on the domesticity of women's lives and voices—three women, her mother, herself the daughter, and their friend, who is also a mother with a small daughter playing in the room while the three adult women talk. Joy begins to understand the interplay of voices and generations by talking with and reading Grace. And I begin to understand them both by listening intently.

These are mere snippets of the conversations that took place during a seven-week period. The conversational reading that I suggest here demonstrates that Joy and Grace together construct knowledge and so represent an integration of theory and practice—higher literacy, socially constructed literacy. We theorize that collaborative classrooms and the portfolios that result will encourage our students to write more and better, to think more deeply, to learn to love and understand the writing process. Reading portfolios conversationally helps me see our theories practiced. I cannot evaluate the work of Joy without also evaluating the work of Grace, and vice versa.

Usually we listen for a single voice, which we might call coherence or unity. But I think that we should also listen for a student's multiple voices, as well as for the intertwining of other voices. Only when we hear the harmonies and the dissonances can we begin to know whether our theories work and whether students have collaborated well. It is a paradox that each of us only achieves a singular, recognizable, authoritative voice by incorporating myriad voices and viewpoints from our particular communities. The singular voice rings true only to the degree that it resonates sympathetically with the chorus of voices near it—just as a literal singer and chorus ring true only as they cooperate. Grace and Joy are learning this valuable lesson. Theirs is not a solipsistic, "personal" knowledge but a synthesizing, generalizing, inductive one.

Grace and Joy are easy to read the way I suggest, because they are often overt about their collaboration. Other students are not so easy. For instance, when I first read the portfolios of another group of women I simply missed the conversations between Nikki and Kenyett, both of whom wrote about Black English. I did not hear that Nikki was defending herself as a speaker of standard English against Kenyett's charges as a speaker of black dialect. I missed the rich, complex interplay between the two, worked out on the field of literacy, the subject both of them chose as their ultimate theme for the semester. It takes a lot of listening, thinking, and numerous conversational readings to hear someone's voice in the work of another—to hear the dialogue, as if in a play. But if I had not returned to the portfolios of Nikki and Kenyett, this time hearing them antiphonally, dialogically, conversationally, and intertextually, I would not understand the implications of portfolios for literacy. Literacy means identity. It means making a writer's voices heard and respected. I would not understand that Grace and Joy are, finally, struggling with the same issues as Nikki and Kenyett.

There are many ways to read. I have found that one of the most productive is to read students side by side, side to side, inside and outside, playing their voices together and against each other—in other words, to read their canons as they have been written.

9

The Connection Between Response Styles and Portfolio Assessment: Three Case Studies of Student Revision

William H. Thelin

Introduction

Classroom portfolios offer more to an instructor than a method of grading. Portfolios allow for a whole process system to be implemented into a writing class, giving instructors the opportunity to establish consistency among day-to-day tasks, writing assignments, and responses to student drafts. Surprisingly, little has been written about instructor goals, varying response styles, and their relationship to portfolio assessment. Jeffrey Sommers notes that portfolios are a "framework for response" (153) and Christopher Burnham discusses response methods in a portfolio system that allow a classroom to become a "writing environment" (137), but neither really discusses instructor goals nor advocates any specific type of response method to best facilitate portfolio assessment. Furthermore, no genuine empirical data collection is offered in support of their contentions.

In the research available, the method of responding and its relationship to the classroom structure are virtually ignored. For instance, from Roemer, Schultz, and Durst, we hear that when the portfolio program was initiated at their university, students still gave "less attention" to comments on their drafts than we as teachers "might like" (463), indicating that portfolios were not substantially changing student behavior during the revision process. However, a specific method of teacher response is not mentioned, and the researchers do not attempt to establish a link between the goals of each teacher in the program, their response styles, and the relative success or failure of the port-folios of individual teachers' students. Sue Ellen Gold, as another example, gives a glowing report on her success with portfolios in her ninth-grade English class, stating that her goals were "to allow the students increased autonomy and to encourage them to experiment, to risk, and to enjoy writing" (21). Her classroom practices and portfolio use were structured around these goals, and Gold looked at students' effectiveness as writers, their ability to make choices, and their metacognitive responses to questions about portfolio use. Unfortunately, Gold does not give any examples of her response style, so no connection between it and the success of the portfolio system can be established.

It would seem reasonable to expect instructors who implement a portfolio system to examine their goals for using the portfolio and then to ensure that their class structures, evaluation criteria, and response styles are consistent with these goals. However, if the research is any indication, I question whether instructors have explored this connection. No report or study I could find analyzed or recommended any particular response style used in successful implementation of a classroom portfolio. Furthermore, no researcher broached the subject of response styles that might have been inconsistent with the goals of the portfolio. Response styles and portfolios simply have not been studied in relation to each other.

On top of this, through my casual observations of colleagues' conferences with students, I wonder whether unfair, inaccurate evaluations might occur due to an inconsistency between grading criteria and the implicit and/or explicit criteria written as comments on student papers. I would see students who were furious when some grading committee had given their portfolios lower grades than the students thought those portfolios deserved. The most frequent com-ment I heard was, "But you didn't tell me about that," referring to some problem that a grader had noted on an evaluation sheet that the instructor apparently had not addressed in class. Even when instructors had graded their own students' portfolios, I still overheard complaints about grading criteria that had not been discussed or emphasized during essay-drafting and revision.

Much of this, I'm sure, can be dismissed as students' inattention in class or to a superficial reading of written responses on their papers. After all, why would an instructor respond to a paper using one set of assumptions and then evaluate the finished product utilizing another? Yet, I feel we must examine this area closely to see if perhaps the students are correct. If such an inconsis-tency crops up in the traditional grading system, the student has a chance to talk to the instructor and clarify the grading criteria. Just the experience of having a paper evaluated can give the student the needed knowledge to do better the next time. With portfolios, however, depending on their classroom implementation, this opportunity might not occur before it is too late. There-fore, an inspection of our response styles and grading criteria would seem to be worth the effort.

Inconsistencies might occur more often than we think, especially when our goals extend beyond grammatical correctness or control over language, and these inconsistencies could interfere with our students' development as writers. In short, I think that instructors need to concentrate on the reasons they choose portfolio assessment and then understand the ramifications of that choice when responding to student papers and establishing evaluation criteria.

In the study that follows, I report on an instructor who did not, in my judgment, fully analyze the connections between her evaluation criteria, her response style, and the reasons she chose to use a portfolio system in her classroom. She used a response style designed to promote critical thinking, and my focus on three of her students examines the effects her response style had on their revisions and the connections to her goals for using the portfolio grading.

Design of Study

This study took place at a major California state university and involved a comparison of various response and grading strategies in Freshman Composition. Ms. Green, the instructor whose students I followed, gave three reasons for choosing a portfolio system:

1. She hoped to reduce the level of anxiety in her students that she felt other forms of grading accentuated during the revision process;

2. She wanted her students to develop a sense of judgment in revising and to learn to make decisions on their own, and she saw traditional grading systems as an impediment to that process;

3. She felt she could inspire the students to experiment with different styles of writing in the drafting stage, so they could discover the style(s) they were most comfortable with before turning towards revision.

All three of the students who participated in my study were members of the same classroom, Ms. Green's Fall Freshman Composition class. Ms. Green had the students write eight drafts, requiring only that the drafts focus on different topics. She would write a one-page response to these drafts on a separate piece of paper, but she would never mark, correct, or note in the margins anything on the actual drafts.

These responses rarely focused on grammatical or syntactical difficulties. In fact, of the 188 units of response I documented on these three students' drafts, none were devoted to punctuation, grammar, and spelling, and only seven concentrated on syntax. True to Ms. Green's goal of critical thinking, the majority of her responses questioned the students' themes or positions on issues, offering suggestions and critiques of their main points and asking for deeper analysis and more specific detail to support their contentions. More telling, I classified thirty-six of Ms. Green's responses as negative or critical reaction towards the students' stance on the subject matter. Of those, twenty-seven confronted the students with strong opposing positions concerning political and social issues such as feminism and social responsibility. More than asking the students to revise for clarification and adherence to Standard Written English, Ms. Green, through her written responses, attempted to raise social consciousness, hoping that the students would see differing perspectives on the issues in question and revise with a critical audience in mind.

From the eight initial drafts, the students were asked to choose three that they wanted to revise. Ms. Green collected a second draft of these three, offered the students conferencing opportunities, and then expected a polished final draft of all three essays in the portfolio. Ms. Green never explained to me what she meant by "polished," and her students were not able to articulate to me what they believed the criteria to be either, but it is safe to infer, I think, that she was looking for a solid mixture of content and prose that demonstrated audience concerns, analytical abilities, stylistic competence, and a tip of the hat to grammatical correctness.

If the students turned in each assignment on time and participated at least marginally in the in-class tasks, the portfolio determined whether the student received an A or B in the class. Until the portfolio, Ms. Green would not add or subtract any points due to the quality of the writing. The students were not asked to turn in a midterm portfolio, and no discussion of grades was allowed during her class or in conference. Task completion was the sole determinant for point allotment until the portfolios were collected.

To study the effects on revision of this particular form of portfolio assessment, I interviewed each of the three students on multiple occasions and reviewed their drafts, revisions, and portfolios. I interviewed Ms. Green, both formally and informally, before and throughout the semester, to supplement and verify my findings. My questions and analysis focused on these five areas:

1. the students' level of stress and anxiety when drafting and revising, especially in relation to grading;
2. their choices concerning how to revise their essays;
3. their choices concerning which essays to revise;
4. the range of their topic and stylistic choices, and
5. the quality of their finished products.

Results of Study

I studied the effects of the portfolio system on individual students. Therefore, I present the data accordingly.

Elizabeth

Elizabeth was an A student throughout high school and was familiar with turning in multiple drafts for an assignment. She had strong feelings about the equity of grading systems. According to Elizabeth, her high school English teacher made suggestions on Elizabeth's drafts that she would follow, only to be marked down on the final paper for incorporating those very suggestions. She felt a burden to get everything right in the first draft and spent hours writing individual paragraphs. Perhaps due to this experience, Elizabeth felt that her essays belonged to her and that they should be revised the way she wanted them to. She stated that it would be unfair for Ms. Green or any instructor to base the grade on the degree of the use of the instructor's comments. She further confided to me that she believed in Ms. Green's ability to evaluate her final products on their merit and not on the viewpoint Elizabeth expressed or on her choices in handling the topic.

If I were to base my findings solely on my interview with Elizabeth, I would have to conclude that Ms. Green's classroom succeeded in removing any anxiety Elizabeth might have otherwise felt during her revisions. Elizabeth expressed to me a feeling of freedom about her writing that stemmed from the absence of quality judgments associated with the first drafts. In fact, Elizabeth admitted to very little stress when it came to the grade. Calling the portfolio grade "important," she nevertheless claimed it had no influence on any of her revision decisions.

My examination of her revision choices make this claim questionable, however. During our conversations, Elizabeth objected to most of the written comments Ms. Green made on two of her papers, one a research paper on rape and the other a salute to the works of Walt Disney. Ms. Green wanted a less clinical point of view on the rape paper and felt that the Disney piece lacked critical analysis. Especially on the Disney paper, Ms. Green's comments might be viewed as confrontational since she felt that Disney characters like Cinderella and Sleeping Beauty were by no means role models, claims that Elizabeth had made. Elizabeth stated firmly to me that she felt Ms. Green had missed the point on both essays and that she would not change them to ensure a better portfolio evaluation. However, when I reviewed the portfolio, Elizabeth had altered the papers in apparent compliance with the views Ms. Green had stated. Elizabeth added to the rape paper a fictional character who had been raped, and deleted any mention of Disney characters as role models in the Disney paper. It is interesting to note, also, that the Disney paper turned into a tribute to Disneyland after Ms. Green, wanting to show Elizabeth a contrasting view about Disney, gave Elizabeth a copy of an essay by Richard Stayton, which documented some inconsistencies in Disney's mandates for the operation of Disneyland. Despite the fact that Stayton was critical throughout, the message that Elizabeth might have inferred by receiving the essay from

Ms. Green was that Disneyland, not Disney, was a more appropriate topic for her essay.

Elizabeth's reasons for choosing to revise these two essays were not clear. She apparently liked them and wanted to continue working on them. Oddly enough, though, Elizabeth chose to revise for her third essay in the portfolio a paper titled "Goddess," even though Ms. Green had failed to give any written responses about it. Although Elizabeth denied receiving any feedback to the other five initial drafts, I had copies of Ms. Green's written comments, so I knew Elizabeth and I were miscommunicating at some level. Since those comments I read were as demanding as the comments on the rape and Disney papers, I theorized that Elizabeth's choice to revise "Goddess" was motivated by those other written responses. She did not want to revise the other five papers due to the level of difficulty in following Ms. Green's suggestions (or perhaps because she wanted to retain ownership of them), so she revised the only one left on which there were no comments to follow. Elizabeth's topic choices were notable for their lack of personal experience and for their use of complete fiction at times. Although Ms. Green suggested, both in writing and during conference, that Elizabeth should talk about herself and avoid writing "creative pieces" in a class concerning nonfiction essays, Elizabeth never varied from this format. The quality of the final portfolio was above average, compared to the rest of the class, but except for minor improvements in editing, the final revisions in the portfolio were not significantly better than the original drafts.

Bart

Bart earned a 3.86 GPA as a high school student, and he hoped to become a teacher some day. He enjoyed writing poetry when he was away from the classroom. His understanding on entering the class was that revision consisted of editing and proofreading, but he didn't flinch at the idea of content revisions and gave every effort to think of revision as a second look at his material. Bart credited Ms. Green for showing him that writing could be a learning device and that multiple drafts could give him a lease on "increased creativity."

Initially, Bart pushed out of his mind worries over the portfolio grade, explaining that the "fast-food idea of just writing" focused him on task completion rather than on evaluation. Towards the end of the semester, though, during our final interview, the reality of being graded hit him all at once. He felt he didn't have enough time to revise, and referred to the portfolio grading system as a way of the teacher "dumping" onto students three assignments in one week, with the "whole grade" riding on those revisions' outcomes. Any anxiety that Ms. Green's system had reduced during the weeks of drafting resurfaced twofold during the revision process.

Bart's revision decisions, not surprisingly then, were designed to please Ms. Green, even when Bart disagreed with her written and oral feedback. In two of the essays he revised, Bart quibbled over some changes he felt that Ms. Green wanted and strongly objected to others. Yet, he always tried to revise along the lines she suggested. He shifted the tone and focus of an essay about teaching math even though he stated that Ms. Green had the point of his essay "kind of backwards." In the other, Bart altered a recurring metaphor about his parents using him as a pawn in a chess game of divorce even though he felt he would lose his narrative voice and alter the point of the essay. This type of compliance with Ms. Green's written comments seemed especially odd because Bart told me early on that Ms. Green had instructed the class to challenge her responses to their drafts rather than to use her suggestions verbatim. He indicated to me at first that he would follow this instruction to challenge her, but as the portfolio deadline drew near, I sensed that he panicked over the grade and abandoned it.

Bart backed away from revising one draft that he had liked because the theme—that fireworks add excitement to holidays and should be legal— produced a strong criticism from Ms. Green. Bart simply explained to me that the essay "didn't go over too well" and therefore that it wouldn't be a good idea to revise it. This resulted in Bart's revising a draft about friendship, one on which Ms. Green didn't provide any written or oral feedback. He did not like the draft and felt that the revision was the weakest in his portfolio.

After starting the semester with more impersonal topics such as the innovations in holograms, Bart based the remainder of his essays on personal experience. He told me this was difficult for him, but that he enjoyed experimenting in the different genres. He also tried different stylistic approaches to the essays he wrote, but this experimentation took place during the revision, not in the drafting stage. His portfolio reflected this experimentation as all of his final revisions seemed to have moved laterally in terms of quality rather than upwards. In fact, although the portfolio assessment resulted in his receiving an A- in the class, I felt some of the earlier drafts might have been stronger than the final revisions.

Michelle

Michelle spoke of positive experiences in high school English and said that she found writing "easy" because her school's curriculum emphasized revision and included multiple drafts for all essay assignments. Like Bart, she wrote poetry in her spare time, and she also kept a journal, a diary of sorts that she had started when she was fourteen. The format of the class made Michelle a little uncomfortable. She felt "antsy" about not receiving written feedback to her second drafts, and the portfolio grade at the end of the class bothered her. She wanted an A and didn't have a clear enough idea of how close she was to it. She said that not receiving any initial grades had helped to reduce stress, but she later expressed that the desire for the A at the end brought the anxiety back as she strove to understand Ms. Green's responses to her essays.

Initially Michelle said that she would not use Ms. Green's revision suggestions just for the sake of getting a better grade—she would have to agree with the suggestions and see that they were "right" before incorporating them. Despite this claim, my later interviews with her suggest that she was trying desperately to use both written and oral feedback with which she strongly disagreed. Furthermore, Michelle had difficulty understanding Ms. Green's written responses, and on the drafts that Michelle revised, she blamed any failures on those same responses. For instance, on a paper she wrote about the art of relaxation, Michelle didn't know whether Ms. Green wanted a "personal" or an informative paper for the revision. Michelle found informative papers "boring" and didn't want to pursue that focus, so she tried to weave the two genres together, leaving her with dubious results. She conferred with Ms. Green often to try to get a clearer understanding of Ms. Green's suggestions, but the oral responses left Michelle equally confused. Yet, our discussions about her revisions indicated she felt a need to adhere to both the oral and written responses as best she could as the portfolio deadline loomed closer.

Although Michelle did not state this, I sensed that she felt little control over which essays she should choose to revise. In fact, on the last paper she worked on before turning in the portfolio, an essay concerning the rock group Winger, Michelle told me that she had felt "forced" to revise that particular paper and that she had done so only to please Ms. Green. This struck me as very peculiar since Ms. Green, in one of our interviews, had demonstrated nothing but disdain for the paper, calling it "trivial beyond words." In another paper, one Michelle chose not to revise, Michelle stated that Ms. Green's written responses were asking her to take a stand on the subject, hypochondria, and Michelle decided not to revise because she didn't want to do that. It should also be noted that Ms. Green was exceptionally harsh in the response to this paper, accusing Michelle of "poking fun" at people with a medical disorder and questioning her compassion. I felt through my conversations with Michelle that she searched for praise and that by sorting through Ms. Green's responses looking for areas where the criticisms were milder, she arrived at her decisions. Thus, she was "forced" to revise the Winger paper because Ms. Green had been the least critical of it.

Michelle experimented with several different genres during the drafting stages, discussing intensely difficult issues such as a time she was kidnapped as a child, while distancing herself in other papers, such as one about the lack of privacy in society. She also wrote one creative piece in which she pretended to be a patient in a coma ward. This pleased her immensely because she fooled the students in her peer response group into thinking that she had actually been in a coma. Her portfolio, however, was disappointing considering her experience with writing. Michelle had referred to herself in one of our interviews as a "perfectionist," but the final revisions showed little improvement from the initial drafts, and unfortunately, were far from perfect. She received a B for the course.

Analysis and Implications

My study yielded results suggesting that the goals of portfolio use in this composition course were undermined by Ms. Green's response style. On the positive side, the students were relaxed and confident during the initial drafting stages of this class, and I saw enough variation in genre and narrative stances to conclude that they experimented with their writing. However, their choices of which essays to revise and how to revise them were ultimately determined by their concerns over the portfolio grade. Furthermore, their anxiety over revising increased as the portfolio deadline grew near, perhaps exceeding the level of stress they would have felt had they been in a different grading system. Finally, the finished essays contained in the portfolio did not demonstrate to me that the students had learned to make mature, independent choices in their writing.

The reasons for these results lie, I believe, in a basic inconsistency between Ms. Green's response style, her criteria for evaluation, and her portfolio system. Ms. Green had an agenda—critical thinking and the raising of social consciousness—to which she deferred when responding to her students' drafts. This agenda, besides taking precedence over her reasons for portfolio use, was further complicated by Ms. Green's desire for polished, final drafts in the portfolio.

Ms. Green's responses to her students' drafts critiqued the students' themes or opinions based on her responses as a reader of the piece. She asked students to look at the subject from her perspective or would question the support or logic in a theme, but rarely would she present her opinions as demands or crucial suggestions for revision. She would give sometimes harsh criticisms, but would call it "food for thought" or the "devil's advocate." Never did she give her students explicit directions about how or what to revise in an essay. She did not want to give the students orders, so she presented herself as a reader and nothing more. However, most of Ms. Green's criticisms included her own political and social agenda—primarily feminism and social responsibility—expressed in varying degrees of explicitness.

As an example, in Elizabeth's paper about Walt Disney, Ms. Green felt that Elizabeth portrayed Disney from a biased point of view (it turns out that Elizabeth, indeed, had a bias since she was related to Disney), and Ms. Green wanted to show Elizabeth that there were sexist and racist elements in Disney's works, elements that could be the basis of another perspective on Disney. Therefore, Ms. Green pointed out the racist portrayal of Native Americans in *Peter Pan* and went on at length to describe the sexist messages in *Sleeping Beauty, Cinderella,* and other Disney movies. She was very explicit and adamant about her opinions, connecting the Disney films with the oppression and abuse of women today, but she qualified her comments at the end by saying they were just opinions that were meant as another perspective. With Michelle's paper about the rock concert, Ms. Green was much more subtle.

She explained to me that she wanted to show Michelle how she was succumbing to traditional gender roles under a patriarchal structure by idolizing the lead singer of the group, Kip Winger. Ms. Green also felt the paper was weak because it lacked focus. In her responses, then, Ms. Green indicated that turning the reader into "the thirteen-year-old schoolgirl type" to help the audience relate to the experience might be an interesting focus to pursue. Ms. Green believed that Michelle would see how she was presenting herself in the essay through this comment.

I should make it clear here that I found nothing wrong with Ms. Green's response style. The majority of her responses were incredibly astute and brought up issues that could have a significant place in the modern composition classroom as we continue to explore the political purposes of our teaching. The undermining of the portfolio goals, therefore, was not a natural outcome of the sometimes confrontational nature of Ms. Green's responses, but an outgrowth of Ms. Green's incomplete analysis of the connection between the response style and the portfolio goals.

The first difficulty that undermined the portfolio goals was that Ms. Green underestimated the demands of this pedagogical system on the students, especially given the time constraints. The students spent well over half the semester prewriting and drafting. Consistent with her portfolio goals, Ms. Green wanted the students to write as often as possible to make them comfortable with writing and to build their confidence. She felt there were bound to be at least three worthy topics from which to choose, and that the abundance of genre and stylistic choices would help in the students' development of writerly judgment. Unfortunately, the students did not start their revisions until all eight drafts were finished. I doubt that this strict separation of drafting and revision is what Ms. Green had in mind, but it was a practical reality due to the structure of the class. So, due to the emphasis on relaxing the students and staving off evaluation and criticism until later, Ms. Green had well less than half the semester first to make the students understand the political issues she was raising and second to help them incorporate them into their revision processes. Through classroom exercises on Rogerian logic and readings on feminist issues to give models of critical consciousness in writing, Ms. Green tried to engender this understanding and incorporation, but even she had to admit that the time limitations were debilitating to her consciousness-raising goal. The result was student anxiety and confusion in revising. Thus the goals of the portfolio and the goal of the response style clashed simply because of the lack of time in a fifteen-week semester.

Second, I feel the content of Ms. Green's responses, couched as they were in the reader response format, undermined portfolio goals. Her questions, perspectives, and criticisms—with their explicit and implicit consciousness-raising agendas—caused confusion, resistance, and anxiety in the students when they tried to revise. Ultimately, these emotions, not writerly judgments, determined revision choices for the students as they consistently avoided the implications of the consciousness-raising comments (witness Elizabeth's revision of the Disney paper, Bart's decision to abandon the fireworks paper, and other choices made by the students). In a sense, the reader response format, although consistent with the portfolio goals, interfered with the students' use of the responses. Since the agenda was established in a system where the responses were supposed to be just another perspective, the responses were not interpreted as instructions or demands. If the students did not want to follow or did not know how to implement the suggestions made by Ms. Green, they did not have to.

The inconsistency here, then, is subtle but incredibly important in seeing how the portfolio goal of promoting choice in revision conflicted with the consciousness-raising content of the responses. The reader response format did not take the edge off Ms. Green's criticisms, if that, indeed, was the intent, and the format helped confuse the notion of authority. Would it be just a mere reader evaluating the revisions in the portfolio or would it be the instructor? Were these Ms. Green's genuine reactions or were they really just an opposing opinion? The content of the responses must have been confusing, also. Ms. Green wanted the students to make judgments in regards to revision, but she also wanted to determine the boundaries of those judgments by introducing her political and social agendas. In other words, if the student had disagreed with or challenged Ms. Green's responses, in which direction were they to go? What choices were there to make once they had chosen to reject her position on the subject at hand? Her response style was not giving the options necessary for the portfolio goal; it was limiting student choices.

This leads to the third element of the conflict, which I think is crucial. The written responses were geared toward Ms. Green's consciousness-raising, yet, the criteria for assessment of the three essays in the portfolio were polished, final drafts. Most of the confusion and anxiety I witnessed in the students was a result of the impending final grade. After having successfully completed the rigorous drafting stage of this portfolio system, the students were guaranteed at least a B. However, perhaps because they had worked so hard up to that point, all three students wanted an A, and they were uncertain how to obtain it. They were confused by the responses, since the comments were not aimed at helping the students polish the drafts. If anything, the responses problematized the essays. None of the students seemed to know how to weave the comments into the process of revision, but the political agenda clearly called for a rethinking of themes and topics rather than for the insertion of details, the restructuring of sentences, reorganization, or other such improvements that would lead to a polished essay. I did not obtain data from the conferences Ms. Green offered the students after the first revisions, but Michelle indicated to me that the conferences were more of the same type of responding, only oral rather than written. Due to the inconsistency between response content and portfolio assessment criteria, I feel the portfolio goal of reducing anxiety was severely compromised.

It seems to me that the positive benefits of both the portfolio and the response style were negated by the inconsistencies of Ms. Green's system. The students did not learn as much as they could have about writing and revision, and I could find little evidence of a raising of social consciousness. What struck me the most, though, was the stifling effect the pedagogical system had on the students. Elizabeth, Bart, and Michelle all seemed to stagnate as writers. These were three students who had positive predispositions towards writing and who had achieved academic success during high school. Yet, no matter what criteria I used in my examination of their portfolios, I could not trace significant improvement from their first drafts to their final revisions nor could I find any indications that they had grown as writers.

I would be remiss, also, not to mention the accuracy and fairness of the portfolio grading, given that the complaints of my colleague's students led me to explore the connection between response styles and portfolio assessment. It should be apparent that if the instructor has conflicting agendas, the students will be confused as to the criteria for grading. Since Bart and Elizabeth received A's, I doubt they would complain about unfairness. Michelle, however, could have raised a legitimate gripe. Michelle struggled to incorporate her understanding of Ms. Green's consciousness-raising responses, assuming, I think, that this would constitute the polish Ms. Green was looking for, and might have given them preference over other revision factors during the waning days of the semester. Since neither Bart nor Elizabeth showed much improvement in the area of critical thinking and still received A's, it seems that Ms. Green did not use this as one of her criteria in grading. In fact, she told me that the final versions of the Disney paper for Elizabeth and the friendship paper for Bart were her favorites among the students I studied. Neither contained the social or political explorations that Ms. Green valued. Therefore, I think it is safe to conclude that Michelle received a B for failing to attend to the other revision factors that go into polishing an essay. Although a B might have been an accurate grade, I have to question whether it was a fair one. Did Michelle know what was expected of her? Did the responses mislead her? Most importantly, would she have gained a better understanding of the grading criteria had a more traditional grading system been used?

For Ms. Green's or a similar response style to successfully and fairly incorporate portfolios, I believe the portfolio itself must concentrate on the process of the rhetorical, political, and psychological explorations in the students' writing and that the instructor must develop a set of criteria for portfolio evaluation that defines quality or polish as an honest attempt from the student to explore these processes. Along with essays, the portfolio could include freewrites, musings, and perhaps summaries of professional articles written on the given subject, all of which could show a student's development of critical thinking faculties. Assigned topics might help also in focusing the students in a particular direction, and the students could compare their struggles with consciousness-raising directly with those of their peers and share insights to guide their revisions. A portfolio such as this would bring into alignment the goals of using the portfolio, the response method, and the criteria for evaluation. A portfolio, then, can work in a class that privileges critical thinking and challenges students through confrontational responses to their writings. Even with the inconsistencies of Ms. Green's system, she had some success in her attempt to promote experimentation in student drafting. With a restructuring or modification of the system, this experimentation that portfolios uniquely allow students could be utilized to promote the consciousness-raising Ms. Green and other instructors are interested in. The students would not have to avoid experimenting with the ideas contained in the responses because a failure in producing a polished essay would not constitute a failure in terms of the portfolio assessment.

The implications of this study do not end here with this particular response style. Every instructor using portfolio assessment must examine her response style, the assessment criteria, and the reasons for using the portfolio to ensure that a sound connection among the three exists. The purpose for using the portfolio cannot conflict with other pedagogical goals without, I believe, impeding students' development as writers and thinkers.

Teachers' Voices

10

Collaboration, Collages, and Portfolios: A Workshop

Agnes A. Cardoni
Rebecca Fraser
Janet Wright Starner

March 1992

So often I get frustrated when I go to conferences or read journal articles because there is a veneer of tidiness—of things working out perfectly. Though the authors would probably say otherwise, when I read their written words I see and FEEL a discrepancy between their students and mine (who can be recalcitrant, bored, absent, dense, etc.) and between their super-organized teaching and my own "felt-sloppiness." It isn't that I don't care enough to put time into my classes, or that I don't organize or interact with my students. No, it is just the actual messiness of classtime. It is a messiness that I have witnessed in every class I ever visited. It is a reality that rarely gets to the surface of published articles or presented papers. (Fraser)

> *   *   *

Portfolio assessment breaks most of the conventional rules for good testing practice: it's messy, bulky, nonprogrammable, not easily scored, and time consuming . . . [Yet] portfolio exams continue to crop up all over the country . . . portfolio assessment alone builds a textured, multilayered, focused measure of the writing ability students can demonstrate when given time to revise papers, and portfolio assessment alone can map the process students go through as they write. (Belanoff and Dickson, Introduction to *Portfolios: Process and Product*)

Theoretical: the collage is a parallel conversation in writing; it captures and includes because it is open-ended rather than formal and closed. Its form mimics the "sloppy" and unpredictable nature of the task-in-progress as well as the raggedness of the portfolio business itself. (Wright Starner)

*   *   *

Sometimes a collage can be more powerful and satisfying than an essay. A collage doesn't have to "say" what it's saying; it can plant seeds in the reader's mind. When such seeds bear fruit, the effect on readers is usually more powerful than if you had told them what you wanted them to think. . . . (Elbow and Belanoff, *A Community of Writers.*)

*   *   *

May 1992

We propose a half-day workshop, the end result of which will be a spontaneously and collaboratively written collage. Our aim is to solicit the experiences—personal, pedagogical, political, and theoretical—of those who have implemented portfolio assessment. This collaborative collage form seems uniquely suited to portfolio products and assessment: opening a multivoiced, sometimes contradictory conversation that does not necessitate closure.

*   *   *

Friday, 2 October 1992

1. In your folder, along with this sheet, you should have permission slips, blank paper, a glue stick, and scissors.

2. Read to each other selected parts of your writing from the last hour.

3. Select the parts of each other's writing to include in your "mini-collage" that will become a section of the larger collage. You may want to select pieces of writing that "speak" to each other, that contrast with or even contradict each other, or provide different views of a common issue.

4. Begin to physically cut up your writing and paste the pieces to the blank paper provided. You'll want to follow your group's negotiated and chosen order. Messiness and chaos counts.

*   *   *

Prompt Number 1

Think about the successes that you associate with using portfolio assessment. Consider those things that work for you and that give you and your students satisfying results. Use some form of narration—story, fable, fairy tale to talk about those successes.

*   *   *

Chris began writing about his black labradors. More and more black lab stories: puppies, breeding, mama labs and daddy labs. Then his first black lab: he had been six or seven years old. And he was being physically abused by an alcoholic father. He ran away with the dog and as they trudged down the highway the dog was hit by a car. Chris had been trying to recreate that dog ever since. He could write about these dogs and eventually about his pain when not confined to a linear semester: sequentially finishing one paper and then the next, the next, the next. Chris found himself weaving in and out of his stories, combining some essays, tossing others out. He began to master a complex process of revision I *never* could have taught. (Fraser)

*   *   *

"Hey, these are neat."
"They look important. . . . I like these labels."
"Looks like more work for us."
"What are we supposed to do with these?"
"Are these instead of our journal folders? . . . our writing folders?"
"Do we all have to have the same color?"
My eleventh-grade Honors class in an on-the-fringe inner city school reacted as I distributed blue portfolios to them at the beginning of second semester. I explained as much as I could—I, too, was a portfolio novice—and asked them to go through their writings—journals, essays, narratives, descriptions, editorials, opinions, poetry—and insert their four best pieces of different writings to date.
Chaos. Marvelous, loud, collaborative chaos. Papers flying. A new set of questions:
"Wow, that's really good. Did you *really* write that?"
"I don't know which one is better, my essay about Huck and Holden or my essay about Dimmesdale. Help me choose one."
"Can we have more than four?" (Doherty)

*   *   *

I read Joe's portfolio in my office at home. Again, the class in fiction writing, this time an advanced class. Joe included an article from *The Writer* about writing murder mysteries. He highlighted a portion of the article in yellow marker for my easy reference. The excerpt is about lifting fingerprints from cigarette lighters. With this artifact Joe includes a page from his first writing of the quarter. On that page he has highlighted a portion in which his main character detective receives information from the lab in which fingerprints were lifted from a cigarette lighter at the scene of the murder.
I am nonplussed. I had no idea that Joe—not one of the more natural talents in class—was working so hard on his writing, using research he had done in magazines, trying to write the accurate, passionate word. (Romano)

*   *   *

It just seems difficult to me to set twenty-five to thirty sophomores free to follow their own pursuits or whatever writing project we're doing. I guess it's the fear of lack of control that I worry about most, or the fear that they won't really be interested enough to settle down and work on their own writing. They are easily distracted. (Quillen)

*   *   *

Grades, I think, distract them, and the portfolio lets me postpone that distraction so that they can concentrate just on my comments and the writing process, not on grades. (Guthrie)

*   *   *

Stephanie made remarkable discoveries about herself as a writer, as a learner. She found that her best writings were those she fought with; the ones that came easily were left in the working folder. Her letter centered around an extended analogy likening her writing process to pregnancy and childbirth—beginning with conception and ending with afterbirth. She did not need a scorer: she knew the value of her performance. (Gooding)

*   *   *

The concern that I felt as I read Chris' story—the therapeutic quality of his process is so obvious. And I wonder: does the portfolio system encourage students to "dig deeper," explore further their psyches? Or is it my nature as a person that will bring this out in any student unless I am very careful? Is "very careful" even desirable? When I had Chris in my class, I was a young, new teacher, as well as a young and fairly naive woman. Something amazing and wonderful did happen for Chris. Yet I don't want to be responsible for what happens when they write about disturbing pasts. (Fraser)

*   *   *

Prompt Number 2

Let's move on to the aspects of using portfolio assessment that are not so successful or satisfying. Bring some of these to mind and write about one or some of them. Try using one of these forms, or something similar: an interior monologue, a dialogue, a letter to a mentor, a letter to students.

*   *   *

What happens when a student loses his or her portfolio? (Schaub)

*   *   *

To: The File Cabinet that holds those midterm portfolios
Forgive me. My hand sticks to my thigh and refuses to reach for your handle and slide open your drawers. Not one drawer beckons me. Those one-hundred portfolios containing five to six drafts of three assignments are too familiar. The intimacy too pungent. I cannot take seriously those pieces designated as a "final draft," or best piece. I am not sure I can teach writing.

Perhaps, Cabinet, I elevated you to keeper of the flame when I directed students to file their work inside you. You feel hot. I think perhaps I'll come back when you cool off. (Trammell)

        *   *   *

The students cannot and will not accept waiting for an end-of-the-year grade based on portfolio contents. Every wonderful piece they write must have a grade, check mark, note, or comment from me. I'm out of time before I even start. (Doherty)

        *   *   *

Can students become obsessed with revision?

        *   *   *

An initial dig into the Wendy's bag revealed a somewhat daunting stack of well-used folders. Notecards spewed out on the floor as soon as I snapped the rubber band from one folder pack. Opening one then another folder, I realized they contained a substantial stack of both typed and handwritten pages, some of them stapled; some in multiple copies; some in neat, precise ink; and some in scrawling drafts. I read here and there, attempting to orient myself to the data. Gradually the contents of these submissions came clearer, as I saw that student-selected essays did, more or less, fit with our suggested list of contents, including papers displaying their writer's sense of the best contributions to substantiate skills of originality, order, and use of evidence. The great variety and difference of these productions amazed me. How might I respond to all this difference? How could I hope to translate this rich confusion to studied reaction?

I phoned and asked, "What do we mean by *assessment?*" (Werner)

        *   *   *

Student Two (Shawn) He had worked on drafts this semester; however, he has not met with the recommended tutor. The dates on his papers show that every assignment was turned in late, and there is very little evidence of revision. Shawn has problems with spelling, sentence structure, awkward sentences, and expressing himself in a coherent manner. He fails the exit exam and retakes the course. (Parrish)

*   *   *

How do we handle the effects of midsemester failure on our students?

*   *   *

Dear Ms. X,

As one of your writing students in Elements of Writing, I want you to know how disappointed I am with my final grade of C for the course.

I feel that I was honest in my final self-reflective writing where we were supposed to talk about strengths that we saw in our writing, areas for improvement, and our growing understanding of our writing process. Then, based on our comments, we were to give ourselves the grade we felt we had earned. As you know, I handed in everything, usually on time, and did most of the revising you asked for. I feel that my greatest strengths were in the areas of organization and correctness and stated honestly that I still needed to work on development of my ideas—but I had come a long way there too from the beginning of the semester.

At our end-of-semester conference you tried to explain why you feel my grade earned was a C instead of the B+ I had given myself. But I can't see it.

Maybe it would have been different if you had graded every paper like my other teachers did. Then I would have known all along "where I stood." But with only your comments and questions through the course and conference at midterm I didn't really understand what I needed to do. I wish you had been more specific about what you wanted. And I'm not the only student who felt this way.

Please reconsider my final grade—you may not know this but my staying in the sorority is determined by my G.P.A.

Student Y   (Bolton)

*   *   *

Would it be better to grade portfolios as pass-fail? You either write satisfactorily or you cannot. (Guthrie)

*   *   *

How much help on portfolios is too much?

*   *   *

Dear John,

No. I can't go out to dinner tonight.

No. I didn't get to the Shop-Rite, so we're out of milk and bread and coffee.

Yes. Thank God, the cleaning ladies were here today.

When you get home and read this, I'll be upstairs in my office with the

DO NOT DISTURB UNLESS YOU'RE BLEEDING FROM AN ARTERY
sign on the door. So don't even try to come in.

When you get home, I will be reading portfolios. I *will have been* reading portfolios since three thirty, when I got in from school.

Yes, I know. That'll be about three hours already. Yes, I know. It's Friday night. But I have to get this done.

And at this point, I'm not enjoying them. It's not the kids' fault . . . the kids did a great job. It's not my fault . . . I can't get any more organized than I am.

I have a hundred and twenty kids, remember? Sophomores and seniors. And it's kinda like you at the theater—the show must go on. I have to have grades by Monday morning.

No. I don't know what other people do, because nobody else at Coughlin does composition this way. And even if they did, I don't think I'd have time to ask them about it.

I'm sorry. I can't go to dinner. Tell Barbara and Steve hello. Have a good time.

Love, Ag   (Cardoni)

*   *   *

My most vivid memory of that first semester is of a particular afternoon in October. To me, my course seemed to have dropped suddenly into total chaos. I'd had my students generate a fair amount of writing, and I'd responded to it, but I hadn't given them any grades . . . oops . . . because that was the point of the portfolio, wasn't it?—no grades until the end. But then, how could I give them the required midterm evaluation? And anyway, they were becoming more anxious as the days wore on: "But Mrs. Starner, what do you want? How will you figure our grade? I want to know how I'm doing!" Yes, well, I could relate to that. I wanted to know how I was doing, too.

Clearly, I had leapt before I looked; with more courage (could that read foolhardiness?) than forethought, I'd jumped into the portfolio boat, but it seemed I'd forgotten some essential equipment, like something to bail with. I could no longer see where we were going; my confidence had been my compass, and that had vanished; my initial flush of good feeling had evaporated. I thought we were all going down together. The only good part was that my students didn't yet realize how serious the gash in the bottom of the boat was. But I knew. We were goners. And it was all my fault.

Whose idea was this anyhow? (Wright Starner)

*   *   *

Prompt Number 3

Let's move on to reflect on the issues you raised in the writing you have done. Then brainstorm a list of questions still unanswered. Circle one or two and try to answer them; speculate.

*   *   *

What are the political or theoretical implications of portfolio use?

*   *   *

Frustrations. . . . formulaic, artificial. Teacher voice writings that show up in capable students' portfolios because of teacher's apprehensions. They, in fear or ignorance, try to reduce writing portfolios to workbook pages, fill-in-the-blank. (Gooding)

*   *   *

Enter the new vice principal into a well-established, traditional junior high school reputed to foster academic excellence. My initial meeting with the teaching staff was the day a new policy of teacher evaluation, professional portfolios, was being introduced by two divisional consultants.

I was assigned to a discussion group. Excited by the possibilities for dialogue that this policy might present, I was eager to participate. The teachers, however, did not share my enthusiasm for the future benefits of this policy:

"Maintain the status quo. I know I'm a good teacher."

"This doesn't lead to increased professionalism; if 'they' want us to keep a teaching portfolio, they should tell us what they want in it."

"Are you going to ask to see this portfolio regularly? What if you don't like what we put in it?"

"Other teachers will lie—how are you going to stop this?"

"When do we write them? We have too much to do as it is." What I had naively assumed would be interpreted as a positive impetus to teacher empowerment was regarded with suspicion and distrust.

Six months later—"Do you have a minute: I want to share my portfolio with you." (Graham)

*   *   *

What do we say to colleagues about in-class writing and the evaluation of it?

*   *   *

I'm sitting in a circle in a room reserved for a meeting of all the teachers of English 1. Now that Rebecca and Agnes have gone, I'm the only one left who uses portfolio assessment in my classroom, or at least the only one publicly identified as such. Rumor has it that at least one other will use it this year, but she hasn't come out of the closet yet.

"How're we doing?" the director of writing asks. After a while, the discussion moves toward grades, the way they seem to become necessary so early, sneaking up from behind both students and teachers. There is talk about the distress of finding at semester's end that three, maybe even four of the grades given don't *really* reflect student "X's" progress—"he's come so far, but here I am, stuck with these grades . . . there just isn't the kind of revision time I feel they need . . ."

I sit silently. The writing director steps into an uncomfortable lull in the conversation and says, "Well, portfolio assessment is *supposed* to solve these problems." Mercifully, he does not require me to defend my practice.

Above the murmuring that follows, a previously silent, bearded fellow suddenly breaks in, "I'd like to know just how this portfolio business *works.* What?! You withhold grades until the end of the semester? How does that play with students? Quite frankly, I don't *trust* my students enough to use this system. I'd need to know more about it." His voice has a nasty edge to it. His implications slice through the air and fly across the room straight at me. (Wright Starner)

*   *   *

What's At Stake?????

- Do portfolios really help manage the paper load?
- Do students' final products really reflect new skills and knowledge?
- How much intervention in the process contaminates the students' real ability, voice, intentions?
- How does a teacher avoid assessing his/her own efforts instead of the students' efforts?
- How do we combat overload? (Trammell)

*   *   *

Dear Colleagues, members of my adjudication committee:

We are the people who will judge my student's portfolios. We will discuss and argue whether each of my first year University writers will pass or fail, whether they'll continue their studies at the University or whether they'll be asked to leave. We are the jury. I'm not impartial. In my mind I am also playing the role of defense counsel in some cases, and prosecuting attorney in others.

When you determine, as you very easily may, that Mohamed Hamed can't write well enough to pass on to English 113, that he should fail, it will be difficult for me to vote along. I know how he started the semester without being able to write a sentence longer than five or six words, and how now he varies his sentence length. I know how he's attended grammar clinic tutorials diligently for weeks. You know none of this. What gives you the right to feel no hesitation when you mouth the vote: "Fail"? (Schaub)

*   *   *

If I were a writing coach instead of a writing umpire . . . (Cardoni)

*   *   *

Do portfolios encourage a particular kind of writing? (No) Do portfolios encourage "deeper" thinking? What is deep thinking? Is it related to the much loved "critical" thinking? How do portfolios encourage critical thinking skills? In what ways does the creation of portfolios by students encourage reflection? (Fraser)

*   *   *

Do they really take more care, or do they just postpone their real efforts? (Guthrie)

*   *   *

What a challenge it must be for you to take each student by the hand and help him/her recognize the value of work-in-progress or help him/her see how coming back to a project or piece afterwards brings new insights and fresh ideas.

But, despite your concerns about assigning grades, don't you feel that the accumulation of work reflected in each portfolio is a much clearer, truer, portrayal of what each student is able to do? Do you not see more specific direction for instruction and intervention in your "teacher/facilitator" role?

I empathize with your frustrations—change is hard work! But, don't you feel that "we're on to something here," something that will modify our view of teaching/learning forever? (Jenkins)

*   *   *

My cranky side says panacea salesmen will always be with us. Maybe I should become one: The Doctor Cardoni Freewriting, Collage-Building, Portfolio-Constructing Elixir and Plantfood, Efficacious for Man or Beast. (Cardoni)

Collage Contributors

- Sandra Bolton, American College Testing
- Agnes Cardoni, Lehigh University
- Carol Doherty, Waite High School, Toledo, OH
- Rebecca Fraser, Nassau Community College
- Joy Gooding, Kentucky Writing Program
- Barbara Graham, Seven Oaks School Division, Winnipeg, Canada
- William B. Guthrie, Wilmington (OH) College
- Carmel Jenkins, South-Western City Schools, Grove City, OH

- Kathleen Parrish, Niagra County Community College, Sanborn, NY
- Judith Quillen, South-Western City Schools, Columbus, OH
- Tom Romano, Utah State University
- Mark Schaub, American University, Cairo, Egypt
- Janet Wright Starner, Lehigh University
- Sandra Trammell, Kentucky State University
- Charlene Werner, University of Toledo

11

Writing Portfolios in K-12 Schools: Implications for Linguistically Diverse Students

Sandra Murphy

Research showing that traditional standardized tests give us a distorted view of the literacy performance, knowledge, and intelligence of students from diverse linguistic and cultural backgrounds is now fairly extensive (Cole, Deyhle, Figueroa, Green, Padilla, Samuda). As a result, educators increasingly turn to alternative assessment techniques such as collections of selected pieces of work in portfolios for solutions to problems associated with assessment of linguistic minority students. In this paper I explore what portfolios have to offer in the assessment of linguistic minority students, particularly their potential for providing more equitable assessments and new approaches in the teaching of writing to linguistically diverse students.

To begin, I discuss the limitations of traditional standardized methods of writing assessment, including indirect methods like multiple-choice tests as well as direct methods like the collection of single samples under timed conditions. Then I address questions teachers often ask about using portfolios to teach and assess writing in K-12 schools: What are portfolios and why bother with them? What can we do with portfolios that we can't do, or can't do as well, when we adopt other ways to go about teaching writing? What can they do for us in assessment where other methods fail?

I focus in particular on four opportunities for portfolio use that have particular implications and promise for teaching and assessing linguistic minority students, including dialect speakers and students for whom English is a second language. These include opportunities to

1. assess and analyze how students write in a variety of conditions, to a variety of audiences, and for a variety of purposes;

2. gather information about processes as well as products;

3. use reflection to uncover the rhetorical and cultural models students bring to the task of learning to write and

4. involve students directly in the assessment process, making criteria explicit so that students can learn from the assessment process itself.

These opportunities can benefit all students, but they are especially significant for linguistic minority students.

Limitations of Traditional, Standardized, Assessment Methods

For many students, standardized tests that are multiple-choice are problematic because for any particular question, there is only one acceptable response, one, nonnegotiable right answer according to the publisher. One of my favorite examples of this is from a story told in Miriam Cohen's book, *First Grade Takes a Test*. In the story, a youngster named George is taking his first standardized test. He comes across an item that asks him to identify what rabbits eat. He is offered three choices—lettuce, dog food, or sandwiches. But of course George knows that rabbits eat something else, so he raises his hand and tells his teacher that rabbits eat carrots. And then, so the test people will know too, he carefully draws a carrot on his test booklet. The point is, of course, that when answers are nonnegotiable, children don't have the opportunity to show what they know.

The nonnegotiable answer format is a problem when assessing all students, but even more so when assessing students with culturally different backgrounds. Let me tell you another story to illustrate what I mean. It's a story about a little girl whose parents were migrants—farmworkers who followed the crops from town to town. In the late 1950s, the parents were working in the orange groves near the town of Redlands in California where my mother taught elementary school. The girl—I'll call her Elena—was a student in my mother's class. For Elena, English was a second language.

As my mother tells the story, Elena was taking the kind of standardized test where you match a picture with a word. On one of the items, the word was *light,* and on the page where she was marking bubbles, there was a picture of a broom, a pot, and a lamp—a traditional kind of lamp on a stand with an upside down "V" shaped shade. Like George, when Elena came to the troublesome item, she raised her hand, asking to talk to the teacher. In those days talking during tests was forbidden. It still is. But teachers often know when to break the rules and this teacher was surprised by what she found out. Like her, you might think that it was the word *light* that was giving Elena trouble since she was an ESL student. But that was not the case. Elena knew what the word *light* meant and she knew how to read it, she just didn't know which image to pick to match with the word. In the trailer where Elena lived in the orange groves, light came from a bare bulb that hung from the ceiling. She didn't have the kind of lamp or lampshade that was in the test. So the test said that Elena wasn't smart, but her teacher knew better.

Standardized tests like the ones George and Elena took don't let students show what they know. In this sense, they aren't fair. But for students like Elena, students who have backgrounds different from the mainstream culture, they are unfair in another way. Standardized tests penalize such students because they don't have the kinds of experiences that are tapped by tests. Although psychologists have tried to create "culture free tests," they have failed (Cole). Tests are not culture free. In fact, as Donna Deyhle says, "Tests are designed for and validated against the values and lifestyles of the middle class, which in turn discriminates against other socioeconomic groups and nondominant cultural groups" (86). Students from nondominant groups then, are not only disadvantaged because they cannot show what they know, they are penalized because what they know is different.

The problem isn't really with the children, of course, it's with the tests, and for linguistically different students, tests present another problem. Students from nondominant groups often struggle with the language.

The "language problem" creates ironic situations in the assessment of linguistically diverse students. Consider multiple-choice exams. On the surface, these kinds of exams might seem a better option than exams that call for actual writing, more fair somehow for students who are not very proficient in producing language themselves. But in fact, multiple choice tests demand sophisticated language skills. They require students to read very carefully and they are filled with distractors—negatives, unfamiliar material, unfamiliar linguistic structures, and other elements that are almost guaranteed to trip students with limited proficiency in English.

Even more ironic, whether the method is multiple choice or direct, when assessment is standardized, students with limited English proficiency are doubly disadvantaged *in the name of* what's fair. Consider traditional assessment methods. People standardize conditions for assessment based on the assumption that by doing so they can create a "level playing field" in which all students, regardless of background, have an equal opportunity to succeed. Multiple-choice tests are timed and in large scale direct writing tests, we also sample writing in timed conditions. We give everyone the same amount of time to be fair. But the real question, of course, is how much time? Many of the current direct tests of writing only sample first draft writing. The National Assessment of Educational Progress (NAEP), for example, has gained notoriety for its nine-minute writing samples; the Scholastic Assessment Test (SAT) allows twenty minutes. Because these kinds of tests don't give students time to revise, they don't reflect what we know about good writing instruction. In a sense, then, these kinds of tests are unfair to all students because they don't let students show what they can do *after* the first draft. But if timed writing tests are questionable for all students, they are clearly twice as bad for students who need more time to show what they can do even at the first draft stage.

Time has been shown to be an important factor in the differential performance of linguistic minority students on multiple-choice standardized tests (Garcia, Mestre, Rincon) and in direct-writing assessment as well. Indeed, when adequate time has been allowed in direct-writing assessment, scores of linguistic minority students have increased so that they approach the scores of mainstream students (Hilgers). Not all playing fields are level.

Assessment Alternatives

Increasingly, educators who are concerned with the problems I've outlined are turning to alternative modes of assessment, like portfolios. Writing portfolios are selections of student work, produced as a normal part of coursework or outside of class, for purposes of instruction and evaluation. The topics for writing may be self-generated as often as they are assigned; the writing is done under a variety of conditions, in class and out, with varying amounts of response from teachers and peers provided during the revision process. The students do the choosing—often with coaching from their teacher. They choose which pieces of their work that they think are best and most representative.

Writing portfolios document performances. They show what a student can do. Performance assessment isn't exactly a new idea. We assess performance when we score athletic events such as ice skating, diving, and so on. We assess performance when we give driving tests, and, although the actual process of the activity is less transparent, we assess performance when we evaluate writing. Portfolios can be used for many different kinds of evaluation purposes, including the assessment of competence or achievement. What writing portfolios *don't* do, though, unless you happen to pick up one of those publisher portfolios, is emphasize decontextualized skills and facts. And they don't depend upon simple "recognition" as multiple-choice tests do. Portfolios contain artifacts of complex performances.

Assessment and Analysis in Various Circumstances

Because portfolios show what students can do in a *variety* of situations, they can give a broader and more accurate picture of student performance. One of the biggest problems in writing assessment is that generalizations about abilities are often based on single samples of performance—as if writing in one situation were the same as writing in any other. Yet we all know that writing a poem isn't exactly like writing an essay and that writing produced in fifteen minutes isn't likely to be as developed as writing produced in an hour, or a day, or two days. Portfolios, then, are potentially a more valid kind of assessment because they accommodate the idea that writing for different audiences and purposes draws on different skills and strategies.

In addition, portfolios accommodate the idea that writing completed in different amounts of time and with different support may exhibit different characteristics. In this respect, at least, portfolios are more fair, especially for linguistic minority students, than other kinds of assessment, if only because portfolios allow students to show what they can do under a variety of conditions. That is, students are not automatically disadvantaged by abbreviated time frames. In addition to increasing validity in assessment, the multiple snapshots of performance contained in portfolios provide some unique opportunities for us in teaching, opportunities to do more than just teach the forms and structures of English. Multiple snapshots invite us to explore how language varies across situations. Using portfolios to understand how language varies with audience, purpose, and across situations is particularly appropriate for students who need to understand how English used for academic purposes differs from other kinds of writing and speaking that they may be accustomed to at home.

Portfolios can help students become more aware of the ways writing varies from situation to situation. To this end, portfolios can include a wide variety of writing categorized in a number of ways. For example, one way to shape the guidelines for selecting portfolio contents is to consider the form, purpose and audience for writing—the what, why and to whom questions that define the nature of the writing task. In considering the "what" question, students might be asked to submit a variety of different genres or forms, such as stories, scripts, letters, narratives, poems, biographies, reviews, or reports. In considering the "why" question, students might be asked to submit pieces written for a variety of different purposes or aims, such as informing, evaluating, interpreting, entertaining, persuading, arguing, or speculating. In considering the "to whom" question, students might be asked to submit a variety of pieces written to different audiences, for example self, peers, younger child, trusted adult, unfamiliar individual, general audience, employer, family member, principal, editor, or celebrity.

Because they contain multiple pieces of writing, portfolios invite teachers and students to conduct a kind of "contrastive rhetorical" analysis by taking a closer look at how texts differ from one another. In this respect, they offer a unique teaching opportunity. For example, when portfolios contain different kinds of writing, teachers and students can analyze variations in the way students treat ideas. Many California students are from immigrant families and write about what it means to feel different. In the following paper, fifteen-year-old Alice uses her own experiences to illustrate a sophisticated idea.

Changes

Ever since I was a child, I have always felt the need to fit in the American crowd. Just to be normal, not asian. Over the years, I slowly began to lose my language as well as my culture. I blamed my parents for not being americans. I didn't want to be the person that stuck out in the crowd. All my friends had blond and brown hair; I had black. I began to only speak English at home. My parents seemed oblivious to the fact that I was losing my heritage.

When I was in the seventh grade, I began my changing process. I seemed to see everything through different eyes. My parents finally forced me to become involved in the vietnamese choir even though I was illiterate. I tried to sing along, memorizing half the words because I couldn't read them. After a long time, I was able to read without having the songs memorized beforehand. Through the choir, I learned how to understand and appreciate my heritage again.

During the time of this transition, I made many sacrifices and decisions. Many people don't realize the advantages of being bilingual until it is to late. I was caught between two cultures that were a world apart. The only way I could have both was by understanding and appreciating my own first.

By itself, this piece shows that when Alice has the opportunity to narrate, she can select and shape details from her own experience to make an idea explicit. Her writing is focused and she speaks with authority. She packs the piece with specifics. But notice what happens when Alice writes about someone else's experience and idea:

Response to *Black Boy*

I think that this statement [" . . . that his resistance to the effort made to mold him has been the means of his education"] means that what he knows, he has learned through life experiences. Experience is not something that can be given to you. Through Richard's efforts of refusing to be molded into the "black behavior," he has gained a vast education on human rights. His experiences have enabled him to write a book of his thoughts and fears in hopes that others will be able to understand a different culture as well as way of thinking.

In this second paper, references to specific experiences are absent, as is the voice of authority. Because the papers showed up together in the portfolio, the teacher—and Alice—could compare the two. They could see that these two papers, while in different modes, were about an idea Alice knew intimately: reconciling cultures. They could note the absence of detail in the piece Alice wrote when she was working from literature instead of from her own experience. And, because the connection was made visible, Alice could be helped to see how a strategy she already possessed in her repertoire—use of specific detail—could be adapted to another situation. She could be encouraged to use her own experience as well as Richard Wright's experience in revising the interpretive paper. This kind of comparative analysis is difficult to achieve when students turn in stacks of papers written to the same assignment. It requires a collection of individual student work—a portfolio.

Collections of work invite comparisons of different kinds of writing and comparisons over time. In this respect, working with portfolios *isn't* like the teaching we know. Instead of correcting stacks of papers written to the same assignment, we have the opportunity to analyze several papers from one student, collected over time and in a variety of situations. In assessment too, when we work with portfolios, our focus shifts away from the individual assignment to the student. That is, we move from the finite nature of a single assignment and the finite picture that assignment gives us of a student's performance to a more complex and dynamic view of a writer's growth provided by many snapshots of performance. This is something that portfolios can do that other assessments cannot.

Information-Gathering About
Processes Along With Products

What else can portfolios do that other assessments cannot? They can provide information about the processes students use to produce their writing. This is useful information for teachers, because it helps them know whether and how well students are using prewriting and revision strategies. Teachers can learn, for example, when students think revision means simply recopying. With this kind of information in hand, teachers can decide when students need to learn a battery of possible strategies that may help them improve their writing. Moreover, because portfolios accommodate and encourage process, they are more in line with what we know about good instructional practices in the teaching of writing.

There are several ways to show writing processes in portfolios. Students can be asked to include both finished works and biographies of works explaining the stages in the development of a piece. In the Arts Propel Project, these biographies include journal entries students have made along the way to reflect on the processes of writing. Portfolios may also include all the notes and drafts telling the story of a piece. In this way, portfolios become long-term records that allow teachers and students to examine how processes change, how students learn to manage them more effectively, and which routines help the student writer. Information about processes can also be gathered by asking students to submit work(s)-in-progress along with plans for revision.

Georgia Garcia and David Pearson suggest that including information about process may be a very important element in the assessment of linguistic minority students. They argue that including information to document the evolutionary nature of the development of a piece may reveal some of the conflicting demands that are inherent in the literacy development of linguistically diverse students. Consider this example from their paper on assessment in a linguistically diverse society:

> *First attempt:* When I am alone, I dream about the man I want to be with. He *a* man that every woman wants, and every woman needs.
>
> *Second attempt:* I daydream alot about what my knight in shining armor will be like. He has to be everything rolled all in one and nothing *suppose* to be wrong with him.
>
> *Third attempt and the beginning of the essay she turned in:* My make-believe man is everything. He is perfect from his head down to his toes. He's handsome, romantic and intelligent.(9)

The excerpts are from drafts of an essay written by a young black woman. The essay was a major prerequisite for entrance into a required rhetoric course at the college level. The excerpts reveal how the student goes about revising her first draft in order to rid her piece of dialect features and create a closer approximation of what she thinks is expected.

Garcia and Pearson point out that the writing in the student's first version, produced when she was not yet worried about dialect features, was more fluid and more complex than the writing in the revised versions. In the first version, the relationships among her ideas were clear, and she wrote with "voice." But Garcia and Pearson also report that when she revised her writing on the second and third attempts, she didn't seem to know what to change and that, in the process of eliminating dialect features, she turned to clichés and broke her thoughts down into simple sentences. The final version, then, was dialect-free, but it was also a choppy piece of voiceless prose.

Without the successive drafts, of course, it would have been impossible for a teacher to trace the evolution of the piece and it would be easy to attribute the choppiness of the last draft to a lack of sophistication rather than to an attempt on the part of the student to make her writing look conventional (Garcia and Pearson, 10). This kind of information from portfolios can help teachers learn why and when students need help in the revision process and it can help teachers learn when the characteristics of writing may be related to misconceptions the student may have about the teacher's expectations.

Reflection, Self-Assessment, Rhetorical and Cultural Models

Portfolios can be used to encourage students to *reflect* on the pieces they write and on the processes they use to write them. In fact, many teachers who have worked with portfolios consider reflection the single most important learning opportunity that portfolios provide. Certainly, reflection and self-assessment are central to good writing. In his paper "How Children Change as Critical Evaluators of Writing," Hilgers claims that a writer's ability to evaluate her or his writing is, after all, the cornerstone of writing skill. Reflection is also central to learning. As Roberta Camp says in "Portfolio Reflections in Middle and Secondary Classrooms," "In writing, as in other performances, we learn in part by looking back on what we have done. In this sense, looking back—reflecting—on the experience of writing a piece or on the written piece itself, is an integral part of our becoming more accomplished writers" (61). Yet the teaching of writing in many of our public schools and classrooms has typically not included many opportunities for student writers to reflect on or to evaluate their work. In fact, when it comes to evaluation, we do it for them. We red ink papers and give comments, grades, points, or even rubber stamps; that is, we respond in ways that let the students know what *we* see and what *we* value. But we rarely ask students to evaluate themselves.

What students have to say in reflective pieces about their writing and their writing processes can be very useful to teachers. For example, when Gwen, a young ESL student, wrote a letter to her teachers to introduce her portfolio, she noted progress, but she also noted clear distinctions between her school and home experiences as a writer. She writes:

Dear Readers,

I have learned alot about my writing from my english class this year, and I really believe my writings has improved.

The most helpful lesson I learned was the writing process. Before, I would start writing when the assignment was given, and start on the first idea that pop in my mind, without giving myself a second choice. Now, I learned to take my time and brainstorm and plan my writing.

Although the writing process has helped my the writings I do in class will never be better, or more interesting that the ones I do at home. Writing on my spare time is to me without pressure of time due, or a bad grade. That was, I feel more comfortable, and my writing would just flow through. . . .

I feel that I would get better grades on my writings if I was writing about subject I am interested in. That way, the assignment won't be boring because it concerns me.

To end this letter I would like to say that I really enjoy writing, and maybe one day, I'll have a career by it.

Sincerely yours,
Gwen

What Gwen clarifies for herself and for us is how she operates as a writer and what she has learned about writing as a process. Combined with the papers that illustrate her analysis, Gwen's commentary dramatizes her need for flexibility in the circumstances surrounding her writing, especially her need for time and for choice of topic. Reflections such as Gwen's can help us learn what is useful to our students and how well they understand what we have tried to teach them. While Gwen was asked to write about her writing process and the kinds of writing she liked to do, other kinds of questions will trigger other kinds of responses that can serve different purposes. Dan Kirby and Carol Kuykendall, for example, use what they call a portfolio audit to help students monitor the processes they go through—and the progress they are making—as writers, readers and thinkers as they work with the writing in their portfolios. Richard Beach, on the other hand, makes *revision* the purpose for student reflection. Before students meet with him in conferences, they divide their drafts into sections and answer questions about their intentions and plans.

All of these good ideas should be useful to teachers with students who are learning to write English as a first language *or* as a second language, since they are simply good ideas for teaching writing. But there is yet another use for reflective questions that should be of particular interest to teachers who have ESL students in their classes. Here, I'm indebted to George Gadda for helping me see another good reason for asking students to reflect on the work in their portfolios. In a chapter from a very insightful and helpful book titled *With Different Eyes,* Gadda reminds us that cultures show a great diversity in the ways they structure writing and in the ways they encourage children to use language. In assessment, this diversity sometimes results in unconscious bias. Indeed, in "Toward an Ethnography of Black American Speech Behavior," Kochman contends that "cultural learning is internalized at the level of the subconscious, so that existing patterns are too taken-for-granted even to be noticed" (290). Thus uninformed evaluators may make decisions that are culturally based without even being aware of how their backgrounds determine their judgments (Tsang). Reflective questions can help us uncover and understand unconscious cultural learning.

Clearly, knowing what ideas our students bring with them to the classroom about different kinds of discourse is useful information in teaching. We need to know "where students are" in order to advise them adequately about "where to go next." But more often than not these days, at least in California, our classrooms are rich mixes of many different individuals from many different cultures. The following report from the Liberal Studies Newsletter gives a sense of the extent of the diversity in California's classrooms:

> In 1989, the State had 4 million K-12 public school students; 52% of these were ethnically diverse. Nearly forty percent of these children enter school with a language other than English and with cultural backgrounds different from "mainstream" America. Latino/Hispanics comprise the largest part of this population but there are ten other major cultural groups (primarily Asian) and one hundred other cultural groups represented. (Vidal 1)

Being informed about the various cultural models brought by children to California classrooms would be difficult enough. However, as Gadda points out, even if you know typical *cultural* models for writing, it is unwise to make assumptions about *individuals*. The solution, Gadda says, is to *ask* our students about the conceptions they have of different kinds of discourse. That is, if the texts the students produce seem to violate expectations in systematic ways, we can ask them why. Gadda suggests that by asking students to tell us how they arrived at texts that we find puzzling, we may be able to learn what conceptions they have that conflict with our own. He suggests questions like the following:

- Why did you begin and end the piece this way?
- How do you think this kind of writing should sound?
- What do you think your readers already know about what you say?
- What do you think you have to tell them?
- How do you expect your readers to follow you from point 1 to point 2?
- What do you expect your readers to understand by this?
- How do you expect this piece of writing to affect your readers? (73)

Gadda's questions are aimed at individual pieces of writing—that is, they ask students what they were trying to accomplish with a particular piece of writing, what kind of a text they had in mind. But I think related questions could easily be aimed at *collections* of writings. Students could be asked, for example, to compare and contrast writing done for different purposes and to trace rhetorical strategies across multiple pieces of writing.

The Assessment Process as Learning Process

Portfolios give us an opportunity to make right some things that have been wrong in assessment. In particular, they offer us the opportunity to make the assessment process a learning process, something very different from the usual assessment scenario.

Just for a moment remember your own experience with classroom assessment. If it was like mine, it usually happened on Friday. On that day, when I was a student, we went to school to fill in and match and check. We were steeped in the paraphernalia and ritual of tests: number two pencils, answer keys, bell curves, points, make-ups, posted results. Once in a while we wrote essay exams. These were shotgun affairs, timed precisely to the number of minutes in the class period, shrouded in secrecy, and weighted with suspense. When we came into class and took our seats, ready at the mark with our pens and pencils hovering over blank paper, the teachers would reveal the topic and the race would start, ending, whether we were ready or not—when the bell rang for the next class. On Mondays we got the tests back—always returned with the grammar corrected and a grade in place. Some teachers gave points. If you got ten points you were in good shape. If you got six you were in trouble. Other teachers gave us A's or B's or C's or D's. But we didn't know why, and we'd complain, "Why isn't this an A?" Reasons for A's and B's and C's remained, as often as not, mysterious to us. Decades later, students are still the recipients of surprise topics and tests and they are still complaining, "Why isn't this an A?"

In all fairness to our teachers, they were only following the lead of larger-scale testing enterprises in the strategies they employed for our assessment. At the time, and still today, most formal large-scale assessment enterprises operate with the assumption that, to be fair, students, like runners, always have to start the race from the same starting line and run the same race. In the direct assessment of writing, this resulted in attempts to universalize the writing experience. Test makers busied themselves formulating topics that could be considered accessible to all students, whatever their individual interests, backgrounds or knowledge. Such tests were supposed to measure "writing competence," the end of the road of writing instruction. They were supposed to be "curriculum independent"; that is, they were supposed to remain unrelated to whatever specific curriculum was the transportation for getting there.

Running the same race meant we all started with the same topic, and it meant that our performance was timed. It's still timed. We usually do more than fill in the bubbles now; even in large scale assessments we write real essays. But again, our pens hover over the paper, waiting for the gate to snap open so the race can start. And the tests are sterile. We make sure that no one sees the topic in advance, just like those classroom tests, except in the large-scale arena people talk about topic "banks." At ETS you have to wear a badge to get into the building. Topic security is now big business. And as in the old days, the veil of secrecy still extends, often as not, along with confidentiality about topics to criteria for evaluation. And after the race, students are still asking, "Why isn't this an A?"

That's a really important question. Like David Pearson, I think that the only real justification for assessing students today is to help them learn how to do it for *themselves* tomorrow. To put it another way, assessment should *teach* students something, not just take time away from teaching.

There are several things we need do to make the assessment process a learning process. First, we need to give students a voice in the assessment process, so that they have some kind of stake in it, a stake for the decisions they are *empowered* to make, not just a stake for the consequences of failure. Second, we need to look closely at the kinds of information we give to students about their performance, so that students have a chance to learn from the assessment process itself. We need to stop relying solely on numbers and begin providing more detailed, individual feedback. And third, we need to make the criteria for evaluation explicit to students, so that they can begin learning how to do it for themselves. All of these things depend on bringing students and teachers together.

Consider what it means to give students a voice in the assessment process —letting students have some say about how they are going to be assessed and on what. I don't mean, of course, that students should be making these decisions without the guidance of their teachers. If that were the case, there'd be no teaching going on. But students do need to be able to exercise judgment in order to learn how to assess a piece of writing or a whole collection of writing.

Asking students to exercise judgment has implications for the way we design portfolios. If the contents of the portfolio are too narrowly specified, students won't have room to exercise judgment, for example, if a portfolio is simply a collection made up of portfolio assignment number one, portfolio assignment number two, and so on. In contrast, when students and teachers are brought together in assessment, when teaching is going on, portfolio guidelines are structured to make the most out of the possibilities for learning. For example, during the first year of the California Assessment Program Portfolio Project, teachers at Mt. Diablo High School in Concord, California, asked students to make selections from broad categories of kinds of writing emphasized in their school's curriculum. They didn't require particular assignments. The students, then, had to exercise some judgment about which of their papers was the best exemplar of a particular category.

During the second year, teachers at Mt. Diablo put even more emphasis on what we might call the learning potential of portfolios. Instead of specifying types of writing—letter, opinion, speculation, and so on, they specified writing strategies. Their instructions to the students sounded something like this:

> Select a piece for your portfolio that *shows* you know how to state and
> support an opinion.
> Select a piece for your portfolio that *shows* you know how to revise.
> Select a piece for your portfolio that *shows* you know how to use writing
> to learn.
> Select a piece for your portfolio that *shows* you know how to reflect.

In other words, the students were invited to select from many different types of writing as long as they demonstrated the strategy in question. They were asked to show what they knew about a particular strategy. These kinds of guidelines help students learn and to know what they have learned. They help students learn to exercise judgment.

There are any number of other ways teachers can encourage students to exercise judgment. Students might be asked, for example, to rank order their papers in terms of personal preference, from best to worst, or on any number of factors or strategies. The assumption is, of course, that teachers and students will be doing something together with the portfolios, not just putting pieces of paper in a folder. Helping students learn how to exercise judgment doesn't mean leaving them in isolation to do it. Along with specific guidelines, then, students need feedback about the judgments they make. Useful feedback, however, doesn't come in numbers, grades, or points. (After all, what good does it do a student to know that he is a two on a scale of five?) Useful feedback comes from detailed response and talk is an efficient and effective way to provide that response.

Expert teachers try to find occasions and opportunities for talking with students about work-in-progress, and working with portfolios in the classroom can provide those opportunities. One of the best things I know about portfolios is that they get teachers talking with students about their writing. But dialogues with students about their writing don't have to be confined to individual classrooms. In fact, it can be very motivating for students to have audiences other than their teachers respond to their writing. What the teachers decided to do at Mt. Diablo High School in California is an example. In this portfolio project, teachers scored students' portfolios at the end of the year according to criteria based on their curriculum. But they also wrote letters to the students, and they made it a point to respond to the portfolios of students who were *not* in their own classes.

These were not easy letters to write, because the teachers were trying to adopt a new approach. They weren't used to fanning out the papers of one writer and responding in terms of questions they had about the whole of a writer's work and work strategies. Questions like

- How does this writer fare across different kinds of writing or writing done for different audiences and purposes?
- How does this writer solve the problems that writers solve?
- How does this writer manage a process?
- In what ways and to what extent has this writer changed and progressed?
- What are this writer's strengths? Weaknesses? Special talents?
- How does this student assess him or herself and by what standards?

For students who received them, the letters were stunning. The students were not used to reading about themselves as writers nor were they used to having their writing read by an adult other than their own teacher. Here is what one ESL student had to say to the teacher who read and responded to his portfolio:

> I have receive your letter today, on my final day. Before I receive this letter, I said to myself, "Oh no, I hope someone who read my portfolio like it." Because this is my first time doing this, and I'm not sure what I write in this is right. When I receive this letter. I was so happy that you like it. I think I'm going to improve my organizing on writing in paragraphs next year. Thank you for take your time to read this.

What this excerpt reveals is that students, particularly those for whom English is a second language, can be somewhat anxious about portfolio evaluation. At the same time, they are eager to establish a writer-to-reader relationship with their evaluators and to commit to making specific improvements. Clearly, letters from teachers have a different effect from a grade or score. Letters treat students as authors while grades or scores do not. Letters instruct and qualify; they do not rank or categorize. Letters are personal; grades or scores are not.

I don't want to imply, of course, that we all have to go out and write letters. What's important here is that the student receive detailed and specific feedback based on analysis. There are many ways to convey the results of that analysis. Some people write letters, others conduct personal conferences, while others hold larger gatherings to which a variety of people, including parents or members of the community may be invited. Whether the audience is large or small, or whether the response comes in the form of a letter, a conference or through some other means, the key element is *interaction* and the focus of the interaction is the student's work alongside criteria for performance.

Criteria come in many forms. They can be descriptions or they can be exemplars. They can apply to individual pieces of writing or to a portfolio as a whole. Some teachers, for example, employ sets of criteria that focus on particular writing situations, each with its distinctive characteristics. The advantage of this approach is that it allows teachers to zero in on specific strengths or weaknesses in students' performance in specific writing modes. The disadvantage of this kind of evaluation is that it focuses more on individual assignments than on individual writers. Some teachers choose to eschew the paper-by-paper approach for its alternative, applying criteria to the portfolio as a whole. In Virginia, members of the Mt. Vernon High School English Department look for particular qualities in the whole portfolio, qualities such as versatility, adaptability, completeness, carefulness, beauty, and power. Teachers at San Diego High School, on the other hand, gear their criteria to what they want to see in students' interdisciplinary portfolios. In social studies, for example, students take into account criteria such as

- uses historical evidence to support arguments and ideas
- uses creativity to approach and convey ideas
- expresses ideas clearly
- connects historical periods with today
- demonstrates an understanding of cause-and-effect relationships.

Although the criteria used by these schools are in some ways very different, they are *employed* in similar ways. In classrooms where students and teachers work together in assessment, there are no surprise topics, sprung on students, and there are no mysteries about criteria for evaluation. Criteria are out there for everyone to see and talk about. In fact in some cases, as at San Diego High School, the criteria *themselves* provide the guidelines for assembling portfolio contents. As students assemble their portfolios, they can refer to the actual evaluation criteria. The portfolio assessment process, then, comes full circle. Selections are based on criteria. Teachers make expectations explicit. It makes sense, because students can only benefit from knowing, rather than guessing at, expectations.

Students with limited proficiency in English, like their mainstream counterparts, can benefit greatly from knowing expectations. And for them, it is much more imperative that we be explicit about the criteria we use to assess.

Less test-wise than their mainstream counterparts, and less familiar with mainstream rhetorical conventions, these students are least likely to be successful at guessing their evaluators' intentions. Only if we are explicit about our expectations can we hope to be fair.

Limitations of Portfolio Assessment

Lest I seem too enamored of portfolios and seem to present them as the panacea for all the problems in the assessment of students with limited English proficiency, let me say what they won't do. They won't guarantee a fair assessment. Consider, for example, this statement by a student named Leticia. She is quoted by Dan Fichtner, Faye Peitzman and Linda Sasser.

> In my country, I was always a top student. But here I get Cs and Ds because of my English. I am so angry because I know I haven't changed. I'm still smart. (143)

Leticia knows she's smart, and many of her teachers know she is smart, but her limited English proficiency influences the way she is evaluated. The quote illustrates the dilemma faced by students with limited English proficiency in content classes, a dilemma that frustrates students and teachers alike. Even work completed in the supportive environment of the classroom will not always reliably reveal what a student knows if language is a barrier.

In assessment situations, whether they occur in the classroom or in a more formal testing context, it is likely that familiarity with a language will always affect the assessment of performance. Everyday familiarity with the language, for example, might not be adequate to ensure that individuals understand the nature of the task they are being asked to perform. On large-scale achievement tests like the SAT, language proficiency has been shown to be a moderator variable (Alderman). But language is not the only problem. Because language-minority persons reflect different cultural and social heritages from those of mainstream American English speakers, there is always a possibility that unrecognized differences in the backgrounds of examinees might clash with the assumptions held by their evaluators.

Sociocultural factors influence evaluators. Tsang, drawing upon the work of Gumperz (*Discourse Strategies* and *Language and Social Identity*) contends that native speakers subconsciously evaluate and interpret abilities and intentions of others through language behavior. According to Tsang, "subtle cultural nuances, attitudes, and values can be miscommunicated and therefore negatively evaluated because of a student's lack of command of the discourse and writing conventions of the language" (239). Moreover, as suggested in *International Comparisons and Educational Reform*, writers from different cultures may have learned rhetorical patterns that may differ from patterns used in academic settings in the United States, patterns that are reinforced by their educational experiences in their specific cultures (Purves and Takala).

In and of themselves, portfolios do not address these problems. More samples of writing, produced in a variety of situations, both in-school and out—that is, portfolios—offer no guarantee against biased judgments. If anything, multiple samples make the judgments we have to make more difficult and more complex. In addition, there is no guarantee that each student will have an equal opportunity for access to the kind of writing experiences and instruction that will allow them to develop complete portfolios filled with a variety of carefully revised pieces. Neither are there any guarantees that the materials students encounter will be sensitive to cultural and gender differences or that fair procedures will be used in scoring portfolios, or that adequate judgmental and statistical procedures will be employed to assess bias. Yet these potential problems are true of all assessments, not just assessments in which students construct portfolios.

Benefits of Portfolio Use

In weighing alternatives, there are potential benefits to using portfolios that clearly tip the scales, especially in the assessment of linguistic minority students. The greater degree of student choice in portfolio assessments—such as topics to write on or projects to conduct—may motivate students and take cultural differences into account. Test anxiety, a special concern for some cultural groups (see Rincon), is less likely to effect performance since work is done as a normal part of the classroom routine and not in a test-like situation. Moreover, students for whom English is a second language are not automatically disadvantaged by abbreviated time frames. In addition, because portfolios provide multiple opportunities for students to show what they can do in a variety of writing conditions, they provide a more comprehensive assessment of performance. In short, they offer opportunities to make the assessment of linguistic minority students more equitable. At the same time, they also offer the unique opportunities discussed in this paper, opportunities that are difficult, if not impossible, to achieve in other assessment contexts. These include opportunities to gather information about processes along with products, to encourage reflection and self-assessment, to increase our understanding of the unconscious models students bring to the task of learning to write, and to make the assessment process a learning process for our students. Potentially then, portfolios can have an enormous impact on the ways students and teachers work and learn, especially when teachers provide formative feedback and students are engaged in reflective evaluation. They offer us an opportunity to put assessment back in the hands of teachers and students to serve instruction and learning.

12

Portfolio Pedagogy: Is a Theoretical Construct Good Enough?

Sharon J. Hamilton

"You mean you *didn't* use portfolio assessment in your Advanced Expository Writing Class this semester?" The brow of our Coordinator of Campus Writing briefly furrowed before she broke into a diplomatic smile. We had worked together on the writing committee that had implemented portfolio assessment in all of our freshman and sophomore writing classes the previous semester. She had, therefore, quite reasonably anticipated that I would utilize portfolio assessment in my upper level classes also, particularly since she knew I had evaluated portfolios in Advanced Expository Writing the previous semester. Her question hung only briefly in the air, yet its import stayed with me. I realized that the factors influencing my decision against portfolio use that semester needed reevaluation and articulation in a broader forum. The 1992 Miami University Conference on Portfolio Assessment provided an ideal opportunity to share my questions and thoughts about portfolio pedagogy with colleagues outside my own institution. My assigned space in the program, last on the last day, enabled participants to enter the discussion already primed with their own questions and reactions to the wealth of perspectives they had encountered. This paper meshes their voices with mine as we explore some fundamental questions about the role of portfolios in teaching, learning, and writing.

1. *What are the theoretical constructs about writing and language learning that inform portfolio assessment?*

When I posed this question, I wanted to examine theoretical connections between kinds of written literacy that occur in classrooms, the process of

157

choosing and the kinds of choices that affect the compilation of student portfolios, and the classroom and course context within which all of this occurs.
Affirmation of these connections permeates the literature on portfolio assessment; similarly, it infused the presentations at the Miami Conference.

Possibly the primary theoretical assumption behind portfolio assessment
was explicated most comprehensively in Pat Belanoff's session, "Portfolios:
Implications for Literacy." Belanoff argued for classroom acknowledgment of
multiple literacies much as Howard Gardner argues for classroom acknowledgment of multiple intelligences in *Multiple Intelligences: The Theory in
Practice*. Belanoff went on to assert that, since student literacy varies by genre
and context, assessment should consider the complexity of genres and composing contexts that students work with and in throughout the year. Assessment of a portfolio of student work can provide an opportunity to acknowledge
these multiple literacies.

Integral to the above theoretical premise is the notion that portfolios *can*
contribute not only to the assessment of multiple literacies, but that they offer
the best means of doing so. Explicit or implicit in virtually every article and
presentation about portfolio assessment is the supposition that, since portfolios
contain texts of various genres composed over time in a wide range of contexts
for a wide range of purposes, they are more valid indicators of writing progress than other forms of assessment. Sheila Valencia has written extensively
on how portfolios are simultaneously a collection of artifacts and a "disposition toward assessment" of these artifacts (4). This disposition exemplifies
a view of assessment that is continuous, multidimensional, collaborative,
knowledge-based, and authentic. She discusses how a collection of student
texts representing a wide range of functional and contextualized literacy tasks
proves to be not only valid, but also far more beneficial to students and
teachers than any set of numbers or one-off writing test. Peter Elbow and Ed
White, in their respective keynote addresses at the conference, generally
agreed with this assumption of validity, though each, in different ways and for
different reasons, questioned whether validity is the single most crucial measure by which to judge the effectiveness of assessment.

Sarah Freedman suggests that even more significant than assumptions of
greater validity is the *capability of portfolios to provide congruence among
classroom instruction, classroom assessment, and large-scale assessment*
(23). Her discussion carries the case for validity one step further, postulating
the potential in portfolio assessment for a kind of integrity between what goes
on in classrooms and how what goes on is assessed at all levels. She discusses
several portfolio-based large-scale assessment programs already in place that
successfully integrate instruction and assessment, such as the Arts PROPEL
program in Pittsburgh—a portfolio project that combines art, music, and
creative writing; the *Primary Language Record* in the United Kingdom—
a systematic collection of examples of and reflections on language growth
of elementary-level students; and the draft of a statewide plan for portfolio

assessment in Vermont. In the climate of statewide standardized testing that currently pervades the United States, portfolio assessment may offer a more complete means of both evaluating individual student progress and monitoring schoolwide, statewide, and even nationwide progress.

A fourth assumption about language teaching and learning that underpins many articles and presentations about portfolio assessment is the belief, as Bob Ingalls and Joyce Jones point out, that writers should remain in charge of their writing (4). Portfolios empower student writers in two major ways: opportunities for revision and opportunities for reflection. Although portfolios are most often (though not always) a compilation of products, in most cases reflection and revision are integral to the process of compiling the portfolio. Miami University, the first institution of higher education in the United States to award entering students credit and advanced placement on the basis of a portfolio of high school writing, requires a reflective letter introducing the writer and the portfolio (Bertsch, Black, Daiker, Helton 7). The portfolio requirements for our writing courses at Indiana University at Indianapolis (IUPUI) focus heavily on reflection as a key part of the process of writing and of compiling a portfolio. For example, the following list includes the minimum portfolio requirements for our three freshman-level writing courses:

W001 (fundamentals of writing)

- writer's statement for the overall portfolio (a "writer's statement" is a one- to two-page reflection on the writer's intentions, strategies, hopes and fears, and text-based self-assessment)
- composition I and writer's statement
- composition II and writer's statement
- process log (reflections on each day's writing throughout the semester)

W131 (freshman composition [I])

- writer's statement for overall portfolio
- personal narrative and writer's statement
- expository essay and writer's statement
- reflections upon the process of writing and writer's statement

W132 (freshman composition [II])

- writer's statement for overall portfolio
- position paper and writer's statement
- critical analysis and writer's statement
- literature review and writer's statement
- annotated bibliography and writer's statement.

This commitment to reflective writing as an integral part of the portfolio has two interrelated benefits. First, the focus on reflection about writing forces students to distance themselves from their writing sufficiently to be able to perceive and then articulate their writerly intentions and the extent of their achievement of these intentions. This need for distance has been shown by Emily Miller and Stephen RiCharde in a study of portfolio-based classrooms presented at the 1991 CCCC to tap students' metacognitive skills as they search for, discover, and explain previously inarticulated connections between early and later drafts of the same paper and between early and later writing within the semester.

In turn, these developing metacognitive skills would seem to enable students to revise at deeper levels of textual—and contextual—meaning. At the Miami Conference, Brian Huot and Kim Lovejoy reported their findings of a study of revision practices in portfolio-based and nonportfolio-based freshman composition classes. Although their results were inconclusive for students at the upper- and lower-achievement levels of the classes, their results showed that students in the midrange of achievement made more revisions overall, and more revisions at deeper levels of textual meaning in portfolio-based classes than in non-portfolio based classes. There is need for much more research in this area; however, there seems to be a growing basis for the hypothesis that connections exist between reflecting on writing and making good decisions about revising it.

Moreover, this reflecting and revising often occur in a collaborative learning environment. Whether talking about teaching portfolios (Stock), student portfolios (Bishop, "Revising the Technical Writing Class"; Harrison, Smith and Murphy) or setting up a portfolio assessment procedure (Freedman, Cambridge, Graham) most educators stress the importance of working collaboratively with peers both to shape and to achieve shared objectives.

In summary, then, portfolio assessment is responsive to the following six theoretical constructs about language learning:

1. There is no single way to define or to assess literacy; teaching and assessment will ideally acknowledge *multiple literacies*. Since student literacy varies by genre and context, assessment should consider a wide range of student writing.

2. Since portfolios contain texts of various genres composed over time in a wide range of contexts for a wide range of purposes, they are more valid indicators of writing progress than other forms of assessment.

3. Possibly more important than assumptions of greater validity is the capability of portfolios to provide congruence among classroom instruction, classroom assessment, and large scale assessment.

4. Writers should remain in charge of their writing.

5. Reflection and revision contribute to writing improvement.
6. Reflection and revision are enhanced in a *collaborative learning environment*.

Notably absent in the literature about portfolios, however, are the darker assumptions one might make about relationships between portfolio assessment and theoretical constructs of language learning. During our Miami session, Russell Hunt countered the positive connections highlighted above with the following equally possible—and equally cogent—theoretical assumptions:

1. Since portfolios are a compilation of products that form the basis of assessment, products must be a reliable indicator of human growth and potential.
2. Writing to produce a product to be evaluated doesn't interfere with or shape the process.
3. Everything a student writes should aspire to permanence, and should be read by an authority.

"No! No!" you quite possibly want to shout, "that isn't it at all!" And you and I (and undoubtedly Russ Hunt) can marshal arguments to dispute all of the above assertions. Just for starters, written products composed over time, in a wide range of rhetorical contexts, exemplifying a wide range of genres, *might* indeed offer at least some indication of writing growth and potential, but surely the processes of selection and revision and reflection that go into the compilation of the portfolio *may* contribute, in themselves, to writing development. Second, of course, writing to produce a product will influence our writing processes, but producing written products is something writers, students, teachers, lawyers, business executives, insurance salespeople, and a host of other people do all the time. Writing to produce a product may not be the only reason to write, but it probably is the most frequent one. Moreover, portfolio assessment *may* encourage a more self-aware, self-reflective process as products, including products-in-process, are selected, rejected, revised, organized, and explicated in a writer's statement, indeed shaping the writing process. And third, the revision and selection/rejection aspect of compiling portfolios, especially when done in a collaborative environment, *might* gainsay Hunt's assertion that portfolio assessment assumes the need for permanence of all texts and for authoritative readers.

However, those qualifying "mights" and "mays" are critical. The intentional irony in Hunt's response to my opening question corresponds with my original conundrum: *portfolio assessment does not, in itself, guarantee either set of theoretical constructs, neither my potentially "benevolent" associations with process pedagogy, collaborative learning, and multiple literacies nor Hunt's potentially "malevolent" associations with unreliable products, distorted processes, and authoritative judgments*. This leads to the second question.

2. *Can these theoretical constructs operate in a classroom that does not utilize portfolios?*

If we take all references to portfolio assessment from the above summary of generally acknowledged theoretical constructs about language and learning that inform portfolio assessment, we are left with the following views of a flourishing language classroom:

1. students are engaged in multiple forms of literacy, working in a range of genres and contexts appropriate to the particular course;

2. there is valid assessment of student writing;

3. there is congruence between what is learned and what is assessed;

4. writers remain in charge of their writing;

5. writers reflect on their writing and have opportunities for revision;

6. reflection and revision occur in a collaborative learning environment.

The learning environment described above is, I suggest, the learning environment that engendered the move toward portfolio assessment, and nurtured its fast-growing popularity. Portfolio assessment does not create the learning environment described above. Participants at the Miami Conference had their own horror stories to tell of systems of portfolio assessment in which students filled a folder with finished products, checked off the accompanying checklist, and had the folder graded like any other finished product. Portfolio assessment in itself is no panacea for anything; it can enhance the learning environment in which it is used; it can maintain the learning environment in which it is used; or it can contradict the learning environment. It does not, in itself, *create* a particular learning environment.

If we answer "yes" to the question, "Can these theoretical constructs operate in a classroom that does not utilize portfolios?" (and "yes" was unanimous in the Miami session I presented), then we need to ask ourselves what *additional* benefits accrue from portfolio assessment. That leads to the next question I raised in the session.

3. *What role does the physical compilation of papers into a packet play in and beyond the classroom?*

Responses to this question range from short-view maintenance of standard assessment procedures to far-ranging visions of reshaping American education.

On the purely pragmatic level, portfolios can confirm graduation status (Brand) and can gain their authors college credit and advanced placement (Bertsch, Black, Daiker, Helton 7). Caroline Stern, in a presentation at the

1991 CCCC, focused on the value of portfolios for keeping track of and revealing the number of all of the drafts students wrote and for indicating patterns of errors and improvement in correcting these errors throughout the year. Leslie Ballard points to the portfolio as an effective inhibitor of plagiarism (46).

Russell Hunt offers the double-edged suggestion that assembling papers into a portfolio plays "very much the same sort of role that assembling paragraphs into a term paper does." My initial interpretation read into that statement "a superficial organization of arguably arbitrary constructs." However, as I pondered Hunt's assertion, I discovered links between it and the assertions of several other educators connecting the organizing of portfolios with developing self-monitoring abilities and metacognitive skills (Miller and Richard), a heightened awareness of accepted standards of a particular discourse community (Graham), and Belanoff's statement that the compiling of a portfolio in itself provides a context for its contents (as—although probably somewhat more than—the organizing of paragraphs into a coherent term paper may provide a context for its contents).

Broadening the scope of potential benefits of compiling a portfolio, Tom Romano, at the 1991 NCTE Spring Conference, portrayed it as an iconic representation of the creative process. At the very least, says Valencia, it is a collection of functional and contextualized literacy acts (6), which, according to Pat Stock, "captures the complexity of written literacy events." Stephen Tchudi writes of how portfolios can lead to social action (112), and Edward White, in his keynote address at the Miami Conference, expressed at least one form of this potential for social action more specifically. He spoke of the power of portfolio assessment to "reshape institutional goals," and of its potential to "change the world of assessment," thereby conceivably "influencing the direction of American education."

These are powerful claims for the compilation of student writing into a packet of prose (or prose and poetry, as the case may be). So, why might anyone hesitate to dive into the current of unquestioning acceptance? That takes us to the next question.

4.What are some potential liabilities in the required compilation of papers into a packet that we label a "portfolio"?

Concern about whose agenda the portfolios were fulfilling dominated the dialogue at the Miami session. I referred earlier to widespread anecdotal "horror stories" of teachers who made a checklist of exactly what was supposed to be in the portfolio, accompanied by a warning sheet of errors that would not be tolerated. A second concern that prevailed in the discussion was apprehension of the belief that portfolio assessment could, in itself, solve problems of assessment while creating an optimal learning environment for writing. As Sarah Freedman writes, just collecting and evaluating portfolios will solve neither the assessment problems nor the need to create a professional climate in schools (17). Freedman goes on to say that only by coupling instruction and assessment in increasingly sophisticated ways will educators using portfolio assessment make a real difference in education (21).

Carol Delco, a participant in the session, mentioned another concern: that portfolios "create an illusion that we understand the creative process because we have collected a series of stages in producing a product." As Terry Eagleton points out, we have no way of knowing the intricate paths and byways through which the mind traversed in its journey toward what is etched on paper (170). Even successive drafts, especially when composed on a word processor, obscure many of the changes of direction that occurred in their composing. Tom Romano's "icon of the creative process" may well be missing a number of critical parts.

Russell Hunt's concern focused on the external imposition of genre and of discourse conformity that may (and often does) occur when the emphasis in compiling a portfolio is on assessment of that portfolio. It was this connecting of the concept of "portfolio" with the concept of "assessment" that had incited my defection from the departmental party line in the first place. Whereas I applaud the theoretical constructs of the rich learning environment that has spurred on the popularity of portfolios, I resist the emphasis on their prime value as a means of assessment. While heartily acknowledging the tremendous benefits of portfolio assessment over other means of assessment for monitoring writing development on a large scale or for university placement, I see the prime value in portfolios at the classroom level related to the processes of their composing and compilation, their celebration of writing achievements, and their potential to show the evolution of a writer's voice in a wide range of rhetorical contexts over a long period of time. Assessment of these classroom literacy events should ideally serve as just one part of the process of an evolving portfolio of student work over a period of years, rather than as the prime reason for using portfolios. That realization led me to the next question I raised during the session.

5. How might we retain the benefits of portfolio assessment while freeing the portfolio itself from assessment?

I offer the following as just one model among many possible alternatives and variations. I envision my writing classroom as a workshop wherein student writers explore the edges of their perceived writing abilities in particular discourse communities, and, by working collaboratively, discover ways to push themselves beyond these perceived boundaries. The sole purpose of portfolios in my class is for students to develop an organizational system to keep account of these explorations and discoveries. That system may take any form that students find appropriate and convenient, since their portfolios are for their benefit and purposes, not mine.

I urge my students to keep all of their heuristic work and successive drafts, not so I can check their work and note the evolution of their thinking and their articulation of that thinking, but so my students can trace for themselves the evolution of their articulated ideas. Each paper that they hand in as a "tentatively possibly final draft" (bearing in mind Robert Scholes' pithy reminder during the 1990 CCCC that "there are really no final drafts, just deadlines") is, in itself, a mini-portfolio, containing catalytic ideas and heuristics (both organizational and conceptual), successive drafts (each of which the other members of their collaborative group and I will already have read and responded to), and a letter of transmittal (which often is more demonstrably indicative of writing improvement—or at least of writing awareness—than the most recent draft of the composition). This letter of transmittal tells of surprises, problems, and insights that occurred in the process of writing the paper, tells if and how intentions changed, points out the parts that students feel best about and why, and the parts they feel unsure about and why, and tells me specifically what they hope I will notice and comment on as I read their papers. I keep these letters of transmittal, but return all the rest, with a one-to-two-page letter of response shaped by a combination of their concerns and mine. I respond to all papers as though they are still in progress, asking questions that may guide or spur possible revisions, while commenting on growing strengths and continuing challenges. Students then write me a letter of response to my letter, telling me what parts of my response were helpful, what parts were confusing, what they wish I might have said but didn't, and whether and how they intend to resolve any of the problems they or I pointed out. These letters of response I file, together with their letters of transmittal and computer copies of my letters of response to them. Students may continue to revise any or all of their papers throughout the semester, and their final paper may, if they choose, be a revision of an earlier paper.

By the end of the semester, after a continual written and spoken dialogue about their writing, the students have a collection of all of their semester's work and five full letters of response from me. I have a collection of five letters of transmittal, copies of my five letters to my students, and five letters of their responses to my letters—a total of fifteen documents reflecting on the writing progress of each student. In their writing groups, they review their collections of evidence while I review mine, and then they write me one final letter of transmittal overviewing their semester's progress. With that letter, they may hand in any supporting evidence they choose: their whole collection (portfolio) of their semester's work; highlights of the semester's work; newly revised work; or just the letter all by itself. The only requirements are that, if the letter is to stand alone, it must fully specify to what parts of the student's writing its major points are referring; if new (previously unseen) revisions are handed in, the letter must guide me through these revisions; and if the whole corpus is handed in, the letter must cross-reference the collection the points the student is making. I write them one last letter of response, describing my assessment of their semester's progress in relation to their overview, any supporting documentation they hand in, and my collected documents.

This model of portfolio assessment-without-portfolios fulfills all of the theoretical constructs of the language learning environment described earlier in the paper, yet militates against many of the possible liabilities mentioned in response to the fourth question. In the first place, although the agenda of the Advanced Expository Writing course is to some extent established before students enter the classroom, each student has plenty of room to establish his or her own agenda under the customary umbrella of the course. There is no checklist of portfolio requirements; students have complete choice over their final bundle of submissions, ranging from just one final letter of transmittal to a complete collection of their semester's work, and that work may range from having no revisions after I have responded to their "tentatively possibly final drafts" to their having revised every one of them.

Second, there is no confusion about whether the portfolio creates the classroom learning environment or whether the classroom learning environment encourages the compilation of portfolios. The portfolios are created by the students as they deem appropriate within the literacy events and context of the classroom and course. They are designed, maintained, and retained by the students throughout the semester, and might never be handed in completely at any one time. Even so, the model sets up a tight congruence between instruction and assessment by having continual written and oral conversations about coursework between student and teacher (as well as within the student-established writing group).

My purpose for developing the portfolio-without-assessment model was to encourage students to design and maintain portfolios for their own purposes and benefit rather than to meet external assessment demands imposed either by me or by my institution. Nonetheless, by developing their own portfolios, students are collecting materials that could be put to departmental service in the portfolios required for their senior seminar, or that could be put to service when they apply to graduate school, professional school, or for a particular job. My intention is to separate the compilation of a portfolio from assessment, in order to emphasize to students that assessment is merely one of several steps in the evolution of a lifetime portfolio of their writing rather than the entire or even prime reason for putting their writing into a portfolio. By not collecting my students' portfolios for assessment, I want to see whether the theoretical constructs that inform portfolio assessment can shape an effective and supportive writing environment without actually assessing portfolios. This brings the discussion full circle to the eponymic question that formed the title of my presentation at the Miami conference.

6. *Is A Theoretical Construct Good Enough?*

A comment by Ira Shor at the Canadian Council of Teachers of English Conference in Montreal in 1991 seems appropriate and applicable at this point:

> Education is not something done to you for your own good; education is something students do for themselves in the company of others.

Portfolio assessment strikes me as something done to or imposed upon students for their own good. Portfolios designed, maintained, and used by students according to their short-term needs and long-term intentions seem much more important at the classroom level than portfolios unilaterally prescribed and assessed.

At the same time, I realize that the option I describe in my portfolios-without-assessment model would not have been nearly so viable or credible a decade ago. Because all of our students begin a portfolio in their freshman writing courses, and refine their portfolios in their senior seminar—the capstone course of their English major—they are already in an academic context that values portfolios, they have been primed to appreciate the value of portfolios, and they are already familiar with procedures of how to go about compiling a portfolio. It is the widespread acceptance of portfolio assessment within my department that enables my resistance to combining portfolios with assessment. What a delightful irony that the increasing prevalence of portfolio assessment may eventually enable us to shift the focus away from assessment as the primary raison d'être for portfolios and toward the rich language learning environment that enables portfolios to flourish.

To conclude, I'd like to rephrase that final question. Considering that the theoretical constructs that inform portfolio assessment can thrive at the classroom level without the actual compiling of portfolios, are portfolios really necessary? Yes, because portfolios go far beyond the classroom. They can represent a lifetime of personal writing development; they can represent writing development in the public schools to the business community, the legislature, and the community at large; they can indicate writing development statewide and nationwide. Yes, because, to slightly change Edward White's proclamation that "portfolio assessment may influence the direction of American education," portfolios have the potential to reshape the direction of education in America.

13

Beyond Portfolios: Scenes for Dialogic Reading and Writing

James A. Reither
Russell A. Hunt

We're going to tell three stories here. We'll begin with two that are fairly brief. The first is about a time we used something that could have been called portfolios to assess our students' performance in a writing program. The second tells how—and a good deal more about why—we stopped using them. We'll conclude with a third story in two voices that tells about practices that developed out of, and are built on, our experiences with portfolios, but that we think go beyond them to solve some of the problems we see with portfolios and with the kinds of scenes for writing that the portfolio method assumes and fosters.

St. Thomas University, where we teach, is a four-year liberal arts college with an enrollment of around fifteen-hundred full-time students. It is in the capital of New Brunswick, a small and not very prosperous Canadian province. Although St. Thomas' faculty comes from all over the world, our students are drawn overwhelmingly from within the province, and their backgrounds tend to be fairly provincial. During the late 1970s and early 1980s, St. Thomas offered its first-year students a many-sectioned, year-long, required writing course, which was taught by faculty volunteers drawn from departments across the disciplines. The key requirement for the faculty who taught the course was that they be active but not necessarily publishing writers, not that they know how to teach writing. From 1978 through 1985, a central feature of that program was that every student in every section wrote at least two (in some years, three) lengthy, research-based essays. The students chose their own subjects. Instruction focused on both process and outcome. The students did some preliminary research, wrote a proposal, and then took their essays through several drafts. As each student wrote and revised, the teacher of her section worked with her, one on one, in the role of coach. To a limited extent, her fellow students worked with her in workshops as collaborators.

These essays, in other words, were not simply written, commented on, and graded. (That, of course, was pretty much the default model of writing instruction at about that time.) Instead, in the context of ongoing feedback from teacher and fellow students, the student wrote, rewrote, and revised until she, her teacher, and her fellow students had negotiated some kind of stopping point: everyone was satisfied that the essay was finished, or the author decided she had done all she could at the time and would come back to finish it off later on.

Furthermore, none of these essays was graded by the student's own teacher. Instead, at the end of the year-long course, each student's essays were assigned ID numbers that hid the author's identity, gathered into a folder, and distributed to the writing program faculty for assessment and grading.

Before the folders were distributed for assessment, the writing faculty participated in training sessions where they learned to assess, rank, and grade anonymous essays holistically. When the folders were distributed, they were shuffled so that faculty received folders from several—perhaps all—of the sections of the course except their own. Each teacher then read and graded each essay. That done, the folders were collected and redistributed, so that every essay in every folder was read and graded by at least two members of the writing program faculty. Essays whose two marks varied by more than a full grade were then read by at least one other faculty member to see if a closer match could be achieved. The grades on the papers in a portfolio were then averaged and the resulting portfolio grade became the student's course grade.

One of our aims in this system of blind, holistic portfolio assessment was, of course, to achieve "reliable" evaluation and consistent grades. In many ways, this was the public rationale for instituting and maintaining this complex process. But what was more important to those of us concerned with the design of the program was that we wanted to change the relationship between writer and reader and writer and teacher. We were trying to structure a writing situation embodying motives for writing that would be different from those in the traditional composition course. Although the students were still writing at a teacher's bidding, their teacher was no longer also their evaluator; they were writing with that teacher's help, but that teacher was not their audience. That audience included not only fellow student-workshoppers, whose expectations they might expect to know; it also included those other teachers-evaluators, whose expectations would be more difficult for them to know. Because we wanted to diminish the value of the strategy of figuring out "what the teacher wants," we were trying to introduce greater distance between writer and assessor. Our thinking was that, if the students were not able to focus their attention on an individual teacher's particular standards and expectations, they would likely shift their focus to the task of writing for a more general audience the most informative and persuasive paper they could write.

We had begun to be painfully aware, moreover, that there were profound differences between the sort of writing activity that seemed to go on when writers were writing "for" someone—especially when that someone was an evaluator of the writing—and the kind that appeared to be happening when the writer was writing "to" someone to explain, inform, move, or persuade. We were beginning to see that when the audience for a text was the teacher, and when the teacher was not only coach and editor but also evaluator and audience, the situation became very peculiar indeed, and so did the pressures on the writer. We wanted to make writing more "real-world" for our students—more like the writing Lee Odell and Dixie Goswami and others were beginning to show us that writers (as opposed to students) do.

Those faculty who finally received the portfolio essays, we naively thought, could act more like real readers than the teacher in the one-on-one, coach-advisor relation to the student. Equally important, we thought that introducing these "real readers" into the situation would help the teacher-coach and student collaborate in figuring out what an audience was likely to know and believe. In this situation, we hoped, the teacher could help the writer learn to use the pressure of audience as a tool for shaping her language "at the point of utterance" (Britton). This pressure would help the writer decide what to foreground and what to background, what to assume and what to state, what to argue for and what to assume as common ground, what to say now and what to put off until later. We thought we could create, that is, the sort of authentic situation Hunt claims supports language-learning ("A Horse Named Hans").

Like many stories of exploration in the teaching of writing, this one sounds as though it has a happy ending, but it turns out that things aren't quite that simple. There's often a second story that has already begun as the cowboys mosey off into the sunset.

During 1985-86, the last year of the writing program, we dropped the whole complex structure of portfolio evaluation, and we reorganized. The faculty teaching the course each chose a subject or theme that the students would study and write about over the year. One instructor, an anthropologist, chose "writing"; another, from the English Department, chose "literacy"; and another, also from English, had his students undertake "an ethnographic study of the rhetoric of teaching." Here the aim of each section was that the students would produce a great deal of writing, most of it in the form of brief reports of research findings, but some of it in the forms of research proposals and feasibility studies. The ultimate aim was for each student to write a single scholarly article that would be "published" in a book of such articles written by the students in the course. Along the way, all of their writing was to be "public"—that is, photocopied, read, and commented on, in workshop, by what Ken Bruffee had called the students' "knowledgeable peers" in the course. None of this writing was to be graded, however. Its function was not to provide material for assessment, but to take the students through (and thus educate them about) a collaborative scholarly process in which writing informed, persuaded, and was used by others in their own writing. As it turned out, instead of each student producing a portfolio of her writings, each course produced a portfolio of its students' writing. As Reither pointed out a few years later, we were putting students into a situation parallel to that of any scholar (cf. "The Writing *Student* as Researcher").

There were a number of reasons for reorganizing in this way. One was that we had become deeply frustrated with the workshopping part of the course. Although we believed in its potential value and wanted to retain the feature in a revision of the course, workshopping—as we had implemented it, at any rate—had not worked for the students or for us. Because the students chose their own subjects, and all wrote on different things, they never became sufficiently engaged in the subjects others were writing about to offer suggestions on anything other than mechanics, syntax, and, occasionally, lines of argument. When it came to the more important question of whether or not the piece would inform or persuade, the students were stymied—everything sounded good to them. And, truth to tell, the faculty were as limited as the students in this respect. Further, the tendency born of this limitation—for the students to see themselves as apprentice English teachers rather than as real audiences—pushed them into a mode of response that often tended to be (at best) condescendingly helpful and (at worst) censorious in the ways described a couple of years earlier by Nancy Sommers in her now-classic article on responding to student writing.

We had other, more theoretical reasons for the specific decision to abandon individual student portfolios. One was that they had failed to solve one of the most important problems we faced—that our writing instruction, like most, created a situation in which the stand-alone written product became the center of everyone's concern. Although the teachers in this writing program had done everything they could to focus the students' attention on the process, in the end what mattered to both students and teachers were the products. Since those products were not, after all, especially interesting to anyone, what *really* mattered was the grade the products in the portfolio received. Here is one stomach-knotting indication that what really mattered was the grade: all who taught the course over the years accumulated huge stacks of students' writing folders. Their authors rarely bothered to collect what they had worked so hard to write. They had their grades, and that, apparently, was what mattered. We now see, with the usual clarity of hindsight, that the problem was that the language in these portfolios had no intrinsic or authentic social function.

A second reason we discontinued using portfolios was that we came to believe that the portfolios only narrowly and peripherally served the students' short- and long-term needs. That is, while they may have served the students' needs to "do well" in their writing so that they could "get a good grade" in the course, in our experience they did not serve the students' rhetorical needs; they did not serve the human need to engage in discourse that is taken seriously by others for what it says and does in communicative, dialogic contexts. In the end, the primary—indeed, all too often, the only and real—function of the students' portfolios was to provide teachers with materials for assessing mastery of content, genre, and "writing abilities." Though portfolios gave teachers more, and more useful, data for assessment, they did not give students opportunities to effect change through writing. For most of the writers and most of the readers, that is, the language in the texts remained object, not gesture; artifact, not utterance; monologue, not dialogue.

A third reason we stopped using portfolios was that the need to assess and grade the products put the assessors in an untenable rhetorical position. In practice, our task was to rank, evaluate, and grade the portfolios. That assignment made it extremely difficult, if not impossible, to give those texts the sort of authentic assessment routinely given to texts encountered in out-of-school situations. The need to arrive at a grade abetted premature closure, limited tolerance for (possibly deliberate) irrelevance, lowered confidence in the voice of the writer, promoted short-term processing, and in general rendered sympathetic, engaged reading—if it could be achieved at all—a matter of continual conscious effort. From a reader's point of view, the language of these essays could not in that situation attain the status of gesture or utterance or dialogue. We took small comfort in realizing that such is the position of all writing teachers engaged in formal assessment and grading, since that was precisely the situation we had been attempting to change.

The upshot is that, while we would not claim that the portfolio-assessment system we used in those years was anything but primitive—even crude—by today's standards, we would nevertheless suggest that, like all approaches that focus squarely on writing *qua* writing, assessment-by-portfolios still assumes a view of language and writing that is necessarily incomplete and inaccurate. The approach extracts writing from communicative, dialogic situations as if all that's involved in writing were the ability to turn out well-organized, clear, and coherent sentences, paragraphs, and essays—and as if qualities like organization, clarity, and coherence were not functions of social situations. The social motives for and functions of writing get lost from view, not only for faculty charged with determining ranks and grades, but also for students charged with completing assignments to fill a portfolio with writing.

It was at about this point in the story that the gods descended in a machine and the writing program ceased to exist as a formal entity, leaving some of the teachers who had been involved to continue exploring these issues in a less formal way. By this time, none of us regretted that we could no longer marshal the forces necessary to conduct even an informal portfolio evaluation structure. We had learned that someone else reading a portfolio wasn't all that different from ourselves reading a term paper: the problem of the role of formal evaluation in the process hadn't been solved, or even much changed, by moving to portfolios and externalizing the evaluation. Thus, it does not really surprise us to read the conclusion of a recent press release on the electronic "Education Research List" announcing a new "pilot study that examines the viability of using writing portfolios as part of a large scale National Assessment of Educational Progress (NAEP) assessment." The conclusion? The U.S. Department of Education says that "even when students were allowed to polish their writing, the pieces were generally not well-developed and did not communicate effectively. The students, for the most part, did not plan, think about, or revise their writing even when they had the opportunity."

Having said all this, however, we would like to make clear that nothing we have said denies the very real opportunities for teaching that can occur in portfolio-driven writing scenes. What we mean to suggest is that, for portfolios to work, everything depends upon having students who ardently and authentically wish to engage with the world through their writing, and who are already capable of effecting improvements through "dummy runs" in which communicative, dialogic reality is set aside, bracketed. For those many students who are not driven by such intentions and motives, there is little that portfolio methodology can do to transform the admonition to be better writers into an effective motive. It cannot help them shape their language at the point of utterance and create the imagined readers they need.

Our third story describes some consequences of our attempt to construct new practices, which build on our experiences and help us move toward situations which better support learning to use writing to get things done. Before we proceed to that story, however, it is appropriate to outline some of the theoretical framework that has come to inform our position. This framework relies heavily on ideas drawn from Kenneth Burke and Mikhail Bakhtin.

In outlining this theory, we do not mean to suggest that there is a one-directional relationship between it and our practice. The theoretical framework is part of the story we're telling: it was in large measure our evolving practice that prepared us to see in these writers (and others) the kinds of ideas that had the power to inform and alter our practice. This dialectical relationship between what we *do* and what we *perceive* and *believe* is itself an important reason for our having adopted the practices we currently employ. If it works for us, the teachers, we suspect it might work for them, the students.

Kenneth Burke tells us in *The Philosophy of Literary Form* that "critical and imaginative works are answers to questions posed by the situations in which they arose. They are not merely answers, they are *strategic* answers, *stylized* answers" (1). For him, "every document bequeathed us by history must be treated as a *strategy for encompassing a situation* . . . as the *answer* or *rejoinder* to assertions current in the situation in which it arose" (109). These claims arise out of his notion of the "scene-act ratio," as outlined in the opening pages of his *A Grammar of Motives*. Burke's notion of the scene-act ratio has given us an important source of explanatory power, helping us understand what we were doing, what we thought we ought to be doing, and how we might go about doing it. In simple terms, Burke's scene-act ratio posits simply that a given scene ("setting," "background," "terrain," "situation") calls for, affords, and enables certain kinds of symbolic acts, and discourages, blocks, and prevents others. The scene, he says, "is a fit 'container' for the act" (3). It does not, of course, alone *determine* the symbolic acts that can or will occur in it, because agents, agencies, and purposes (the other terms in Burke's Pentad) are also determinants. However, "from the motivational point of view, there is implicit in the quality of a scene the quality of the action that is to take place within it. This would be another way of saying that the act will be consistent with the scene" (6-7). The scene thus "contains" a likelihood, a potential that certain kinds of symbolic acts will occur in it: certain symbolic acts are likely, appropriate, or proper, while other symbolic acts are unlikely, inappropriate, or even disallowed.

Burke's scene-act ratio helped us understand something about our own scenes for written acts. An academic journal, such as the *Journal of Advanced Composition* or *Rhetoric Review,* calls for, affords, and enables certain symbolic acts: statements of editorial policy, scholarly articles, publishers' advertisements, notices of special issues, calls for submissions from other journals in the field, letters responding to articles in previous issues, notices of upcoming meetings and conferences—those sorts of things. Because academic journals provide scenes in which the members of a field of practice carry on the academic enterprise, neither the *Journal of Advanced Composition* nor *Rhetoric Review* is likely to include in its pages advice to the lovelorn, barbecue recipes, romantic fiction, furniture or automobile advertisements, how-to electronics articles. (One of our favorite journals, *PRE/TEXT,* might, but not the *Journal of Advanced Composition* or *Rhetoric Review.*) The scene which is an academic journal in the field of composition studies is a "fit 'container' " for academic, scholarly symbolic acts. It is not "fit" for a wide range of other kinds of symbolic acts.

Not at all incidentally, this understanding offered us the materials for a critique of what we were doing and of portfolio assessment more generally. It would run something like this: a central problem with portfolios is that, because they occur in and help create scenes that focus students' attention upon the production of stand-alone written texts for assessment and evaluation, they work against students learning more than superficial lessons about writing for other purposes. Portfolios constitute scenes that do not obviously "contain" the ways in which a text's meanings evolve out of relationships with other texts. Portfolio-driven scenes thus deflect students' attention from such fundamental issues as a writer's motives for writing, where texts come from, who writes them, who reads them, and why. In sum, portfolio-driven scenes obviate serious examination of what it means to be a writer or a reader; they render invisible (if they do not actually eliminate) the communal and consensual interaction among writer, world, text, and reader that is involved in authorship.

Our reading of Burke in the context of our writing program's problems afforded a way to think about them that suggested that what we needed was a different scene in which writing could occur, one that would not only be different, but be seen to be different by the writers. Reading Bakhtin in that context gave us a way to think about how that scene might work.

The work of Bakhtin (or of the Bakhtin circle) in which we're interested is not that which deals mainly with theories of literature, with studies of the novel, and of Dostoevsky. The work we found particularly engaging concerns the ways in which language and languaging are social and is found in *Marxism and the Philosophy of Language* and (especially) in the essays collected in *Speech Genres and Other Late Essays*. This is where we found the claim that the *utterance*, not the phoneme, the word, the sentence or the text, should be taken as the basic unit of analysis for understanding language. It is work that made clear to us that no categorical differentiation between written and oral language needs to be made. Bakhtin begins with speech rather than writing, with *parole* rather than *langue*, with the contingent and context-bound rather than the clear and stable. He makes spoken, conversational language the norm in terms of which other kinds of language can be understood (it is almost as an aside, as though it were so obvious it hardly needed to be said, that he notes that "everything we have said here also pertains to written and read speech, with the appropriate adjustments and additions" [*Speech Genres* 69]).

This is where we hear that the utterance is invariably created, formed, and shaped *as a response* to a previous utterance or utterances, and that it is always created and formed and shaped *in anticipation of a responding utterance*. It is from this work that we learn that no piece of language is ever final, finished, polished and perfect; Bakhtin insists that all language is occasional, provisional, incomplete, open. Language, he tells us, is an unending dialogic web of cross-connected utterances and responses, each piece of writing or speaking, each utterance, depending on its occasion and context for its very existence, for its comprehensibility. The meaning of an utterance, he insists, is connected not to diction and syntax but to dialogue, occasion, intention or social relationships and processes. The same string of signifiers, he reminds us, can mean absolutely different things when uttered in different situations. Our speech, he is often quoted as saying, is filled to overflowing with the words of others—and the phrases and sentences and discourses and texts of others, as well.

As we came to read him in the context of our evolving practice in classrooms, Bakhtin's view implied, for us at least, a dramatic change in the way we thought about the status of texts. In large part because of this reading, we take with increasing seriousness the idea that language is inherently dialogic and inextricable from its contexts of use; we have moved toward understanding it as what Bakhtin calls "continuing speech activity between real individuals who are in some continuing social relationship" (quoted in Bialostosky 220). As one of us has said elsewhere, it seems "more and more clear that talking about the properties of texts is like talking about the properties of reflections on water—they clearly do have properties, but we are forced to be more and more circumspect about what we call properties and what we must acknowledge to be products of the viewer's angle of sight, the objects reflected, and the wind on the water" (Hunt, "Speech Genres").

Instances of language, then, cannot be understood in the abstract or out of their contexts of use. Even more important, Bakhtin's work implies that the sentence (or phrase, or word, or text) becomes, when moved from one context of use to another, a different utterance, and thus observations about it cannot be transferred back to the original context. We are never not engaged with an instance of language; we can never be only observers of it. Our readings of Burke and Bakhtin enabled us to understand that our goals as teachers ought to organize course and classroom scenes that would be "fit containers" for language that was truly communicative and dialogic—scenes that abetted students in their efforts to understand the full dimensions and complexities of literate discourse.

A key tool in our kit-bag for setting such scenes is a written course description we give our students at the beginning of each course we teach. These course descriptions all have three main objectives: to provide an overview that tells the students what they will be studying in the course; to describe the method we call "collaborative investigation" by which the students will undertake their study; and to describe our evaluative practices —what gets evaluated and how it is evaluated. All three objectives tie in with this overall teaching objective: to provide a scene for dialogic action by engaging all the students in the same project—the same collaborative scholarly investigation—that calls upon them to learn by pooling information and ideas. Here, in Russ Hunt's voice, is a brief narrative telling what has happened during the first couple of weeks or so of this year's introductory literature class.

English 1-200, Introduction to Literature

To create in an introductory literature class a scene in which authentic dialogue is the central issue for everyone involved, each year I write a lengthy, thoughtful, and complicated course description, which attempts to make everything we're going to be doing as explicit as I can make it. During the first class session I introduce myself and explain that my intention is to make writing and reading do as much of the work of the course as I can, and that wherever possible I'll substitute them for oral language. I then hand each student a copy of the document and also another, one-page document titled "In Class Today," that simply asked the students to read the longer document carefully, mark confusing, interesting, questionable, or threatening passages, and then to take a sheet of paper and write for ten minutes, saying whatever seemed important to say about the course introduction. It also made clear to the students that what they wrote would be read by others in the class.

When everyone had time to read the document and about ten minutes to write, I formed them into groups of five or so and asked them to read each others' work, reminding them that it's to be expected that most of what was written wouldn't be of great interest, and their aim should be to find what was and ignore the rest.

Finally, after everyone had read each document, each group discussed them and decided on two or three marked passages that they thought needed to be brought to everyone's attention. A member of the group other than the author was designated to read the passage or summarize it. We went around the class from group to group and each raised a concern or an issue for discussion by the whole group and response by me or another class member. Among the issues marked by more than two readers this term were the following:

- If this is what the year is going to be like, how can a person learn about literature without a textbook or lectures?

- . . . but if no one is marking or correcting my papers how may I know my mistakes? If all we are doing is writing to discuss topics how can our writing styles improve?

- To think that there will be no grammar lectures is great.

- This course seems very straightforward. Is it as useful as a more "old fashioned" English course, i.e., grammar, essays, etc.?

- I'm here to work. This course seems to fit right in with that plan. I don't know if I need it or not, but I want it.

The scene in which this writing and reading activity occurs affords, in my view, a rather different relationship to written texts than the usual class situation. Here, the texts are embedded into dialogic transactions: responses are invited to the writer's textual intentions rather than to the status or quality of the text. My original texts are either understood or not, and people deal with them not by evaluating their quality as texts or trying to help make them better, but by engaging with them dialogically. They understand or they don't; they decide to do what they suggest or else to argue that other things should be done. Similarly with the students' own texts: they express puzzlement, or confusion, or a desire for information, or hostility, and the response they get is clarification, support, commiseration, etc. When we're done with the texts they are either discarded or serve further functions; they're not revised, improved, and ultimately evaluated. They function, that is, as tools for learning.

This year, the first assignment in that class (after everyone had a chance to make sure she understood the course and how it would work, and to switch to another section if that's what she wanted) was to go out and find a text that she recommended that everyone read. The student then wrote a recommendation of it for class reading and decision, and brought a copy of the text to class. (Again, the assignment was explained in writing.)

During the next class session, I formed random groups and asked each group to give all its recommendations to another group, who read them and asked questions that they thought would help them make a choice of what to read. The questions were to be in writing, attached to the recommendations. The original recommenders then answered—again in writing—as many of the questions as they could in a few minutes, and gave the answers back to the questioners, who made their choice, obtained the original of the text from the owner and made arrangements to make copies and read it.

Again, one of the central aims of this activity was to create a different scene for writing and reading, one in which the intentional substance of the text was the focus of attention, rather than its quality; where the text was used as the medium for dialogue rather than the object of study itself. If your recommendation was persuasive, its readers were persuaded; that was your evidence of its success.

In one case, for example, Ulrike (all the names have been changed) recommended a story called "Chicken," which she described as dealing with "a stolen chicken brought home for food and feathers" which, after its head is cut off, "jumps up as if it still has a head and mind of its own." The group asked her why she decided to read it, and she conceded that "actually I was kind of appalled by the story. I felt that it could be a story that would raise quite a bit of discussion." The group ultimately decided to read the story because, as they said, "we are curious about what makes this short story different."

In the event, after reading the story and writing individual responses that they shared in the next class, the group was deeply divided about the story. The division is reflected in their responses:

Emily: "Reading about a chicken running about without its head was awful."

Tracy: "It is a story that gets its message across clearly . . . No one actually wanted to kill the chicken, in fact you could say they were 'chicken' to kill it, but everyone in the story knew it had to be done. I believe it will bring to the class the true knowledge of where some of our food actually comes from, a knowledge that we distance ourselves from when we drive through our local McDonalds."

Kelly: "When I first read the recommendation for the story Chicken I decided I didn't want to read it. When our group received the responses back, I liked the answer and I was curious about what kind of story this was. . . ."

It has a meaning, although you may not see it at first. This story gets you thinking about how people like to get things easy."

Trevor: "This story is dull and boring. The idea of people killing chickens and somebody making a story up about the event is hard to understand. . . . I cannot imagine wishing this piece of literature on some innocent by-stander."

The consensus document the group arrived at in turn reflected their division:

> As a group we had different opinions. In some ways we thought the short story was awful, but then again it has a lot of meaning. For instance, one thought it would bring the class to the true meaning of where our food comes from. Another person thought it was awful that an innocent bystander would have to read such a story. It was difficult to read a story about a chicken with its head cut off running around. We all hoped that the chicken would get away, and live forever, instead of ending up on our dinner tables.

Ultimately, on reading the document, the class decided not to read "Chicken." But the fact that reading the document had actual consequences changed how it was written and read in ways that Burke and Bakhtin help us to understand. This is a scene that affords dialogue. The class would continue to use writing and reading—the students', mine, that of professionals—in ways similar to this throughout the rest of the course.

But this narrative addresses only one of the issues lying behind the question of portfolio evaluation. It may deal with the problem implicit in a scene where portfolio-writing is a central purpose, but it does not address the more critical problem: what gets evaluated, if not product? And if language is agreed to be, as Bakhtin insisted it was, provisional, temporary, and incomplete—incomprehensible out of its dialogic ecology—how do we decide when to extract a core sample for evaluation, or when to take our photograph to freeze the process for analysis?

Burke tells us that for most of our students, especially the ones who need our help the most, evaluation creates a scene that makes evaluation itself the central purpose for the product in the first place. This means that we need another strategy altogether.

We think we have one. Although each of us manages the details of evaluation in ways that are slightly different in detail, we all follow a basic pattern that dispenses with lectures, teacher-guided discussions, textbook readings, assigned term papers, and exams. Although our students write in and for almost every class, this writing takes the forms of proposals, recommendations, progress reports, informal feasibility studies, reports of findings, inkshedding, and the like. Although the goal of writing a course book (our version of a kind of course portfolio) is always in mind, much—perhaps most—of this writing is meant to be used in the investigation and then set aside as the investigation goes on. Some of it will be revised and used in the course book, and much will be thrown away, but all of it—even the course book—is for the students' use; and the teacher, who often does not even see it, neither comments on it nor grades it.

In our courses, then, evaluation takes a radically different form than in the traditional university writing or "content" course. The following tells how evaluation was handled in one of Jim Reither's recent courses.

$$*\qquad\qquad*\qquad\qquad*$$

English 2-394, Selected Themes: Writing and Reading about Literature, was a one-semester course offered primarily to second-and third-year students. In the written description I gave my students at the beginning of the course, I told them that

> I hope it's obvious [from what's come earlier in the description] that this course will challenge students to develop and extend their abilities to communicate with others in persuasive ways, to listen to others and encourage them to speak and write, and to help others teach and learn—in short, to cooperate and collaborate. The course will not put the usual premium on competition—on "doing better" than or "beating" others. . . . Since there are no tests, exams, or term papers in the course, and you will often be working with others when I'm not present, we need alternative ways to evaluate student achievement. I will devise an evaluation form which asks questions about participation (e.g., whether or not a student shows up for meetings with assigned work done; takes part in the work of the group; listens to others; offers information and suggestions; . . . and about leadership (e.g., understands what we are studying; helps set an agenda for the group; . .). This form will also ask about students' goals and their perceptions of one another (How do you want others to see you? How do you think others actually see you? How do you see others?)

I went on to explain that full participation in the course—coming to class, doing the assignments—would guarantee a grade in the C range, but that a grade of B or A would require both full participation and clear evidence of leadership. Participation would be measured quantitatively: I would record attendance and give students credit for every activity or assignment they took part in. Leadership would be measured qualitatively, by the students, since only they could know what they have learned from one another. To get access to what they know about one another, twice in the course I asked students to fill out a version of the questionnaire mentioned above. This year, in an effort to tell my students very specifically what participation and leadership mean in my courses, I devised a questionnaire that began with self-evaluation by asking the students to tell how they hoped others would see them and how they think others might actually see them. The questionnaire then listed every student in the course and asked the student filling out the questionnaire to

Figure 13–1

[Name of student] _____

	Yes	Sometimes	No	Don't Know
Participation				
Comes to meetings with assigned/written work done				
Offers information and suggestions Contributes without dominating				
Listens to others; reads what others have written				
Participates without interfering				
Helps write group reports				
Leadership				
Understands what we are studying				
Regularly helps get an agenda for the group				
Regularly tries to involve everyone in the work of the group				

Comments: If you can, describe what, or what sorts of things, you learned from this student. In particular, tell what you learned from this person's writing. How has this person's writing helped you learn and write?

indicate how she saw those students, using a version of the form shown in Figure 13–1.

What we are trying to do with questionnaires like this, of course, is redefine and reshape the way the students see themselves and learning. Other teachers who use this method use different questionnaires. But there is general agreement, among those of us concerned, that what we want is to use our methods of evaluation as part of an attempt to set new scenes for our students to write in, scenes that will redefine and reshape the way the students see themselves, their relationship to one another and the teacher, and the process of learning. What we seek is a method of evaluation that will not infect the scene for writing with secondary motives, but which will still allow us with some confidence to tell the rest of the university, and our society, that our students have achieved a certain level of competence. We are, that is, attempting to take audience into account in our evaluation procedures: we need to tell something to our students, to each other, to ourselves, and to the world outside (represented first by the registrar's office). This strategy, we believe, allows us to do this.

There, then, are our stories. Like all stories, what their points are and how they'll be understood and passed on is a function of the situation in which they're told, the tellers, and the audience: the scene. We hope that they open the doors to further dialogue.

Teacher Training

14

Portfolios for Teachers: Writing Our Way to Reflective Practice

Chris M. Anson

In 1986, George Hillocks published his now well-known work, *Research on Written Composition*. This was the first "metaanalysis" in a maturing field, a sign that the study of writing had reached a critical mass sufficient to let us stand back and assess how far we had come and to find out what works in the teaching of writing. The result was a useful set of delivery modes that described the dominant ways in which composition classrooms are organized and taught, followed by an empirical assessment of these modes' effectiveness.

If Hillock's painstaking synthesis clearly reflected our preoccupations, then formal inquiry into composition had been driven by a hunger for abstractions, not by a desire to understand what happens in the minds of individual teachers who are influenced by personal experiences and act on self-constructed theory. As Susan Miller characterizes this focus on the abstract, it has left little room for "interpretive theory in composition, an approach that privileges the subject in, and the subjectivity of, composition as an intellectual pursuit" (120). Such an approach relies on accounts of teaching that weave through the thoughts, ambitions, and struggles of individual teachers as they breathe life into their own personal curriculum.

Unfortunately, the scholarly research community often devalues storytelling as a type of inquiry. In *The Making of Knowledge in Composition*, North defends the practice even as he acknowledges that "its credibility, its power vis-a-vis other kinds of knowledge, has gradually, steadily diminished" (21). In an effort to raise the intellectual stature of narratives about classroom experience, Brannon argues that it is primarily through storytelling that we come to know about teaching. Proposing a dialectic between the "softness" of classroom narratives and the "hardness" of scientific truth that has dominated our scholarly journals, she argues that it is time for each to inform the other, time to rediscover "reliability" of our own reflected practice. Brannon is not alone in this belief. Recent work such as Witherell and Noddings' collection, *Stories Lives Tell: Narrative and Dialogue in Education,* as well as extensive research by Lee Shulman, suggest a growing awareness of teachers' reflected practice as an arena of authentic study. These voices challenge us to redefine what should count as knowledge of the writing classroom and ask why it is that teachers' stories are not widely written and heard.

Recently, through such organizations as the American Association of Higher Education, teachers and administrators have taken a keen interest in an innovation that places personal accounts of teaching at the center of instructional development: the *teaching portfolio* (see Edgerton, Hutchings and Quinlan). Teaching portfolios invite teachers to tell the story of their work and in doing so to become more reflective of their own practice. As such, teaching portfolios respond directly to calls, like Brannon's, to legitimize classroom experience and wed teaching and instructional inquiry.

To composition scholars, teachers, and administrators who have campaigned vigorously for student portfolios, the teaching portfolio makes good sense. Yet we still have much to learn about the method, both as a tool for appraising teachers' performance and as a way to encourage faculty development, collaboration, and professionalism. This chapter describes the teaching portfolio and its goals, offers a rationale for its centrality to our profession, suggests some ways in which it can be adapted to specific kinds of writing programs, and raises questions for further exploration and study.

The Nature and Structure of Teaching Portfolios

Most approaches to teaching portfolios define them as a collection of materials, assembled by a faculty member, that document or reflect teaching performance. Some approaches emphasize the "communicative" goals of portfolios as a way to share one's teaching, others stress its role in assessment, still others its potential to encourage development. Wolf's description in "The School Teacher's Portfolio" perhaps best sums up these various functions:

> A [teaching] portfolio can be defined as a container for storing and displaying evidence of a teacher's knowledge and skills. However, this definition is incomplete. A portfolio is more than a container—a portfolio also represents an attitude that assessment is dynamic, and that the richest portrayals of teaching (and student) performance are based upon multiple sources of evidence collected over time in authentic settings.

While the portfolio may seem at first glance like a typical faculty "file," it differs from standard dossiers in important ways. First, although it can contain personal material, it benefits from agreements among a community of teachers about what it should contain and what purposes it should serve. Individual faculty dossiers, by contrast, represent mostly private efforts (often symbolically "off-limits" in a locked department file). Second, the teaching portfolio is not simply a repository of the outcomes of teaching; it contains documents that show teachers in action, both creating their teaching and reflecting on it during moments of introspection. Finally, the teaching portfolio may contain much more material than might be forwarded to a hiring committee or faculty evaluation team. The portfolio may become several portfolios, each displaying different materials depending on its purpose and audience.

Ideally, a teaching portfolio should contain both primary and secondary documents. Primary documents are actual materials from classroom instruction, including, but by no means limited to, the following:

- Syllabi
- Course overviews or descriptions
- Assignments of all kinds
- Exams
- Study Guides
- Student papers, perhaps with teacher comments
- Classroom materials such as overheads or handouts
- Innovative instructional materials (computer programs, etc.)
- Logs from class visits
- Student evaluations

Secondary documents are materials that demonstrate active, critical thinking about instructional issues and materials. They might include the following:

- Reflections on peer-observations or videotapes
- Reflections on course evaluations
- Self-evaluations of all kinds
- Narrative accounts of problem-solving
- Responses to case studies and scenarios about teaching
- Journals documenting thoughtfulness about instructional issues
- Goal statements and philosophies
- Letters of assessment from others

From a developmental perspective, these secondary documents are essential if portfolios are to be used for something more than what Wolf, in "Teaching Portfolios," calls "amassing papers." Instead, they must be *structured* around key dimensions of teaching, such as planning, teaching, evaluating students, and professional activities. . . . [T]he portfolio should be more than a few snapshots, but should reflect a person's accomplishments over time and in a variety of contexts" (2).

Most published descriptions of teaching portfolios also stress their collaborative potential. Portfolios should not only bring teachers together to talk about and share in the activity of teaching, but should also represent the influences of colleagues, students, and theorists. They should, then, be understood first as something programmatic or anchored in a community, not as a "file" stored away in a department cabinet.

Teaching Portfolios at the Center of Writing Programs

Teaching portfolios seem especially well-suited to the field of composition, whose scholars and teachers are experts in writing assessment just as they understand and strongly promote the use of writing as a mode of learning. Three important subject positions of teachers among our community nicely match the less discipline-specific goals of the teaching portfolio.

Teacher as Writer

More than in any other teaching-oriented field, composition celebrates the value of writing for improved instruction and deeper reflection. In most nationally prominent workshops on the teaching of writing, participants' experiences drafting, sharing, and revising their own texts become the seeds of personal and professional growth. Such experiences "enact the belief that the best writing teachers are teachers who write" (Faery); participants learn how to teach writing "from the inside out" (Healy).

As Durst points out, however, many teachers write less than their own students:

> For most elementary, secondary, and community college teachers . . . writing is not a necessary part of the job. On the contrary, the responsibilities of their jobs generally work *against* finding time and energy for writing. And, of course, there are few job-related rewards for being a teacher who writes. (262)

Institutions that expect publication do, of course, encourage their faculty to write. Yet to survive in these settings, the faculty may end up working exclusively on articles and books unrelated to teaching.

Teaching portfolios must be *written*. While most primary documents placed in a portfolio have an independent life as part of classroom instruction, the portfolio casts a new light on such documents and gives their creators a different sense of audience. Through the imagined eyes of a colleague or administrator, the college teacher now rethinks the overly dictatorial tone in her course syllabus. Anticipating the scrutiny of a hiring committee looking at his portfolio, the recent Ph.D. wonders whether his sample assignment seems clear enough to demonstrate his best work. Knowing she will soon be sharing her comments on student papers with her peer teaching team, the instructor at a community college begins reflecting on her style of response. The various audiences invited into these teachers' portfolios inspire them to think in more principled ways about how their teaching materials are written, and this process leads to revision, new thought, and new action where perhaps otherwise there would be little change.

But it is the secondary documents that really encourage teachers to write. Teaching philosophies, observation reports, discussions of course designs, explanations of assignments, analyses of comments of student papers, reflections on sets of student evaluations—these become the threads of a narrative, a kind of professional autobiography of a teacher's classroom life. It is difficult to imagine anyone invested in their daily work as a teacher giving short shrift to a statement of their beliefs about how best students learn and how best we might teach them. Ideally, teachers can meet in small focus groups to circulate and discuss drafts of their reflections and philosophies. Revisions of primary or secondary documents can then lead to changed attitudes and improved teaching strategies.

Teacher as Scholar

The dominant rhetoric in higher education unnecessarily splits teaching and scholarship, often through systems that reward one more richly than the other. "Research universities" stand in stark contrast to "teaching colleges." In spelling out the criteria for success, promotion and tenure codes usually separate the activities of "research and scholarship" or "publishing" from the activities of "teaching and advising students," as if the two were unrelated. In its report on the rising costs of higher education, the U.S. House Select Committee on Children, Youth, and Families argues that "the focus on higher education today is on research, not teaching" (3). Offering statistics that show the decline of attention to teaching and advising relative to the rise in emphasis on research, the report suggests that

> conducting research has become such an overwhelming focus on today's campuses that those professors who still manage to teach more than a few hours a day are actually looked down upon by their peers, to say nothing of the negative effect teaching has on their chances for tenure, pay, and promotion. (3-4)

Such dichotomizing characterizes teaching as a deliberately unscholarly kind of work requiring the endurance of tedium in contrast to the more demanding and intellectually rewarding work of research. In a valiant effort to tear down this barrier between the personal life of the laboratory or office and the public life of the classroom, Ernest Boyer offers four specific ways in which teachers can be scholars: through the scholarship of discovery (such as research), the scholarship of integration (such as writing a textbook), the scholarship of application (such as consulting), and the scholarship of teaching. Uniting all the professional activities of college faculty under the banner of scholarship restores teaching to its rightful intellectual place. "At bottom," Edgerton, Hutchings and Quinlan claim, "the concept entails a view that teaching, like other scholarly activities . . . relies on a base of expertise, a 'scholarly knowing' that needs to and *can* be identified, made public, and evaluated; a scholarship that faculty themselves must be responsible for monitoring" (1).

By creating and developing teachers' base of expertise through inquiry into the real problems and experiences of the classroom, teaching portfolios encourage this scholarly view of teaching. In the field of composition, "teacher research" has already gained prestige as a kind of inquiry rooted in classroom experience but branching into the world of theory and investigation. As William Schubert argues, even the teacher lore so often denigrated as unprincipled chit-chat is actually highly relevant to "the theory and practice of curriculum, teaching, supervision, and school improvement. . . . To assume that scholarship can focus productively on what teachers learn recognizes teachers as important partners in the creation of knowledge about education" (207).

Teacher as Professional

Faculty members in higher education, particularly at research-oriented universities, often define their professional lives in terms of scholarship. In spite of the increased demand for a stronger commitment to teaching in American universities, the public itself perpetuates the image of experts in disciplines whose intellectual missions exist at some remove from teaching. The popular press stereotypes "absent-minded professors" as intellectuals immersed in the stuff of their disciplines. TV shows and movies depict faculty as distant, hard-to-reach scholars who hurry from their lectures for fear of being harassed by students. Much rarer are images of compassionate teachers willing to sit down with students and help them to learn, and who think conscientiously about their own instruction.

This tendency to privilege field-specific knowledge as the grist of one's professional life systematically devalues teachers (especially in public schools) whose professions are necessarily rooted in classrooms. Howard Gardner has described this situation as a paradox: "Few societies have paid as much lip service to the importance of education . . . yet it seems necessary to say as well that education—and particularly the schools—have often held a dubious position in the value scheme of the larger society" (98). Perhaps no sign more strongly defines the belief in professionalism-as-scholarship than the organization of the faculty vita. Publications, research grants, conference papers, and other artifacts of scholarship almost always appear before (and more prominently than) lists of courses, names of advisees, instructional innovations, and other outcomes of teaching.

Teaching portfolios not only display a teacher's best work but invite readers into the teacher's studio, where strategies for principled instruction are conceived and created. Portfolios provide glimpses—and sometimes longer, studied gazes—of teachers at work as professionals. In this sense, the portfolio encourages teachers to think of themselves as experts whose decisions are reflected in the professional artifacts of their instruction. Their expertise as *conveyors and orchestrators* of specialized knowledge stands side-by-side with that specialized knowledge itself.

Adapting Teaching Portfolios to Specific Contexts

Most of the literature on teaching portfolios agrees that portfolios give teachers a way to work on and document not just the outcome of their efforts but also their reflection, improvement, and growing expertise. Individuals or committees charged with evaluating teachers (for performance appraisals, merit pay, or hiring) come away from a portfolio with a much clearer and more comprehensive picture of a teacher's work than brief testimonials and statistics from student evaluations. And, in composition, portfolios define a space for teachers to work on their own writing or, with other teachers, collectively focus on a large area of their professional lives.

Yet in spite of this conceptual agreement about teaching portfolios, important practical questions remain. Without decisions about the contents and uses of portfolios, they can become merely random repositories—haphazardly organized collections of student evaluations, old syllabi, and hastily photocopied handouts. And if they are used solely for assessment, teachers may soon look on them with feelings of fear and doubt rather than a sense of personal ownership in their work.

To be effective, portfolios must be adapted to teachers' and administrators' specific needs. If a program of faculty development wants to emphasize teaching style, the documents might go so far as to include a videotape of all or part of a class session along with a self-analysis. If participants in a writing-across-the-curriculum program want to improve the way they read students' work, then the portfolio might contain some examples of students' final and/or draft papers representing a range of quality, along with the teacher's commentary on those and an accompanying reflection on the nature of the teacher's responses. Specific questions can be designed as prompts ("Characterize your response style by examining a classful of your papers, and include a sample; what are your goals in responding to student writing? How do your comments achieve those goals?") If a department wants to work in a given year on the principles of effective writing assignments, the portfolio might include three sample assignments with accompanying descriptions of their place in the scheme of a course and a rationale for their design. The following year, the focus might shift to advising students—and the portfolio contents for that year should reflect the shift. Central to the adaptation of portfolio contents is the constant need to guide reflection and encourage change in keeping with the missions of particular departments and institutions.

To illustrate this adaptive potential further, let's consider three fictitious writing programs where teaching portfolios play a role in faculty development and the evaluation of teaching. Each site uses portfolios for different purposes among quite different teachers.

Site 1 is Jonesville College, a small liberal arts school with a strong writing-across-the-curriculum program. The program is supported by teaching portfolios among all faculty assigned to "writing-intensive" (WI) courses. WI courses have a smaller class size than most other courses and also carry a special incentive bonus paid by the central administration. New teachers of WI courses meet monthly throughout their first year to participate in workshops, discuss the integration of writing into their coursework, and share ideas and samples of student writing. Coordinators of the WI program use portfolios initially to support faculty development. However, because competition to teach WI courses is keen, faculty are reappointed to these courses yearly. An evaluation committee coordinated by the director of writing across the curriculum examines the portfolios of present WI teachers who wish to continue teaching the following year. Criteria for reappointment include evidence of principled assignment design, integration of writing fully into the coursework, reflections on the nature of students' writing, and year-end self-assessments with commentary for further improvement. At Jonesville, therefore, the portfolios begin cumulatively and developmentally for teachers-in-training, and turn recursive and evaluative in future years. Model portfolios from experienced WI teachers provide ideas and techniques for teachers new to the program and demonstrate the principles of reflective practice.

Site 2 is the English department at Smithtown Community College, a midsize campus near a major metropolitan area. The department coordinates a single first-year composition course staffed largely by annually renewed instructors, some of whom teach at other local colleges and spend little extra time on campus. Five years ago, the instructors lobbied the department to examine its rather haphazard process of faculty evaluation after several younger instructors were eliminated following a budget cut. The chair decided to begin a teaching portfolio program as a way to assess the instructors' performance and create a better community of more committed teachers.

The model he chose is recursive: each portfolio must include, at a minimum, a full syllabus for each course taught, along with a two- or three-page rationale for its design; three samples of student writing from each course in the categories "strong," "typical," and "weak," along with the original responses and a one-page analysis explaining the papers' relative strengths and weaknesses and how the responses encouraged revision or further learning; two-page post-course self-assessments for all classes taught, with accompanying student evaluations from one of those classes; and a cover essay articulating a philosophy of teaching. Optional but strongly encouraged are informal write-ups of conference sessions, workshops, or readings relating to teaching.

The portfolios represent Smithtown's mission by focusing on student performance relative to strong, student-centered teaching. In successive years, teachers must revise or replace these documents but must refer to the changes they have made in their methods or beliefs. The chair discusses the portfolio with each instructor at the time of reappointment. It is generally understood that seniority will not count as much as a continued commitment, demonstrated in the portfolio, to change, renewal, and improvement in teaching. While the instructors continue to lobby against the inequities of annual renewals, they feel that the portfolios more fairly reflect their abilities at the time of reappointment.

Site 3 is a large composition program at Johnson State University, staffed almost entirely by teaching assistants pursuing Ph.D.s in the Department of English. As part of its TA development program, the program begins teaching portfolios in the first year of the TAs' five-year appointments. The model shown in Figure 14–1 is cumulative: the directors feel that as TAs move through their teaching appointments, they naturally attend to different concerns at different levels of instructional sophistication. Since most of their new TAs have never taught before, Year 1 focuses on strategies for leading discussions, running small groups, working individually with students, and managing time. All TAs are given a common course design that they may slightly modify after consultation. During the year, each TA must visit another instructor's class at least twice and be visited at least twice. Small teams discuss, revise, and enter into the portfolio their write-ups of these visits, as well as reflections on samples of student writing. At several points during the year, the instructors write "teaching reflections" in which they analyze specific successes and failures in their classroom instruction. The writing program administrators and their assistants respond to the portfolio entries as they are cycled into the portfolio.

In Year 2, the TAs begin designing their own versions of the composition courses offered at JSU. Now the focus is logistical. Documents placed in the portfolio include a full syllabus, an accompanying rationale, and extended descriptions of each assignment along with explanations of its goals, contents, and sequence in the course. Instructors also write narrative-like philosophies of teaching. By the time they move to Year 3, the TAs must begin reading more extensively in the area of composition theory and research. A graduate course optionally supports this new theoretical focus. Now the TAs must reinterpret their classroom activities, course design, and philosophy through the new perspectives offered in their readings. Documents include

Figure 14–1
A Cumulative Model for Teaching Portfolios

	FOCUS	ENTRIES
Year 1	Experiential	Reflections on visits Teaching reflections Responses to student writing
Year 2	Logistical	Syllabus with rationale Extended descriptions of assignments with rationales Narrative philosophy of teaching
Year 3	Theoretical	Revised philosophy of teaching New rationales based on theory Student surveys of techniques, with analysis and reflection
Year 4	Experimental	Post-course self-assessments Analyses of experimental techniques Revised philosophy of teaching
Year 5	Professional	Best samples of all work (new portfolio for job search)

revised statements of philosophy, deeper rationales for pedagogical choices, and at least one carefully administered student survey focusing on a specific technique used in the classroom, along with an analysis of the results.

In Year 4, TAs move into a more experimental stage during which they try out new and often innovative ideas in the classroom. In addition to post-course self-assessments, each TA must place into her portfolio at least two analyses of experimental or innovative instructional strategies. The best of these are photocopied and circulated among all the instructors. Finally, between Years 4 and 5, TAs prepare a professional teaching dossier from the materials they have accumulated in their teaching portfolios. These include the very best examples of syllabi, assignments, descriptions of innovations, reflections, post-course self-assessments of students' evaluations, and teaching philosophies. In this way, JSU's program uses teaching portfolios initially as a development tool and gradually "professionalizes" them to support teachers' job searches when they complete their graduate programs.

Clearly, each of these sketches raises concerns just as it suggests innovations. Most such concerns, however, will not arise from the "developmental" potential of teaching portfolios but from their use in the evaluation of teaching. No one will argue against creating a space for deeper reflection, greater collaboration, and more effective instruction. But many will question the method as a way to make judgments about teaching ability. To this issue we now briefly turn.

The Problem of Assessment

At the heart of the teaching portfolio lies the belief that excellent teachers possess a special expertise, what Shulman calls the "pedagogy of substance," that allows them to transform discipline-specific material into learnable concepts and methods. Shulman's research suggests that it is possible to gauge or measure this expertise and the attempt to achieve it. Because it provides rich descriptions and actual materials from teachers' instruction, the teaching portfolio opens up that possibility for measurement in a way that has excited many educators concerned about the public cry for accountability in higher education.

As experts in the assessment of student writing and thinking, compositionists interested in teaching portfolios as an evaluation tool face the mixed blessing of working out criteria for successful performance. Primary documents appear to be the easiest to codify in this way: most teachers can distinguish between an especially strong course syllabus and an undeveloped or quickly drafted one. The unimaginative or thoughtlessly written assignment stands in stark contrast to the assignment that reflects clear goals and will interest and motivate students. Secondary documents, on the other hand, present more interesting puzzles. How might we measure "the ability to reflect"? What really counts for good response to students' in-process drafts? How might we sort strong from weak rationales for specific writing assignments?

Consider, for example, excerpts from the observation logs of two teaching assistants in the early years of their teaching careers. The teachers, both women, have observed the class of a colleague, kept a descriptive log of what happened during the class, and met briefly with the teacher to discuss the log.

Excerpt 1

[The teacher has visited a colleague's class on a day when the students worked on rough drafts of papers in small groups.]

Four of the five students apparently had little difficulty with the assignment, although not having read the papers I could only judge by watching their interaction. The fifth was out of her element, a high-school student who did not understand the assignment or seemed unable to carry it through. The teacher was extremely empathetic to her and gave her many openings to verbalize her understanding of the assignment and the essay she was analyzing; however, she was unable to do so. He finally excused her by saying she was apparently just "letting it sit for a while."

The quality of the students' comments varied, but they stayed quite general. The high-school student offered no contribution, except to say that she could not read one copy of the rough draft that she had been given. The teacher, unquestioningly the main critic here, offered comments and questions to each of the writers. All of the information flowed through him, rather than from student to student.

Paper 1. The paper was more analytical than evaluative. Student comments were made on clarifying audience, using more detail, and asking for elaboration and expansion at specific points. The best student response came for this paper, which was apparently quite funny. The teacher pointed out that the rhetorical strategies needed clarification. . . . Paper III. This "undeveloped" paper has already been mentioned. The instructor's tact was impeccable, and he gave her a chance to start over if she needed it. In the postobservation conference, the instructor related that this student did not ever take his offers of extra help. Her attendance is good, although she is in over her head. *I would infer that because this student is in high school she probably thinks that if she continues to come to class she will pass, regardless of her written performance. . . .*

Excerpt 2

[The teacher has visited a colleague's class on a day when the students have brought in short responses to a chapter about journal writing.]

. . . At this juncture, X solicited responses from the class. "Ok, what did you think about the reading? How did you react to it?" There is general silence; students flipping through the pages. X tries again. "Was this useful, do you think, as a way to start writing?" Students seem to nod in assent, but still no response. X starts talking about the concepts in the chapter. Two ways to use the techniques, as learning tool to explore material, and as writing tool to gather thoughts and draft. 7 minutes; X still talking. Then he asks if there are any questions. A student says she keeps a journal anyway, and can she turn in pages from it in this journal or somehow do both at the same time. X cracks a joke that loosens up the class a little. Then he sobers, advises her to do more academic kind of work in the course journal. Leave other stuff out. One student doesn't see the difference. He explains; focus is always on course or paper. Then quickly moves to transition into his explanation of the next assignment.

Two issues emerged for me from this part of the observation. The first is the questioning style and the silence. I find this so typical in my own teaching. You throw out a question and . . . nothing. I think X lost a chance to capitalize on the s's freewrites. Maybe by prefacing: "Take a look for a minute at your freewrites about the chapter, and star or circle any responses that stand out for you." Give them 30 seconds or so, then follow up. If the response seems limited, maybe just call on them, or do a safe-circle round-robin kind of thing, so everyone has a voice. X filled in the silence, but in our pre-ob he said he was trying to make his course as active as possible. So this wasn't a case of mini-lecture, of presenting vital information, but it came off like a lecture.

The other issue (a little thornier?) is the journal. The most exciting part of the first part of the class came when the student asked about her own journal writing. Then #10 thought there wasn't any difference between the two types (actually he asked, but it was almost an implication). I might have let this run a bit. The journal is slippery; maybe X could have asked #6 to describe what sort of stuff she writes in her personal journal, to gauge if it could fit into the course journal. Also, if the initial class discussion had been richer, the question might have come up in that context, instead of a "Is it ok to do such-and-such" question. I know how X felt. There hadn't been any discussion, he was put off, had other stuff to cover, and maybe just shut down a potential theoretical problem with the journal. He did loosen them up, which seemed a wise move if you're uncertain yourself. I'm not sure. But the openness he wanted didn't seem to be there. In my own use of journals in the classroom, I try to . . . [paragraph].
After describing the next assignment, X asked students . . .

As shown in the italicized material, the first teacher provides almost no reflection on her observation. She is witness to, but not interpreter of, the classroom she observed. In contrast, the second teacher stops in the middle of her account to discuss her own use of journals and how she might have handled a moment of silence. If we assume that the presence of such meta-commentary reflects positively on a teacher's ability to monitor her own teaching and continually improve her instruction, the second teacher would seem far ahead of the first.

Anyone who uses such material for assessment, however, will soon have the gnawing suspicion that the presence or absence of reflection may not predict teaching ability—just as talking a lot in class may not predict a student's intellectual acumen, ability to write, or accumulated knowledge. Critics in the creative arts have long claimed that artistic ability may be largely unconscious. Writers, painters, and composers are often unable to say exactly what made them describe a scene in such lugubrious words, choose burnt umber for the edge of the moon, or suddenly shift to the minor key in the middle of a movement; yet they may still create brilliant works.

Comparisons of what defines "quality" in teaching—between individual teachers, between departments, or between disciplines—can also illustrate quite clearly the present dubiousness of specifying universal criteria or standards for such quality. Edgerton, Hutchings, and Quinlan, for example, include in their monograph *The Teaching Portfolio* a sample entry from Harvard University history teacher James Wilkinson. Wilkinson's entry includes a student's typed book review, on which Wilkinson has made marginal annotations and an end comment. In his reflective statement accompanying the student paper, Wilkinson describes his reasons for writing what he did, and what the sample tells him about his own practice. This and other examples of portfolio entries are reproduced in order to "look at the particulars that might comprise [a teaching portfolio]" (13).

From the perspective of a history department, Wilkinson's entry no doubt shows a concerned faculty member who takes the time to design good assignments, read his students' work carefully, and write useful comments. While not intended to be a model of excellence, Wilkinson's entry clearly reveals a dedicated teacher at work, someone able to stand back from his teaching enough to know that he is offering "encouragement, even where there is need for improvement," and not "writ[ing] out what [students] should have said, but instead giv[ing] them general guidelines" (39). Most advocates of writing across the curriculum would react enthusiastically to such an entry, inspired that writing can be used effectively in all disciplines.

But if we switch the setting for purposes of illustration, the history department's criteria seem more localized. From the perspective of a faculty member teaching advanced composition, Wilkinson's commentary may seem inadequate, or "differently adequate," lacking developmental insight or advice about the writing process in order to draw the student's attention to the material of history. From the perspective of a psychology department with large classes void of writing assignments, Wilkinson's response may seem absurdly diligent. Once we acknowledge such multiple perspectives coming from widely different disciplinary, departmental, or institutional settings, the problem of establishing universal criteria for "good teaching" takes on considerable complexity. Perhaps evaluating teaching using documents in a portfolio (especially secondary ones) may have to remain the responsibility of individual departments within specific universities.

To release themselves of such dilemmas, most administrators argue that specifying exactly what should be in the portfolio and then describing strong and weak examples of those contents *encourages certain kinds of thinking* conducive to good teaching. This privileges neither the "science" of teaching, which assumes an objectivist and sometimes clinical view, nor the "art" of teaching, which often resigns ability to intuition, magic, and God-given dispositions. Reflection blends the two approaches by assuming that teaching can be discussed and improved consciously even if it can never be understood entirely clinically. If the ability to reflect on and problematize teaching activities really is associated with expertise, then evaluation programs can play a powerful role in improving instruction across entire campuses by raising to consciousness at least some of those decisions, actions, and experiences that lead to success in the classroom.

Without explicit, theoretically informed criteria for such portfolio contents as observation logs, reflections on student evaluations, or rationales for assignments, teaching portfolios can still encourage accountability, which in turn can be linked to assessment. A program of faculty or TA development, for example, can list documents that must be placed into a teaching portfolio over a certain time period. More ambitious programs can provide models of

15

Graduate Writers and Portfolios: Issues of Professionalism, Authority, and Resistance

Nedra Reynolds

Graduate students probably learn more about the academic profession from each other by way of stories, anecdotes, and gossip than they do from a typical or traditional graduate seminar. Storytelling and gossip are legitimate forms of knowledge production, but their need arises because of the ways in which professional practices and expectations have been mystified. To borrow John Clifford's term, "discursive mystifications" surround issues of speaking and writing for professional or disciplinary audiences. Some of these mystifications can have more serious consequences than simple regret about "all the things they don't tell you in graduate school" because they determine issues of authority: who gets to speak and who gets published. I want to present a case for trying to de-mystify a few common writing practices by incorporating writing portfolios into graduate courses. This paper is a first attempt to explore what kinds of writing these portfolios might include that would help graduate writers find their own ways towards professional savvy and discursive authority.

Discursive authority, in my view, comes from a writer's subjectivity, experience, and location. Acknowledging my own subject position, therefore, contextualizes and qualifies the claims I make here about graduate writers. As a second-year assistant professor, I do not yet have the distance from my own graduate school experiences to feel nostalgic; I feel, instead, the need to analyze while I still occupy a position from a valuable perspective: simultaneously I am still "outside" many realms of the profession, yet "inside" enough to understand the stakes. I understand that writing successfully is one of the highest stakes, but having never practiced conference proposals, abstracts, grant applications, or query letters in graduate courses, I am just now becoming a writer in this profession. At the same time, I find myself in the position of teaching and advising graduate students who want to figure out the ways and means of writing for audiences in rhetoric, composition, and literary studies.

Represented most keenly by exams and the dissertation, *writing* is the single most anxiety-producing part of the graduate students' experience, and this anxiety is heightened by the lack of attention to writing in the graduate curriculum. As Patricia Sullivan's study of graduate writing, discussed below, so thoroughly demonstrates, we need to pay more explicit attention to the expectations, demands, and realities of writing for the profession from a distinctly marginal position.

Studies of Graduate Writers

Until quite recently, graduate studies and their students have been a grossly neglected area of research and inquiry. An attempt to remedy this neglect occurred in 1987, when first a conference and then an MLA collection focused on *The Future of Doctoral Studies in English* (Lunsford, Moglen, Slevin). However, this text, and the conference that preceded it, are blatant examples of the exclusion of graduate student voices. Not as an oversight, but by design, graduate students were left out of these discussions. (By the way, no assistant or untenured professors were invited either.) James Slevin is one of the only contributors who acknowledges the glaring absences. The collection also fails to analyze the multiple, shifting, and complex subject positions of graduate students. Familiar to all of us, but rarely analyzed, are the layers of contradictions with which graduates contend; they are asked to be financial wizards, dedicated students, and equally dedicated teachers, while never neglecting their families. We ask them to follow institutionalized practices in their own classrooms but to question them in ours; to be open-minded readers but to pick a theoretical camp; to align themselves politically but to protect their chances at scholarships or awards. They are caught between the positions of novice and professional, and this in-between stage is most evident as they write.

In their roles as teaching assistants, rather than in their roles as writers, graduate students have been the focus of countless meetings and memos, if not actual scholarly publications. When the concerns are motivated by administrative matters, TAs do receive considerable attention. Too often, writing program administrators are the only ones in a department who concern themselves with the teaching and professional lives of graduate students. Unfortunately, this concern can take the form of "policing" the teaching of TAs—a disciplinary function that does little to question how their teaching locates them institutionally.

It takes a graduate student, of course, to blow the whistle on these problems and lapses: in the May 1992 issue of *College Composition and Commu-*

nication, Eileen Schell demonstrates the ways in which the 1991 CCCC "Progress Report" underrepresents the problems of TAs, including the misnomer of the title itself. Schell is right to point out that graduate students "are increasingly being asked to assume a more 'professional image' by reading professional journals, giving papers at professional conferences, and publishing their work. These demands contrast sharply with the relatively unprofessional status that GTAs occupy as low-paid wage workers" (165).

Today's graduate students, operating in a tight job market and a changing profession, are painfully aware of this demand for increasing professionalism; candidates can no longer distinguish themselves by teaching experience, conference presentations, and publications, since these have become the norm rather than the exception. The very real demands that graduate students be or quickly become professional writers clash, then, with the paucity of research about them, especially compared to the numerous studies of first-year writers that have helped to legitimate the study of writing as a discipline. (As Sullivan notes (298) early research into the process movement put English majors and graduate students automatically into the "experienced writers" pool, with little attention to what that experience includes.)

Let me note first, however, two important and quite recent exceptions. In 1988, Carnegie Mellon researchers Carol Berkenkotter, Thomas Huckin, and John Ackerman designed a sophisticated case study of entering graduate student "Nate" to discover how he "attains advanced literacy in the context of graduate school" (10). Nate's texts were closely analyzed, using a variety of approaches, to measure or indicate "the *visible index of his initiation into an academic discourse community*" (11). And in a very recent article in *Written Communication,* Deborah Brandt applies an ethnomethodological approach to a writing episode of a graduate student drafting a conference proposal.

These two studies are exceptional in that they do not assume that graduate writers already know "how to write" and simply need a spit of professional polish to get them published. As both the Berkenkotter and Brandt studies show, at issue for all kinds of novice writers—and we are all novices in some contexts—is the ability to negotiate particular discourse conventions, especially as various communities converge or conflict. However, what these studies do wrongly assume is that these novice writers will surely get writing experience—and direct writing instruction—in their courses or seminars.

Patricia Sullivan presents a forceful case, however, that writing is virtually ignored in graduate-level classes. In stark contrast to the presence of contemporary theories of reading and writing in English graduate courses stands the absence of any pedagogical guidance on writing for the profession. Sullivan demonstrates convincingly that this disjuncture between theory and pedagogical practice causes problems in invention and argumentation for graduate writers (289-93).

Sullivan conducted a two-part study; she surveyed graduate students in English at six universities and then followed up the survey with four case studies. Of the one hundred students who completed the survey about their writing experiences in graduate English courses, nearly all reported that the term paper of fifteen pages or more was their most typical assignment. The fifteen- to twenty-page term paper is "perceived as preparatory to the scholarly essay or journal article," but Sullivan argues that the term paper is not taught at all; it is merely assigned (294).

> Less than ten percent reported that their professors had asked to see or respond to drafts before the final version was evaluated, had asked students to share their written work with other students in the class, or had specified an audience or suggested a forum other than the professors themselves. (286)

In this typical scenario, writing becomes, in Sullivan's words, "a matter of individual performance, a solitary act rather than a social or collaborative experience. . . . acts of writing are both marginalized and privatized in the graduate classroom" (288).

Sullivan concludes by arguing that graduate students must see themselves as makers of history and culture through their acts of scholarship (297-98). It's no accident that Sullivan ends her essay with a reference to authority, for issues of authority are at the heart of graduate writing. They are also at the center of discussions about portfolios.

Implementing portfolios in graduate classes can address Sullivan's findings and serve three goals. First, their use places at the center of the course the kinds of writing that the profession expects, demands, or rewards, as well as those discourses it tends to silence or discourage. Second, the use of portfolios allows students to "try on" certain discourses, and different identities, finding those that feel more comfortable; in doing so, they learn how connected identity and authority are. Finally, portfolios give graduate students some safe space for experimentation and play and perhaps a site to explore resistance of varying degrees to dominant forms of academic discourse. In any case, like all portfolio designs, their use in graduate classes provides the chance to take risks since the one-shot seminar paper has been eliminated.

One Portfolio Design for Graduate Courses in English

The best portfolio systems evolve from a local context and several stages of experimentation. In my effort to design a professional yet flexible portfolio method for use in graduate seminars, I have made several adjustments and will make many more, but the goal is an end-of-semester portfolio that contains a variety of documents representative of the "actual" writing done in the profession—writing that gets the work done. I've suggested the following on a recent syllabus for a rhetorical theory class: a one- to two-page research proposal, directed to me, about a longer project; a two- to three-page position paper that takes a stand on an issue encountered either in the reading or in class discussion; a proposal to give a conference presentation (accompanied by the call for papers); an abstract of an article or chapter not on the reading list; an annotated bibliography; or any project students wish to design and run past me, including any collaborative arrangements. More recently, I've added or considered adding collaborative dialogues or electronic discussion transcripts, teaching statements, and letters to editors. The goal is for graduate writers to explore a number of different, experimental, fragmentary, or contradictory short pieces that will allow them to dip into a number of issues or try a number of genres. With more options and more room, these writers are freed from committing themselves to a full-blown argument before the course is even half completed.

Whatever the combination of entries, prefacing them all is the cover letter to the portfolio, which asks students to conduct some "self-assessment" as they introduce the contents of the portfolio to readers, explain how the entries represent their interests and their work in the course, and describe the processes by which one or two entries were produced.

Graduate Cover Letters and Authority

Of all the "parts" to the portfolio I assign, the most fascinating and richest area for inquiry is what I call, along with others, the cover letter. As Kathy McClelland, Kerry Weinbaum, and other portfolio researchers attest, cover letters, in some form or by whatever name, are documents of self-assessment directed to the portfolio's readers (Belanoff and Dickson). In their function of self-assessment, cover letters are crucial, if not fundamental, to the portfolio method. Cover letters or their equivalent become sites where issues of professional identity and authority are played out.

In its explicit function to introduce the contents of the portfolio, the cover letter also introduces (more implicitly) the *writer* of the portfolio, her identity as a writer. In fact, from my own experience as a portfolio rater in assessment situations, the cover letter can tell us so much about the writer that reading the rest of the portfolio contents can seem redundant or unnecessary—at least in changing our initial judgment of the writer. In the fall of 1989, as a rater in Miami University's Portfolio Assessment project, a group of us were training to score portfolios submitted by entering first-year students who were hoping to earn up to six hours of credit in college composition. In the holistic training session that preceded the actual rating of portfolios, our group of raters became intrigued by the first required document in these portfolios, what the Miami team had named the reflective letter. I remember quite vividly the impact on the group of one reflective letter in particular (Stager). This letter, we were convinced, was written by someone who had constructed a comfortable identity for herself as a writer, one she was able to assert with relish. (See Robert Brooke, *Writing and Sense of Self*, for discussion of how student writers negotiate the various identities offered to them in both traditional and workshop writing classes.) With such sentences as "I've got the five paragraph essay down like rain" and "I spent pages of journal-writing trying to come up with my big life-meaning paper," this young writer was so confident address-ing her audience of writing teachers that she risks irony as well as emotion. She convinced us that she is capable of meeting any writing task with experi-ence and self-awareness.

This ability to assert one's identity as a writer and the importance of doing that in a writing assessment context came back to me as I encountered the cover letters to my graduate students' portfolios, which raised certain questions for me. What might these cover letters tell us about graduate writers and how they go about constructing an identity for themselves? How do they present them-selves as authorities when they are typically marginalized in a professional context? Since I have encouraged acts of interrogation or resistance in our class discussions, what evidence can I find in these cover letters of "resistance"?

In a careful reading of the cover letters written by several of my rhetorical theory students in the fall of 1991, I located trends or patterns that do indicate something about how these writers see themselves as subjects in relation-ship to the class, to me, or to rhetorical and writing theory. Two categories of statements or claims appear quite regularly in these cover letters: first, those that reinscribe the writers' subject positions as students—institutionally situ-ated near the bottom of the academic hierarchy—and second, those that assert a writer's identity and an emerging authority.

At what might be considered the lowest level of commitment or engage-ment, many of the writers summarized, if only briefly, the contents of their portfolios, highlighting what I could expect to find as I turned the pages. Two of the weakest cover letters, in my view, stayed only at the level of summary.

A more interesting strategy these writers used to introduce their port-folios, especially as an opening line, was to claim how much they had learned in my course: "In introducing my portfolio I would first like to say that I have learned quite a great deal this semester." (I'm quoting directly from the students' cover letters, after receiving signed permission slips.) This is the strategy, I think, that highlights their subject position as students and reveals their perceived relationship to me as a hierarchial one. In addition, the "I learned so much this semester" comment reminded me that they were keenly aware of the function of the portfolio: to evaluate their performance as writers and thinkers and as rhetorical theorists.

Another strategy had to do with the degree of satisfaction they felt about the work, how happy they were or were not with the final product: "I am not totally happy with all the work enclosed—revision is an ongoing process." This kind of statement illustrates the function of self-assessment in the cover letters; several students understood or accepted that function and were able to step back and be critical about their own work. With awareness of the evalu-ation involved and in their role as good students, they often reiterated my own emphasis on revision.

Another, different, set of rhetorical strategies struck me as I read these cover letters: those that did not depend on the good student image but asserted something of an emerging professional identity and sense of purpose.

First, a few of the students talked about their projects as continuing beyond the course, as issues or conversations they would pursue or be involved in: "I see this research continuing for me. I say continuing because I plan to go on teaching." And: "I would like to do two things with this project. I'd like to do a proposal for the RSA [Rhetoric Society of America] conference, and I am thinking about this as a chapter of my dissertation. . . ." This desire to extend projects or seminar papers beyond the assignment is nothing new, but giving students a forum in which to articulate it might be, and asking them to consider what comes next reinforces the profession's expectations that the work never ends.

One of the rarest and most sophisticated comments, I thought, was one that asserted the writer's perceived contribution to the field or to the study of rhetorical theory:

> I am also pleased with what I think has been my contribution both to our class discussions and, if I may be so presumptuous, to what should be the continual goal of rhetorical theory (what still needs to be done). This contribution includes my continual questioning of accepted discourse, my recognition of the politics inherent in all kinds of rhetoric, and my commitment to addressing the oppression of women in both discourse (the discourse which they construct and that which constructs them) and in their day-to-day lives. This, I would submit, has been my contribution.

I find this passage especially interesting because of the qualifier—"if I may be so presumptuous"—within what is otherwise such an impressive, authoritative statement of purpose. This writer is concretely aware of her position as student, but she is also ready to take on rhetorical theory! This makes for a fascinating tension and a good illustration, I think, of the in-between stage of these writers, caught between novice and professional, aware of the evaluation that controls their futures but able to assert some authority nonetheless.

These references to ongoing work or newfound commitments demonstrate the emerging professionalism and authority of these graduate writers. Not all of the cover letters, however, looked the same or followed the same format. In contrast to cover letters that opened with "I have learned so much this semester," the writer of the cover letter reprinted below feels very little obligation to address the specificities of the course or even to address me directly, which most of the writers did. This letter in particular addresses the issue of resistance because of the way in which this writer positions himself in relationship to so-called "professional writing" and in the ways he—intentionally or not—subverted my expectations.

A Slightly Impersonal Introduction

Having spent the first ten years of my life locked in a closet has forced my mind into a rather abstract mold. Assimilation of, and assimilating into, larger structures escapes me, and the propensity for both amazes me further. Perhaps, too much aestheticism combats corpuscles within my blood stream, and this battle leaves my brain oxygen-less, and numb.

This portfolio is a cell in the latter stages of its replication, for this reason the work it contains continues *to be* formulating and reformulating with every turn of the page. *HyperText(s),* too is such a cell only beginning to divide from a formative nucleus. Pages twirl helix-like among themselves, surrounding a rather general concept—that of cognition; or, how we come to understand, as well as the transmission of understanding.

Post-script: as a slightly ironic aside, the piece *HyperText(s): Developing multiple textual moments writing with technology,* was basically rejected by the desktop publishing program used to create *Hypertext(s).* The article suggests that composition utilizing technology opens and frees the text from its material positioning. However, the Express Publisher program felt my article did not deserve freedom.

Because I do want to invite students to "try on" various discourses and identities, I couldn't very well say that this was unsuccessful as a cover letter or as a piece of writing in general. At the same time, however, I felt compelled to point out how most readers in "the profession" would react to it—probably quite negatively. Still, I can understand the position this writer wants to occupy in his portfolio and how he hopes I will "read" him: as a writer of fiction and fan of deconstruction.

What I now see in this cover letter, with considerable help from current writers on the concept of resistance, is that this graduate student's cover letter conflicted with the modernist conceptions of writing (coherence, clarity, logical order) and the modernist conceptions of writers (unified, also coherent, and rational) that shape modern composition studies and that, in turn, affect my pedagogy (Faigley, *Fragments of Rationality*). Robert Brooke also explains the mechanisms of underlife that provide important resistance points along the way to developing an identity (25). Brooke defines resistance this way: "the need of people on the margins to refuse to assent to definitions of self and reality which dominant institutions seek to impose on them" (122). Graduate writers are clearly on the margins, subject to a number of definitions of self and reality that the university and their profession (just to name two) seek to impose on them. But once again we find them caught between two positions: that of graduate student, eager to critique and resist institutionalized demands (especially if invited to do so); and that of emerging professional, driven to secure a position and begin contributing to research and scholarship.

Thus, this "resistant" cover letter pinpoints my ongoing dilemma: how do I help graduate writers figure out what will get them accepted to a conference or get them a publication while at the same time trying to encourage their interrogation of or resistance to certain conventions of academic discourse, especially from their marginal position? How do I help to initiate students into professional discourse and simultaneously encourage them to resist?

I think the answer lies in acknowledging the contradictory and conflicting positions graduate students and other marginal members of the profession occupy and the concomitant tension that accompanies what they write. John

Clifford, in his recent essay "The Subject in Discourse," explains the theoretical relationship between contradiction and resistance: "inevitable contradictions within subject positions can be a catalyst for resistance and counter-hegemonic thinking" (41). Once we think of writers as sites of contradiction (39), we can begin to move toward agency—a state of self-consciousness that can lead student writers to resistance. Clifford points out that students—and I would emphasize how much truer this is for graduate students—are "eager to become willing participants in the university's discursive mystifications" (46). My goal is to make students aware of the discourses that carry power and to introduce them to certain "discursive mystifications," *not* so that they can become "willing participants" in reproducing the institutional ideology but so that they can become *agents*—"critical agents capable of making their own history" (Trimbur, "Cultural Studies and Teaching Writing," 5)—who are aware of their own contradictory subject positions but able to claim those contradictions for authority.

These issues of resistance are not easily resolved, but after using a portfolio method in graduate courses for two semesters, I am convinced that it does make writing and writing pedagogy more central to the course, whatever the other subject matter. Portfolios will not truly have made their mark on graduate pedagogy, however, until they are implemented at the level of graduate programs themselves. Bonnie Hain writes in the Belanoff and Dickson collection about using portfolios for the master's exam, and her suggestions can be modified in a number of ways to suit various programs. Surely portfolios, in their invitation to variety and their opportunities for students to negotiate and practice a number of identities, offer an exciting alternative to the several-hours-locked-in-a-room syndrome of many comprehensive examinations.

One of the most encouraging signs that this system works comes, of course, from the students themselves and the evidence I find in their writing. One graduate writer opens his cover letter with what might be an apt metaphor for the discourses of portfolios: "Bakhtin refers to the asylum ignorantiae in *Marxism and the Philosophy of Language* as 'the place where all unresolved problems, all objectively irreducible residues are stored away' (930). This portfolio is just such a place, stuffed with the rhetorical residue of theoretical and pedagogical struggle." That's what I want portfolios to be: sites of struggle, where even residue has potential. Authoritative discourse grows out of pieces, tidbits, leftovers, and scraps—just as authoritative writers become agents of change through moments of struggle, glimpses of conflict, and in-between stages.

16

Make Haste Slowly: Graduate Teaching Assistants and Portfolios

Kathleen Blake Yancey

Readiness

Yesterday I worked with a group of high-school English teachers in Davidson County, North Carolina. They care about their students; they know their subject; they want to work to improve learning for all their students. They are drawn to portfolios because they like what they see: a chance to bring pedagogy and assessment into alignment in a way they design, they implement, they review. The teachers also like portfolios because so far, no one-size-fits-all-mold has been advocated by state administrators or delivered by publishers or copyrighted by university people.

At the end of the day, one teacher laughed as she showed me the novel she had brought to the workshop but had forgotten to read.

These teachers are ready to use portfolios.

In this essay I wish to make an argument with which I am not entirely comfortable, and which, in its basic premise, runs counter to my own philosophy of teaching as well as to my own practice. I wish to argue that new graduate teaching assistants, who of course are not assistants to other teachers at all, but rather teachers of writing themselves, should wait to try portfolios until they have taught for a term. As they wait, and before they try portfolios, they can learn to teach, focusing on how to help writers develop, on how to read student writings, and on how to respond to those writings. Alternatively, in the absence of this best case sequence, if TAs must use portfolios, they should do so *only* when a prescribed set of conditions obtains.

(I wish to make this argument in spite of its anti-TA or anti-portfolio appearance.) I understand that it seems to contradict much of what I say I believe in—in teachers as agents of change; in teachers as the designers of the links between curriculum and assessment; and in an assessment of writing of the kind that we do see in portfolios, that is cumulative and developmentally based. Worse perhaps is the hierarchical distribution of agents implied above, with the line of demarcation drawn between the "new" teacher and the one not-so-new, a dichotomy that ordinarily I oppose.

My proposal also runs counter to what is rapidly becoming conventional wisdom for people who prepare teachers and for people who advocate portfolios in the teaching of writing. Don't Peter Elbow and Pat Belanoff recommend portfolios as an excellent vehicle for staff development? Hasn't Chris Burnham suggested that TA training benefits from portfolios? Didn't Wendy Bishop assert that teacher trainers "*should* consider" (my emphasis) portfolios for TAs specifically? Indeed, in this volume, doesn't Irwin Weiser make a persuasive case for portfolios' serving the needs of **both** students and new teachers? In a word, yes—to all four questions.

As will become clear, however, my argument doesn't oppose portfolios (quite the reverse, actually), and it certainly isn't intended to exclude my new colleagues. On the contrary, it's an argument in favor of both beginning teachers and portfolios; in favor of the kinds of support that will help all three —new teachers of writing, students, and portfolios—succeed. Put simply, those kinds of support are three in number:

- time to develop
- resources to draw upon
- guidance to shape their own portfolio writing classroom.

I will first consider these one at a time, and then connect them to the concept of readiness.

How Much Time Might New Teachers Need?

New teachers of writing, and in particular new TAs, often come to their teaching "underprepared." Some, if those at Purdue University and University of North Carolina, Charlotte are at all typical, have never taken a freshman writing course, so they haven't an experiential model of what to do or of what not to do. Most of them have taken no teacher-preparation courses, nor have they completed related coursework in rhetoric, literacy, or assessment, for instance, that might help them bring a "schooled" theoretical or philosophical background to their early teaching. Many of them have not taught before, so they can't work from classroom experience or from experience with adults or returning students. Some of them will not want to teach writing at all; they won't bring the enthusiasm and commitment we'd like to see in all colleagues.

But here they are, new writing teachers planning to work with our students, needing to learn quite a bit, quite fast, often in a mere four or five days.

Presumably, these new teachers need to learn something about rhetoric, assignment-making, keeping a gradebook and organizing the workload, developing a syllabus, leading a discussion, establishing peer work, practicing evaluation and response, conferencing with students, and oh, yes, something about how to run the cranky ditto machine in the small office around the corner. In short, there's a lot to learning how to teach writing, even without portfolios.

If portfolios are to be *added* to the agenda, will more preparation time be allowed? And will it be enough to prepare the TAs adequately? Several accounts of teachers' development of portfolios—for example those of Sandy Murphy and Mary Ann Smith, Catharine D'Aoust, and Roberta Camp—emphasize that even for experienced teachers, time is crucial: time for preparation so that portfolios work within a curriculum and lead to an assessment that students (and teachers) understand; time for ongoing monitoring while students are creating the portfolios; time for review of both portfolios and classroom instruction when the portfolios are submitted. Building in the time necessary for these processes helps ensure that teachers will bring perspective to their teaching, to the student learning, and to the portfolios. It seems self-evident, therefore, that if experienced teachers need time to plan for portfolios and to review them, so too will new teachers. Simply grafting portfolios onto an unchanged TA preparation program probably won't work: it won't help the TAs be better teachers, and it won't help the students write better. Even with the benefit of a well-prepared practicum, it's not clear that TAs will continue to use portfolios once they are on their own either, if Wendy Bishop's observations are typical (227). The program either has to change or has to be capacious and flexible enough to admit the changes that portfolios bring.

At UNC Charlotte, we do have such a program. *Before* TAs enter the classroom, they take a semester-long, credit- and grade-bearing graduate course in The College Teaching of English. In this course, TAs have the time to read in rhetoric, survey composition texts and journals, plan a syllabus, quarrel with the cranky ditto machine, *and* think about portfolios: why and how they might want to use them and then to plan for them if they choose to use them. In identifying this kind of preparation, I'm not saying that new TAs need a course before teaching just so they can use portfolios, although preparing new teachers through coursework before they enter the classroom has much to recommend it, in and of itself. (I can't help noting that such coursework also has precedent in our preparation for undergraduate teaching majors, whose difference chronologically from their graduate student colleagues is frequently merely a matter of months and whose task is presumably no easier. This, however, is another argument.) What I claim here is that if new TAs are to use portfolios, they ought to be assured that they won't be asked to do this as well as all the other things they already don't have time for, and in the same time frame. Rather, just as with a portfolio writing class, where students are provided with the gift of time to develop, new teachers too should be provided with the gift of time to develop first as teachers, perhaps then as teachers who use portfolios to help students learn.

Are New Teachers Provided With the Resources to Succeed?

This question might sound a little odd. Since students create the portfolios, what resources do new teachers need? If we consider resources from the point of view put forward by John Dixon, then we see them not so much as synonymous with physical implements, like paper and pencil, but as experiences:

- seeing a writer develop over the course of a term, not in a linear fashion from poor to better to best, but recursively, circuitously, from average to poor to great to poor again
- designing an assignment that clearly signals the writers as to the reader's expectations
- reading numerous papers and trying to comment insightfully and helpfully on each one
- seeing which comments motivate which writers and why
- seeing revision in action, sometimes successfully, sometimes not.

In sum, experiences like these help new TAs learn on the job—how to assign writing, how to read it, how to respond to it. Frequently, of course, TAs read sample papers, comment on them, and share those comments with their peers before they teach and during the course of a term, and this is valuable preparation. But as one commercial had it, there's nothing like the real thing, in this case the experience a real teacher has with real students composing real writing, ultimately for an all-too-real grade. For each real paper, the teacher performs multiple roles, as Alan Purves has so carefully explained in his seminal article "The Teacher as Reader: An Anatomy." We don't just read and respond; we act as editors, coaches, critics, graders, sometimes as gatekeepers, and we do this for different kinds of papers as well as for different students. The expectations we have for a piece of expressionistic prose do not replicate those we have for transactional discourse; negotiating and articulating genre specifications, the expectations readers bring to such discourses, and student enactments of them are also part of what the new teacher learns on the job. In other words, by making different kinds of assignments, reading student work, responding to it, and by learning from all these activities, the new teacher acquires the experience that permits her to read variously—to read her students, to read their work, and to read their development.

Portfolios, some will say, don't change these tasks. And that may be true, at least until the semester's end, when the portfolios are read *in toto*. Reading these collections, it's worth suggesting, may not be the same task as reading a single essay: it is, presumably, *another kind of reading*. In commenting on the demands of portfolio reading, for example, Chris Burnham describes its special difficulty, particularly for the teacher seeking to *grade* the portfolios:

> Reading a portfolio honestly requires considerable forgetting. Beginning to read a portfolio with preconceptions about a student's ability and potential can lead to reading only to find evidence to confirm those preconceptions. This violates the purpose of the portfolio. Instructors need to read the portfolios to evaluate the writing in front of them, not to defend evaluations built up through the semester. (134)

In other words, reading a set of works at the term's end is not the same as reading a single work, even when that work appears in multiple drafts. Presumably, these *kinds* of readings—the reading of a single paper and the reading of a set of papers—call for different skills and require different dispositions. I say presumably, because the research that might confirm this supposition has yet to be produced. As Sandra Stotsky observes in the October 1992 issue of *Research in the Teaching of English*, there is an "absence" of research studies on portfolio assessment (246). In the interim, we would do well to honor Burnham's conclusion, remembering that if we plan for our new colleagues to use portfolios in their teaching, we need also to plan for them to learn to *read* portfolios.

Unfortunately, the conditions of teaching compound the problem of portfolio readings. The timing on them for us all, but for first-term TAs particularly, could hardly be worse, at the end of the term when their own papers and exams come due. Is this a reasonable request to make of new teachers, that they try a new kind of reading (about which we aren't too certain ourselves) at this point in the semester? Will they be able to bring to the task the kind of perspective and focus that go into a "good" reading?

Yet another problem with making haste too quickly to bring TAs to portfolios goes to the issue of a baseline, for that's what all new teachers develop through practice. In the case of a writing classroom, it is this baseline, this firsthand knowledge of how writers develop, that helps to account for the confidence with which a teacher can say, "Yes, you do need more and more specific support. Let's try this method of invention; it has worked with other students in the same position as you" or "No, I don't think that's an error; do you have any strategies for proofreading that might help you here?"—in sum, to give the advice and directions on which portfolios are built. Through the resource of experience, teachers are creating their own baseline, one that will allow them to relativize with some confidence the papers they will read the next semester, to see student work developmentally, and thus to assure students that the teacher's advice should be followed. Implicit in this analysis of what new teachers learn and of the complex task of teaching writing, a task whose complexity we sometimes forget, is a compromise position: that new teachers of writing focus in their *first term of teaching* on reading and on responding to various kinds of writing as they teach, but that they *consider* as they do *how their evolving practice might change were they to use portfolios.* Designing teacher preparation for portfolios this way, making haste slowly, takes advantage of a doubled perspective: first, that of the teacher considering what is taking place now; second, that of the teacher considering what would happen if the single but major change of portfolios is put into place. Questions like "How might this assignment be different in a portfolio program?" and "How might you change your grading in a portfolio program?" can offer another perspective to the first-term teaching experience, while at the same time building in the TAs a kind of readiness for portfolios and preparing them, in some cases implicitly, in others quite explicitly, to come to portfolios the next semester in a thoughtful and informed way.

What Kinds of Guidance Might Be Provided to New Teachers of Writing as They Begin to Use Portfolios?

Answers to this question could constitute this entire essay, but there are some basic questions that new teachers—and not so new ones, for that matter—will need to consider before they begin. Taken together, these questions form a heuristic that helps us determine if the conditions for success are in place.

- Nothing happens in isolation. What is the context in which the teacher works? Is there a strong set of departmental guidelines for the freshman writing program? Are departmental goals relevant? What are the points of intersection between the writing program and the department?

- What does the teacher believe to be his or her goals in the classroom? How do these fit with the department's goals?

- How informed are those goals by the current literature? How informed by experience?

- How much opportunity do teachers have to shape their classes? Will they develop their own assignments? Will they decide all/some/any of the portfolio contents? Will they set the portfolio standards? If yes, when?

- Who will work with the TAs? In what capacity? How often?

- What are the stakes in the TAs' use of portfolios? Will the assessment of their teaching hinge on their willingness or ability to use portfolios?

Exploring these questions with the new teacher of writing will help ensure that the TA is vested in both pedagogy and assessment and that he or she appreciates the nature of the undertaking. It will also address a need articulated by Wendy Bishop based on her work with new TAs and portfolios. She suggests that if portfolios are to succeed with these new teachers (as well as with their students), the TAs may need to participate in the process of curricular design, "may need *actively* to adapt materials and methods to their classroom" (Belanoff and Dickson, 225), which, as she comments, not all new teachers are knowledgeable enough or willing to do. As one of her TAs recommends,

> "I don't know. I don't think that the Portfolio thing is a total disaster. It just didn't do anything for me this time around. If I wanted it to work for me[,] I guess I would have to re-structure my entire class plan." (225)

It's not necessary that TAs *restructure,* if they use the first term to plan for the second; then they can *structure.* During the first term, the TA sees the range of writer accomplishment and the kinds of writer development, and the way that development is situated within the context of that department and institution. She or he can consider how portfolios can serve such writers, can be integrated into the classroom, can be assessed. And during this process of planning and structuring, specific kinds of guidance can be provided: a review of the increasing body of the materials available on portfolios; a survey of portfolio models and response mechanisms and rubrics; and collaboration on the development of syllabus, curriculum, and standards consonant with the model chosen or designed. At the conclusion of the first term, then, the TA is ready to introduce and implement portfolios in the next term, and in the process he or she has also learned something about curricular design and student assessment.

Some Concluding Thoughts: Issues Avoided, an Issue Engaged, and the Significance of Readiness

This essay argues that new TAs should not make a hasty approach to portfolios and that if the TAs and the portfolios are to "work," certain kinds of support are required: adequate time for preparation; resources; and guidance. Embedded within this argument are several other issues, however: one I want to avoid (it can't be resolved universally, and I don't think it persuades); one that others have told me to avoid (so I know it doesn't persuade); and two more that are germane and can be resolved. While developing the first two is thus beyond the scope of this essay, they should be mentioned because they—especially, the first—are at the heart of the argument: if, how, and when TAs will use portfolios.

The first issue, perhaps the central if unspoken one, has to do with authority, the tension surrounding it represented in the title we use for the graduate student/teacher: teaching assistant. That designation is one that most of "us" wore, too, in graduate school; we remember its feel, its ability to constrain as well as to empower, its resistance to categorization. How much are these teaching assistants teachers? How much are they assistants? Put directly, how much authority do these teachers of writing exercise in the courses that they teach? Do they design their own courses? Should they? What is appropriate in this context, and why? My assumption in this essay has been that teaching assistants should have some voice in the classes that they teach, that if we want portfolios to work short-term and long-term, after TAs are on their own, we need to work within a portfolio program that allows all its participants, teachers as well as students, some choice, some authority in what happens to them.

A second, more theoretical issue has to do with the nature and reading of portfolios. More than one person has suggested that portfolios are more than the sum of their parts, and thus that reading them requires a kind of expertise; that portfolios rely on an expert system in the sense that the fair reading of them is contingent on the reader's familiarity with student work and with compilations of student work. This makes sense to me, but in exploring this line of reasoning, I've been at odds with several whose judgment I respect, so here I raise it as an issue to be explored and resolved. What goes into the reading of portfolios? And is such a reading different from, the same as, or similar to our other kinds of reading? And (how) is it complicated when the reading is attached to grading?

The third issue can be more easily addressed: the grading mechanism to use if one isn't working with portfolios. To this issue, I am particularly sympathetic, having come to portfolios myself out of a frustration with a grading system that "averages" performance that often isn't averageable at all. As Irwin Weiser explains, portfolios can alleviate this frustration because they help us defer grading until the end of a course or sequence, so that we award a grade that speaks to the quality of the work *at that time*. But if new teachers defer using portfolios, won't they have to resort to the averaging practice just critiqued? No. There are several options available, as a quick conversation with a group of high school English teachers will demonstrate. Let me mention here just one, suggested by Peter Elbow in his keynote address at the New Directions in Portfolio Assessment Conference: a contract. This contract specifies the kinds of behavior required for students to pass the course: class attendance, submission of acceptable work, and so on. This kind of contract operates independently of portfolios, it focuses on writing, and it diminishes the malignant effects of averaging. At the same time, it does something else: it offers new teachers of writing a chance to develop a readiness to use portfolios.

I am borrowing the concept of readiness from the well-known and recently revitalized Head Start Program. Founded during the 1960s, the Head Start Program helps underprepared youngsters develop a "readiness" (ability, preparation) to undertake school learning, chiefly by broadening the experience that enables reading. This concept, the idea of readiness, is one long overlooked, if not universally undervalued. What it presupposes is that human beings can always learn and develop—when they are provided with enough time, appropriate resources, and wise guidance.

Readiness is a concept, I think, that applies in many other situations, including that of the new teacher of writing. If we introduce the idea of portfolios—rather than requiring the practice of them—in the first term, if we allow the new teacher of writing to consider them in the context of that first term—in their implications and their potential—if we allow our new colleague at least some of the freedom and responsibility and authority that we so fiercely cherish ourselves, and if we work with him and her throughout that term, we build a readiness that is critical for success: a readiness to see a disjunction between what might be called traditional grading and portfolio grading, between a grading that is product-based and a pedagogy informed by process and reflection, between a teacher-driven practice and a student-centered one. Seeing these disjunctions speaks to the motivational issue raised by Wendy Bishop; it makes portfolios not just palatable but desirable.

Building readiness also makes sense when we remember the content in which new TAs tend to work. Many if not most of them are new to graduate school as well as new to teaching and find the juggling act we call graduate education a bit breathtaking. Allowing these teachers to be students in their own courses and of their own teaching practice also builds a readiness to take on more when the more assumes a concrete shape, when a student's writing portfolio can be visualized, when the move from a working portfolio to a pre-sentational portfolio can be anticipated and prepared for, when the new teacher can predict and respond to the rhythms of a term.

In sum, if we work to create a readiness in our new colleagues, if we make haste slowly in preparing new teachers to use portfolios, if we assure that the conditions for success are established—that sufficient time, appropriate resources, and collegial guidance are provided—we will be working for the benefit of all: students, teachers, and, I think, teacher preparation programs. In the best case scenario, we may even find that our new teachers of writing ask us not to make haste too slowly, after all.

17

Portfolios and the
New Teacher of Writing

Irwin Weiser

In recent years, writing teachers and writing program administrators have become increasingly interested in the use of portfolios as a means of evaluating student writing. The Miami University conference, along with the recent publication of Belanoff and Dickson's *Portfolios: Process & Product* and Yancey's *Portfolios in the Writing Classroom,* attests to that interest. Much of the initial attention has focused on the use of writing-portfolios for program-wide assessment of student writing, particularly as substitutes for existing or proposed proficiency tests that do not include direct measures of student writing.

My interest in portfolios, however, lies in their use as an extension of process pedagogy. Writing teachers no longer assume that good writers are capable of producing polished work on their first try. We know that writers do not often "get it right" the first time; instead, we teach students strategies for planning, drafting, revising, and editing their work, recognizing that practice of these overlapping parts of the writing process enables students to produce better final papers. Portfolio assessment is a natural extension of our emphasis on process, reflecting that writing can always be made better and that writers can always improve. In particular, portfolio evaluation counters the sense of closure and finality, of separation and fragmentation, that grades on individual papers encourage. Students whose work is constantly being seen in-progress, unfinished, and under revision can make connections between papers and be encouraged to reflect on their progress-and-learning. Also, portfolio systems of evaluation remove the often punitive element that comes from grading work too early in the writing class, before students have begun to benefit from process-based pedagogy and practice. For that reason, portfolio evaluation is not only consistent with current theories about how people write, but is also consistent with what Phelps has recently called the "developmental attitude" towards student texts (53).

Despite the general support for portfolio evaluation, both in its program or course assessment guise and as a pedagogical approach for individual teachers, some contend that new teachers of writing should not be encouraged or required to use them. Elsewhere in this volume, for example, Kathleen Yancey, herself a proponent of portfolio evaluation, suggests that portfolio evaluation is not appropriate for beginning teachers who lack the necessary experience as evaluators of writing to use portfolios. She argues that new teachers need time, resources, and guidance before they can effectively use portfolios in their classes (see Yancey, "Make Haste Slowly" pages 210–18). While I do not disagree with her premises, neither do I agree that they support a case against new teaching assistants using portfolios. In the pages that follow, I wish to show how writing teachers with little or no prior experience in evaluating student writing can use a portfolio approach. I will describe a teacher-preparation program that provides the kind of support for which Yancey calls. In addition, I will point out benefits of portfolio evaluation both to teachers and students, and discuss issues that need to be addressed in teachers' preparation if such an approach is to be effective.

The Context: The Teachers and the Course

Undergraduate writing courses at Purdue are taught almost exclusively by teaching assistants and part-time faculty. All teaching assistants new to Purdue, whether or not they have previous teaching experience, enroll in a year-long practicum in the teaching of composition. Practicum groups are limited to eight teaching assistants. Groups meet in the fall during the week prior to classes and weekly throughout the year. In recent years, we have had four groups, each taught by a faculty member in the rhetoric and composition program, each of whom selects texts and designs the syllabus for his or her group. Thus, while our goals are common, our specific approaches differ. The new teaching assistants I work with are usually first-year master's students in literature, creative writing, linguistics, and American Studies, none of whom have taught before. Although our Developmental Writing Program has used portfolio grading since 1983, I had, until two years ago, resisted incorporating portfolios into the practicum group. Instructors in Developmental Writing all had taught composition in our program for at least year, thus all had experience with evaluating and grading student writing before they began to use portfolios, but the instructors I work with in the practicum have no such experience. However, the success of the portfolio system in the Developmental Writing Program and discussions with Kathleen Yancey, who at that time was at Purdue and teaching one of the practicum groups, persuaded me to begin using portfolios with these new teachers. The contradictions between the process theories driving the course and the summative evaluation of individual papers were too great not to do so.

Portfolio grading has led to several changes in the structure of our course and in the focus of the practicum. Instead of grading at the time of their initial submission each of the six course papers completed by students, instructors now assign a single grade to a portfolio of writing that students submit towards the end of the semester. The portfolio contains five of the formal papers the student has written for the course, including the required written planning assignments, the drafts that have been read and critiqued by classmates, and the initial revision of each paper that has been read and responded to by the instructor. Towards the end of the semester, students meet with their instructor and select three of these papers, which they then extensively revise once more before they submit their portfolios. The portfolio counts for approximately 70 percent of the student's course grade, with the major emphasis of the grade determined on the basis of the three re-revised papers. The remaining 30 percent of the student's grade is based on his or her participation in class, other classwork and shorter assignments, attendance, and a final, longer paper that serves as a culmination of the work done over the semester and, in the first-semester course, a bridge to the focus on academic writing in the second semester.

Several features of this system bear elaboration. While the largest part of the student's portfolio grade is based on the three selected and re-revised papers, all of the papers must be resubmitted in the portfolio. We require that all of the work be resubmitted for two reasons. First, we want to make sure that students do not get the idea that they only need to do half of the papers assigned in the course—that they can skip a paper or two since most of their grade will be based on the papers they revise specifically for the portfolio. They understand that only complete portfolios will be graded, that a portfolio with fewer than five papers is not complete. Second, and more importantly, we want to emphasize that improvement in writing comes from writing frequently and working with that writing. By requiring students to submit all of their work, we hope we are encouraging them to realize that every paper they write contributes to their improvement. We also hope they learn that they will not be equally satisfied with each piece of writing they do. One of our goals is to help them see their own development over the course of the semester, not only as they realize how much better they can make an earlier paper by revising it again, but as they look at the total body of writing they have produced.

A second feature of this system is the emphasis we place on the selection and revision of the main portfolio pieces. Much of the two weeks prior to the submission of the portfolio is devoted to a combination of teacher-student conferences and revision workshops. Students come to conferences having tentatively selected pieces they intend to revise further for their portfolios and to discuss their choices with their instructor. They are expected to be able to talk about why they have selected particular papers for inclusion and how they intend to improve them. The instructors offer suggestions both about selections and revisions. Students spend much class time during these two weeks reading one another's revisions—the latter a practice throughout the semester—

so that writers receive as much advice as possible about their revisions. Our intention is to encourage students to help one another demonstrate the best writing they are capable of doing and to produce portfolios that represent what they have learned during the course. Thus the emphasis remains positive and motivational.

Third, the portfolio grade is the major but not the exclusive grade for the course. It is clear that the major objective of the course is to help students improve their overall writing ability and thus the grade should reflect how well they write at the end of the term. However, one of the assumptions of the course is that writers improve by working with other writers, particularly by reading and discussing work-in-progress; therefore, part of the grade is reserved for what falls under the general umbrella of "participation." This includes regular attendance since much of the class time during the semester is spent in group discussion of one another's writing or in workshop activities. The course grade also includes the grade on a final paper of greater length and complexity than those students had been writing previously. While it would, of course, be possible to include this paper in the portfolio as well, we have chosen not to do so for three reasons. The first is practical. By excluding the final paper from the portfolio, we can ask students to submit portfolios two weeks prior to the end of the semester, and instructors will have an opportunity to read them before they are engaged in finishing papers and preparing for exams in their own courses—we can reduce their work load at what is their busiest time of the semester. The second reason for excluding the final paper from the portfolio is that students would not have time to revise it following their instructor's comments. Finally, the inclusion of the final paper, the longest, most complex writing assignment in the course, would probably lead us also to require that it be considered one of three papers upon which the bulk of the portfolio grade is based, thus undercutting students' responsibility for selecting their best work.

A final point concerning our system is one that distinguishes it from many others that use portfolios: the portfolios are read and graded only by the students' instructor, not by other instructors or a formal evaluation committee. My decision to use portfolios was not intended to remove either the responsibility or the authority for grading from the instructors, whom I believe have the best insight into their course goals and their students' progress. While evaluation by readers other than or in addition to the instructor has value in training teachers to be more effective and consistent graders, and while external evaluation is necessary in programs that use portfolios to determine subsequent placement or as exit criteria, these are not the goals in our program. In fact, over the years, we have recognized that portfolios have as much value in supporting the instructional goals of a process-oriented composition course as they do in addressing the difficulties of grading the work of students in basic writing classes. Portfolios have come to serve primarily an instructional purpose and only secondarily an evaluative one.

The use of portfolios has led to some changes in the practicum, some of which bear directly on the fact that the instructors I work with have neither taught nor graded writing before. In the first place, during our initial meetings prior to the start of the semester, we not only discuss the theoretical and pedagogical approach to our course but also the rationale for using portfolio grading. Although occasionally some of the students in creative writing have had some experience with writing portfolios, for most of these first-year teaching assistants, using portfolios seems like one more complexity added to their new responsibilities. We talk not only about how the portfolio system fits the course pedagogically, but also how it will fit practically—when they should require portfolios to be submitted, how the syllabus is designed to allow time for conferences and for their reading of portfolios prior to the time when they will be immersed in their own end-of-the semester papers and exams. Most importantly, we discuss how they can introduce students to the use of portfolios so that the students' worries about their grades are decreased. I have written a sample statement on grading that I encourage teaching assistants to use or adapt for their course policy statements, one of the central sections of which is entitled "How to Know Where You Stand." In this section, students are encouraged to read their instructor's comments on their work carefully and to talk with their instructor if they have any questions about the comments and suggestions they find. They also learn that they will have midsemester conferences with their instructors at which their progress to that point will be discussed. Finally, students are given the option to request, at any time during the semester, that their instructor give a tentative grade to one of their papers. It is made clear that this grade is not binding—that it will not be recorded in any way and that further revision may affect the instructor's assessment of the paper. We have learned, interestingly enough, that very few students take this option. The offer of a tentative grade seems to relieve most students' anxieties about their performance sufficiently that they do not request it.

Of course, it may also be that another shift in the emphasis of the practicum has contributed to students' comfort with the portfolio system. While, like all such teacher preparation courses, we have always spent quite a bit of our time reading, commenting on, and assessing student writing, we now try to split our focus between summative comments that emphasize what a student has accomplished with a given draft of a paper and formative comments that suggest what he or she might consider doing with the paper to improve it for the portfolio. Both types of comments take on greater importance when students are not going to receive a grade on each paper. In the first place, students have to rely on comments rather than the grade to tell them if they have done well or poorly, and in the second place, students need the comments, which suggest how they can improve their work. Instructors thus have to learn that they can not rely on a grade to clarify any mixed signals they may be sending students in their comments. Their desire to use praise to motivate and encourage students has to be tempered so that they do not inadvertently lead students to believe that their paper is more successful than it really is. Specificity becomes even more important than it usually is, and as we discuss samples of student writing, we talk a lot about how to describe a strength or weakness and how to suggest revisions. And we write and discuss sample comments.

Advantages for Teachers

Perhaps the most significant advantage of a portfolio system from the teacher's perspective is that it allows teachers to separate, at least temporarily, the two frequently conflicting roles assigned us by the institution: evaluator and instructor. Under conventional evaluation systems, the teacher-as-evaluator role is dominant. Teachers and students alike understand that the teacher's job is to read papers, mark errors, comment on strengths and weaknesses, and assign a grade. And it is the grade on each paper that goes into the grade book and is eventually made part of the student's course grade and academic record. The grade becomes all-important in the student's mind, and the teacher is perceived as a grader, more or less benign according to how satisfied the student is with his or her grades. And of course, with grades come disputes over them—students questioning not only why they received a C instead of a B, but also why they received a C instead of a C+. Portfolio systems allow instructors to defer grading and thus defer such disputes. In some systems, those in which the portfolio is evaluated by people other than the class instructor (for an example of one such program, see Belanoff and Elbow), the grader role is entirely removed, but even in programs such as ours in which the class instructor ultimately assigns a grade for the portfolio, the teacher-as-grader role takes a secondary role to that of teacher-as-instructor or writing coach or professional editor trying to help a writer achieve his or her goal. Another benefit of deferred grading is that teachers no longer feel the very real pressure to write comments which justify or explain a grade. Instead, comments on papers can be formative and instructive, offering students advice about specific revisions before the piece is submitted as part of the portfolio and about what the student might wish to concentrate on for the next paper.

A portfolio system also allows teachers to emphasize progress in writing in a way that is more difficult to accomplish in conventionally evaluated courses. When even the first papers in a course are graded, everything the student writes counts towards the summative final grade. This kind of grading is problematic because the written text as an evaluated product can be assessed by a large number of overlapping criteria. Writing is not like math: in math students can get good grades by mastering discrete skills necessary to get the correct answers to easy problems early in the course and can learn additional skills which will enable them to do more complex problems correctly later. The difficult problems are assigned after the students have studied the concepts necessary to solve them. But in writing, all of the complexities of planning and developing and expressing one's ideas are present in every writing task. There are no "easy problems" in writing, especially for inexperienced writers. Writing can go wrong in numerous ways. Teachers feel the frustration of not being able to teach everything before they grade, of wishing that their students knew at the beginning of the course what they will know at the end. They see problems and weaknesses they know will be addressed later in the term and are faced with the decision about whether or not to overlook them at first or to base early grades on different or fewer criteria than they will at the end.

Portfolio systems allow teachers to address this problem by withholding the assigning of grades until the end of the course, and thus they can more easily focus the course on writing as a learnable craft rather than as a talent or a static skill. They need not worry that because they have not addressed a particular concept, students will not be able to write well. The emphasis is on an accumulation of writing abilities, not on those the student brings to the class. Such an emphasis is particularly reassuring to new teachers who are themselves just learning how to read and respond to student writing and whose concerns about being fair to students and providing them with sound advice are greatest early in the semester. They feel less pressure to "be right," to give "correct advice" to students, to "catch everything" in a system that recognizes that improvement in writing takes time and that students can only address a small number of problems in their writing at one time. And they are free from concerns about grading too harshly or generously, about labeling students too soon as strong or weak or average writers. Thus, and I would argue particularly for new teachers, portfolios provide a means to encourage process and progress in writing that grading individual papers does not. Nor do some other means of assigning grades, such as the contract method suggested by Peter Elbow. Contracts emphasize and reward writerly behavior rather than writing and the development of writing ability, since grades are based on the completion of a specified number of assignments or pages within a specified amount of time, with little concern for the quality of the writing, either as initially submitted or revised.

Advantages for Students

For students the major advantage of a portfolio evaluation system is that it allows them to put aside, at least temporarily, the paralyzing effect of grades and concentrate instead on improving their writing. As all writing teachers know, when students receive graded papers, the first thing they do is turn to the last page to see what their grade is. For many students, looking at the grade is *all* they do when a paper is returned to them. If they are satisfied with the grade, they see no particular reason to look at marginal or terminal comments, and if the grade is low, they may find in it confirmation of what they already suspect: they cannot write. The instructor may have written careful, detailed comments, offering specific suggestions for improving the next draft or next paper, but frequently these comments go unread once the students see their grades. Hayes and Daiker have suggested that students frequently misread the comments, even to the point of finding criticism in positive comments if the paper has received a grade with which they are not satisfied. Under a portfolio system, however, students must consider the comments carefully, not only because there is no grade on the paper, but also because the comments provide them with suggestions for improving the paper before it is submitted as part of the portfolio at the end of the course. And because the comments are directed towards improvement, students can read them as advice, not as criticism, as something to prompt further action, not anxiety about a grade.

Indeed, an emphasis on improvement is the second major advantage of a portfolio system. In conventional evaluation schemes, each paper receives a grade and each grade is factored into the final grade the student receives for the course. Though teachers often modify such schemes by allowing students to revise papers for higher grades or by dropping the lowest grade or by weighting the grades of later papers more heavily than earlier ones, these modifications still have the effect of privileging the grade, not the progress or improvement the student has made. The evaluation is summative; that is, the grade and the comments that accompany it serve to summarize the student's performance on a discrete task. With a portfolio system, on the other hand, all comments are formative, functioning as advice and guides to the student for future performance. Comments on each paper not only identify specific strengths and weaknesses of that effort, but also serve to inform the student about how he or she might want to revise that paper and approach later assignments. Of course, many teachers use such comments whenever they evaluate writing, but when the comments are accompanied by a grade, the grade has precedence for the students. They realize that once a paper has been graded, that grade will affect their final course grade, whether they improve on later papers or not. However, when students know that their course grade will be determined primarily by how well they can write at the end of the term, they find both greater incentive to improve and greater reason to consider the comments they have received as advice to help them do so. Such formative assessment thus motivates students to learn to improve their writing and to continue to revise it, underscoring the process orientation of our course.

A third advantage of this portfolio system for students is that they are not penalized for an occasional weak paper. As was pointed out earlier, in the version of the portfolio system used at Purdue, students, in consultation with peers and their instructor, decide which papers will form the core of their portfolios and revise those papers extensively. In other versions of portfolio systems in which all of the student's work for the course is in the portfolio, the work is nevertheless revised before the portfolio is submitted for a grade. In either case, students have the opportunity to revise weak papers before they are assigned grades. The advantage of the selected portfolio over the comprehensive portfolio is that the former approach acknowledges what all professional writers know: not every effort deserves publication. In a writing course in which students are assigned anywhere from six to ten papers, it should not be surprising that some students will find some assignments more difficult than others. Perhaps the topic is not one that the student is prepared to address. Perhaps the student has not attained the skill or knowledge necessary to do well on a particular assignment. Perhaps the assignment assumes a certain kind of experience the student has not had or a developmental maturity the student has not reached. Perhaps, as sometimes happens, the student has done poorly because he or she has tried to do more, has stretched to or beyond his or her limits. If not every paper is to become part of the portfolio and thus part of the grade, such papers can be acknowledged by the teacher and accepted by the student as experiments that failed but, like all failed experiments, from which one learns. Students, in fact, can be encouraged to experiment, free from the fear that an unsuccessful effort will lead to a lower grade. Not only does this ability to take risks benefit motivated students, but it also releases writing apprehensive students from some of their anxiety and encourages them to write without fear of failure. Both stronger and weaker writers are provided risk-free opportunities to attempt more difficult, ambitious writing. Thus, in one more way, portfolio assessment supports the notion that writing is a process involving development, growth, and learning.

Portfolio Evaluation and Teacher Training

My emphasis thus far has been on the benefits to instructors and to students of portfolio evaluation. Clearly, I am convinced that a carefully designed portfolio evaluation system supports and extends contemporary pedagogical theory. One issue I have not yet addressed is how instructors who have no prior experience as graders and who have not been grading papers during the semester can be prepared for the inevitable moment after they have read a student's portfolio when they must assign it a grade. Indeed, it is this very issue which lies at the heart of my disagreement with Kathleen Yancey's argument that new teaching assistants are not ready to use portfolios. For while, as I noted earlier, I agree with most of her premises, I also believe that the approach to portfolios I have outlined here provides for these needs. In particular, and most importantly, portfolios provide new teachers with the time to develop all of the multiple-reader-roles Yancey mentions, including the last two, grader and gatekeeper (Yancey, "Make Haste Slowly" this volume, page 213). And because portfolios allow teachers to defer the last two roles until they have had nearly a semester of experience developing the other roles—of editor, coach, critic—grades, when they must finally be assigned, are based on *more* experience in these crucial roles than occurs when teachers assign grades to writing within the first few weeks of the course and their teaching. While the actual time spent reading and evaluating portfolios is significant, and while it often does come at exactly the time teaching assistants are busiest, the selected portfolio approach outlined in the early pages of this paper offers suggestions for lessening the burden, most notably the submission of portfolios two weeks prior to the end of the semester. In practical terms, this allows the instructors a little over three weeks (the last two weeks of classes and final exam week) to read, evaluate, and grade portfolios, at a time when they are better prepared to make decisions about grades.

We achieve this preparation by beginning, about a third of the way through the semester, to assign grades to the sample papers we work on in the practicum. Our approach is similar to that of any grading session, including those we have been conducting without grades, but we extend it by discussing what grade the paper would receive if we were assigning one. Thus by the time instructors assign grades to the portfolio and to the final paper of the course, they have the same experiences of "calibrating" themselves as graders as they would have had they been grading each paper throughout the semester. A collateral benefit of this approach, however, is that the instructors have gained this experience without exposing themselves or their students to the very real problems new teachers' uncertainty about grades can cause—early grades that are either too low or too high. Because the instructors have the opportunity to practice assigning grades before they actually grade students' work, they are less likely to err in either direction, and students are neither penalized by overly harsh nor misled by overly generous grades early in the semester.

Conclusion

In the two years I have required first semester instructors in my practicum to use portfolio evaluation, I have been pleased to see that both instructors and students have been satisfied with it. As Director of Composition, I am the person students see when they want to appeal their grades, yet in two years, only two students from portfolio sections have come to discuss their grades with me and neither decided to initiate an appeal. Student evaluations about grading fairness in general and the portfolio system specifically have been positive. And while not all of the instructors have continued to use portfolio evaluation, most have. My experience, then, has been that new teachers of writing can indeed successfully incorporate portfolio evaluation into their teaching, and both they and the students they teach can reap from it its widely accepted benefits. While incorporating portfolios into the preparation program for new teaching assistants does, as Yancey points out and I have described, require modifications to that program, these have not been difficult to incorporate, nor have teachers found portfolios cumbersome or excessively time-consuming. In urging us to "make haste slowly," Yancey emphasizes that portfolios cannot simply be "graft[ed] . . . onto an unchanged TA preparation program" (Yancey, "Make Haste Slowly," this volume, page 212), and here we agree. But an implication of making haste as slowly as Yancey suggests is that new teaching assistants and their students are better served if teachers assign grades to individual papers. Our experience, both at Purdue and as reported by others whose work appears in this volume and those I cited earlier, suggests otherwise.

Part Three:
Large-Scale Portfolio
Assessment

Issues in Portfolio Scoring

18

Writing Like a Woman and Being Rewarded for It: Gender, Assessment, and Reflective Letters from Miami University's Student Portfolios

Laurel Black
Donald A. Daiker
Jeffrey Sommers
Gail Stygall

In 1990, Miami University began to place students into first year composition classes on the basis of a portfolio of writing completed in high school. We believed that writing portfolios which consisted of multiple samples of student work composed over an extended period of time with ample opportunity for revision and reflection address the concerns that a number of researchers have raised about the validity of traditional, single sitting, single sample essay exams (Charney; Huot, "Reliability, Validity, and Holistic Scoring"; White, "Teaching and Assessing Writing"; White and Thomas). Portfolios reflect, too, a growing realization of the teacher/evaluator's need to have a sense not merely of the student's writing, conceived of as a set of discrete, definable and reified skills, but a sense of the student *as* a writer—a more holistic, complex view of writers, readers, and writing.

Despite our assumption that portfolio assessment is inherently more fair than essay exams, the program at Miami has shown a pattern over the last three years that indicates it is particularly attractive to female students. Further, until 1992, women were significantly more successful than men in receiving advanced placement and credit through the program. We've begun to explore these differences, focusing first on the reflective letters with which students introduced themselves and their portfolio to readers.

Issues of gender difference and notions of "good writing" intersect in the field and act of assessment. Those who teach writing are as much concerned with the writer as they are with the writing. When we describe good writing, for example, we share terminology with psychologists; we talk about maturity and development. As Peter Elbow has pointed out, we "embody" the writing, speaking of its voice, how it "touches" us (unpublished ms.). The substance of the writing becomes inseparable from the substance of the writer.

The issues of identity and language are important in writing assessment. Recent feminist examinations of the work of William Perry and Lawrence Kohlberg have criticized findings that considered women to be less complex than men in their moral development (Gilligan; Belenky, Clinchy, Goldberger, Tarule; Lyons). Central to many of these critiques is the work of Nancy Chodorow, who explored the mother-child relationship. Chodorow argued that because of our culture's childrearing practices, daughters remain much more closely bonded to the primary caregiver—the mother—and so develop a sense of identity that is focused on connectedness. Males, on the other hand, are forced to differentiate themselves from the person who usually most represents nurturing and connectedness, and so develop an identity that stresses independence and autonomy.

Carol Gilligan shifted the discussion from identity to language. Applying Chodorow's theories of identity to current ideas about the relationship between language structures and belief systems, Gilligan examined the language used by males and females to describe the relationship between themselves and others. She identifies two "voices": the male voice, which focuses on individual achievement, independence, and autonomy, and is centered in an ethic of rights; and the female voice, which focuses on connectedness and attachment to others, and is centered in an ethic of care.

With its more complex view of cognitive development and its resistance to norming one population against another, such research reflects recent changes in the fields of composition and assessment. Increasingly, researchers in composition are examining the writing of college students within the context of gender difference. For example, Jo Keroes' central premise is that "If . . . men and women perceive and respond to the world in identifiably different ways, . . . then the themes that characterize their distinctive ways of viewing the world should be evident in the way they write about certain personal issues" (245). Keroes examined two hundred essays written by students, one hundred each for two prompts. The first prompt was designed to elicit "autonomous" responses, the second to allow for a more "connected" response. What Keroes discovered was that, overall, a greater number of autonomous than connected responses occurred for both topics, but women accounted for the majority of the connected responses.

Elizabeth Flynn, also working from Gilligan and Chodorow and informed by the work of Belenky, Clinchy, Goldberger, and Tarule, examined narrative descriptions of learning experiences written by traditional age college freshmen. She writes: "The narratives of the female students are stories of interaction, of connection, or of frustrated connection. The narratives of the male students are stories of achievement, of separation, or of frustrated achievement" (428). Geoffrey Sirc finds similar differences in his study of narrative descriptive essays, calling the writing of male students "apocalyptic," "epic," and "lurid." In contrast, he describes the writing of women as "banal/anticlimactic." Sirc asserts that "the textual results of gender show its mechanisms to be a primary, systematic determinant in the student writing observed" and argues that these writing patterns reinforce predictable and harmful cultural patterns: self-aggrandizement in men, self-abasement in women. As a possible way of disrupting this "stunted cultural replication," he calls for reflection. And yet, as our examination of the reflective letters from Miami's portfolios seems to indicate, many of the patterns noted by researchers are as evident in student writers' reflections as in their narratives.

The issue of "writing like a woman" is an important one for these portfolios. Feminists argue that for a variety of cultural and social reasons, the characteristics and structure of "strong" writing have reflected culturally constructed characteristics of masculinity. Strong writing is concise and moves linearly toward "achieving" closure. It is driven by a demand for thesis and evidence, for proof rather than exploration; it positions reader and writer in an adversarial relationship and moves from the particular to the universal. Weak writing is, of course, the polar opposite, and is identified by characteristics culturally ascribed to women: recursive and expansive, imbedded in particulars, driven by exploration rather than proof, tentative, not controlling. Where feminist literature intersects with composition studies, the disadvantage of "writing like a woman" is often asserted. Yet in Miami's portfolio program, we seem to see perhaps the opposite.

The overall pass rate for women ("passing" meaning that a student received either three or six credits and advanced placement) was strikingly higher than for men in both 1990 and 1991. (See Figure 18–1.) Not only that, it increased for women from 1990 to 1991, while it dropped overall for men. By the end of the third year, however, the pass rate for women had dropped slightly, and the pass rate for men had risen dramatically.

By the end of the second year, it seemed imperative to explore these differences, beginning with the reflective letters. The instructions of the reflective letter for 1991 gave students a number of options.

> This letter, addressed to Miami University writing teachers, introduces the student and the portfolio. It may describe the process used in creating any one portfolio piece, discuss important choices in creating the portfolio, explain

Figure 18–1

Pass Rate and Participation of Students by Gender
in Miami University's Writing Portfolio Program

	Males	**Females**
Number students, 1990	102	175
Overall Pass Rate, 1990	37.4%	48.5%
3 Credits—1990	25.7%	26.9%
6 Credits—1990	11.7%	21.6%
Number students, 1991	116	253
Percent increase	13.7%	44.5%
Overall Pass Rate, 1991	33.5%	49.6%
3 Credits—1991	20.7%	36.8%
6 Credits—1992	12.8%	12.8%
Number students, 1992	154	311
Percent increase	9.5%	8.1%
Overall Pass Rate—1992	47.3%	44.3%
3 Credits—1992	35.7%	33.7%
6 Credits—1992	11.6%	10.6%

the place of writing in the student's life, or use a combination of these approaches. The letter should provide readers with a clearer understanding of the student as writer.

As the initial piece in the portfolio, the reflective letter provides us with our first impression of the writer, answering unspoken questions and raising others. What should we know about the writer and the portfolio pieces she has selected? How is writing important (or is it?) to this student, and what kinds of writing has s/he done? How have we been positioned, and how does the student position herself? Most importantly, is this person a "writer"? How will we know? What counts for evidence of that?

We selected a total of fifty-eight portfolios (approximately 15 percent of the 369 portfolios received)—twenty-nine each from males and females—representing the full range of possible scores. Portfolios had been scored using a three point scale: a 0 from a reader meant that the student should receive no credit and be placed into the standard composition sequence, a 3 meant the writer should receive three credits and be placed into an accelerated class, a 6 meant the student should receive six credits and exemption from the first-year writing sequence. (In years one and three, we used a 6-point scale, with 1 being low and 6 being high. The 6-point scale gave us greater flexibility in determining credit and placement, while it reduced the number of discrepant readings. The return to a 6-point scale also reflected the discomfort many readers had with the three point scale.) We read through the letters from these portfolios, looking for recurring strategies and topics. What finally resulted was a long list of categories, including a catch-all one entitled "other." In creating categories, we tried to describe the action or strategy or statement and to avoid the kind of adjectival categories that were problematic in other researchers' work. For example, Sirc describes the topics selected by female writers as "banal/anticlimactic." Both of these terms have negative connotations and rely heavily on the reader's perceptions. Still, while some of our categories, such as "commenting on the high quality of their English program of class" seem relatively unproblematic, others were more difficult to determine. When a student states that writing forces the author to "interpret what he/she knows," is that equivalent to "organizing thoughts"? Or is it more properly placed in the category of "using writing to understand and learn," or in "reflection"? Problems of categorization aside, there were a number of differences between the reflective letters written by males and those written by females (see Figure 18–2).

These differences are largely consistent with the findings of Gilligan, Lyons, Flynn, and Sirc. Female writers position themselves in relationship to others in these letters. They mention family and friends, collaboration, and team work. They write of learning to be dependent, of "yearning to serve" after getting to know an elderly, lonely woman. They write letters to friends, pass notes in school ("ceaselessly" one woman writes, even though it's "illegal"), and offer characterizations of themselves in the context of their ability to form relationships with others. One writes that her "most endearing fault is repetitious storytelling." Another characterizes herself as shy, and writes: "I have faced the fact that I will never be a blooming socialite who influences every person with calculated chatter. I have never had any desire to talk to people, but I will always have something to say."

Women use writing to care for themselves and others. Writing is a form of therapy for them (and for men, too, but to a much lesser extent, based on these letters), an outlet for frustration. One woman writes:

> There are some things I write that I don't show to anyone. I purge myself onto paper. I could be found many times in my room crying, writing about the horrible day I had.

Another explains her need to write this way:

> Most importantly, writing allows me to sort out my thoughts, express my feelings, and vent my frustrations. You see, I have kept a diary since I was thirteen years old, and I do not think that I have ever realized how much I *need* to write in that little pink book. Writing has become a therapeutic habit for me.

In caring for others through their writing, women write out what they have to say and share it with someone who has hurt them or angered them, believing that their words will be more accurate, careful, less harmful.

Figure 18–2
Gender Differences in Reflective Letters

Men are more likely to:	Women are more likely to:
Refer to the quality of their English class or program.	Refer to the difficulty they have experienced in writing.
State they are coming to or have been accepted to Miami.	Refer to Miami's evaluation of their portfolio.
Refer to their portfolios as a way for readers to know the student as a writer.	Express a lack of confidence in their writing ability.
*State that the writing in the portfolio is representative of their usual quality and/or style.	Make references to family and friends.
	Refer to years or a history of writing.
Refer to the ease they experience in writing.	Refer to writing done outside of school, especially *notes, *letters, and poetry.
State they are looking forward to being at Miami or taking English at Miami.	Mention they have experienced growth in writing skills.
Discuss the difficulty of selecting pieces for their portfolio.	*Refer to collaboration, group work, or team work.
Mention writing editorials, argumentative pieces, or using writing to state opinions.	Assert that writing plays an important role in their life.
Positively self-evaluate their writing.	Refer to awards, contests, and publications.
Say they use writing to generally "communicate."	Discuss the way they use writing, especially as emotional release or therapy, *for archival purposes, organizing and expressing thoughts and emotions, for reflection, and to improve their writing in other contexts, particularly school.
Characterize writing as good when it comes from strong emotions.	
Evaluate the authors/texts or topics they choose.	Stress the importance of reading to their lives or to writing.
Refer to themselves as writers.	*Mention the risk of others reading their writing, or a fear of readers.

Figure 18–2
Continued

Men are more likely to:	Women are more likely to:
State the writing included meets Miami's requirements.	Offer a characterization of themselves (such as shy, curious, or sentimental).
*State that most/all the writing they do is school-sponsored.	Negatively evaluate their writing.
Give a detailed description of their writing process.	State what their favorite kind of writing is.
Praise Miami's portfolio program.	Refer to emotions and emotional experiences.
	*Say they visualize their writing as part of the composing process.

*The other gender has no entries in this category.

> If I get angry with someone I write that person a note telling her exactly how
> I feel . . . Writing it all down gives them the chance to read it, crumble it up,
> think about it, straighten it out, read it again, and respond accordingly.

Women also use writing to share joy or happiness with others. One writes that
she puts on paper whatever it is that makes her happy and shares it with her
peers, family, and friends.

With so much that is personal invested in their writing, women also
express a fear of criticism. One writer eloquently describes her vision of the
relationship between reader and writer.

> You have asked me to compile this portfolio . . . I realize that in doing that,
> you have also asked me to share a part of my life with you. Every piece of
> writing allows you a glimpse into myself and my life through my style, my
> language, and the subjects I have written on. Allowing you or anyone else
> this glimpse can be a risk because it invites someone to judge me or a part of
> me . . . If I am ever given the chance to look into someone else's life through
> their writing I'll understand the risk they've taken and the trust they've
> placed in me.

Because for many of these women the relationship between the writing and the
self is extraordinarily close, the relationship between reader and writer becomes one of trust. They write confidently, even passionately, about their
private writing. They are less confident and more concerned, however, about
the public airing and evaluation of their work. They ask for a compassionate,
responsible reader.

A look at the list of what male writers are more likely to do in these
reflective letters shows a very different orientation toward the reader. Males

generally posit a public relationship with the scorers, not the private one constructed by the women. Their emphasis remains on the portfolio itself and on institutional contexts.

> As a graduate of Parkway Central High School, I feel the writing experiences and English courses that I have been exposed to have been very beneficial. Parkway Central, a national recognition school, has taken pride in their exceptional English Department.

Men praise the Writing Portfolio Program because it offers them a chance to "showcase" their work and gives them a use for their writing.

> The Miami University Writing Portfolio Program is a tremendously innovative and beneficial concept. It is unique in that credit hours can be earned by the satisfactory submission of a portfolio of the student's writing efforts. This, in the long run, will free the students and teachers from an unneeded burden.

Within the guidelines of the portfolio—indeed, within school sponsored writing generally—they are confident of their abilities.

> I am a multifaceted writer. I hope you can see that in my selections. I consider myself to be diverse in what I write. I chose these selections to send to show my diversity . . . My editorial about gang violence should show that I can be fairly intimidating in my writing.

Men position themselves as separate, connected not to other people but to a disembodied institution and a set of guidelines. It is not their selves being evaluated, as so many women seem to feel, but their writing, an object they evaluate positively and then present—rather than reveal—to the reader.

Because discussions of gender difference often tend to become essentialist, it is important to remember that there were very few categories that had entries from only one gender. It's highly likely that examining all the portfolios would not produce a single gender-exclusive category. Further, while what prompted this study was the fact that more women than men were receiving credit, they weren't receiving credit because of their sex but because of the cultural artifact that is a portfolio and our culturally inscribed ways of assessing that artifact. We don't say, this is how men write or how women write; we say, this is how these predominantly white, middle- to upper-class seventeen- to nineteen-year-old students constructed their portfolios and how a predominantly white, female, middle-aged, middle-class group of readers evaluated them. We can make it more complex. What kinds of books had these students read? What television shows? What was their curriculum? What kinds of writing do they value? All of those issues are important but beyond the scope of this study.

Because these portfolios were created for an evaluative situation, it was important to connect gendered differences in writing to assessment, something too rarely done in such studies. And so, looking at the strategies that were successful in both male and female portfolios, two appeared to be particularly significant in the context of our program: referring to the self as a writer and referring to out-of-school writing.

Let's return to what Miami asked students to do in their reflective letters. Whichever of the many options the student chose, "the letter should provide the readers with a clearer understanding of the student as a writer." We did not ask for a clearer understanding of the student's writing skills. We asked students to show us how they play a role, how they adopt and fit themselves into a persona. What does it mean "to be" a writer? When we say someone is a lawyer, perhaps we mean that at a minimum, she or he has followed a somewhat rigidly prescribed course of study and passed the bar exam. We can go on to qualify or evaluate this (particularly problematic is the issue of "practice," "doing" as opposed to "being"), but what is fundamental is that the person has met some particular set of characteristics or requirements that, for this culture, defines him or her as "lawyer."

But what characterizes a "writer"? This is more problematic, for there is no real credentialing body. A writer does not necessarily possess a specific set of experiences, nor has s/he successfully completed a prescribed series of courses. Nor is it the simple act of writing, for many people write daily in various ways without considering themselves or being considered "writers." We assert that "being" a writer requires minimally two things: stating that you are a writer and writing frequently either by choice or out of a strong, almost visceral need. This is a simple definition ignoring issues of publication, degrees conferred on graduates of "writing programs," and the like, but it is a beginning which allows us to proceed in our investigation of these letters.

Relatively few students explicitly referred to themselves as writers in these letters, and then more men than women. However, looking closely at the catch-all category of "other," we discovered something important: instances of women *depicting* themselves as writers. Here is how one woman depicted herself as a writer.

> Writing has always been my greatest passion. There was never an item so appealing to me as a new, blank notebook waiting for me to scribble stories in it. Often I have postponed schoolwork in favor of reading or writing, and I owe many sleepless nights to story or poem ideas that demanded to be written down. When an idea gets into my head, I feel a driving need to write it down before it goes into hiding again. My best stories and poems seem to develop at about two in the morning.

Writing for this woman is not just a physical act but an emotional, perhaps even an erotic act. Writing is a passion and a blank book is the object of desire. She writes by choice, postponing school-sponsored writing in order to work on creative writing, postponing even sleep in order to write. She recreates here one of our culture's strongest images of a writer: a person working alone, struck by the muse and driven to write at the possible expense of her health and in defiance of more traditional forms of writing. Another woman creates for us a similar scene:

> My best stuff seems to come late at night. When everyone else is tucked away in their warm, cozy beds, my creative juices begin to flow. Looking at the clock, right now it is 1:48 a.m.

There is an immediacy and power in her construction of this image, with its reference to on-going writing and its use of the present tense. While the image of the writer as solitary and driven has been challenged as composition and literature have embraced collaboration, moved into social construction and deconstruction, and incorporated many voices into one piece, it continues to retain its power. Significantly, too, in addition to depicting themselves as solitary writers, women were also more likely to discuss collaboration in writing.

Letters from successful portfolios—and successful letters—also demonstrate that the writer writes by choice. Women not only asserted much more frequently the importance of writing in their lives but went on to provide evidence of its importance. In all but one of the categories for writing outside of class, such as journals, diaries, letters, notes, poetry, and fiction, women had more entries. Additionally, women were much more likely to specify the ways in which they use writing: seventy-five times to men's total of forty-two. Women created scenes of themselves writing in their journals, writing letters to friends, writing thank-you notes, putting together a collaborative book. Where men asserted that they wrote out of class, with the exception of those who called themselves "creative writers," they did not go on to provide the same kind of evidence as the women did.

Edward White discusses the two conflicting functions of the writing teacher: to socialize and to individualize. He points out that in American schools, while we prize creative ideas and reward originality, we are not so excited by creative spelling or punctuation. As Daiker, Sommers, and Stygall (forthcoming) point out, the contents of a portfolio reflect the direction toward which the institution leans, either toward socialization or toward individuation. Although it is possible to submit to Miami's program (and many students have) a portfolio whose contents are highly conventional, the guidelines discourage "how-to" writing and traditional research papers, and encourage personal writing, exploration, and choice. In this way, the program leans toward individuation.

This emphasis on individuation, in conjunction with what Chodorow and Gilligan see as the male model of development and the male voice—autonomous, independent, individualized—would seem at first to draw readers from Miami's English program to the writing more typical of men. But Miami is strongly committed to process writing. Elizabeth Flynn points out how often the descriptions of process writing seem feminized: an emphasis not on the final product but on the process of creation, the recursive nature of writing, and the collaboration that is part of most process classrooms, allowing many voices into the final paper. And this emphasis on process writing appears in the scoring guide used in training readers. The following description guided readers in their judgment of a "6" or excellent portfolio:

> A "6" portfolio is a very good to excellent one. It is characteristically substantial in content (both in length and development) and mature in style. The writer demonstrates a sure control of language. Voice is usually strong, and there is a clear sense of audience and context. Often, there will be a close connection between the writer's sense of self and the writing and/or a thematic unity within the four separate pieces. A "6" portfolio typically takes risks that work—either in content or style—and challenges the reader by trying something different.

Miami's description of an excellent portfolio includes not just the product but the writer; the portfolio itself is not merely a static collection of pieces to be evaluated but an actor "taking risks" and "challenging the reader." The process of writing is explicitly merged with the process of reading.

If the readers' notions of good writing include not just the product but the ways in which the writing comes to be, then women's descriptions of writing in journals, of collaborating with one another, of discussing books with a parent, or of comparing the process of writing their own poetry with the poetry they read in class, all provide something important to the reader. Male writers, who are more likely to simply present the product to the reader, may leave a process-oriented reader looking for more. In yet another way, our institutional notions of good writing advantage women. Key phrases in the description of an excellent portfolio stress the writer's voice and sense of connection to the pieces submitted. The reflective letters written by women were more likely to make that connection, to see evaluation of writing as equivalent to an evaluation of the self, to blend the product with the producer. They were more likely to offer characterizations of that self than were men, who offered instead characterizations of their writing or their institutions.

Women writers also took what could be perceived of as "risks." A preliminary look through the rest of the portfolios indicates that while men were more likely to submit editorials, persuasive pieces, or research papers in fulfillment of the explanatory essay requirement, women were more likely to submit a narrative piece: for example, a story about a friendship that has lasted for years as an explanation of the concept of "friendship." This kind of response presents information in ways that are less familiar, less "academic" to us within the genre of explanation. Men were also more likely to use classroom heuristics or traditional structural approaches to textual analysis, for example, looking at the character of Beowulf in the context of a received set of characteristics of an epic hero. Women, on the other hand, frequently wrote very personal responses to texts, or looked at the roles characters played in a larger, social context, for example, exploring the way in which Hester Prynne was forced by the community to sin. These are ways of taking risks that might advantage women writers.

Finally, more women than men indicate in their reflective letters that they keep journals and diaries. These forms of private writing usually involve reflection. Thus the reflective letter, the one piece of writing that must be specifically written for the portfolio—not just drawn from class assignments—is of a genre that is more familiar to women. It is writing in these journals, an activity about which women feel passionately, that provides the heart of many reflective letters. Women state in their letters much more often than men that they use private writing to improve their school writing and writing in other forms. In some ways, then, they have been practicing for the demands of a portfolio, blurring some traditional boundaries. The journals and diaries they keep have provided them with both content and practice in writing that appears important to the success of their portfolios. Portfolios provide a site where "writing like a woman," in its active sense as well as its descriptive sense, is rewarded.

But these rewards may be short-lived. Over a three-year period, while the pass rate for women has dropped slightly, it has risen dramatically for male writers. In 1992, men had a slightly higher pass rate than did women. We've not yet had a chance to examine what's occurring in the most recent portfolios, but we have one hypothesis for the shift. Miami's approach to first year composition has, until recently, been grounded in the expressivist school, with students looking within themselves for the content of their essays and finding answers from that inner search. Under the guidance of a new Director of College Composition, the suggested standard syllabus has shifted to one grounded in social constructionism, examining how, through language and other symbolic systems, we are culturally inscribed. The focus has shifted from a private voice that has served women well in the program to a public voice, from the personal to the academic. This instructional shift was indicated by the negotiation that occurred in the most recent calibration session, where new definitions of "developed" and "substantial" were being debated, where issues of position, location, and discourse communities grew out of discussion of what is meant by "audience" and "sense of self."

Such a shift will certainly change the ways in which readers receive the "voices" of the writers who participate in the Portfolio Program. While the data from 1992 in Figure 18–1 seem to indicate we may have achieved something close to equity in our program, we are nonetheless suspicious, given our research on reading portfolios (see chapter 19, this volume). What is needed to provide a more complex picture is a multi-year study which examines features of writing in relationship to gender, the scoring rubric, calibration discussion, curriculum change, and patterns of scoring.

Large scale holistic assessment, with its discussion of scoring guides and sample papers or portfolios, has made painfully clear the subjective and cultural basis of notions of "good" and "bad," "right" and "wrong," "successful" and "unsuccessful." When we talk about evaluation, then, we are talking not only about writers and writing but also about readers who bring their own cultural and gender constructs to their evaluation and understanding of student texts. What any institution strives for is a system of evaluation that is fair, sensitive to both the strengths and weaknesses of students' abilities, and staffed by evaluators who understand the political and pedagogical implications of their definitions of "strengths" and "weaknesses." This paper serves as a reminder that as we begin to explore the ways in which the form of assessment evokes different responses among different genders—and races, and classes, and ages—we must also understand ways in which such responses advantage or disadvantage one group against another.

19

Gendered Textuality: Assigning Gender to Portfolios

Gail Stygall
Laurel Black
Donald A. Daiker
Jeffrey Sommers

When we first proposed Miami's Portfolio Assessment project to the Fund for the Improvement for Post-Secondary Education in 1990, one of our hopes focused on the idea of assessment equity—assessment that would allow *all* students the greatest range and opportunity for the best possible performance in writing. Gender especially has been a site for exploration from the outset of the project. Women students had, traditionally, fared less well on standardized tests. Miami University's own exemption testing program seemed to put women at some disadvantage, although it was unclear whether the disadvantage was due to the form of or to the topics on the impromptu exam. Using portfolios as the means of measuring exemption credit for first-year composition, we hoped that the opportunity to choose one's own topic and timing would remove any disadvantage women students had been experiencing. We did find changes that suggested women were faring better with portfolios. Male and female students were now passing the exemption exam in nearly equal numbers, and there were now more women students submitting portfolios for exemption credit than had taken the impromptu exam in the past. But were women students really faring better?

This paper is a cautionary tale, warning of the dangers of using assessment to correct social wrongs in education, in this case, portfolio assessment, rather than seeking remedies in the social context from which and through which inequities arise. This paper is also a preliminary exploration of how gender is assigned to a reading of portfolios. We use the term gender rather than biological sex because, as feminists, we believe that gender is a socially imposed category. But we also want to suggest, as Judith Butler does, that gender is not just a binary category, reliably assigned to sexed bodies. Similar to Butler's theoretical analysis, we want to point to the performing of gender, rather than being gendered-performed, enacted, and inscribed by the writers submitting portfolios and reenacted and reinscribed by the raters. Thus, this paper also explores how gender can prove to be a problem for feminist empirical research in writing and composing. Our simple assertions that gender is a two-valued system may not fairly represent the written constructions of gender that we read.

The sense of our experience—that women students fared less well in academic rhetoric—was widely reported in the discussions within the field. In 1979, for example, Thomas Farrell asserted that academic writing is generally male. In the 1980s French feminists declared that academic writing is fundamentally male in nature at the same time they tried to subvert and undermine it. Similarly, feminist empirical researchers located women's problems in academic reading and writing in gender differences, resulting in studies such as Elizabeth Flynn's "Composing as a Woman," Linda Barnes's "Gender Bias in Teachers' Written Comments," or recently Donald Rubin and Kathryn Greene's "Gender-Typical Style in Written Language." Women's whole approach to writing—to speaking, *to language*—was less highly valued than that of men.

In the first year of our FIPSE-sponsored program we were delighted to find that women submitted portfolios at a substantially higher rate than sitting for the exemption exam, from well below 50 percent in the exemption exam to well over 50 percent in the first year of the portfolio project, climbing to 66 percent by the third year of the project. In examining the transcripts of the calibration sessions in the first and second years of the project, however, for both the impromptu proficiency exam and the portfolio session, it was clear to us that gender was somehow still being assigned to the exams and portfolios read. As raters discussed the various anchor papers, they gave the student writer a gender, using gender-specific pronouns, occasionally saying, "well, he writes about . . . I think this is a he . . ." What, we wondered, was contributing to this understanding of gender and writing? And what did it mean? Though the second year of the project did not yield the phenomenal gains for women students submitting portfolios as the first year did, women students, nonetheless, continued to submit portfolios at a higher rate than they had chosen to sit for the exemption exam.

We conclude from our exploratory results here that actual assignment of gender to student writing is usually stable and conventional, and that reader/raters are influenced by stereotypical gender features in student texts. But the complexities and particulars of the assessment context allow for several other kinds of performances of gender in which social gender and biological sex are matched and unmatched, from the female writer who performs gender as a stereotypical male with hard, objective argumentation, to the male writer who, perhaps knowing Miami University's English faculty preference for a self-disclosing, expressive writer, performs conventional female gender. After discussing the specific results, we will examine two texts in which the raters were consistently unable to identify the writer's sex. In the third section, we will make a number of observations about the ratings and suggest that portfolios are only more equitable if and insofar as the specific local context is equitable. Although portfolios do provide all students, male and female, with an extended opportunity to make a case for the best possible assessment, they cannot override the notions of gender embedded in global or local institutional contexts. Performing gender, by both writers and raters, continuously shifts the possible ground for redistributing educational opportunity.

Rating Writers' Gender

Finding it unlikely that the text itself firmly and irrevocably announced either the sexed body or the social gender of the writer, we turned to the readers as the source of that gender assignment. Working from the same sample of scored portfolios from the second year's submissions used by Black, Daiker, Sommers, and Stygall (see Chapter 18), a group of trained raters at the University of Washington read and assigned gender to the writers. Because the first two parts of the original portfolios—the cover letter in which students were asked to give a description of themselves as writers and the narrative/descriptive piece —seemed likely to provide more obvious clues to gender, these raters read only the explanatory and text-analysis pieces of the portfolio sample. Raters had originally been trained and calibrated on portfolios in the course they were taking on composition theory. Most of these raters were fifth-year, undergraduate, English education majors or returning teachers in the Master of Arts in Teaching (MAT) program. Asked to read quickly for the gender assignment, the raters were then asked to reread the two pieces for cues as to the most prominent reasons for their assignment. All sets of papers were read at least twice, but over the same period of time, more sets by female writers were given three or more readings. This suggests that raters could assign and account for female gender more easily than male if speed of reading and response is a factor.

Figure 19–1 presents the overall results of the rating. The accuracy of gender assignment for the entire group was just under 70 percent, higher when split out for the gender of each writer. When the writer was female, raters were accurate 72.6 percent of the time; when the writer was male, the raters were correct 73.3 percent of the time. We can assume that this is well above the chance level of probability, given that sex, in standard statistical analysis, is a two-valued system, yielding an equal probability that either gender would be accurate. Raters were slightly more accurate when rating writers matching their own gender.

And what was it that made the raters assign gender in these ways? Figure 19–2 lists the ranked reasons, by frequency, given by the raters for their gender assignment. *Topic* was overwhelmingly the primary reason given by

Figure 19–1
Overall Rating By Gender

Female Writers

	RATERS' CORRECT ASSIGNMENT OF SEX			RATERS' INCORRECT ASSIGNMENT OF SEX	
	FR	MR		FR	MR
	48	5		15	5
Total	53		Total	20	
	72.5%			27.4%	

Male Writers

	FR	MR		FR	MR
	28	16		13	3
Total	44		Total	16	
	73.3%			26.6%	

FR=Female Rater
MR=Male Rater

raters for assignment of gender. Women students, the raters felt, were far more likely to write about relationships, interconnectedness, and the so-called arts of living—dance, friendship, cuisine. Male gender was assigned at the first mention of sports, even if the writer gave other indications of female gender. More ominously for English teachers was the consistent assignment of gender based on the author or character foregrounded in the portfolio's text-analysis assignment. If the author was female or the character analyzed female, gender was assigned by the raters as female. This was in fact not always the case. One male wrote about Jane Eyre, but the assignment was consistent. Likewise, male authors such as J. D. Salinger and Kurt Vonnegut were assumed to be discussed by male student writers. Though we, too, believe that *Catcher in the Rye* is definitively a male-oriented coming-of-age novel, we knew that students were often simply reproducing the high-school curriculum with which they had been presented and there are few female coming-of-age novels to be found in any standard curriculum. Many of the raters were aware of this as well but found it an irresistible match, apparently feeling that if a student liked Caulfield well enough to write a text analysis about his character in the novel, the writer must be male. Similarly, anything that had to do with direct action or aggression was assigned to the males—politics, war, electroshock therapy, gangs, violence in general.

The second most frequent category on which gender assignment was based was the author's stance toward the topic. Women writers were thought to be emotional, sentimental, connected to other people and to larger communities,

Figure 19–2
Ranked Reasons for Gender Identification

Female Writers	**Male Writers**
1. TOPIC	1. TOPIC
love relationships	baseball
connectedness	sports
process	cartoons
dance	heroes
cliques	electroshock therapy
social relationships	war
female characters	politics
female authors	gangs
weight	violence
babysitting	male authors
cheerleading	male characters
2. STANCE TOWARD TOPIC	2. STANCE TOWARD TOPIC
emotional	individualistic
sentimental	unemotional
connected	analytical
belonging	detached
nonlogical	logical
3. EXEMPLIFICATION	3. EXEMPLIFICATION
constrained within female	minimal
experience	distanced
maximal within experience	
4. WORD CHOICE	4. PRONOUN USE
adverbs	exclusive use of masculine pronouns
feeling words	generic "man"
"frisky"	
5. PRONOUN USE	
inclusive pronoun use	
exclusive use of feminine pronouns	

and nonlogical, associative in their reasoning. Men, on the other hand, were assumed to promote individualistic values, were detached and uninvolved with their topics, cool and analytical, logical and reasonable. Males, if perceived to indicate bonding at all, were "wolfpacking" in several raters' estimation. This aspect for gender assignment is probably the one most closely associated with the difference Jo Keroes attempted to isolate in her study of gender in writing proficiency exams at San Francisco State University.

Keroes, applying Carol Gilligan's assertions about female connectedness and male autonomy, found women writers to be more likely to produce essays evidencing connectedness, but not at the rate she anticipated (255). Keroes concludes that the college setting and the culturally relevant moment of separation from family makes women's production of autonomy themes more likely (256). Similar observations could be made of Miami's students. However, because these essays from the portfolios were written before students left home for Miami University, women's production of autonomy themes may be less relevant.

Exemplification was closely related to the connectedness-autonomy axis and constitutes the third category. While women writers seemed to be constrained by subject areas of this culture's stereotypical female experience, when writing about that experience, they were maximally detailed. Knowledge of details about high-school dances, readying oneself for a date, selecting clothing, details of thorough cleaning and even the subtleties of color symbolism in novels were all thought to be direct indications of female gender. Males were more distant and less-detailed as indicated in stance, and this distance resulted in minimal exemplification and little drawn from personal experience, except in the case of sports.

Word choice appeared as a fourth category for women and not at all for men. For the raters there were no words assigned just to males, but there were many words found to be female-specific. A number of raters declared that writers who used adjectives and adverbs extensively were more likely to be female. Others found specific words as clear indicators of gender. One rater said "No male student I ever had ever called a poem 'endearing'." We might add that she was wrong in this particular case. But other words were nominated as gender indicators as well—frisky, outfit, fabulous, calling high-school-aged males "boys" rather than "guys." Most interesting, though, is the fact that there is no such corresponding category for the papers assigned male gender. This is what linguists call markedness. Typically, the most common linguistic feature is unmarked, "author," for example, as opposed to "authoress." The latter is marked, requiring a suffix to declare the writer's female gender. As Dale Spender has long asserted, women are always the marked case. Likewise, then, the vocabulary male-perceived writers used is unmarked; any male-associated vocabulary is entirely unremarked, while females are thought to be "marked" by particular usages.

The fifth category for women and fourth for males was the issue of pronoun use and generic "man." If a student writer used inclusive language, in any way, the rater assumption was that this was a female writer. If the student used a so-called generic masculine third person pronouns, raters assigned male as the gender. This appears to be yet another case of markedness; use of inclusive pronouns is the marked case and seems to signal female gender. Several raters wrote that although they themselves had been taught to use the masculine third person singular pronoun, they could not help assigning male gender when they read it in a student text. They were right to be cautious, because many female writers did use the masculine third person apparently generically.

Rhetorical Cross-Dressing

So what can we observe from these sorts of results? First, 70 percent is a level of high accuracy and suggests that raters in Washington shared a number of stereotypical gender assignment strategies; we will return to this point in the next section. But 30 percent of the gender rating was inaccurate and it is to that grouping that we turn next. In order to examine the inaccurate gender ratings, we will discuss two papers in this section, one in which a female writer was judged to be male in gender, and one in which a male writer was determined to be female. Both essays received scores high enough from the original Miami raters to result in some college composition credit. But each is, in its way, an occasion for rhetorical cross-dressing, a successful parody of gender expectations. It is because gender is inaccurately rated in such a large number of readings that we might want to rethink our categories, indeed our identity politics, as feminist researchers.

Feminist critics have pursued two related issues in the past decade. First, there was the problem of the relative lack of a feminist political agenda for women, an agenda shared widely by women with quite different problems. Critics pointed to the feminism of the second wave in the 1960s and 1970s as relevant only to educated, upper-middle-class English-speaking women. For women of social and economic classes other than upper middle, different in color, ethnicity, and sexual orientation, the political agenda of second-wave feminism seemed pointless. Moreover, the agenda did not recognize that demographic categories overlapped and interacted. Being a woman of color and of the working class was different from being a woman of ethnicity and alternative sexual orientation. Second, and more fundamental, is the question of identity. Is "woman" definable in global, unified terms? Is the term even possible without reference to the binary relationship with *man?* Empirical, feminist research in the social sciences has only recently addressed either set of issues. Instead, the simplified analysis of gender being socially assigned, usually in tandem with the sex of the body in question, provide the appropriate research category. To answer the first set of concerns, researchers may statistically correlate "gender" with "race" or "ethnicity" or "sexual orientation." To answer the second set, researchers struggle with differences between such aspects as psychological gender and the sex of the body, as do Donald Rubin and Kathryn Greene in their study of gendered features of student writing, a study to which we will return shortly. The possibility of gender being multiple is simply not addressed except in concessionary remarks to sexual orientation.

Judith Butler's *Gender Troubles: Feminism and the Subversion of Identity* provides an extended discussion of the problem of binary relations between sexed bodies and our understandings of gender in current feminism's identity politics. Butler argues that an identity politics for feminism, founded on a prelinguistic, prediscursive self who has only sex but not gender, is in and of itself a problem for feminism. She suggests that the effect is to leave all those who fit the category of "Other" (as women usually do) in the same position from which they began. That is, feminist identity politics will inevitably fail, because a binary notion of biological sex—the "true" body sex—will lead relentlessly to a repetition of a binary notion of gender—the socially enacted outer sex. For many people, common sense notions of biology usually intervene, and thus many resist the idea that sex and gender may be more than binary oppositions. There are only two, right?

Michel Foucault raises the question of biological sex in his introduction to the journals of *Herculine Barbin,* in which he describes the problematics raised by a hermaphroditic body regulated by a two-valued sexual categorization. Drawing heavily from Foucault, Judith Butler delineates the discursive distinction between the body's interior and exterior. Only through the soul/ body distinction of much of Western philosophy, Butler argues, can the idea of gender remain so heavily regulated and disadvantaging to those somehow different (136). Parody, Butler suggests, using Esther Newton's analysis of camp, drag, and cross-dressing, exposes the fabrication of sex, identity, and gender. In drag and cross-dressing, gender begins to multiply: the "outside" is dressed as one gender, with the "inside" the body sex of the actor; the "real" bodily appearance is the sex of the actor, and with the "inner essence" the psychological gender is yet again different. So a cross-dresser may "feel" female inside, while having the body parts of a male, or the person in drag may be dressed as a male while having female body parts and still "feel" female inside. What gender is the cross-dresser or person in drag? Is "he" really a "she" or is "she" a "he"? Or is he/she (she/he) another gender altogether? Butler concludes by suggesting that parody of gender represents a truly subversive and potentially corrective practice.

Our original research gesture in this study—to correct problems of social gender—inherently contains the problematic Butler addresses. What happens if gender turns out not to be two-valued? What if we have portfolios written by men that are consistently thought to be women by raters? What if we have portfolios written by women that read as male in gender? Do we push and shove readings that are incorrect back into "correctly" gendered lines? Isn't that the very thing we were trying to avoid? In the two essays from portfolios partially reproduced in Figures 19–3 and 19–4, we have the appearance of gender multiplication.

In Figure 19–3, we have a female writer scored as a male by five different readers. In Figure 19–4, we have a male writer scored as female by four different readers. In both cases, there is little in the way of linguistic features that would signify the assignment of gender. As with Rubin and Greene's search for textual features of gender, we found little in these portfolios to point to gender.

Figure 19–3
Inaccurate Rating #1

"An Unrecognizable India"
Paragraphs 1-5

The India of today would be unrecognizable to a character in E.M. Forster's *A Passage to India* (hereafter, PI) because the social and political climates have greatly changed. Forster himself suggested this when he said,

> I began to write the novel in 1913, but the first world war intervened and it did not get published until 1924. Needless to say, it dates. The India I described has been transformed politically and greatly changed socially . . . (Beer 50)

Shortly after her arrival, Englishwoman Adela Quested, one of the main characters of PI, expressed the desire to see the "real India" (24). She had not met or had any contact with natives except her servant. Throughout PI, the Indians are almost invisible, accurately reflecting that the British had as little contact with them as possible. Mrs. Moore, Adela's chaperone, shared her uninitiated enthusiasm: she, too, wanted to see the "real Indian," though Adela's beau laughed at such a wish. Fielding, a schoolmaster, suggests the ladies "Try seeing Indians" (26). When she and a group of ladies began to discuss the prospect of doing so, one of them tells Adela that Indians are "disrespectful" (27).

Mr. Turton, one of the government officials, had a "bridge party" which was supposed to bring together the British and the Indians socially. However, the party was not a success because the Indians kept to themselves, and, likewise, the British stayed in their clique. After a while, the British ladies tried to talk with the Purdahs, but the conversation was awkward. I suspect that one of the reasons for the failure of the bridge party is that, simply, the British did not want it to work out. One of their strengths in ruling was the separation and imposed superiority over the Indians. To unite with them would be to weaken their rule.

Here, and throughout the novel, there is evidence that the British considered themselves superior, and therefore, remained isolated from the Indians. They superimposed their culture onto the Indians, forcing them to be subservient. The English said that the Indians were all alike, and the Indians said the same about the English. So disrespectful of the Indians were the British that Forster's Mrs. Callendar felt, "Why, the kindest thing one can do to a native is to let him die" (27).

The British moved into India never intending to stay permanently, nor intending to win the Indians over to their way of thinking. They were, instead, only there to govern and to do business (Tully 14). In India they attained cheap labor and raw materials. In this time in British history, the nation was expanding and forming colonies in many parts of the world. The British believed it was their right to take over India and use it and its people to their best advantage.

Figure 19–4

Inaccurate Rating #2

"For Better, Or Worse"

Paragraph 1-2

"I had three chairs in my house: one for solitude, two for friendship, and three for society." So said Henry David Thoreau in *Walden Pond, Visitors*. Those three chairs still exist today only in a modified form. There are still the three original chairs representing the upper, the middle, and the lower classes, but tucked in between those are three more chairs representing the upper middle, the lower middle, and the lower lower classes. If you picture these chairs all lined up on a staircase the upper class would be perched in solid gold, red velvet throne—not the short, round, white ones—on the first step, the upper middle classes would be sitting in a bronze throne covered in jewels on the second step, the middle middle class would be seated in a leather Lazy-Boy recliner on the third step, the lower middle would be sitting in a corduroy winged back chair on the fourth step, the lower class would be squatting on a wooden bar stool on the last step, and down on the landing at the bottom would be the underclass sitting on the floor. There are two questions to answer: what chair am I sitting in now and what are the chances that in fifteen years I will be sitting in a better chair than my parents?

To determine upon which chair I sit I need to measure my social status, or rather than of my family. To measure my social status I used a checklist of class indicators. 1) Income: father and mother: above $100,000. 2) Occupation: Dad-Doctor of Dental Surgery (dentist), Mom-design consultant: both self-employed. 3) Residence: Shorewood Hills, Madison, Wisconsin, U.S.A. 4) Schooling: Dad: eight years of college-Doctorate in Dentistry; Mom: six years of college-Masters in Design. 5) Clubs/Teams: Nakoma Country Club (twenty years), John Poweless Tennis Club (five years), Madison Club (three years), and Cherokee Club (two years). 6) Sports: golf, tennis, raquetball. 7) Drinks: wine coolers, LaCroix, champagne, wine, occasional beer. 8) Hobbies: golf, skiing, jogging and reading. Just about any activity that is outside. 9) Shopping preference: Marshall Field's, The Watertower, Nieman-Marcus, Wooldenberg's for Men, Jan Byce's, Laura Ashley and Eddie Bauer. Along with all that we do a lot of traveling, drive a limited edition 1989 Honda and a 1989 turbo powered Saab convertible. It seems to me that the above facts indicate that I am sitting on a very large, red velvet throne. The question still remains as to where I will be in comparison to my parents in about ten to twenty years.

Rubin and Greene found only seven of the original seventeen proposed gender markers present in the texts they studied, and three of those seven features became evident after screening for psychological gender was factored in (via a version of the BEM Sex Roles Inventory). The seven features sensitive to gender were

1. orthographic intensifiers [exclamation points, underlining];
2. the discourse move of acknowledging another side;
3. women using more "I"s in expressive segments;
4. men editing hedges in argumentative segments;
5. men using more of the "other" first person pronouns [we, our, us];
6. psychological "males" using more illustrator markers [for example, for instance]; and
7. psychological "males" having greater sentence length (27-29).

The screening for psychological gender done by Rubin and Greene represents an acknowledgement of the problem of simple binary gender. Rubin and Greene included a psychological screening as an attempt to account for "weak findings in previous research about writing and gender" (16), a weakness they argue comes from the "essentialist fiction" of two-valued gender. Yet they, too, end up with student texts that they are unable to explain because they are working from, though suspicious of, a two-valued system.

In these two portfolios, we will find few distinguishable features of gender as described by Rubin and Greene. The student whose work is excerpted in Figure 19–3 included essays on the topics of the nation of India, from the India described in E.M. Forster's *A Passage to India* to contemporary Indian government, and Shakespeare's *Hamlet*. It was primarily because of its stance toward the topics that raters assigned a male gender to this writer. As one said, "these papers are entirely unemotional toward the subjects." Though the essay on Forster and India eventually directly discusses the dangerous sexism embedded in Indian society, no rater considered the writer to have been female. "It's very distanced and objective," reported another rater. The *Hamlet* paper tries to develop a tripartite scene of emotional states in the main character: ignorance, knowledge, and confusion. It is a distanced discussion, quoting passages that the "reader will interpret." What we have, we would argue, is the successful rhetorical cross-dressing that many female student writers find necessary for academic success. Though this writer's topics edge into conventionally "female" arenas, the writer manages to stay uninvolved, dispassionate, and distanced. "Dowry death," "sati" in Indian terms, the ritual burning of widows on the husband's funeral pyre, is not an occasion for outrage and grief as a female writer. Instead, it is just "another modern problem," an analytic category. But the writer "scores" with the original raters at Miami, rhetorically "dressing" herself as the autonomous male, these papers contributing to the garnering of some college composition credit.

The student writer whose work is represented in Figure 19–4 provided more problems for the gender raters. The two essays read by the raters involved topics that seemed inherently male in gender: success and public and private morality. It was the execution, the level of detail and description that seemed to force the readers' rating this male writer as female. "For Better, or

Worse" contains a novelesque assortment of detail about chairs, material, drinks, places to shop, life styles: only a woman student writer (or more implausibly a male would-be novelist) would notice these items. As one rater pointed out, "What self-respecting eighteen-year-old male knows about velvet thrones and Laura Ashley?" The desire for material wealth throughout the initial essay, though tempered with generational reality, reads female to the raters. One rater says, "males should want power. This writer wants the things that come along with power, not power itself." In this student's second essay, entitled "Founding Fathers," it is the writer's "placidity" toward issues of morality that earn the writer a female-gender rating. The essay concludes with the writer claiming, "I translate that into meaning that there is a need to allow yourself both vices and virtues but there is a middle road to travel while attempting to obtain the goal of 'perfect' morality." Unlike the previous portfolio, this writer produces "I" in abundance, another marker of binary gender. Yet this is a male writer, and the writer who receives the highest evaluation in the original scoring. Oddly enough, while in the previous portfolio, there were no absolute markers of gender—no sex-specific name, no reference to athletics, to same-sex friendships—there are several in this portfolio. The writer identifies himself by name at the end of the first essay and mentions his athletic involvement in the second. Raters, nonetheless, ignored it and scored the portfolio as female, another successful rhetorical cross-dressing.

Observing the Written Performance of Gender

So what does happen to equity in assessment when gender multiplies beyond the binary? We want to make some observations in closing that we believe bear further thought and analysis. These observations relate both to the accurate *and inaccurate* ratings of gender. We want to suggest, finally, that the use of portfolios for writing assessment means that we need to make substantial changes in the ways we calibrate and prepare to assess and score portfolios.

First, the construct for gender used by the raters when they were accurate is fundamentally similar to the hypotheses offered by Robin Lakoff in the mid-1970s on women's language. To linguists who are also feminists, this is an ominous correlation. Lakoff's work has been considered controversial to many empirically oriented women sociolinguists, in part because her findings were not grounded in actual observations. Lakoff observed her own speech and that of her friends as the basis for her findings, typical perhaps for the theoretical linguist but atypical for the sociolinguist. Tag questions, hesitations, hedges, polite forms and perhaps hypercorrectness, and greater depth in the lexicon for color terms formed the base for Lakoff's premise that women's language was different. Linguists in the following decade set out to disprove most of Lakoff's observations, finding tag questions, for example, could indicate a power difference in any social context, rather than a specific form only women used, and that the modal used in tag questions was more sensitive to gender than was the use of tags alone. Hedges also differed in frequency by context, as did polite forms and hesitation phenemona. Nearly all of these particular forms were extremely sensitive to power differentials. Thus, tag questions are as familiar to the teacher in the classroom, coming from her students, as they are in male-female cross-sex conversation. More problematic in sociolinguistics is the continuing assumption that the search for women's language will eventually yield a universal description, "true" for all women.

But what if what Lakoff was describing was not empirically true but socially true, true as a socially shared construction of gender and speech? What raters may be doing then is applying a socially shared construction of gender to writing. And what student writers may be doing is putting forth a set of gestures—in writing, unmoored from any physical or visual check—that can be read and interpreted as gendered. But this unmooring and slippage of signification also means that written gender can be manipulated, parodied as Butler suggests. Because we rarely provide opportunities for discussion of these issues in assessing writing, the raters were free to apply conventional social judgments. Likewise, the writers could choose rhetorically to mine those conventional social judgments for the most value. Consequently, there is no "true" gender equity possible because there is no way to "make" student writers adhere to gender norms, nor would we want to make them do so.

Nonetheless, we should remember that, in the eyes of female students, we have improved the material conditions of writing assessment. As we suggested at the beginning of this essay, males participated more readily in the proficiency exam before the study initiated portfolio submissions. Females, presumably, felt that there wasn't much point in trying since the format wasn't one they liked or at which they felt they could succeed. After we switch to portfolios, we suddenly have equal numbers of female and male students participating. Why? We have to assume that female students felt that this kind of assessment was one at which they could succeed. Moreover, these participation rates for women have held steady over the three years of the study. These participation rates give us considerable reason to believe that female students' perception of equity in assessment is stronger with the portfolio than it was with the proficiency exam.

Second, the local context for the writing and submitting of the portfolios has subtle gender effects. Miami University's portfolio assessment program asked for personal, expressive, self-disclosing writing, perhaps of the kind that women writers are thought to be more comfortable producing. We requested it in the portfolio cover letter in which we asked students to describe themselves as writers and we invited it more obliquely through the narrative/descriptive pieces. In short, we asked for what women are thought to be able to do; at the same time we asked them to mark themselves extensively for gender. If we stereotypically assign female gender to personal, expressive writing, then we are actually inviting writing that rhetorically cross-dresses these male students. For female students, we perhaps invite greater risk-taking because writing in academic contexts is almost never in these "female" forms.

A third observation comes from the ESL readers on the west coast. Once gender is assigned by a reader, it is extremely difficult if not impossible to budge. On at least four portfolio sets in this sample, the ESL students, mostly Asian in background, observed the writer's own specification of gender in the paper. They noticed phrases like "as girls my age often do," "a teacher said I was a girl who . . . ," "I was looking for those who wear ties to spend my evenings with," all giving clear cues at the phrase and word level that the writer was female. In each of these cases, some non-ESL raters had assigned male gender and did not notice the error. This confirms Stygall's earlier work in the ordinary understanding of expert knowledge, in which jurors ignored some parts of the evidence they heard once they had decided on a narrative explanation of the cases they heard. If it didn't fit, they ignored any new information. Readers here performed a very similar procedure. Once gender was assigned, specific evidence to the contrary did not change that assignment. One male reader, in his sympathy with the difficulties of dating, read the ties phrase as an indicator of male solidarity. Non-native readers apparently weren't distracted by culture and read only the textual cues available to them correctly. This suggests the power of the assignment of gender for native speakers.

Do portfolios provide the opportunity for more equitable assessment of student writing? Is gender equity possible in writing assessment? We are somewhat less hopeful now about the method providing the correction than we were when we started this work. We believed then, as we do now, that it is important to provide that proverbial even playing field. But even playing field notwithstanding, judgments about gender remain prominent in any reading of student writing, blind, as in the assessment situation or full-faced, as our own classrooms provide. Not making gender visible in the scene of assessment did not remove it from our view in rating portfolios. Consequently, we have come to believe that gender equity is a locally-generated value, integral to calibration and rating, and not something that just happens to come with a portfolio assessment package.

When we laud the benefits of assessment means such as portfolios, we believe we must be careful in describing the values of our own writing communities. At Miami, for a number of years, experiential, expressivist writing was believed to allow students more freedom, more creativity, more choices in their writing. Nonetheless, we asked for academic writing, not for new categories of feminist rhetorical forms. No paper we examined, nor any paper any of the raters at UW examined, evidenced French feminists' calls to subvert male academic discourse by the presence of *jouissance,* nor did any of these portfolios evidence the rupture of the presence of Kristeva's semiotic. Though we adjusted in subsequent years some of the content of the portfolios to reflect the kinds of writing that we were receiving, and of necessity that reflected the higher female participation rate in portfolio assessment, we didn't set out to provide a forum for radical changes in students' high-school writing.

Set against the possibility of a truly different feminist rhetoric, we neither encouraged nor received portfolios that opened new frontiers of academic writing. What we did receive—and we believe it is cautionary for us all—is evidence of a kind of rhetorical cross-dressing that invites difference only within conventional frameworks. To disrupt this conventionality, we might want to consider the possibility of changing the way we address gender and other social categories in the calibration and scoring of portfolios as a better means of affecting change than the portfolio assessment alone. Portfolios bring to the moment of assessment a much larger sample of the students' writing. In attempting to address the constant tension between the institutional demands of assessment and our classroom practices in teaching writing, we seem to have overlooked how compelling the urge is to "construct" a student as we are reading. There is considerable evidence that this construction already occurs in holistic scoring sessions of single essays. The wider variety available of the students' work in the portfolio may well make the "construction" unavoidable. And inevitably, once we begin to construct, we begin to specify gender, race, ethnicity, class, and sexual preference. Yet our method of scoring—calibration through a training session toward single scores—either denies the construction is taking place or ignores it. A calibration session in which raters explored their constructions of student writers would allow us to examine our stereotypical assignment of social categories and to understand what effects those assignments may have on our scoring. Even if we use portfolios, we remain locked in a scoring system that privileges "objectivity" and distance over local, situated understandings of student writers. Reliability achieved at the price of disregarding our own understandings of student writers is too high a price to pay. The gender assignments described here raise critical questions for portfolio assessment. Has a student writer who switches rhetorical gender achieved something more than a student who matches her rhetorical gender with her body's sex? Is it more difficult for a male student to achieve female rhetorical gender than it is for female students to achieve male rhetorical gender? Does a student's sexual orientation affect the choice of rhetorical gender? That we as raters assign value to these rhetorical genders is unquestionable. What remains questionable is how we choose to deal with it. Portfolios, as a tool for writing assessment, not only open new possibilities to us in developing more equitable assessment, but they also require us to reconsider fully the rest of the assessment practices we currently use.

20

"Portfolio Scoring": A Contradiction in Terms

Robert L. Broad

> Certainly any theory of aesthetic value must be able to account for continuity, stability, and apparent consensus as well as for drift, shift, and diversity.
>
> Barbara Herrnstein Smith,
> "Contingencies of Value" (19)

Suppose we were to take up Barbara Herrnstein Smith's challenge in the specific context of communal portfolio assessment. How might we account meaningfully for both consensus *and* diversity among our evaluations of student writing? How would we have to change our attitudes toward evaluative disagreement in order to make sense of that disagreement?

In the noble tradition of Galileo, let's conduct an imaginary experiment. Subject A walks into a room full of writing-assessment specialists and utters this speech: "When people *agree* in their evaluations of student writing, things are working just as they should. Their agreement constitutes useful information about the text being evaluated and about the group conducting the evaluation." What response does Subject A's speech elicit? Friendly nods, pats on the back.

Now Subject B walks into the same room and pronounces the following: "When people *disagree* in their evaluations of student writing, things are working just as they should. Their disagreement constitutes useful information about the text being evaluated and about the group conducting the evaluation." What reaction might Subject B expect? Cold stares, turned backs.

Disagreement is a fly buzzing crazily around the clean white room of communal writing assessment, and we seem bent on exterminating the insect no matter what precious objects we break and no matter whom we bruise in the process. Dominant voices in our field consistently portray "discrepant" readings as the result of incompetence or ill intent: "Excessively rigid teachers or those who are insecure often have difficulty adopting group standards, and faculty who take pride in their differences with their colleagues may resent the entire process" (White, *Teaching* 157). In the name of "fairness" and "science," they exhort us to seek ever higher levels of numerical agreement among scorers, a goal well known to us as "inter-rater reliability."

Edward M. White, for example, *defines* reliability as fairness (*Teaching* 22), and has stated flatly that "A reader who scores differently from everyone else is wrong" ("Portfolios"). We shouldn't be surprised, then, when White censures Peter Elbow's recent suggestion that reliability may not be worth what it costs us. Reviewing Belanoff and Dickson's *Portfolios: Process and Product,* White admonishes Elbow and other skeptics of reliability in ominous tones:

> We do not have to throw away fairness to be honest in our measurement, and we make ourselves irrelevant to serious measurement if we assert that we must . . . Unreliable measures are merely subjective impressions by disparate individuals and we have more than enough of that already . . . (Review 538)[1]

I advocate communal writing assessment precisely because I agree with White that we have "more than enough" teachers grading as "disparate individuals" in isolation from one another. I must, however, protest White's disparagement of disagreement as "subjective impressions" and his appropriation of the weighty terms "fairness," "honesty," and "serious measurement." I want to re-appropriate each of those terms and propose a substantial shift in our theory and practice of communal writing assessment.

We need to transform our notions of consensus and difference in the context of communal writing assessment much as John Trimbur has transformed them in the area of collaborative learning:

> We need to see consensus . . . not as an agreement that reconciles differences through an ideal conversation but rather as the desire of humans to live and work together with differences. The goal of consensus . . . ought to be not the unity of generalizable interests but rather what Iris Marion Young calls "an openness to unassimilated otherness." ("Consensus and Difference in Collaborative Learning" 615)

As the culmination of twenty years' rapid movement toward more and more enlightened evaluation of writing, portfolio assessment cries out for just such "openness to unassimilated otherness"; yet "difference" remains a dirty word in most large-scale evaluation settings. In my view, portfolio assessment both deserves and demands that we reconsider the meanings and merits of evaluative disagreement.

Let me begin with a few critical observations regarding the nearly universal twin practices of scoring portfolios and demanding evaluative consensus.

For starters, I propose that quantification and the demand for agreement intertwine theoretically and reinforce one another practically; quantification and statistical reliability make perfect partners. I further suggest that those twin practices not only contradict our best theoretical insights—including those that undergird the very practice of portfolio assessment—but also lead us to deceive our students and to abuse our colleagues and ourselves.

Everything I argue here follows from a single premise: that the construction of textual meaning depends upon social context. While this axiom has so far been much more commonly discussed among literary theorists than among compositionists, I nevertheless understand it to be widely accepted by those in both the literary and the rhetorical subfields of English. In the opening pages of *What is English?*, Peter Elbow recounts as the "main conclusion" of the 1987 English Coalition Conference that " . . . we see the same *constructive and social activity* [of making meaning] as the central process at all levels of the profession of English. . . . At all levels we stressed how this central activity is *deeply social*" (18, emphasis added).

Below, I group my initial premise with several corollaries that follow from it, and illustrate each statement with examples.

Main Premise: *The construction of textual meaning depends upon social context.*

The "OK" gesture, interpreted in U.S. culture to signify cheerful agreement, in Mediterranean cultures is taken as an insult with clear references to aberrant sexual behavior. Similarly, the phrase "make love" encountered in a 17th-century lyric poem likely refers to various acts of courtship (including the composition of love poems), whereas the same phrase found in 20th-century verse likely suggests activity subsequent to courtship (and probably exclusive of literary pursuits).

Corollary #1: *Textual value, being inextricably bound up with textual meaning, also depends upon social context.*

In "Contingencies of Value," Barbara Herrnstein Smith proposes an inquiry that would foreground the link between textual value and social context: "The type of investigation I have in mind . . . would seek to explore the multiple forms and functions of literary evaluation, institutional as well as individual, in relation to the circumstantial constraints and conditions to which they are responsive [including] specific local conditions . . ." (14).

Corollary #2: *We can establish no single, fixed meaning or value for any text.*

Laura Bohannon's "Shakespeare in the Bush" offers an entertaining illustration of the mutability of value and meaning. Recounting the story of *Hamlet* to members of an un-Westernized African culture, she is startled when her listeners not only radically re-interpret the tale, but also correct the "mistakes" Shakespeare made in telling the story and impugn Shakespeare's literary capabilities.

Corollary #3: *Differences of interpretation and evaluation are not only inescapable, they are downright wholesome elements of everyday rhetorical experience,* elements that we do harm to ourselves and our students in trying to conceal or extirpate.

The powerful concept of "interpretive community" is often invoked to explain why evaluators in a given large-scale assessment must agree in their judgments of a given text. If, however, such an "interpretive community" includes—as it often will—rhetoricians, literary types, Africanists, Marxists, feminists, creative writers, technical writers, New Critics, New Historicists, grammarians, expressivists, graduate students, adjuncts, and tenured faculty, then we achieve agreement only by bleaching out the kaleidoscopic quilt of values which comprises the *true* community of many English departments. A bit later, I present the story of "Martha" by way of example.

Working from this theoretical basis, I believe we can and should change our attitudes toward difference in large-scale writing assessment. And nowhere is the need for this change more urgent than in the realm of portfolio assessment.

The peculiarly 20th-century hunger to quantify writing ability and demand interrater agreement has never, in my view, served teachers and students of writing well. In the current context of the portfolio assessment boom, that penchant for quantification and homogenization seems even more questionable. Figure 20–1, "A (Very) Brief History of Large-Scale Evaluation in the Department of English at Miami University," illustrates why.[2]

Compare the striking developments in "evaluative INPUT (what the students do)" to the puzzling stasis of the "evaluative PRODUCT." The changes in the nature of evaluative input from multiple-choice testing to writing portfolios are two-pronged: a surrender of strict control over the writing process and a movement to broaden and enrich the context for composition. We've abandoned the effort to make students' writing the same in favor of letting students make the differences among them into resources for writing. So difference and context are transvalued from "confounding variables" (as in the discourse of psychometrics) into useful, stimulating elements in the process of evaluating writing.[3]

But where are difference and context when it comes to the evaluative product? To what exactly does the number assigned to a writing portfolio refer? How can requiring all readers to produce the same number in response to the same texts account for the differences among raters and their varying responses to the powerful content and context offered by the writing portfolio?

Figure 20–1 illustrates that, while our work in portfolio assessment has made the ground fertile for context, choice, difference, and multiplicity in the area of students' evaluative *input,* we persist in stripping context and quashing difference when it comes to our evaluative *output.* In other words, in equating interrater disagreement with "unfairness," we cling to what are for most of

Figure 20–1
A (Very) Brief History of Large-Scale Evaluation
in the Department of English at Miami University

→ → (historical time, 60's through 90's) → → → → → ↑

	Multiple-choice	Impromptu essay	Portfolio
evaluative **DESIGN**	evaluators write all questions and all answers, designating a single right answer to each of their questions	evaluators compose and field-test prompts, making room for a variety of approaches to their topic	evaluators compose formal guidelines, leaving choice of topics, audiences, and approaches to the student
evaluative **INPUT** (what the students do)	select the correct item from among test-makers' answers (to test-makers' questions); strict time limits imposed	actual WRITING (first-draft, single-genre) on a topic of the test-makers' choice; strict time limits imposed	actual WRITING (revised, multiple-genre), featuring choice of topics and audiences, collaboration, revision, and research; writer sets context for her writing using reflective letter; no imposed time limits
evaluative **PROCESS** (what the evaluators do)	feed answer sheets into the scoring machine	actual READING, requiring interpretation and evaluation	actual READING, requiring interpretation and evaluation
evaluative **PRODUCT**	single score quantifying "writing ability"	single score quantifying "writing ability"	single score quantifying "writing ability"

→ → → the evaluative process → → → → → →

us outmoded and discredited ideologies: foundationalism and scientific positivism.

I am aware that I must handle the term "positivism" with caution. In "The Legacy of Positivism in Empirical Composition Research," Carol Berkenkotter traces the history of that term to illustrate how complex are the positivist and post-positivist traditions within science, and to resist the notion that any attempt by composition researchers to be "scientific" is necessarily positivist. A further restraint against employing the term as a critique of mainstream writing assessment is that the literature of holistic scoring appears resolutely social-constructionist, rife with references to Stanley Fish and "interpretive community."

I persist in applying the term to the predominant discourse of writing assessment because it accounts for the otherwise inexplicable circularity, rigidity, and authoritarianism of "interpretive community" as it is practiced in large-scale assessment events. Only if one believes that a given text "has" a certain value and that some people know that "true" value better than others— and only if one believes that *community* and *value-pluralism* are mutually exclusive concepts—does it make sense to demand that a roomful of readers agree in their evaluations of a given text.[4] The story of "Martha and Portfolio 354" will help to illustrate the problems inherent in our single-minded insistence upon evaluative consensus.

Portfolio 354 was chosen to serve as an anchor portfolio in the 1992 Writing Portfolio Program here at Miami University. This means that during our "calibration" discussion, the entire group of forty or so evaluators read this portfolio, discussed its strengths and weaknesses, and scored it. Since inter-rater reliability was equated with "fairness" throughout, our goal was to see whether we could agree about the value of portfolio 354. For the most part, we did. But what interested me most, and the reason I'm telling this story, was a moment in which one reader offered a notably different reading of portfolio 354.

A friend of mine, whom I'll call Martha, had the job of recording the evaluators' comments on the chalkboard at the front of the room. First we discussed what we saw as the portfolio's strengths, then we discussed its weaknesses. During the first part of the discussion, Martha silently recorded the strengths and didn't speak up until the very last moment, just as the chief reader was getting us ready to talk about weaknesses. I make a point of the timing of her comment because I had two strong impressions about it: first, that it almost went unspoken, and second, that it significantly shifted the group's assessment of this student's writing abilities.

Martha's comment referred specifically to the third piece in the portfolio, an essay about Dr. Martin Luther King, Jr.'s "Letter from Birmingham Jail." In that piece, the student writer first examines King's arguments about the failure of the white church to confront racism and join in the civil rights struggle, and then traces the implications of "Letter from Birmingham Jail" for the present-day church. Everyone in the group-grading session had read that essay, and they had also read the student's "reflective letter," which introduces and sets a context for the other pieces in the portfolio. Among the forty or so readers in that room, however, *only Martha pointed out the connection between the topic of third piece and the audience for which the reflective letter had said the piece was originally written*: the admissions committee at the University of Notre Dame, a Catholic university.

"You could," Martha observed, "call it [the student's selection and handling of the topic for that piece] audience awareness, given that he sent it to Notre Dame."

After Martha spoke there was a brief pause, and then an audible and visceral reaction from the entire group: "Mmmmm!" "Aahhh!" People nodded their heads thoughtfully; others shook their fingers in a gesture I interpreted to mean: "good point!" or "touché!" The chief reader gazed at the ceiling with a mock blank expression, brought his index finger to his forehead, then cried out "Bing!" as the light bulb suddenly switched on. He laughed and said, "Nice, Martha."[5]

Martha had apparently made a strong point in the writer's favor that the other forty readers in that room (including me) had simply overlooked. Since the scoring rubric prominently featured "a clear sense of audience and context" as a criterion for judgment, it seems likely and appropriate that Martha's comment shifted the group's evaluation of the portfolio upward to some degree. The crucial point of the story is that under the ideology that drives mainstream quantitative assessment, in her evaluation of portfolio 354 Martha was "different from everyone else," and therefore, according to Ed White's formulation, "wrong."[6]

Martha's story spotlights how getting people to discuss their evaluations prior to scoring helps to open up the conversation and make room for divergent perspectives that are often squeezed out under the pressure for numerical agreement. Our usual reliance upon *numbers*—as opposed to the positioned readings that "produce" those numbers—and our ardent pursuit of numerical *agreement*—at the expense of conversation about why we do or don't agree—corrupt portfolio assessment and prevent it from being as serious, fair, and honest as it could otherwise be.[7] Thanks to the way that calibration discussion was handled, Martha's story ended happily: her divergent reading carried the day, and that student's portfolio appeared to receive a more favorable—and, if we consider the scoring guide, a more fair—reading as a result.[8] Unfortunately, the ideology that criminalizes discrepant readings is rarely so kind to students and teachers.

In the context of our department's optional "team grading" system (in which instructors evaluate each other's students' papers), I have seen my students become deeply disturbed when their writings received widely discrepant evaluations, and I have asked myself "Why?" Evidently we have taught our students that evaluative disagreement signals sloppiness or malice:

if readers' assessments conflict, someone must be wrong. Worse yet, evaluative diversity leads some students to believe that writing assessment is a chaotic, meaningless, arbitrary process. Should we be surprised, then, when students turn cynical about writing assessment, concluding that they have absolutely no control over the reception their writing receives? These are the students whose only interest in the evaluation their work receives is the grade. As teachers of writing we complain bitterly about such students, yet I wonder how seriously we've considered our complicity in "educating" such students into their depressing relationship to writing assessment.

What about us? How does the drive for interrater reliability affect the lives of administrators, instructors, and evaluators involved in large-scale assessments? Participating in and researching holistic scoring sessions at three different institutions over a span of ten years, I have encountered a number of situations that give me reason to worry. Here are a few examples:

- Evaluators complain of a contradiction between their experiences in "calibration" or "norming" sessions and the way administrators represent such sessions. While administrators will usually portray such an event as a *democratic* process articulating the values of the entire group, many evaluators experience it as an *autocratic* process requiring the large group to adopt the evaluations of the leaders. This incongruity leads one participant to label such sessions "a hoax" and another to comment, "I was surprised that 'consensus' was so often imposed on the group. I think discussions (and my sense of calibration) suffered because of it." A third evaluator says she felt "extremely frustrated" during the calibration discussions because the anchor group "had all the answers beforehand."

- Faced with several discrepant scores for a particular portfolio, a chief reader invites the anonymous discrepant readers to take a job other than grading, explaining that their lack of calibration may undermine the group's interrater reliability. One of these discrepant scorers finds this invitation "disconcerting," particularly because he was well "calibrated" in evaluating most of the other portfolios that day and didn't see himself as a defective reader. Another participant—not one of the discrepant readers in this scenario—comments that she "felt frightened" by the chief reader's invitation.

- Administrators monitor individual scorers' rates of discrepancy and compose a list of those who will not be invited to participate in future sessions due to their discrepant tendencies.

- In the course of a norming session ostensibly held for the purpose of "building consensus," and despite principled arguments from the minority for passing a particular portfolio, a chief reader states that the portfolio "absolutely cannot pass."

By no means do I mean to suggest that such painful anecdotes tell the whole story of communal assessment. Scorers often speak of how encouraged and gratified they feel when their evaluations correspond with the majority; being told that you are successfully "normed" can mark a genuinely euphoric moment. The crisis on which I focus here arises from our treatment of the minority. My personal experience and the experiences of many of the scoring-session participants I've interviewed is that incidents like those described above severely undermine instructors' sense of professionalism, dignity, intellectual integrity, and community. Interviewees use words like *oppressed, silenced, intimidated, frustrated, angry, depressed,* and *insulted* to describe such episodes. If these are the feelings of some of the people whom we attempt to draw into our "interpretive community," we might want to begin asking ourselves just what sort of community it is, and whether the rules for belonging are due for a change.

Ultimately, I judge the stupendous energy pumped into achieving statistical reliability in holistic scoring sessions (see Charney; Charles Cooper; Huot, "Reliability, Validity, and Holistic Scoring"; White, *Teaching & Assessing Writing*) to be a waste of precious resources, destructive to our students, to our colleagues, and to our project as teachers of literacy. If we let go of the quantification of writing ability in large-scale assessments, we could also dispense with our fixation on statistical reliability. Rather than allowing a number to be the evaluative output of what is otherwise a rhetorically sophisticated process, we could offer something more useful and more appropriate theoretically: positioned, situated, or located assessment.

In an essay entitled "Traveling Theory," Edward Said warns against transporting theories into new situations without sufficient consideration of the circumstances that gave rise to those theories in the first place. When I argue for positioned or located evaluation, I make a parallel argument: I believe that the circumstances and process of any evaluation are crucial to understanding the outcome of that evaluation and putting that outcome to ethical use. The quantification of writing ability radically simplifies what a reader has said about someone's writing and frees that reader from responsibility for his or her evaluation: "Oh yes, she's a *B writer.*" Simplification and freedom from responsibility are the two elements that make quantification both appealing and appalling. Located assessment is more difficult to transport, manipulate, and flatten; from my perspective as a teacher of rhetoric, that is its great strength. In practical terms, then, what would it mean to provide situated, positioned, or located assessments?

First, we could offer *institutional* location. Rather than asking evaluators to provide scores that are later translated by administrators into institutional action, we could restore to evaluators responsibility for making the institutional decision at hand, whether pass/fail, 0–3–6 credits, or otherwise. This shift would represent a gain not only in professionalism (since it would put the decision in the hands of the teacher-experts) but also in accountability, since teachers would need to face the consequences of their evaluations: "I am failing this student," or "I am granting this student an entire year of credit; she may never take another writing course in her life!"[9]

Second, we could offer *axiological* location.[10] Contrary to the irresistible implications of quantification, the evaluation of writing is a critical and creative act carried out by some human beings upon the critical and creative work of others. The key here is that *not everyone's values are the same.* In fact, even in an apparently homogeneous group of evaluators—the infamous "interpretive community"—astonishing differences in interpretation and evaluation sometimes arise. During last summer's portfolio assessment here at Miami University, for example, forty college English instructors gave one portfolio all six possible scores. Foundationalist ideology makes such a circumstance chaotic, meaningless, or corrupt: "What is their problem that they can't get their evaluations *right*?" Constructivist ideology, on the other hand, makes evaluative differences meaningful, instructive, and useful.

In "The Idea of Community in the Study of Writing," Joseph Harris offers a metaphor which helps clarify the contrast between foundationalist and constructivist portraits of "community":

> The metaphor of the city would allow us to view a certain amount of change and struggle within a community not as threats to its coherence but as normal activity . . . We need to find a way to talk about [the workings of communities] without first assuming a consensus that may not be there. (20)

We often hear from people who were as writing students either terrified by or furious about the fact different instructors valued different things in students' compositions. In the "city" of positioned evaluation and constructivist community, differences would be less threatening; they would constitute a crucial part of one's rhetorical education.

What would truly constructivist, post-positivist assessment look like? In *Embracing Contraries* and *What is English?,* Peter Elbow proposes what strikes me as the most moderate (and therefore the most likely) first step: multiple scales of evaluation (*Embracing* 171, *What* 256). From the perspective of valuing context and difference this is an obvious improvement over the single scale, yet multiple quantitative scales still tempt us to "average" them into a single number, as in the notorious example of grade-point averages. The virtue of narrative and qualitative evaluative output, by contrast, is that it can better resist these reductionist temptations.

Brief narratives like those used at Hampshire College, Evergreen College, and the University of California at Santa Cruz can replace grades very successfully in a classroom context. For the purposes of large-scale assessments, however, narratives are nearly impossible to manage. Most of us have experienced how draining the relatively quick and superficial act of marathon scoring can be; those who have tried offering actual commentary along with a number have found that approach to be even more grueling. Yet I've argued here that numbers undermine our purposes. So what's the best option for large-scale assessments? A number of people have experimented with a form for "positioned evaluation." It indicates the institutional decision (pass/fail,

0–3–6 credits, etc.) but also offers a substantial checklist of writing qualities such as "organization," "humor," "detail," "tone," "correctness," and "surprise." Evaluators can check off those qualities that most affect their decisions, and indicate with another quick mark whether that quality figures in as a strength or a weakness. Without adding much time to the old approach of producing a number on a scale, such a checklist proves more informative and professional than scoring. Figure 20–2 shows such a checklist, this one designed by Shannon Wilson for the Miami University English Department's Team Grading process.[11]

To me, the most compelling alternative to quantification is one about which Brian Huot writes in "Reliability, Validity, and Holistic Scoring." Huot describes William Smith and his colleagues at the University of Pittsburgh sitting around a table, reading the writing of incoming students *not* to judge them but to place them. The question ceased to be "How shall we quantify and rank these writings by 'quality' or 'ability'?" and instead became "With which of us four instructors will this writer grow and learn best?" By institutionalizing the fact of evaluative and pedagogical diversity, Smith and his colleagues achieved the most creative, most honest evaluation process I have encountered (or imagined), an approach wholly untainted by what Stephen Jay Gould calls the twin fallacies of reification and ranking.

In my argument for post-positivist methods of writing assessment, I've stuck close to the particular concerns of teachers and students and their lives within educational institutions. Yet I believe the implications of the conflicts I have traced here go well beyond the classroom or the holistic scoring session; I see these issues as seamlessly bound to questions of culture and politics.

Would it be extreme to say that the discourse of positivism and the exclusionary version of "interpretive community" which guide the drive for statistical reliability are ill-suited to democracy, regardless of how congenial and liberal most of its advocates may be? Would it sound grandiose to claim that narrative, positioned assessment better supports democratic culture, whether in the classroom or across society? Perhaps. Consider, however, this paragraph from Pat Belanoff's "The Myths of Assessment":

> We need to realize that our inability to agree on standards and their applications is not something we need to be ashamed of . . . far from it, [that inability] is a sign of strength, of the life and vitality of words and the exchange of words. For, if we agreed, we could set up hierarchies and fit ourselves and others into then and then all could dictate to those below them and follow the orders of those above them. And in fact, in such a set up there would have to be an autocrat at the top who knows what's best for us and who knows what texts are best. Then someone would know what sort of texts to write and to teach and the variety would leave our profession and along with the variety, the richness. (62)

This tendency toward the devaluation and extermination of difference is what troubles me most in the discourse of mainstream writing assessment. I have

Figure 20–2

PAPER #_____   GRADE _____
GRADER# _____

The criteria below were derived from the anchoring session responses. Some of the qualities are specific to particular assignments (i.e. discourse analysis and reflective narratives); others are more general.

Check three to five qualities that were key in the grade determination.

+	–
_____ asks good questions	_____ appropriates research
_____ aware of methodological influence on research	_____ cliched
	_____ difference denied
_____ clear	_____ difference not examined
_____ challenging topic	_____ disjointed
_____ complex ideas	_____ disorganized
_____ contextualizes	_____ doesn't fulfill assignment
_____ depth	_____ doesn't explore issues raised
_____ describes method used	_____ doesn't consider own location
_____ engaging	_____ ends where it should begin
_____ focused	_____ essentializes
_____ includes data	_____ formulaic
_____ incorporates discourse in analysis	_____ generalizes
_____ in-depth analysis	_____ importance of topic unclear
_____ interesting topic	_____ incompetent mechanical skills
_____ interesting use of language	_____ location is superficial
_____ locates/positions self in relation to social	_____ "normal" goes unexamined
_____ mechanical competence	_____ not self-reflective
_____ organized	_____ overstated conclusions
_____ provides examples	_____ passes judgment without considering location
_____ reflective	_____ plagiarism
_____ resists generalizations	_____ proofreading
_____ resists pat ending	_____ repetitious
_____ specific	_____ superficial
_____ style	_____ surface analysis only
_____ takes risks	_____ takes on too little
_____ thoughtful	_____ takes on too much
_____ uses humor	_____ topic nebulous
_____ uses research/data	_____ undefined terms
_____ uses quotes	_____ unfocused
_____ voice	_____ unorganized
_____ well-developed	_____ voice
_____ other _____	_____ weak connections
_____ other _____	_____ other _____
_____ other _____	_____ other _____
	_____ other _____

proposed that we replace it with the more rhetorical, more theoretically engaged, and more educationally holistic practices of positioning our evaluations and (trans)valuing our differences. We can make our theories and practice—both educational and political—truer to what we as enthusiasts of communal portfolio assessment really believe.

Notes

1. Although I focus here on Edward M. White as one of the most influential voices in the field, he is not alone in his dim view of evaluative difference; throughout the literature on communal evaluation, disagreement is represented as inherently problematic.

2. I sketch Miami's history of large-scale assessment because it is the institution I know best. The overall historical movement traced in my "Very Brief History" is, however, common to a large majority of the educational institutions of which I am aware.

Two elements of Miami University's Writing Portfolio Assessment Program may insulate it from part of my critique: Miami's is a voluntary program, not one required of all students in the institution, and it awards advanced placement and credit, rather than functioning as a proficiency measure. I accept these as qualifying factors even while I maintain doubts regarding the push for agreement and the quantification of writing ability, both of which are key features of the Miami program.

3. For the concept of "transvaluing difference" I am indebted to Linda Brodkey's editorial.

4. Too late to integrate it more fully into my essay, I discovered Michael M. Williamson's remarkable article, "An Introduction to Holistic Scoring: The Social, Historical, and Theoretical Context for Writing Assessment." Williamson's article serves as the introduction to *Validating Holistic Scoring for Writing Assessment,* a volume he recently co-edited with Brian Huot. In that opening chapter, Williamson traces the historical and theoretical geneology of holistic scoring. He strongly affirms that the mainstream tradition in holistic scoring carries with it assumptions about knowledge and value that he calls "positivist" and "psychometric." Lamenting the "simplistic and dated views" from which specialists in writing assessment often operate, he exhorts us to develop our practices out of an evolving theory of writing rather than out of a "fossilized" theory of assessment.

5. Details and quotations of this event are taken from videotapes I made of the session for research purposes. I wish to thank participants at two different research sites for opening their portfolio assessment programs to my inquiry even when they knew that I brought to the research a critical point of view.

6. In his keynote address to the Miami University Conference on New Directions in Portfolio Assessment, White told a similar story. Having found his evaluation of an essay on Faulkner's *The Sound and the Fury* discrepant, White realized that his score was discrepant because he had read the novel and knew that the writer was misrepresenting it. Since none of his fellow readers had read the novel, they were quite satisfied with the essay.

7. Fortunately, a number of programs have found ways to open up the conversation and to legitimate evaluative differences. At SUNY Stonybrook, for example, instructors *talk* about portfolios when their evaluations disagree. At Miami University, the aggregate score for a disputed portfolio includes all three evaluators' scores, including that of the "discrepant" evaluator. Unfortunately, during the calibration and norming sessions I've witnessed, discrepancy is still usually treated as failure, as the anecdotes on page 270 illustrate.

8. The difference between the anchor group's and the calibration group's scores for portfolio 354 supports my hypothesis that Martha's comment boosted our estimation of the portfolio. In the anchor session, "audience awareness" was never mentioned as a strength of this portfolio; most anchor-group members gave portfolio 354 a "3 minus" and one scorer gave it a "2," so the portfolio was rated there as a "low 3." At the conclusion of the calibration discussion in which Martha spoke, most raters gave the portfolio a "3," but more scored it above a "3" than below it. So where "audience awareness" was credited to the portfolio, it ceased to be a "low 3" and became a "solid 3" at least.

9. The leaders of the Miami University Portfolio Program tried this once. In 1991, they replaced their standard scale designating six levels of writing "ability" or "quality" in favor of an institutionally located 0–3–6 scale indicating how many credits the evaluator of a given portfolio felt the writer ought to be awarded.

Unfortunately, the resulting distribution of scores did not allow administrators sufficient flexibility in designating who would place out of first-year English; administrators knew that in order to meet budgetary constraints and keep down class sizes they need to exempt "X" number of students, but the composition instructors' evaluations were telling them to exempt "Y" number. In the name of "economic realities," the six-point scale was reinstated the following year.

10. *Axiology* refers to the study of value judgments.

11. The team running the Miami Portfolio Assessment Program is also experimenting with ways of providing more location of and information about instructors' evaluations, including checklists like this one.

21

Maintaining a Portfolio-Based Writing Assessment: Research That Informs Program Development

William Condon
Liz Hamp-Lyons

Introduction

Portfolio-based writing assessment has gained so much momentum over the past few years that we can safely say it is here to stay. In its latest incarnation, portfolio assessment has been championed by no less a personage than Peter Elbow, who, both alone and together with Pat Belanoff, has authored several important articles establishing the advantages of the portfolio over the one-shot writing sample. And in a recent address before the Conference on College Composition and Communication, Edward White called portfolios "the future of writing assessment." Two conferences, four books, and a spate of journal articles also attest to the power of this trend toward establishing portfolios as the preferred instrument for writing assessment.

At the same time, many have begun to notice the dearth of empirical research establishing the effectiveness of portfolios as an instrument for writing assessment. To date, the portfolio has simply been accepted on faith, on writing specialists' *feeling* that the portfolio is better. At the recent conference on portfolio assessment, held at Miami University, Brian Huot characterized publications about portfolio assessment as "show and tell," publications that describe the process of portfolio-based assessment, but provide no real evidence that establishes the portfolio as a more valid or reliable assessment instrument. Indeed, Edward White, in his keynote address at the same conference, while endorsing portfolios, indicated nevertheless that we need to ask some hard questions about this new instrument, questions that speak to its reliability and validity, of course, but also questions that lead us to examine the assumptions underlying our current practices.

In a recent article in *College Composition and Communication,* we report on a study of the portfolio reading process that examines some of those assumptions: assumptions about the advantages of multiple texts and multiple genres; about the degree to which portfolios integrate assessment and instruction; and, most important for our present purpose, about how extensively readers attend to all the texts in a portfolio. Briefly, we asked twelve readers to fill out "Reader Response Questionnaires" as they completed reading the first, middle, and last portfolios in the set of thirty-two portfolios they were assigned. The surveys revealed that readers do not attend equally to all the texts in a portfolio. Self-report after self-report indicated that readers arrived at a strong impression of a final score during their reading of the first paper. Some readers reached a tentative score after the first or second paragraph of the first text. Other readers postponed any decision until the second piece, but quickly settled on a score within it. The self-reports suggested to us that readers sought a "center of gravity" and then read for confirmation or contradiction of that sense. However, no reader reported altering that early impression, meaning that students were being scored not on the basis of four texts, but at best on one and a small portion of another—but most often on the basis of the first text in the portfolio only. Given the nature of these data, we hypothesized that as the portfolio assessment became routine, readers went on a kind of "automatic pilot," leading them to become less attentive to the whole portfolio. We felt that if we could increase the reader's investment in the portfolio—raise the stakes by giving the readers more contact with each other, more information about each others' classes, and more input into what sorts of text went into the portfolio—then we could change readers' behavior so that they would once again attend to the portfolio as a whole.

Although the reformation of the reading groups is significant in and of itself, in this paper we focus on the process of investigating important questions about portfolio-based assessment and the ways that research helps reform both the assessment and the writing program. Specifically, problems that arise in the portfolio assessment generate questions to investigate. Deciding how to investigate—how to gather the data that form the basis for a decision—forces a deeper analysis and understanding of both the assessment and the curriculum that gave rise to it. Additionally, the investigation itself yields information that shows how to reform both assessment and instruction. As a result, decisions based on this information produce changes in the course, which, in turn, become the basis for reforming the assessment, constantly making it a more stable, more reliable, and more thoughtful assessment.

Materials and Methods

The results of the first study challenged our assumptions about the effectiveness of the portfolio as an assessment instrument. If our well-trained readers, all experienced in writing assessment, were so strongly affected by their first impressions of a student's writing, then the possibility existed that portfolio readers could not be expected to attend to all the writing in a student's portfolio, thus calling into question the whole basis for portfolio assessment. If readers score on the evidence of only one text, then students are not able to benefit from demonstrating a range of abilities across several texts, and portfolio assessment would represent no significant improvement over a standard holistic assessment based on a single sample of a student's writing. In order to discover whether this behavior could be overcome, we designed two measures: one that we hoped would produce a change in readers' behavior and one that would help us determine whether the change had indeed occurred.

In the fall of 1991 a second set of readers (consisting of nine from our original twelve, together with fifteen new readers) went through the redesigned set of reading procedures.[1] As usual, teachers read portfolios in groups of three, but this time the portfolio reading groups took a more active role, and they began their work in the second week of the term. Reading groups were set to gain the maximum benefit in faculty development. One member of each group was a veteran of at least five years of teaching in the Writing Practicum, one was new to this course, and the third had at least one year of experience in the course. This composition allowed the groups to serve a mentoring function for faculty who had not taught this course before, and it ensured that veteran faculty would be exposed to new ideas from teachers whose approaches had not had a chance to harden over years of teaching the Practicum. In their first meetings, the groups were allowed to decide what sort of impromptu writing would go into their students' portfolios and what the reflective pieces would look like. Groups could not alter the two revised pieces, one of which had to be an argument while the other could be any non-fiction essay. In addition, members of the group visited each others' classes at least once, meeting after the visits to discuss any issues that arose as a result of the visits. Finally, in addition to the whole-group standardizing that we continued to conduct about a week before portfolios were collected, each portfolio reading group met to standardize on at least one "live" portfolio from each instructor's class. This small-group standardizing occurred as soon as the portfolios were collected, but before the teachers had begun reading and scoring them. These measures were designed, first, to improve teaching in our Writing Practica; second, to heighten the instructors' sense of investment in the portfolios from their own and their colleagues' classes; and, third, to lead instructors to attend more closely to all the writing in the portfolios they read.

We designed two measures to test whether we were getting the desired results. First, prior to the reading, each instructor received a sealed envelope. Instructors were asked to read several portfolios and then, putting away the last one they had read, they were to open the envelope, where they found a Recall Protocol (see below), designed by Hamp-Lyons. Immediately after reading that portfolio, the reader put the portfolio away, opened the sealed envelope, and answered the following questions:

Close the portfolio you have been reading and do not open it again. Which portfolio did you have?

1. What was the first essay in the portfolio about?

   Write down everything you remember reading in the first essay. Try to recall the issues, arguments, and support. Try to write your recall in the order the student used. Used the student's word whenever you remember them.

2. What was the second essay in the portfolio about?

   Write down everything you remember reading in the second essay. Try to recall the issues, arguments, and support. Try to write your recall in the order the student used. Use the student's words whenever you remember them.

3. What was the third essay in the portfolio about?

   Write down everything you remember reading in the third essay. Try to recall the issues, arguments, and support. Try to write your recall in the order the student used. Use the student's words whenever you remember them.

4. What was the reflective page about?

   Write down everything you remember reading in the reflective page. Try to recall the topic(s), analysis, and information. Try to write your recall in the order the student used. Use the student's words whenever you remember them.

Clearly, any reader who did not attend to the whole portfolio would not be able to answer all the questions with equal fullness; indeed, if the pattern from the earlier study held, we expected to see full descriptions of the first text in the portfolio, but increasingly vague and brief responses to texts two through four. However, if the readers could describe all four texts in equal or near-equal length and depth, that would indicate that they had read and attended to the four pieces equally.

As a second test of reader behavior, we performed a simple manipulation of the texts in the portfolios we used for the whole-group standardizing session. Each of the three portfolios were "borderline"; that is, they had caused split scores when they were originally read. One portfolio's scores placed it on the border between placement back into the Practicum and placement into Introductory Composition, the next higher course. The other two sample portfolios had received scores that put them on the border between a placement of Introductory Composition and Exempt from Introductory Composition. One of these had resulted in placement into Introductory Composition, while the other had earned a score of Exempt. In each case, these portfolios were selected because there was a marked difference in quality among the texts, ranging from a text which seemed consistent with placement at the higher level to a text which seemed consistent with placement at the lower level. We then rearranged the texts in the portfolios so that half the readers (twelve) received versions with the stronger texts first and the other half of the readers (twelve) received versions with the weaker texts first. We collected scores from the readers before discussing the portfolios in the standardizing session so that the discussion would not taint the scores. If readers' scores differed according to which essay came first in the portfolio, then the test would confirm that the earlier pattern had persisted; if, however, the scores were similar for both orders, then we could say that readers were attending to all the texts in the portfolios and that they were taking the quality of later texts into account in their scoring.

Results

The questionnaires indicated that these readers attended equally to all the texts in the portfolios. The length of responses, measured in number of sentences and in number of lines, was similar for each piece in the portfolio, as Table 21–1 indicates.

The results from the whole-group standardizing session suggest to us that readers considered evidence from all the pieces in the portfolios. No matter whether readers had the strong-to-weak order or the weak-to-strong order, the scores they assigned were similar, well within expected levels of disagreement. In Table 21–2 we record the number of readers at each scoring level for the three portfolios. In each case, Order A represents the high-to-low order, while Order B represents the low-to-high arrangement of texts.

Table 21–1

	Number of Sentences (Avg)	Number of Lines (Avg)
Piece #1	5.1	6.9
Piece #2	5.2	7.0
Piece #3	4.9	6.7
Piece #4	5.3	7.1

Table 21–2

	Portfolio 1 (Exempt)		Portfolio 2 (Intro. Comp.)		Portfolio 3 (Practicum)	
Scores Received	Order A	Order B	Order A	Order B	Order A	Order B
Exempt	9	8	4	3	0	0
Intro Comp	3	4	7*	9	3	4
Practicum	0	0	0	0	8*	7*

*Lower n results from undecided reader(s).

Discussion

Put simply, both tests indicate that our restructuring of the portfolio reading procedures did change reader behaviors. The responses to the Recall Protocol demonstrate that readers were able to remember all four texts in the portfolio equally well, helping dispel any fear that readers still attended closely to the first text but not so closely to the other three. On the actual form, readers had eight lines in which to describe the portfolio from memory, and they consistently used almost all the available space, using between 6.7 and 7.1 lines. In addition, the number of sentences in the descriptions remained constant for all four texts in the portfolio, whether the text was one of the two revised essays, the timed impromptu, or the one-page reflective piece. The determining factor in how much a reader wrote on the Protocol seems to be the amount of space allowed, rather than the amount the reader could remember. Finally, when we compared the actual portfolios with the protocols, we found that readers had been able to reproduce the students' language in their summary descriptions, and that the ability to do so remained constant for all four texts. Since readers attended to all four texts closely enough to be able to describe them similarly on the Protocol, it follows that they attended to them closely enough to use all four texts as the basis for their scores.

The results from the whole-group standardizing session also suggest that readers scored on the basis of all four texts in the portfolios. Since both groups produced almost identical scores, readers must have been weighing the relative quality of later texts, which means that all four texts counted in the scoring process. This result was confirmed as readers discussed the portfolios. In one reader's words, "After I read the first essay, I was sure this would be a Practicum placement, but the impromptu and the second revised essay changed my mind." In fact, the scores on this measure were surprisingly close. Since each of the three portfolios had produced split scores when they were originally read, we expected to see a high degree of disagreement from readers. These portfolios, we felt, would test the boundaries between our placement levels, as well as give us the chance to check our hypothesis about readers' scoring habits. In spite of our expectations, though, readers were able to agree fairly closely on placement. All three portfolios received scores which, in the aggregate, duplicated their original placements, and in each case, the order of the texts in the portfolio made no significant difference. If readers had been attending closely to the first text only, and skimming or skipping later texts, then we'd have expected scoring patterns to be reversed for orders A and B, since we had arranged the texts in A so that readers saw the strongest text first, then the next stronger, and so on until they read the weakest text last; while the texts in B were arranged in just the opposite way. Instead, as Table 21–2 shows, the scores on all three portfolios were similar for orders A and B. Thus, readers must have made adjustments to their early impressions as they read the subsequent texts, meaning that our adjustment of the emphasis we placed on the portfolio reading groups did result in more careful readings of the portfolios.

Conclusions

These results are encouraging for several reasons. First, we were able to use empirical methods to locate and then to solve a problem in our portfolio assessment. The first study alerted us to the fact that readers did not attend to all the texts in a portfolio equally; the follow-up study indicates that the measures we took to ensure that readers would weigh all the texts worked. This success stems from the ability to break down a portfolio assessment into its component parts and examine those parts closely. We believe that similar studies could reveal much more than we have about the process of teaching to portfolios, the process of compiling them, and the process of reading and scoring them. Based on our experiences in the first and second studies, we can describe a kind of research spiral: reader protocols turned up problems in readers' behavior; discussions followed about what measures might assure that readers would attend to more of the writing in each portfolio; these discussions led to changes that not only improved the quality of the assessment, but had a positive impact on the teaching/learning environment in the course as well; finally, changes in the purpose and structure of the portfolio reading groups produced the desired result, as the later protocols demonstrated.

Second, we note that problems with our assessment are essentially local problems; that is, they stem from characteristics of our program. Other programs may not have the same difficulties with reading procedures, even though our context suggests that some sort of difficulty is likely: our readers are experienced in holistic and portfolio assessment, and the first study was done after three years of using portfolios as the instrument for exit assessment in our Writing Practicum. In addition, most of our readers (approximately 80 percent) are full-time faculty, a cohesive group sharing a pleasant central office complex that provides numerous opportunities for teachers to communicate with each other about common objectives, teaching methods, standards, and so forth. Readers with less experience, less training, or less sense of community are probably even more likely to employ reading habits that result in less reliable judgments or that, in effect, render the portfolios less valid as instruments for assessment. In each case, however, our experience leads us to believe that these problems can be identified and solved on the local level by searching for ways to collect data that can account for what actually happens at each stage of the portfolio assessment process.

Third, our experience demonstrates that collecting these kinds of data pays off in more ways than just assuring a more accurate assessment. Our solution did make our assessment more accurate, and thus more fair, but it also improved the effectiveness of the Practicum as a whole. The chain of events allows us to draw some conclusions about the kind and level of maintenance needed for portfolio-based writing assessment. We have reported elsewhere that portfolios allow us to integrate assessment and instruction, and that integration yields information that allows certain problems to surface. Problems that remained hidden before we shifted from single-sample assessment and that would also remain hidden in a system in which individual instructors issued grades became apparent when we began reading portfolios from each others' classes. This factor, together with the questions raised by the data we collected in our earlier study, allowed us to conclude that portfolio assessment requires constant maintenance, which in turn requires the constant collection of data about the various components of the assessment: instruction, curriculum, methods, reading and scoring behaviors, and so forth. This level of maintenance helps assure a careful, accurate, and fair assessment.

Fourth, the information we gathered about problems in our assessment led us to make changes that produced a better assessment by ensuring that the theoretical advantages of portfolios are realized in practice. More important, the changes we made in order to make the assessment somewhat better helped us strengthen the element of faculty development that is naturally a part of the process of participating in a portfolio reading group. Teachers collaborated more closely, meaning that they shared their theories and practices to a greater extent than before. Younger, less experienced instructors benefited from close contact with veteran English Composition Board faculty, while the veterans had the opportunity to be jogged out of their complacency by the energy and new ideas of the younger faculty. Class visitations increased this exposure, giving each member of the reading group an opportunity to receive feedback on her/his teaching in a low-risk setting (observations for the purpose of formal evaluation were conducted separately, by faculty from a different reading group). Thus, the portfolio reading groups became a focal point for faculty training and development, producing a wealth of new ideas, assignments, and methods, as well as an opportunity for faculty to re-examine their teaching practices in a supportive, low-risk environment.

Finally, our results encourage our belief that portfolio assessment can be a richer, fairer, and more accurate instrument than anything else that is currently available to us. It also confirms our sense that along with the benefits to assessment come other important benefits. Portfolio-based assessment, carefully and thoughtfully conducted, helps reform courses and curricula, it provides a forum for faculty training and development, and it creates an environment that encourages faculty to perform continual self-evaluation. Even if portfolios were no better than the standard one-shot writing sample, these ancillary benefits would be so valuable that they would make portfolio assessment worthwhile. However, with continual, careful observation of our portfolio assessments in action, and with both reactive and proactive research into the elements of portfolio assessment, we can provide convincing arguments and evidence that portfolio assessment is superior to traditional direct writing assessment.

Notes

1. By this point, Liz Hamp-Lyons had moved on to the University of Colorado at Denver, so Condon was working with Emily Jessup, who succeeded Hamp-Lyons as Associate Director for Assessment. Condon and Jessup worked out the re-designed reading process, while Hamp-Lyons designed the procedures that would reveal whether or not that process had in fact counteracted readers' tendencies to focus so heavily on the first text in a portfolio.

22

Portfolio Negotiations: Acts in Speech

Russel K. Durst
Marjorie Roemer
Lucille M. Schultz

When we evaluate student writing, we consider diverse and at times contradictory evidence, reducing multiple factors such as voice, elaboration, organization, coherence, diction, and usage to arrive at a single, unequivocal judgment of the student's work. Sometimes our internal struggle with conflicting claims is intense, but this struggle is usually a silent one. We pause over the page, and then we write the verdict. However, in our version of portfolio scoring at the University of Cincinnati, which emphasizes group discussion of student work, we seek to make these internal struggles outward and visible. In debating the merits of particular papers to arrive at pass/fail judgments, we engage in speech-acts, performing our judgments in open discussion, subjecting our decisions to debate and possible revision. These discussions reflect something of J. L. Austin's category of the performative, where "the issuing of the utterance is the performing of an action" (6). What we seek to do in these discussion groups is to make our actions, normally carried out in isolation, into language that is open to interrogation, not merely in terms of true or false, or right or wrong, as if the judgment reflected a description of the paper's absolute value, but in terms of evaluations to be contested. Our portfolio process thus makes writing evaluation a more multivocal project and at least reminds us of the complexity of considerations that the letter grade or pass/fail judgment represents.

The idea of talk, of discussion about students' written work, is central to our notion of the value of portfolio assessment. From the time we first considered adopting this form of assessment in our Freshman English Program in 1987, to our early pilot studies familiarizing ourselves with portfolios, to our 1989 decision to adopt them program-wide, we have seen portfolios as providing invaluable opportunities for teachers to get together and discuss student writing. In our program, these discussions have centered around such key issues as establishing criteria for evaluation, gauging signs of writing development, and examining questions of dialect interference and control of standard English. Discussion is particularly important in portfolio assessment because portfolio evaluation, as we are coming to understand it, is a fluid form of assessment that requires negotiation not calibration, a form of assessment that moves away from absolute judgments about writing into more shaded, nuanced understandings of difference.

In 1991, we published an essay in *College Composition and Communication* entitled "Portfolios and the Process of Change," which looked at the challenges and benefits of implementing portfolio evaluation in a large freshman English program. In this chapter, we move into "second stage" research, examining what happens once the system is up and running. In particular, we look closely at the kinds of discussion and negotiation that take place around student writing in portfolio norming sessions. We examine, first, a conversation among new teaching assistants and their practicum teacher about the difficulties of juggling what Peter Elbow refers to as the conflicting roles of coach and judge. We next examine a discussion by experienced instructors and a program administrator on the complexities of determining evaluation standards. These discussions illustrate ways in which, for both beginning and experienced instructors, portfolio negotiations can serve as an important means of faculty development, can help ease anxieties about grading and passing judgment on students' work, and can provide a forum for teachers and administrators to re-think the goals of a freshman English program.

A brief description of our portfolio system and how it fits into the Freshman English Program will provide a context for the examination of portfolio discussions that follows. Ours is a large program in which approximately three thousand students annually go through a year-long, three-quarter course sequence. The program employs about sixty FE instructors, a diverse group including teaching assistants, adjuncts, and tenure-track faculty. We, the program administrators, decided to adopt portfolios, replacing a long-established, sit-down exit exam at the end of the sequence. We did so because portfolios put the emphasis where we felt it belonged, on students' writing development over time. With portfolios, as opposed to a timed exit exam, students are judged on their best work, on a number of different pieces of writing, on writing produced within the context of the course, not writing tacked on at the end. The portfolio system is much more consistent with our philosophy and our curriculum than was the exit exam, fitting our emphasis on process, multiple drafting, the development of self-reflective powers, and encouraging students to take more responsibility for their own growth as writers. In addition, we felt that portfolio evaluation had the potential to empower teachers, and we wanted very much to decentralize our program, giving teachers more of a say in determining standards as well as more opportunities to meet and discuss writing.

Under our portfolio system, every student taking the first quarter composition course keeps a portfolio consisting of clean copies of four essays, chosen from the five essays required for the class. Teachers form trios, exchange portfolios within their trios, and give a pass/fail evaluation to each other's student portfolios. They do so at midterm for diagnostic purposes and at the end of the quarter to determine which students will actually pass or fail the course. Before the mid-and end-of-quarter evaluations, teachers meet in groups of about twenty for norming sessions facilitated by one of the program directors. They read a range of anchor portfolios in advance, then discuss at the meeting whether they would pass or fail the portfolios and the reasons for their judgments. Both these norming sessions and the trio meetings provide opportunities for lively and at times intense discussion of critical issues in writing evaluation. What follows are two meditations on conversations that occurred at norming sessions.

Conversation One: Marjorie's Group

"But I Thought We Were Teaching Process," *or Teaching TAs To Give Grades*

This first conversation (actually pieces of two conversations) emerges from work with a group of nineteen teaching assistants. They are teaching English 101 for the first time and so are just being initiated into the mysteries of becoming authority figures in the classroom and the awful responsibility of giving grades; for this reason, they are a particularly striking group to study. In our earliest phase of the development of portfolios, we emphasized the process of developing this kind of assessment as an institutional practice. We said then: "We learned that because the portfolio system depends on negotiations and adjustments, it is a system that will always be subject to further negotiation and adjustment." Now, a year later, we have more experience with some of the forms these negotiations take.

Early on, Peter Elbow provided us with a useful way to describe a central conflict for every teacher of writing, the tension between the dual roles of being both coach and judge. Portfolios allow us, as Elbow said, a way to look at that double function and, in some measure, to clarify the division. As classroom teacher, we coach; as portfolio team member, we judge. But nothing in our lives is that simple (not these days, anyway). These categories, like all categories, leak. Our coaching always rests on certain kinds of judgments we have made, and our judging is the judging of teachers. It is part of our work as coaches, part of our pedagogic function.

The TAs were grappling with the issue of standard-setting and gate-keeping for the first time, and their responses are dramatic. As a group, the practicum class had responded eagerly to our early pep-talks about process writing and generative strategies. They were stimulating their students to gather "telling facts" and "fabulous realities"; they were "looping" and "brain-storming," "collaborating" and encouraging "feedback," and then came October 23, the day of our midterm norming session. Here's an excerpt from the discussion that followed examination of one piece of student writing:

Graham: In this paper they use some ridiculous word choices . . .

Martha: Engfish.

Alison: . . . not exactly.

Graham: It looks like they went wild with a thesaurus, but he did have a certain number of details that helped it move along. The presence of the details made me doubt whether it was a fail.

Cassy: I passed it in the vote, but I have an enormous criticism that the resolution doesn't follow what the thesis proposes.

Samuel: Well, wait a minute. I was drawn to this paper for two reasons, because of its details, which I emphasize in class. Its malapropisms are correctable. It's correctable. Somebody could work on it.

Betsy: But this is a final, revised version.

Bernie: For me, this is a much clearer fail than the other. This person isn't paying attention, is flinging language around like a bag of seeds.

Florence: It's really out of control.

By the end of the hour, Karen Slaper, our graduate assistant and the observer/recorder at every norming session, made the following observations. (She has given each participant a number.)

#6 and 8 look troubled—hands drawn over mouths, wrinkled brows.
#14 is rubbing head
#17 is obviously upset, says: *"If this paper fails, I have twenty-five failed students right now"*
#11 says: *This session was sobering; now I have to think about what to tell my students.*
#5 says: *I thought we were teaching process; now all we're talking about is product.*

A few days later I asked the TAs to write some responses to these sessions. Here are two such answers:

#1

It scared me. Then I realized I had better enlighten my students quick. Took in "Gold" and the Florida trip papers—passed them around—we went over each one and decided what we liked/didn't like about them. Then what was wrong, mechanically-speaking. Had lively discussion, with most students understanding the drawbacks of each paper—regarding form—content—grammar—"flow"—etc. (only abstractly, I don't much use technical terms). Told them some would be failing at midterm—not to think that would keep them from ultimately passing the course—emphasized the course is a developmental one—they can't be expected to perform perfectly with only two papers. Afraid my encouragement is too gushy—they're so tender—but I told them college was tough—professors would not accept error in "real" classes—they must write effectively to move on successfully. (Success is a word that usually perks up their ears.)

#2

I felt reassured with the norming class; I found that I was on the same wave length as the majority of instructors in the group. I became concerned about my students, though, when I realized that my portfolio group may recommend passing an essay which I really feel should not pass. I don't think it's to a student's benefit to pass work which doesn't bode well for his/her progress in other courses. I'm concerned I may feel myself in disagreement with my portfolio group and still be inclined to follow my instincts. Attitude entrenchment.

Perhaps norming session might be useful earlier in the course? My impression was that many in the practicum felt upset because they felt they may have misled the students about their progress up to that time (having already dealt with essay one).

There are many themes we could trace in these responses to what one of the TAs called the "norming shock." There is concern in the last one about loss of teacher autonomy, a very real concern for teachers; there is the usual paranoia of the freshman English program about what "real" teachers in "real" classes will demand and about how well we can prepare students for these demands to come; but most of all there is the jolting move from coach to judge, from process to product. The trauma of this experience seems largely unavoidable, and better faced head-on as a group than left to private terrors and individual nightmares. It is hard to combine the desire (and need) to reassure, to encourage, to stimulate, with that other responsibility, to establish and assert standards. For me, both roles are a part of the job and both are integral to our roles as instructors (and sometimes as coaches and judges of other people's instruction).

While this October 23 meeting was a little bit hairy, in the end I think it was very useful. Some TAs thought we should have done more of this work together earlier in the quarter, but I'm not really sure of that. I think it was reasonable early on for the TAs to experience the excitement of their ability to encourage, to inspire, to liberate their students' writing and that the atmosphere of these classrooms promoting fluency made for a very rich beginning of the course. The process of learning to teach, like the process of learning to write, can't start with evaluation. Four weeks into the quarter, this first time around, was time enough for us to begin thinking together about where all this writing would have to take us if the freshmen were to be successful in the tenth week.

So, we survived the midterm, and in the tenth week of the quarter we began our portfolio norming. The following conversation is part of a transcript from the second norming session, held at the end of the quarter. We have been looking at a very difficult portfolio by a student we will call Marvin. Marvin's portfolio was difficult in part because his in-class essay seemed much stronger than his take-home writing. This student's work was chosen as an anchor portfolio because of its problematic status, and it has engendered much disagreement and some very strong feeling. (Two papers from the portfolio appear in the appendix at the end of this chapter.)

In the transcript we will see Betsy has just said, "What about asking students whether they think they are ready to go on to 102 (that is, to pass this 101 class)? Can they become part of the process in this way; is there room for negotiation?" Garth saves me (momentarily) by offering his response to that question. Then I "answer."

Garth: I think there is because I had a student who . . . um . . . she . . . I . . . I . . . she is one of the cases where I just could not figure out what was going on . . . um . . . her papers were always underdeveloped. They looked like they . . . the paper had been rolled into the typewriter and something had been banged out and brought in, okay. Whether or not that was true, I don't know. But she avoided coming to see me for her conference at midterm time. And she waited around, she disappeared. I kept telling . . . generally a blanket statement to the class . . . come see me, come see me, because if you haven't received your midterm grade you may want to see it, okay. Then she comes to me . . . I got another paper like this and I just put on it "see me." You know, I was tired of talking about the whole thing. She came and I told her, look you were failing at the midterm, you know, I don't know. Her fourth paper was better and it looked like she was going to make some improvement. But I just stopped and said, do you think that you're ready to go on to 102? And she said, no. And I said, okay. I said, you're going to be in 101 next quarter, and there's not much . . . I said, I could, you know, go to bat for you for this and try to get the graders to change their mind, but if they've already failed you and you haven't made any development; if they failed you at the midterm and you've haven't changed much since the midterm I can almost guarantee that you're going to fail the class. And she said, that's fine, I understand.

Marjorie: What if she hadn't said that?

Garth: If she hadn't said that then I would have tried to have persuaded her that it would have been better for her to repeat the class.

Marjorie: I guess, I don't know the answer to your question, Betsy. And, I
mean, I certainly don't want to pretend there are no gray areas and there
is no room for negotiation. What I'd like to suggest is that we want as a
group to get fairly clear standards, as clear as we can get. We want to have
those portfolio teams fail the papers that look as though they are not
securely in control of the language. If you are in a team, and your other
reader . . . this is your portfolio and you feel very strongly that it would
serve the student well to go forward and your other . . . I mean that's what
happened with this one actually; this portfolio was sent to me; . . . what
would you do? what do you think? . . . so, I mean, clearly this was a
problematic portfolio and one around which a certain amount of negotiation could take place. So, I think it's important, at least for the original
reading of the portfolio group to have clear standards. If there is some
reason why we feel that this is a borderline case and it should go this way
instead of that way, then I think that has to be negotiated out, and I think
teachers' judgment counts. I think you have hunches and intuitions, but I
also think that it's very important to send a pretty clear message to
students that is not sentimentalized, you know, that is not some kind of
liberal guilt thing, but that is really: look, here are the standards for
success in this field and we're going to uphold them and press to see that
you have a chance at speaking in this conversation.

As you can see, I miss part of the original question, and, in fact, answer a
slightly different question—one about negotiation, but not directly about
students' participation in the process. Perhaps the confusion and the complica-
tion of this exchange is some indication of just how many sorts of negotiations
are going on here at once. We, as a group, are negotiating standards together;
we are trying to square those with some sense of "programmatic" or "departmental" standards, and we are negotiating with our students, trying to engage
them in the process of framing acceptance of the standards that inform our
community. This moment on the tape captures with embarrassing clarity the
inexactitude of our calibrations. We are trying very hard to be fair and to be
helpful. We want to do what we think will help students, but we are not always
sure, either individually or as a group, what that is. We have to read between
the lines, to "concretize" the text of a student's progress as best we can. What
story of emerging skill do these essays tell us? Why do we each read the story
differently? These are reader-response issues. I would like to suggest that
while our readings are never identical, they can be mutually illuminating. I can
learn from your reading and you can learn from mine. Just as in the study of
other texts, the reading of a group can be richer and more nuanced than the
reading with which each person began the discussion.

Some years ago I participated with a group of lecturers from the University of California at Santa Barbara in a project that we called the videocell. We
videotaped our classes, viewed and discussed them together and then made a

tape of clips from our classes and bits of discussion about the clips. One of my freshman classes knew about the project and asked to see the final, composite tape. I showed it, and they got to see a group of teachers talking about teaching, disagreeing sometimes, negotiating. My class loved it, and at the final class meeting when we were evaluating our class together, many of them referred to the video to clarify what they thought the course was all about. I had the distinct impression that they had learned more about the course from the video than from the course itself. Perhaps work like this around portfolio evaluations will need to be done more and more in classes to bring students into the process, to help them to participate in the multiple, complicated, shifting, inexact, but powerful readings that constitute the knowledge, the standards and the authority that we create in the community of our discipline. (This account is, then, a belated answer to Betsy's question . . . yes, students can be, and must be, a part of the process; that is our best way of teaching them what our discipline is.)

The fumblings and the inexactitude of our coming to consensus in these sessions can easily be seen as weakness: if we were all good teachers and expert graders, we'd all agree absolutely all the time. Once we abandon that position and see grading papers as another act of reading, as complex and varied as all acts of reading, then we can begin to consider that complicated process of reading papers as part of the knowledge that we must share with beginning teachers and writers, part of the content of our freshman writing classes as well as of our teaching practica.

Conversation Two: Lucy's Group

"I'd Like To Slit Your Throat," or
Words We Might Not Have Heard Spoken

This was a ninety-minute conversation among sixteen experienced writing teachers on 2 December 1991; also present at the meeting were a program administrator and a graduate student observer/recorder. Some of these teachers had taught in the program for more years than any of the program administrators, some had won teaching awards, some had long-established personal and professional relationships with each other; some shared offices, desks, and telephones; most of them shared the rank of adjunct faculty. While adjunct faculty as a group are in many ways marginalized in the department as a whole, their voices were the center of this conversation. And the voices were strong and powerful; they were the voices of teachers with strong personal commitments to teaching writing and, in most cases, a long history of classroom success; the graduate student who observed the group wrote in her notes, "This group seems very self-confident and sure of themselves."

Exactly because of this confidence, however, teachers seemed able to invest freely and heavily in the conversation; they spoke out of their own belief systems, the personal values and standards by which they read/evaluate student writing, and they stood their ground. It is the value of that kind of exchange of views that we point to and interrogate and celebrate here.

First, to place the conversation. In preparation for this meeting, each member of the group had read four portfolios. At the beginning of the meeting, with a show of hands, the group quickly agreed—unanimously—that portfolios one and two were passing and that portfolio four was failing. Portfolio three, discussed earlier in Marjorie's group, was more complicated. While, finally, fourteen people judged it failing, and two judged it passing, the tension over its merits was clear even in the voting process. The observer noted, "While voting, a number of teachers asked for a possible borderline category. They then asked for a few minutes to decide. And while doing so, they conferred among themselves." It's interesting that the impulse to talk about this portfolio was there from the beginning—and so it was about this portfolio that the conversation centered, and in this conversation that one teacher said to another, albeit in jest, "I'd like to slit your throat." (Two of the four papers from Marvin's portfolio appear in the appendix to this chapter.)

What emerges from the transcript of the conversation and from the observer's notes is that teachers who judged the portfolio failing did so for very different reasons. What also emerges is that the groundwork was laid for the sparks to fly as teachers disagreed with each other. One teacher, for example, reflected, "Well, I think that what made me want to fail it finally was thinking, this student's going to have to go to arguments next quarter, and I can't see that he's ready—even though the last paper is the best one. . . . [Argument] is going to require some skills that I just don't think this student has." Another teacher, however, was concerned that the papers weren't long enough, and that became her reason for failing the portfolio. Pat said, "This is just a matter of standards alone. Half the papers in this portfolio aren't even the minimum length requirement." It was Pat's comment that drew the first round of sparks in the conversation. Interrupting her as she was still working out her thought, another teacher, Jane, bolted in with, "Pat, that's your idea." To which Pat replied, "But I'm saying why I failed [the portfolio]." Jane then wanted to know if the department had a standard length requirement and called on the facilitator of the conversation to arbitrate, and the observer reported that Jane "seemed upset" by Pat's having introduced paper length as a standard of judgment. The transcript shows that the facilitator talked about the importance of uncovering difference, not to force each other to conformity, but to recognize what was real: "what is so interesting . . . is that teachers do have different ideas for doing things and we're not here to sweep them under the rug or to come up with a single voice, but to let come out what some of our differences are so that we can talk about them, so that we can hear what they are and listen to them." Jane allowed as how this was "all right," but in the next breath, and in jest, added, "but I plan to slit [Pat's] throat."

Obviously what this points to is the passion with which teachers claim their reasons for responding to papers as they do. And even more obviously, that teachers—good, solid teachers—don't always agree. The disagreement over this paper opened up in another important way. The issue, not surprisingly, was the importance of superficial correctness. Here are two portions of the transcript that reflect the disagreement and the attempt of the teachers to listen to each other:

Jane: I think that the least important things [in a student paper] are surface correctness and length. That's the way I feel and that's that.

Tom: What do you mean by surface correctness? Grammatical sentences?

Pat: You mean mechanics?

Tom: You mean syntax? Sentences? Aren't sentences pretty serious? Run-ons?

Jane: No. I mean punctuation of sentences. Not what Bud pointed out before, which is a failure of thought and style. I mean a failure of squiggles.

Amy: They're forever using any word that looks something like the right word . . . Any word that sort of starts with the same letter and looks like the same length will do in place of the right word—and I see an awful lot of that.

Tom: Well that's in the liberal view, and that side of the room [here Tom points to the side of the room where Jane is sitting].

Amy: Words have meanings and they don't have any old meaning and not any old word will do.

Tom: I expected somebody to pass this portfolio, but I don't think I would— just because maybe I agree a little more with you, Amy, than I do with Jane on this. But I can see going both ways.

Jane's statements "having drawn fire from across the room" (the observer's words), Jane at this point reenters the conversation, reclaims her voice and space and continues to make her case on behalf of passing the portfolio, a stance that even Tom thought was possible. What the conversation points to, again, is that people have strong investments in their decision-making about student writing. Superficial correctness, as a concept, means different things to different teachers, and different teachers weigh differently in their judgments. For Jane, it's almost non- issue. For Amy—who in some way deflects the conversation to her issues about language choice and diction—sentence level matters are much more important, and her take, finally, on the paper is, "I do see things that show me that the student doesn't attach any importance to what he's doing."

In some ways, there is no resolution in this kind of conversation, at least not the kind of submissive coming to agreement that we have come to expect in holistic norming sessions. That is, the facilitator does not work toward agreement, and experienced teachers do not fold their hands. What does happen, though, while perhaps harder to see, is in many ways more significant than what does not happen. What does happen is that in a public, safe, and carefully designed space, teachers have the opportunity to articulate for their own sake and for their information of their colleagues, the standards that they invoke and apply in private. Not to name these differences does not mean they don't exist; it simply means that we deny them. To name them, it seems to us, is to name the reality of difference and of diversity that informs, enriches, and enlivens our work.

In addition to naming and arguing on behalf of those standards teachers are committed to, the portfolio conversation also allows teachers to name and to reflect on their uncertainties, the areas that are puzzling to even the most experienced teacher. In this conversation, for example, teachers debated whether or not to pass this portfolio that had two kinds of papers in it, some papers written in "school language" and some in more dialect-inflected prose. One teacher, speaking out of what seemed to be very real frustration, made this passionate statement as part of her argument to pass the student: "We're not doing anything about why the kid . . . went back upon himself, violated his world. I mean, why would he do this? Why did he write two papers in school language and then suddenly decide . . . to write these two papers in the mother dialect? Why? What do we do about it?" The unstated implication is that in spite of the students' serious work, they are caught by conflicting forces and sometimes in impossible situations, and that teachers have to assume at least some of the responsibility for changing that dynamic. So while the initial question was whether to pass or fail a particular portfolio, what emerged was an opportunity for teachers to reflect on ways in which their own standards can evolve and be modified in this process of a portfolio conversation.

From these conversations, teachers also have the opportunity to serve as resources for each other. In this meeting, teachers traded information about the ways they worked with international students and about little known tutoring resources on campus for various student populations. This was a genuine exchange; information was teacher-to-teacher, and resources came with firsthand recommendations. If teachers have much to gain from these conversations, so do students. Surely it is to their advantage to study with a teacher who is more broadly informed as a result of participating in these discussions.

Program administrators also have a great deal to gain from this group-talk. On one level, we learned that in spite of massive amounts of print information, numerous large and small meetings, and pilot programs that ran for a year, some members of the faculty still had major misunderstandings of how we were doing portfolio assessment, and what their role as classroom teachers was. One teacher in this group, for example, thought we were still putting grades on individual papers, rather than deferring grades until the mid-quarter and end-of-quarter. In some ways, these misunderstandings were surprising in that we thought we had saturated teachers with information;

in other ways, it wasn't surprising given that ours is a large program, that portfolios were new, and that teachers have different levels of investment in change. Clearly, the major value for program administrators is the opportunity such group-talk provides for hearing what is important to teachers: gripes, desires for change, different approaches to evaluating student text. This kind of conversation is one of the few set-aside spaces where the voices of teachers are central.

Conclusion

The portfolio struggles we have been describing are certainly apt for a cultural moment that takes all meaning to be the product of negotiation and construction. The more we study portfolio negotiations, the more information we will have about how we read differently from one another and how we come to change our minds, or to see eventually what at first we did not see. We think of Tom Newkirk's wonderful essay "Looking for Trouble" where students go through several readings of a poem with different colored pencils in hand and then produce the story of their successive readings of a text, and we think that we will need to develop such stories of the reading of students' papers. The portfolio process opens up a range of possibilities for new research on how teachers read and evaluate student writing, and how group discussion in its many manifestations can lead to new interpretations, changed positions, or what one TA cited earlier referred to as "attitude entrenchment." Portfolio negotiations are an ideal site in which to examine how we in composition build consensus and at times resist such consensus and instead challenge authority.

What is powerful about portfolio reading is that it provides us with a place where differences in reading "count"; they produce different consequences. As in Linda Brodkey's work with legal texts, differences of interpretation are here not just matters for idle conversation about "style"; here "readings" have palpable effects, both on the evaluation of individual students' portfolios and on the development of group standards.

In establishing a program-wide portfolio system, especially in a large institution, one wants to set the rules, the structure and procedures, clearly. Yet the actual work is always messy and muddled, a tangle of conflicting claims and concerns that in the old days might be the private psychomachia of the instructor, but in the more public world of the portfolio scoring team has now become an enacted series of pushes and pulls, gives and takes, an articulated duel of competing claims, a committee meeting.

From the perspective of someone directing a program, or leading a portfolio team, there is, as we said, a need to establish the standards, to ensure that the program is accountable to something and that the students in it have equitable treatment. On the other hand (and there is always another hand), there is the danger of coercion, using the pressure of the group, or of the majority, or the authority of the leader, to police judgments in ways that violate individual teachers and their particular styles and ways of reading and teaching. How far can we tolerate the imprecision, or the multiplicity, of our judgments; how comfortable are we with the real differences among us as graders? These questions are the kinds of questions that assault us from every corner of our postmodern lives. Most of us are reconciled to the demise of Truth in its singular, capitalized form. But can we and our students tolerate facing the ultimate indeterminacy, the indeterminacy of the freshman English grade?

To offer one answer to that question is impossible, but we can call attention to the way the portfolio system—in the group form that we've adopted it—allows us to view, and we hope to study, the complexities of our assessment processes. Just as process approaches to writing have allowed us to externalize and make available to observation some of the stages of composition, our continuing work in portfolio teams will allow us to study in more detail the layers of competing claims that struggle in the judgments that we make when we assess student writing.

Appendix
Two Papers from Marvin's Portfolio

Paper One

This essay is a profile of an organization. Students had two weeks to write a rough draft, receive peer and teacher feedback, and revise the essay.

Voices of Youth

There we were, James Lynch and I walking down the deterring sidewalk slowly approaching the enormous Alms Hotel; the home of the infamous Voices of Youth.

We finally reached our destination, yet there was still another obstacle to overcome. There was a huge corroded steel door covered with a thin layer of light-blue paint; nevertheless, a meer attempt to cover the enormous amounts of corrosion on the door. James knocked softly as if he feared that the paint would flack off. The blue door slowly creeped open and we walked in. The radio station WAIF is nothing like I imagined. WAIF is located in the basement of this enormous hotel. When we entered, I first notice this dull brown and white fake leather couch. From just a glance I could see the layers of dust and dirt covering it, and yes, to top it off I seen a mouse on the arm of the couch. James just walked on pass as if not even seeing the mouse. There was a long dark erry hall that we had to go through to get to the equipment room. There was only one red light, and the walk seemed endless. When we finally entered the equipment room, and we quickly entered. There was a lot of dirty looking equipment, but it was all clean. There was not a speck of dirt anywhere. That really shows that the members of Voices of Youth took pride in what they were doing. Although there was a lot of old looking things such as: that big silver digital clock which has some numbers that do not light up, and that 1972 Pioneer eight track player, also, an antique recod player. They also had a couple of modern systems.

The thing that I thought was very ironic was that the ten members of this proud orgination ranged from the ages of thirteen to twenty-four and one senior adult. That seems so ironic to me for all the success they have been having for the past seven years. That just shows what hard work and dedication can do.

Voices of Youth is a nonprofit volunteer organization. "The main purpose of our organization is to raise the social consciencesness of our listeners, and to help them become aware of what is going on in our society", said James.

From listening to the topics which were discussed, gave me a sense that an organization of this kind received satisfaction from knowing that they help spread the knowledge that most places are afraid to talk about today. For example, topics such as: The African American Woman, Racisom on Campus, Words from Louis Farrakhan, and knowledge about the success and contributions of African Americans in our history.

All in all, Voices of Youth have proven to me that they are a positive organization striving for awareness, but there is still a need for participation. They feel that they can have more participation because of the vastness of African Americans in our city, yet there isn't a mistory to be solved.

Paper Two

This essay is an evaluation handwritten in class during the last week of the quarter.

Strictly Unorganized

The textbook, Calculus with Analytic Geometry, which is used in the freshman calculus courses, is in need of yet another revision. The present edition, the third edition, inhibits students from learning, it lacks organization and useful appendices.

First, the authors, Robert Ellis and Denny Gulick, have arranged the information in the book poorly. The authors scatter related material throughout the book, instead of building on material covered in previous chapters. Professor Levang, a professor of freshman calculus, expressed his discontent with the textbook by saying, ". . . it looks as though an editor looked over the final copy of the book and handed the authors a list of traditional calculus textbook material. They took it and stuck it in where it doesn't really belong." For instance, the second chapter of the book, "Limits and Continuity," covers the limit process. The students finish the chapter thinking that they know all that they are required to know about the limit process. However, later, in the fourth chapter, the book adds more information about limits in a section entitled "Limits at Infinity".

The material learned in the second chapter is not fresh in the student's mind. Consequently, the professor must waste time going over material that has already been covered. For instance, in most calculus classes chapter two was covered during the second week of the quarter. However, later, during the eighth week of the quarter, the professor was forced to review the material covered in chapter two so that he could teach the seventh section of chapter four, "Limits of Infinity". Moreover, the material following "Limits of Infinity", section 4.8 is entitled "Graphing" and is, at most, remotely related to the limit process. This arrangement of the material only serves to confuse the student. In preparing for class, a student previewing the assigned text would be unable to connect the new material with the old material (from the previous section). In addition to being disorganized, the book contains no helpful appendices to aid the students in quick reference situations. For instance, in reviewing for a test or quiz, a student must search through a lot of pages trying to find a single definition or theorem. This searching is a big waste of time and once the student finds the information, he must deface his book by highlighting. The text does not contain a list of the major theorems, such as the Mean Value Theorem and the Intermediate Value Theorem, which would help the students considerably. Also, it fails to provide a glossary of terms where important words such as "inflection point" and "partition" could be defined.

A number of proofs, definitions, and theorems incorporate the use of Greek letters, but the book lacks a table listing the Greek alphabet. Specifically, in section 2.1 where the authors define a limit: " . . . then a number L is the limit of f(x) as x approaches a if for every number E $>$ 0 such that is $0 < [x - a] < E$, then $\{f(x) - L\} < \sigma$." A student cannot begin to ask a question because he does not know what a "E" (epsilon) or a "σ" (delta) is or how to pronounce it.

As a whole, the freshman calculus book is not all bad. One must understand that in order to avoid publishing a calculus book which resembles a telephone book, the author had to omit some old material to make room for the new. Still, rearranging the material is essential.

Note

We wish to thank especially Karen Slaper for her assistance in our portfolio program and the following composition teachers who participated in these conversations: Abigail Albert, Alice Bolstridge, Susan Boydston, Tony Chiaviello, Doug Connell, Cynthia Crane, Judy Dehan, Laurie Delaney, Beth Duley, Harriet Edwards, Val Gerstle, Shirley Gibson, Greg Griffith, Jerry Hakes, Patton Hollow, Darrell Hovious, Ron Hundemer, Omar Johnson, Lee Kellogg, Barbara Kuroff, Ellen Lauricella, John Maddux, Lou Marti, Elizabeth McCord, Jim Schiff, Elaine Singleton, Laura Smith, Suqin Song, Taunja Thomson, Jean Timberlake, Rebecca Todd, Lisa Udel, Kevin Walzer, Pam Whissel, Lise Williams, and Bill Zipfel. Teachers' names used in the transcripts are pseudonyms.

Issues in Portfolio Administration

23

A WPA's Nightmare: Reflections on Using Portfolios as a Course Exit Exam

David W. Smit

Scene One

She pauses at the open door and then asks politely, stumbling over her words, "Are, are you Professor Smit?" Her eyes are dull, her shoulders slumped.

"Yes," I reply. "What can I do for you?" And I wave her to the chair beside my desk. But I already sense what her problem is: I get two or three cases every semester.

"It's not fair," she says.

"Oh?" I reply. "Tell me about it."

So she begins. It's about the portfolio evaluation: she failed.

"Oh," I say, "I'm sorry. What happened? Tell me about it."

Well, she says, several of the papers in the portfolio failed, and it's not fair.

"How did that happen?" I ask.

Well, two of the four required papers just weren't good enough. She quickly skims over the fact; she does not even try to defend her work. The papers just weren't good enough.

By now I have confirmed that I am dealing with the problem I immediately recognized, and so, with a pang of anxiety, I go through the litany. "But surely you had enough time to prepare," I go on. "After all, you had the entire semester to put the portfolio together."

She grants that she did. She takes full responsibility for her work.

"And wasn't your instructor helpful? Didn't she explain your problems? Didn't she give you a chance to revise?"

The student has nothing but admiration for her instructor, who was helpful and considerate and often helped her revise a paper four or five times.

"So what's the problem?" I ask, disingenuously now, for I now know what the problem is better than she does, and I catch my breath waiting to see how well she can articulate the cause of her distress.

"It's just not fair," she says. "My instructor thought some of my other papers were passing, but I couldn't submit those. The portfolio guidelines say we have to submit an informative piece and a research report. I don't write those kinds of things as well. If it weren't for the fact that I failed the portfolio, I might have gotten a C in the course."

I wait, but that is as far as she can go, and once again I am safe. So I haul out the old arguments and rattle them off: "You see, although portfolios are designed to give you a chance to submit your best work under the most helpful, most naturalistic conditions, we still have to be sure that you can write in a variety of genres for a variety of purposes for a variety of audiences. There is not just one kind of writing or one way of writing. Which is why we have the restrictions in the portfolio guidelines. Which is why we teach writing different kinds of things for different purposes and audiences. Which is why we require you to hand in a number of different kinds of writing in the portfolio."

All of this is true, but there is still the possibility that she will see the fundamental problem, the fatal flaw, in this reasoning. And I wonder, in a brief attack of panic, what would happen to me and my writing portfolio program if a student close to the university president or a member of the Board of Regents failed the portfolio exam and then realized the implications of what I had been arguing. I envision a sea of students outside my window, some of them waving placards that read "Down with the portfolio" and "Portfolios Discriminate" and all of them chanting, their faces contorted with rage, their chant building to a crescendo of anger and frustration: "It's not fair, it's not fair, IT'S NOT FAIR."

I have come to understand that what my disgruntled student senses but what she cannot articulate, what she calls the unfairness of the portfolio, is inherent in our use of portfolios as a course exit exam. In a broader, more philosophical sense, what she senses but cannot articulate is the question of VALIDITY, of whether our portfolio exam measures what it is supposed to measure.

And what is our portfolio exam supposed to measure? Since we use portfolios as an exit exam, we often claim that it measures the general sense of competence that our students should have demonstrated in the writing they did for our courses: Expository Writing I, a course in expressive and informative writing, and Expository Writing II, a course in writing persuasively and in response to literature. In Expository Writing I, for example, our students learn how to write any of the things they can submit in their portfolio: personal narratives; descriptions of people, places, or events; observations, news articles and feature stories, reflections and meditations, personal essays and literary nonfiction, interviews and profiles, how-to pieces, process analyses, and informative research reports. The individual pieces of writing in the portfolio need not meet any predetermined standard of form or content, and no individual portfolio need necessarily be like any other—with one exception: in our system, each portfolio must contain one expressive piece, one informative piece, and one researched piece, as well as an in-class writing that can be either expressive or informative.

But if both a personal narrative and a reflective essay can satisfy the requirement for the expressive piece, and they can, and if a journalistic profile of a public personality and a description of a process on how to tune a carburetor can satisfy the requirement for an informative piece, and they can, then just what does competence in these cases look like? And why is the ability demonstrated in these pieces a better indication of a writer's competence than the pieces she did not submit?

In his foreword to Belanoff and Dickson's *Portfolios: Process and Product*, Peter Elbow argues that portfolios have "improved validity" over other kinds of writing tests because they give a *better picture of students' writing abilities*" (xi). That is, Elbow thinks that portfolios are valid because they show what students can do in a variety of genres written under naturalistic conditions. Now, in one sense, of course, no one can argue with Elbow's assertion. Most of us who have studied writing agree that people generally write differently under different conditions, for different purposes and audiences, and that their abilities in various modes and contexts vary considerably. But in this sense Elbow's assertion is true by definition: all a student has to do to demonstrate competence is to write a number of pieces in different genres for different audiences.

In another sense, however, Elbow's sense of validity begs the most fundamental question: how do we recognize the competence demonstrated in a portfolio? What does such competence look like? If we can't articulate what such competence looks like other than to say that pieces in the portfolio will be written differently, we will have no way to tell whether the writing in the portfolios is any good or whether one portfolio is better than another. If students can submit such a wide range of writing, each for a different purpose, each for a different audience, each following the format and conventions of a different kind of discourse, it hardly seems possible to evaluate such different pieces of writing by a common standard, some general sense of overall competence.

In our program at Kansas State we struggled to develop a scoring guide or rubric that would fit all the possible kinds of writing that could be submitted in our portfolios. Commonly used criteria, such as a clear purpose, an organizational structure that is easy to follow and clearly marked, substantive detail or evidence, an appropriate style or tone, and error-free editing, seemed to be too general and of little help in evaluating such diverse products as, for example, a reflective personal essay and an informative piece on how to tune a carburetor. In addition, we found it impossible to develop a set of "anchor portfolios," a set of model portfolios to guide us as to what a superior, average, and unacceptable portfolio would look like. We were simply allowing our students to submit too many different kinds of writing in their portfolios for a single set of portfolios to work as a guide or model of what all portfolios should look like.

On the other hand, we sensed that if we adapted criteria to the individual demands of each kind of writing submitted in the portfolios, we would wind up with a measure of very specific demands that could not be used to compare portfolios with each other; that is, we would wind up with a criterion-referenced test, one that measured how well each piece of writing met the demands of a very task-specific definition of writing quality.

We finally settled on the five general criteria I mentioned earlier for our initial reading of portfolios: purpose, organization, evidence/detail, expression, and mechanics, more out of a sense of futility than anything else. And in the overwhelming majority of cases, some general sense of competence has been enough to allow us to agree in our judgments. I am always amazed that we do not disagree more. Perhaps it is our training program. Perhaps it is that we tend to require the same kinds of writing and often share assignments. Perhaps it is that we only pass or fail portfolios—we do not grade them—so our judgments can be rather rough. Or perhaps it is the grace of God.

But to help us deal with the significant number of borderline portfolios about which we could not agree, we decided to require that each piece submitted in the portfolio must be accompanied by an assignment sheet listing more particular requirements. And for these hard cases, our primary criterion became how well the pieces in the portfolio fit the assignments.

In some ways this is an attractive solution. Our readers have to balance general criteria with the specifics of the assignment, to see how the general criteria are to be manifested in each piece of writing. To fulfill the criterion of evidence or detail in an *expressive narrative,* for example, the assignment sheets usually call for a dramatized key moment with sensory detail and dialogue; but for evidence or detail in a *profile* the assignment sheets usually call for anecdotes and quotations from the subject of the profile. In fact, we might argue that these assignment sheets are just particular rubrics, which help guide our readings of particular papers.

Such an argument may look like a triumph of ingenuity, but it is not. It is a defeat. For much of the theoretical justification of a portfolio system is that it measures some general sense of competence. What we were admitting is that in many ways we did not know what that competence looks like or that competence can be demonstrated in so many different ways the concept is meaningless. What we have instead is a criterion-referenced test: we are measuring how well students meet the requirements of a predetermined set of very specific assignments.

Having gone through the difficulties of trying to articulate what our portfolios measure, I have abandoned the attempt to claim that our portfolio exam measures "writing competence." "Writing competence" is analogous to such concepts as intelligence: we can only recognize them in concrete and particular situations anyway. "Writing competence" is simply an attribute we assign to writers whose work we admire for very particular and very different reasons. I think of our portfolio exam as a collection of individual criterion-referenced tests. Each paper in the portfolio is a sample of what the student was required to do in the course, and to pass the portfolio the student must pass two of the four papers. In these terms, the issue is whether the student fulfilled the requirements of the course, not whether she demonstrated some sense of competence above and beyond those requirements.

So if the disgruntled student had argued that the portfolio was invalid because the range of writing illustrated by her passing papers was sufficient to demonstrate her competence, that an adequate research report should not be a litmus test for a writer's competence, I would only have been able to nod and sympathize and even in one sense agree with her. But my counterargument would have been that we are not measuring competence; we are simply measuring whether students have fulfilled the requirements of the course.

Scene Two

A chubby man with a military haircut comes into my office. He introduces himself as a colleague from a science department. He is outwardly affable, but I sense that he is wound up tightly and trying to keep himself under control. He makes it very clear that he has not come to complain. He tells me that his daughter received C's in Expos I and II, but he has no quarrel with those grades. He admits that his daughter is not a great writer.

However, he *is* very concerned, he says, and in a rambling and often incoherent conversation I come to understand two things: first, this man's daughter has been taught in our program by two different instructors with two very different teaching styles, and second, her portfolios have been read the first semester by a self-selected group of experienced instructors and the second semester by two less experienced instructors paired by one of our advisors. During the course of our conversation, the professor manages to keep himself under control, but just once he allows a certain amount of anger to bubble up and the point he is making at the time is this: it is not right that we conduct an exam that is ostensibly organized to be fair and consistent in such an arbitrary way. We should not allow our teachers to teach in such different ways—even though the results may be the same—and we definitely should not allow our groups of readers to be so variable and arbitrary. To be fair and consistent, we need to group our readers randomly.

When the professor leaves, I have another nightmare flash: what if a major political figure or influential alumnus had the same reservations and decided to pressure the English Department into dropping the portfolio system? How would I defend myself?

Although the professor did not use the term, he was arguing about our RELIABILITY, about whether his daughter's portfolio would receive the same rating with a different set of readers. Ironically, he did not use his daughter's experience as an example of the inconsistency he predicted. His objections were entirely theoretical.

Some background might be helpful here. For the past four years we have experimented with various ways of grouping our portfolio readers: we have read in pairs, in triads, and in larger groups; we have read in pairs, triads, and larger groups that mixed new instructors, second- and third-year instructors, and our old hands; we have read in pairs, triads, and larger groups that have been limited to readers with the same years of experience in the program. We have also allowed our old hands to organize themselves into pairs or groups. In a survey we conducted after all this experimentation, our instructors indicated overwhelmingly that they preferred to read portfolios in triads with instructors with similar experience, which is the system we are using now. Our advisors organize the groups for the first-, second-, and third-year people. Our old hands organize themselves, although I insist that they change groups each semester.

Of course, this system is not ideal by any stretch of the imagination, and by the standards of many experts in testing and evaluation, it is horrendous. Edward White, for example, strongly recommends that portfolios be read in the same room at the same time in order to enforce common standards:

> Experience with essay tests has shown that reliable readings can take place only in controlled sessions, with all evaluators reading at the same time and place, under the direction of a chief reader. This experience may not hold true for portfolios (they are still relatively untried for assessment in writing), but it probably will, as the scoring of portfolios seems in every way even more difficult than the scoring of essays. (Assigning, Responding, Evaluating 69)

Our system is not ideal, but we adopted it because it was politically feasible. When we instituted the system, our instructors and graduate teaching assistants (GTAs) were more concerned about the amount of extra work the system would take than with any other issue, a valid concern considering that we were not offering them any more money. In addition, a large grading session at the end of the term was a sensitive matter for GTAs with papers to write and their own exams to study for. Allowing groups to trade among themselves and read at their convenience was a trade-off we felt we had to accept in order for us to have a portfolio system in the first place. In order to increase our reliability we have five grading sessions a year, three for the entire program and two in small groups, in which we read papers together and try to arrive at a common understanding of how we should rate them.

Table 23–1

Surprises in the Trial Run of the Portfolio System at Kansas State University

	Fall 1989	Spring 1990	Fall 1990	Spring 1991	Fall 1991	Spring 1992
Total # of Portfolios	2,859	2,069	2,493	1,913	2,460	1,542
Surprises	30	29	54	34	94	50
—as % of portfolios	1%	1.4%	2.2%	1.8%	3.8%	3.2%

On paper we seem to agree most of the time, which is what I told the complaining professor. Every semester we conduct a trial run, in which students submit one paper to an outside reader. If that paper passes, the students are guaranteed that at least one paper in the final portfolio will pass. The trial run introduces them to the way the portfolio works, and for the great majority of students it builds their confidence.

The trial run is just that—a trial run, practice. Whether students pass or fail has no bearing on their grades, and so we have no appeal system if the instructor disagrees with the outside reader. We counsel our instructors to inform the students of their disagreements, so that the students can get a sense of how and why people disagree about writing and use that information not only in preparing their final portfolios but in the writing they do for the rest of their lives. Despite the fact that we do not keep records of those who pass or fail, I do ask instructors to let me know the results of the trial run, some of which are shown in Table 23–1.

One of the things I ask for is surprises, the number of failing papers instructors would have passed and the number of passing papers they would have failed. As you can see, the results vary from 1 percent to 3.8 percent, a rate that is rather small. The only thing ominous is that the rate of surprises has gradually gone up over the years. So far so good.

We have also kept records of the number of portfolios that have passed and failed, and the number of failures that have been appealed by the original instructor, indicating that the readers could not agree on a judgment. These results appear in Table 23–2, and whether they are something we should worry about is a matter of interpretation.

When I am on the defensive as with the complaining professor, I always cite the following figures: as a percentage of all portfolios, the number of disputed portfolios is very small; from .2 to 1.7 percent. What I conveniently do not mention is that as a percentage of failing portfolios the number of disputes is very high indeed: from 9.6 to 42 percent. However, I might note that both the highest and lowest figures come from the 1989–1990 academic year, the first year the portfolio system was in effect for all of our instructors.

Table 23–2

Appeals in the Portfolio System at Kansas State University

	Spring 1989	Fall 1989	Spring 1990	Fall 1990	Spring 1991	Fall 1991	Spring 1992
Total # of Portfolios	1,582	2,662	1,869	2,427	1,830	2,399	1,541
Failures	58	73	31	70	60	114	50
Appeals—as % of failures	24	42	9.6	20	18	14	22
—as % of portfolios	.09	1.2	.2	1.7	1.6	.7	7
Total # of Instructors	49	64	57	62	52	59	46
Number of instructors appealing	5	7	2	9	6*	4	5
—as % of all instructors	10.2	10.9	3.5	14.5	11.5	6.8	10.9

*Not including one instructor with special difficulties who appealed 18 portfolios

During that year we were still getting used to the system, and a number of instructors resisted the idea that they should have to accommodate their standards to the larger group. The main battle was fought in the fall, and in the spring we retreated to lick our wounds. If we eliminate 1989–1990 as an anomalous year, the percentage of disputes ranges from 14 to 24 percent. The most noteworthy thing about these data is that despite our best efforts at training our instructors to read papers in similar ways, our rate of disputes is not going down.

What is of more concern is why the number of disputes is not going down. We get some clue from the percentage of instructors involved: from 3.5 to 14.5 percent, or if we eliminate highs and lows, about one out of every ten instructors. These percentages indicate only the number of instructors who appealed the outside reader's or group's judgment. The objection might be made that it takes at least two people to disagree, so the figures should be at least twice as large as they are. To which I would reply, in most cases, no. The reason I think that only one instructor need be counted in these disputes cannot be conveyed by facts and figures. It is a matter of interpretation. Let me explain.

Our program is staffed entirely by about forty-five graduate teaching assistants and fifteen part-time instructors. No tenured faculty teach in the program unless they want extra employment during the summer or unless they are new comp/rhetoric faculty who want an inside look at how the system works before they assume an administrative task. That is not because our comp/rhetoric faculty shun teaching lower-division courses. It is just that we are terribly understaffed and have no one else to teach upper-division writing courses and graduate courses in composition theory and rhetoric.

Although we are pushing our GTAs to complete their degrees in two years, most of them take three years. Thus, we have a turnover of instructors of about 30 percent every year. With such a large staff and such a large turnover, we are bound to get a certain number of GTAs and part-time instructors who have difficulty teaching or whose skills in reading, commenting, and editing are less than we might like.

Although I have not kept accurate records, I believe that the large majority of disputes over portfolios generally occurs for this reason: an instructor originally grades a paper much too quickly or carelessly and either gives the paper a passing grade or does not adequately inform the student how to improve it. When the weakness of the paper is pointed out to the original instructor by the outside reader during the portfolio assessment, she has to appeal to protect herself from the wrath of the student or in the hope that the final reader will take into account her original assessment in order to be fair to the student. In effect, what is in dispute is not the quality of the papers in the portfolio but the judgment of the instructor and the adequacy of the instruction the student received. This is why I do find the rate of disagreements so intimidating: about one in ten of our instructors seems either incapable of recognizing bad writing or unwilling or unable to tell the students how to improve their writing.

The complaining professor was right, but for the wrong reasons. It is not the nature of our groupings that produces our disputes. It is the lack of attention or inability of certain of our instructors. This problem has been constant, and I see no way of making it better. If our program is attacked by disgruntled parents for its lack of reliability, I can always defend the portfolio system by arguing that the percentage of our disagreements is very low, considering the total number of portfolios. But my heart will not be in it.

Is our system unreliable? I do not know. I am not sure I know what the term means in our case. Most of us, including the complaining professor, have been conditioned to think of reliability in terms of classrooms that have been carefully set up to control a number of variables, training in holistic scoring, the apparatus of monitored large-group grading sessions, and high reliability coefficients. But even commonly accepted methods of achieving traditional notions of reliability have their problems (see Charney; Huot, "Reliability, Validity, and Holistic Scoring"). To me "reliability" only means what I have told you: we cannot achieve unanimity in our judgments because a number of our instructors are not very good at evaluating and commenting on papers. What then is an acceptable rate of disagreement? I do not know that, either. But as long as people think of reliability the way my complaining professor does, our program will always be vulnerable to the charge that our portfolio system is not reliable. The only defense I can muster is that we ought to be more flexible in our notions of reliability, that we ought to think of reliability in terms of particular circumstances.

Unless we do achieve some sort of flexibility in understanding reliability, when push comes to shove, I will not defend our system because it is reliable. I *will* defend it because it helps us to teach writing the way I believe it ought to be taught: it forces both students and instructors to take revision seriously. It forces both students and instructors to confront the fact that evaluating writing is often a messy, subjective, and even quarrelsome business.

In particular, it forces us to tell students with weaker papers that although we, as their instructors, might pass the particular piece of writing, another reader may have some difficulties with certain areas, and the students ought to really work to improve those things in the next draft. That is, the portfolio system allows us to play good cop, bad cop. In this sense, the very potential for disagreement becomes a pedagogical device for motivating students to revise and polish. We hope that, if nothing else, our students will learn what a complex and multifaceted thing writing is and that honorable people can disagree about what constitutes acceptable writing. And we hope that our students will recognize that often they will have to write for different audiences with different standards and expectations. Our portfolio assessment is then a metaphor for what they will confront when they leave our classes. College is not too early to learn how messy life really is.

In addition, the portfolio system forces our weaker instructors to confront the fact that someone else will be reading their papers and helping to decide whether their students should pass. That puts a certain amount of pressure on them to learn what the standards of the group are and to help their students as best they can. I hate to imagine what these weaker instructors would be doing with their students' papers if they were not required to fit into the portfolio system. For this reason, portfolios are a way to protect students from arbitrary and uninformed judgments.

I suspect that many other programs around the country are like ours, struggling to make their evaluation systems as good as they can be. And I also suspect that if we continue to accept only the notions of validity and reliability promoted by national testing services that evaluate single essays, we will always be held to a standard that we will have difficulty meeting. I think we need to allow individual programs to develop notions of validity and reliability which take into account their particular goals and methods.

In any case, our programs will only be as valid as the claims we make for them. When I talk about our portfolio system to other members of the Kansas State community—students, faculty, and administrators—I am careful to claim only that the system helps us to guarantee that at the end of our courses, our students can indeed write at least three papers that most people would accept as literate and worth reading. And I point out that our portfolio system seems to be more of a criterion-referenced test than it is a measure of competence. Perhaps because we have not made exaggerated claims for what our portfolio system can accomplish, it has achieved broad support on our campus.

About our reliability I am more concerned. But until that utopian day when universities start relying on trained specialists in composition and rhetoric to teach all of their writing courses, we will continue to rely on GTAs and instructors who come and go with disheartening regularity, many of whom will not be as knowledgeable, as perceptive, and as dedicated as we would like. And until that day when universities pay instructors enough and provide GTAs with the time to balance teaching and learning, we will continue to have ad hoc arrangements for reading portfolios. Our portfolio system cannot change our fundamental situation; it can, however, encourage a sense of community and common standards, and it can provide some pressure on weaker instructors to perform better than they might otherwise.

I suspect that portfolio systems will always have problems with validity. I see no clear way to prepare anchor portfolios or to achieve common standards for the wide range of writing portfolios allow. But I look forward to further research on this matter.

I also suspect that the conditions of universities will always work against portfolio systems such as ours becoming more rigorous in their reliability. But at least portfolios systems can encourage instructors to do justice to the writing of their students, which is a step in the right direction.

24

Climbing the Slippery Slope of Assessment: The Programmatic Use of Writing Portfolios

Charles I. Schuster

From 1977 until 1992, the University of Wisconsin-Milwaukee required undergraduate students to pass an English Proficiency Essay Exam to graduate or—since 1986—to attain junior status. The Exam was typical of the proficiency genre: students wrote an argumentative essay in ninety minutes on a blind topic in blue books. Those responses were then scored holistically on a four-point scale by composition instructors, in our case mostly teaching assistants and lecturers. During the 1991–1992 academic year that situation changed, largely as a result of a seven-year effort on my part to alter the way we conceived of "writing proficiency." The story of that change—and the key role that portfolio assessment played in it—is the topic of another essay. I want to focus here on the challenges that our new writing requirement poses for teachers of writing. Those challenges are bound into portfolio assessment methodology and are not, I think, specific to one university; but beyond those difficulties I want to address the pedagogical and theoretical difficulties that large-scale portfolio assessment introduces into a writing program, and ultimately the programmatic difficulties of binding the testing of writing within the teaching of writing.

UWM offers a four-semester writing sequence at the freshman level: two non-credit, basic writing courses (English 090 and 095), which emphasize confidence, fluency, coherence, and control; and two credit, college-level courses (English 101 and 112), which engage students in analysis, critique, and argumentation. Students must earn a C or higher in a course to take the next one in the sequence. Once they complete English 112 with a C or higher, they have satisfied the new English Composition Requirement which, for most students, replaced the old English Proficiency Essay Exam. Currently, portfolio review is mandated for all 095 and 112 students. For fall semester, 1992, those courses represented more than two thousand students. In addition, 70 percent of our English 101 instructors also participate in portfolio assessment, adding another eight hundred or so student portfolios to our reading load. Thus at the end of each semester, we will evaluate two to three thousand portfolios to determine if students will successfully complete our composition courses. Whether we can survive this work load logistically and psychically remains an open question; in our second-semester course alone, portfolio assessment demands a minimum of six to seven hundred person-hours of reading, evaluating, and reviewing. That there are benefits to this method of assessment for students, instructors, and the entire writing program is obvious, but it also exacts considerable costs, especially in regard to time and compensation: underpaid and overworked teaching assistants and lecturers perform most of this labor, although I have found some ways to compensate them exclusive of salary adjustment.

The UWM portfolios consist of one in-class essay, two out-of-class essays, and an out-of-class reflective letter. Different courses demand different kinds of writing: English 095 basic writers include narrative-descriptive work in their portfolios; English 112 portfolios, on the other hand, must contain essays that make explicit arguments offered through a close reading of whole, nonfictional accounts by writers like Paul Fussell, Frances Fitzgerald, and Jonathan Kozol. Although narrative and descriptive writing can play a part in these 112 portfolios, they cannot represent a dominant mode of writing. (Note: we don't believe in the modes as a way of teaching, but we find their usage inescapable in describing the written products students write.)

The benefits of portfolio assessment have been well articulated by Elbow, Belanoff, and many others (Belanoff and Elbow, "Using Portfolios to Increase Collaboration and Community in a Writing Program"; Murphy and Smith). They include increased collaboration among instructors, an emphasis on both writing process and writing product, an increased sense of democracy in that students choose—to some extent—the terms by which they will be evaluated, etc. As Grant Wiggins has noted, portfolios may be the closest we will ever come to creating "authentic assessment" (703–4) in writing programs. We agree with these benefits; portfolio assessment—as we have articulated it in our own unique circumstances—has greatly improved our teaching, and, we know, helped us to maintain standards.

But we are also struggling with significant problems that may well doom portfolio assessment programmatically within our writing curriculum. Those problems fall into four main categories: 1) Recycling Paper; 2) Appropriating Essays; 3) Fictionalizing Authors; and 4) Mediating Differences. Let me say from the outset that these problems largely arise from the fact that our assessment process replaced a proficiency exam; as such, it must (at least for now) perform a parallel testing function. It must pass some students and fail others; it must discriminate between capable and incapable writers, promoting the former and demoting the latter. During our first full semester of portfolio assessment, more than 25 percent of our students failed to earn grades of C or higher in English 101 and English 112; all those students are required to repeat these courses, since completion of 112 is a requirement for junior status. For students, therefore, our portfolio system is high stakes; their graduation depends upon successful completion of one, two, or three separate writing portfolios. With so much depending upon each portfolio, the writing program operates under significant constraints. We must be certain that each portfolio represents the student's abilities and receives an appropriate score of either C or higher, or C- or lower. Given these factors, the kinds of problems I outline below take on significant resonance.

Problem 1: Recycling Paper

Let's begin by examining a portfolio by a freshman student named Desiree. For her English 112 class, Desiree submitted exclusively argumentative essays. Desiree's portfolio received a high score, a result she might expect given her self-assessment: "I don't consider myself a writer," confessed Desiree when interviewed about her writing, "but I am very happy with my papers." As it turns out, these essays should be good ones, for Desiree has been in a very real sense writing them for several semesters. Desiree freely states that she first wrote the essay on abortion for her 095 class a year earlier and recycled that paper for English 112. Says Desiree: "I turned the abortion paper back in because I think it's a very good paper, and then . . . I redid a paper on suicide," a paper that she first also completed a year earlier in 095. Thus Desiree has in some sense been writing these essays for three semesters, a potentially troubling fact since we are applying a one-semester perspective when we evaluate them. This may be a problem for us, but it is not one for Desiree. On the contrary, she is pleased with herself and under no circumstances considers that she is engaged in unethical or inappropriate behavior. And perhaps we should be similarly pleased: from a purely instructional perspective, most composition faculty would commend a student so committed to a paper and a topic that she is willing to rewrite it successively for two or three semesters.

Desiree's use of previously-written essays is probably endemic within freshman composition courses; undoubtedly, some students do so because they are lazy, unmotivated, and unethical. But others, and I think Desiree is one of them, find certain subjects compelling. Like professional essayists, they return to an essay repeatedly over a period of months or years in a successive effort to get it right. As a writing instructor, I want to encourage this kind of long-term commitment and revision; as upholder of portfolio assessment, however, I almost certainly will discourage it. To evaluate an essay written over two or three semesters by the same criteria as one written over five or ten weeks is unfair and unacceptable.

We could inhibit such paper recycling by creating course-specific assignments tied to particular texts or ideas; indeed in English 112 we are doing precisely that, and we may follow suit throughout our curriculum. In more paranoid fashion, we could collect and file all the previous essays that students wrote in our courses until they graduated, or install video cameras in their dorm rooms, or insist that each assignment be notarized. My point is that our portfolio assessment, with its high-stakes emphasis on two to three out-of-class essays, will likely encourage students to work on essays that have already proved successful in other writing classes, or that have proven unsuccessful in their earlier incarnations in previous sections of the same course. We have yet to resolve the problem of paper recycling so as to best serve the interests of both teaching and evaluating.

Problem 2: Appropriating Essays

In "On Students' Rights to Their Own Texts: A Model of Teacher Response," Lil Brannon and Cy Knoblauch consider the danger of teachers overwhelming student writing with comments, suggestions, and explicit recommendations for changes in sentence structure, ideas, organization, and correctness. They do so, argue Brannon and Knoblauch, because teachers possess an authority lacking in student writers, thus giving control of the text to the teacher-reader rather than to the student-writer. Thus "the teacher more often than the student determines what the writing will be about, the form it will take, and the criteria that will determine its success" (158). Portfolio assessment exaggerates the tendency among instructors to efface student authors and appropriate texts. In essence, the student disappears as writer, or at the very least produces an essay initially authored by the student but revised and edited by the instructor.

In encouraging, nay, demanding, extensive revision from students, the portfolio process demands that we consider these issues of help, collaboration, and appropriation. UWM instructors stress the importance of writing groups; similarly, they encourage all writers—from freshman to faculty—to visit the Writing Center for tutorial help. We conceive of such help as fundamental to growth in writing; most of our instructors spend many office hours working individually with students on their drafts. I would imagine most writing programs are similarly committed to such instructional support.

When piloting English 112 with its mandatory portfolio assessment, we discovered that many students demanded intensive, one-on-one help from instructors; many students met with instructors ten, fifteen, even twenty times in an effort to improve their portfolio essays. Such help exhausted the instructors, but it greatly helped the students; the pass rate among students was close to 90 percent, far above expectations given the low test scores these students had attained during their years at UWM. Our question is, therefore, what kinds of teacherly help are appropriate, and what kinds of help end up appropriating the student writing? The play on words is significant: given our high-stakes system, we must negotiate that difference between "appropriate" as an adjective and "appropriate" as a verb. We must determine how teachers can best help students without undermining portfolio evaluation. In the final analysis, our system requires that we determine with a fair amount of certainty whose essays those are in the student portfolios.

To return to Desiree for a moment, we can see the problem reflected in her statement about teacher help. Stated Desiree:

> basically I read through what she [the instructor] says, and the majority of it I agree with—some of it I don't so I just leave it my way— . . . she's really helped me because I have for my portfolio given her my papers like . . . it had to be at least 10–15 times and she's proofread them over again and given them back, read them over again, and given them back, read them over again, given them back, read them over again, given them back. So I am happy.

Desiree's writing has been significantly appropriated by her instructor, but that appropriation has served a useful pedagogical purpose. Desiree likely learned from the repeated responses of her instructor; through her teacher's example, Desiree may well have improved her own revising and editing abilities. Unfortunately, it is impossible to determine with any certainty whose mastery is being evaluated in the Desiree's final portfolio. Nor is this an isolated case. When another student, Norm, was describing his process of revising and editing, he stated:

> I don't find them [the mistakes in my essays]. Either friends or my professor—they find them. My instructor . . . gives good choices or she gives her opinion like what I should say or what words I should use. I use a lot of her advice, and then I give it back to her again and then she gives other suggestions. She crosses things out and puts things that she would have said, and gives suggestions like do this or try to make the sentences more varied, and then you just go on your own.

Our composition program is devoting considerable attention now to theories of commenting and exploring options like minimal marking and marginal interrogation to help instructors cope with this difficult pedagogical issue. We have asked instructors to refrain from extensive editing and improving of student writing, and some students complain now that instructors do not provide enough specific help in terms of focus, coherence, the development of an argument, the nuts and bolts crafting of a piece of writing. A parallel concern, however, is appropriation by tutors, friends, parents, and paper mills. We have always had some problem in this regard, but our old system did not emphasize the production of essays in this way. Since we initiated portfolio review, our plagiarism cases have multiplied four-fold, and we are now cautiously developing ways to protect against conscious and unconscious appropriation.

Problem 3: Fictionalizing Authors

In my experience, readers who evaluate writing in large-scale assessments such as ours reveal a strong tendency to create a portrait of the author based on the writing. Readers offer comments such as, "You can see that this author would have considered this argument about the sexist nature of advertising if only she had had time" or "I can just see this writer fumbling through his dictionary trying to find another four-dollar word for a ten-cent idea" or "I think this essay works because the writer obviously is a great listener."

Some of this fictionalizing is unavoidable; some of it may aid in portfolio assessment. But in my view the overall effect of this extrapolating is destructive to fair and measured evaluation. In effect, fictionalizing student authors moves readers away from normed criteria, replacing careful evaluation with reader response. Readers of student portfolios cannot presume to know what authors intended but did not do, what students look like, what their personalities are, how they feel toward the course, whether or not they are good, upstanding, sincere, loyal, and patriotic. Presumptions concerning personality, intention, behavior, and the like skew readings or turn assessment into novel reading. By fictionalizing authors, readers add an obscuring psychological or psychoanalytic layer of interpretation to their analyses. Instead of reading the writing, they read the writer, a tendency that can only complicate and undermine the assessment of writing. The probable origin of this tendency may be in the reading histories of the assessors: they are graduate students in English who have spent their lives reading and interpreting narrative literature, figuring out the intentions of characters and the consequences of actions. Such fictionalizing serves a useful purpose within a classroom: by doing so, instructors individualize and humanize their students, or at the very least, create narrative explanations and justifications for student work. Writing assessment, however, demands that we exclusively evaluate what the student has produced on the page in the portfolio. Fictionalizing in this context can only obscure judgment.

Once again, Desiree provides some insight here; she claims that the predominant characteristic of her writing is that she is emotional:

> I let all my emotions out when I write. I'm not an emotional person, but that's what I like about writing. You can bring everything out of you. It's easier to write about it than to say it. . . .

Desiree also finds that it is "easier to persuade people by bringing in emotions." Such a statement is considerably at odds with Desiree's essays that, although written about "emotional" subjects such as abortion, teen suicide, and drunk drivers, are largely flat, understated, factual, and distant in voice and perspective. In her essay on alcoholism, for example, Desiree writes:

> The most important causes of suicide are emotional. Young people who try to kill themselves usually have trouble developing relationships or

keeping them. They are often described as "loners." Lack of self-esteem and no real sense of self-importance also hurts these teenagers. They often feel that they don't matter to anyone. They may simply want someone to say, "I love you! I don't want you to die!"

Another cause of suicide attempts among young people is the pressure to succeed. This is often the result of having insecure parents who set unrealistically high standards for their children. This may lead . . . (etc.)

Desiree's work mainly projects an informational, almost clinical attitude toward her subjects; she, conversely, thinks she is emoting all over the page. What is most important, however, is that all portfolio readers hold in check their impressions of her purpose and personality so that they can evaluate her work on the basis of the criteria and standards that have been explicitly articulated and shared with students and other readers.

Problem 4: Mediating Differences

My final concern is whether we can form valid and reliable holistic judgments of portfolios that consist of two or three different kinds of work produced in dissimilar settings. Since the portfolios at UWM consist of an in-class essay, two out-of-class essays, and a reflective letter, we are struggling to negotiate differences, say, between problematic in-class writing and perfectly acceptable out-of-class writing, between essays written on easier subjects and others exploring more complex and abstract lines of reasoning.

In our classrooms, we frequently discover that students produce uneven work over time. Most of us have observed cases in which a student plummets from an A essay to a D essay, or handles one subject brilliantly on an in-class response and then utterly flops on her next out-of-class assignment. In these situations, we can meet with the student, request draft materials, work to discover problems and solutions. In a single portfolio, however, little information is forthcoming: other than the reflective letter, evaluators have no way to determine contexts and case histories.

How, for example, are the differences between the in-class and out-of-class writing exhibited in the following portfolio by an English 112 student to be mediated? The hand-written essay shown in Figure 24–1 represents the student's in-class response to Frances Fitzgerald's *Cities on a Hill,* one of the two required texts for the course. The essay indicates what the student is able to accomplish in fifty minutes on a general topic concerning the ways Fitzgerald represents different communities. I include only the essay's first two pages. Most composition instructors, I think, would agree that the level of writing/thinking ability in these pages does not merit a grade of C or higher in a second-semester college-level composition course. The garbled syntax, the lack of coherence, the surface-level problems, the inability to create a focus and context for the writing point to basic problems in composing—especially

Figure 24–1

Frances Fitzgerald explains in her book | reader think that those communities are wrong.

Cities on a Hill different types of commu- | In the Sun City chapter Fitzgerald

nity that exist in United. ~~It was expecting~~ states where I read books | explained with details what was that

When I read the book, I was expecting | community about. For example, where it

to read an objective book where the author | is located (Florida): who are the members,

describes without her opinion each communi- | what they do: Sun City is a community

ty characteristics. I was ~~white~~ wrong. While | of retired people who ~~according to Fitzgerald~~

I was reading some of ~~the~~ its chapters of | are wealthy enough to afford living there, according

~~Cities on the Hill~~ I noticed that you can | In addition, that is not black people living there and not jewish

perceive the author's opinion. It was like | to Fitzgerald. When the author mention this

reading between the lines. Fitzgerald's | I think she is tying to tell us that no matter

examples about each community make the | if they are a community apart from the rest of

when we remember that this student has spent much of the term reading, writing, and discussing Fitzgerald's text. After all, such a student may well be asked to produce a spontaneous piece of writing at work; an employer seeing this poor quality will attack the low standards of the composition program.

I think we respond much differently, however, to this student's out-of-class writing, a typical page of which reads as follows:

> In the past few years, our society has witnessed the increase of teenagers who spend most of their time in the malls. An interesting fact is that they are there by themselves or with other teenagers. They spend their time there walking inside the mall or sitting in a specific corner of the mall. This situation was not expected because malls were constructed for adult convenience when they do shopping, and not for teenagers to walk around. As William Severini Kowinski mentions in his essay *Kids in the Mall:* "the presence of so many teenagers for so much time was not something mall developers planned on".
>
> Kowinski gave two examples related to this matter. One example is about the kid who made his mother drop him off at the mall after school everyday until closing time. The other example is the kid who rode his bicycle five miles everyday to get to his old neighborhood's mall. Therefore, I think there are reasons for kids deciding to go to the malls instead of their homes. I think those reasons come from their homes. One of these reasons

is that kids are missing their parents' attentions so, being at the mall is a way for kids to escape from home.

Most parents are too busy working or with their problems. Therefore, some kids are not receiving the necessary attention and affection. I believe that because I have a cousin who used to go to the malls after school. Her parents would complain about it, but she would not stop going there. In addition . . .

The out-of-class writing is clearly stronger; although not overly sophisticated in thought or style, it represents a student able to think through a subject, articulate some of the major issues, and integrate library research into her/his own perspective. I think such a student should pass the course, much as I would want him/her to take additional writing or writing-emphasis courses.

Is it appropriate for a student to fail a course on the basis of one fifty-minute in-class essay rather than two fourteen-week out-of-class essays? That is, is there a standard for in-class writing below which no student should fall? Should all students who receive the lowest possible scores on in-class writing fail the course, no matter how good their out-of-class work? How do I mediate the differences? Is such mediation possible in any meaningful way? The question becomes more complicated when different portfolios are compared to each other, when we attempt to form programmatic judgments as to the relative qualities of students in different courses producing radically different essays—but all judged by the same absolutist criteria. Although we can normalize instruction to a greater extent by creating a uniform syllabus and eliminating variability in terms of texts and modes, we do so at our peril: instructors must be invested in their teaching if assessment is to have any value or credibility. Perhaps the most essential question of all is what do we mean by writing ability and how best is it demonstrated? We know writing is individual, multiple, social, collaborative. We know that capable writers demonstrate their abilities in a wide variety of settings, purposes, and audiences. But what modes and contexts and purposes should we validate? What do we mean when we decide for our university that a student is a good and capable writer?

At UWM, we moved to portfolio assessment because the ninety-minute blind topic exam undercut writing instruction, distorted what is important in writing theory and pedagogy, and tended to penalize groups of students, particularly second language and minority students. In shifting to portfolios, we intended to honor the entire process of writing, and we are still bathing in the warm glow of our achievements in persuading the University to change from a test-driven composition curriculum to one that is course-driven. But the problems we face in portfolio assessment—recycling paper, appropriating essays, fictionalizing authors, and mediating differences—perplex our writing program and will likely continue to do so. They evade solution, in part because the cures, useful as they are, have the unfortunate consequence of making the patient sick in ways that are unforeseen and possibly unmanageable. That is, we can eliminate most paper recycling by excluding all out-of-class writing from the portfolio; we can eliminate problems arising from appropriation by dissolving collaborative writing groups and closing our writing center. Such solutions are really dissolutions.

The problems are stubborn because they represent an essential contradiction between who we are and what we are required to do by virtue of institutional mandate. Whether proficiency driven or portfolio driven, freshman composition, at least at many public institutions, is a course that certifies students, an academic version of water dunking, the primary means by which students demonstrate that they are either clean or unclean, deserving of a place within the university or ejected from the land of promise with its allure of economic and social upward mobility. This instrumental use of the writing curriculum is seriously at odds with writing pedagogy, and no amount of portfolio assessment can set this relationship right. To teach writing, we must work with small numbers of students in interactive, collaborative ways that promote a rhetorical relationship. We must create a context for writing and rewriting; we must offer both the structures and the means by which students learn how to invest themselves in their writing and rewriting. We must, moreover, take a long view, knowing as we do that students learn how to write incrementally, over years and not just semesters, that writing is situational and that writing improvement is alinear at best.

All of these principles are at odds with assessment, even portfolio assessment. Teaching is hot; assessment is cold. Teaching constructs students; assessment deconstructs student writing. No matter how creatively we fashion our means of assessment, it will remain at odds with our disciplinary and pedagogical principles as long as composition is certification, as long as it is the primary means by which some are chosen—and some are not. Portfolio assessment works best when the stakes in a course are a grade, not graduation. It works best as the means by which a student can produce her own best work, rather than an end product read in isolation for the sake of life or death judgments. Portfolio assessment, in contrast to a proficiency test, greatly increases validity, but reliability has a tendency to disappear. For all its usefulness, portfolio assessment cannot ameliorate the problems we face in large-scale composition programs, for those problems derive from the uses of writing to determine aptitude and acceptability. Those problems are structural, and they place on composition a burden it cannot bear, even with the improvements offered by portfolio assessment. The struggle of portfolio assessment may well be to retain the fundamental value of helping students construct a writerly self through the authoring of a portfolio while simultaneously finding ways to deemphasize and contextualize its evaluative consequences. Whether this kind of teaching and testing can be held productively in balance is still very much of an open question.

Note

As part of my research on portfolio assessment, Kristi Yager, my Project Assistant, interviewed Desiree, Norm, and several other students about their portfolios. I wish to acknowledge her able assistance in providing me with useful and important material that I have used in this essay.

25

Beyond the Classroom: Using Portfolios to Assess Writing

Brian Huot

Most of the burgeoning scholarship on portfolios (Belanoff and Dickson; Graves and Sunstein; Yancey and others) focuses upon their use in the classroom. This is understandable, since portfolios were first used in composition classrooms to provide a means for both teaching and assessing writing. This focus and orientation on pedagogy and practice reflect the strength of the grassroots movement associated with portfolio use in the area of composition. More important than the publications themselves is the continuing and widespread use of portfolios in writing classes from K through college. Simply, portfolios make sense to the composition teacher who tries to create a literate environment for her students within the composition classroom. Portfolios postpone and limit the evaluative nature of the teacher's role and permit students to write for meaning and over a period of time, allowing more opportunity for reflection and revision. Portfolios give students more responsibility for preparing a body of work, and in some cases students actually choose which pieces are to be included for evaluation. Overall, portfolios have been lauded for their ability to defuse the importance of grading (McClelland), since they encourage a focus on the importance of discovery, experimentation and the learning that accompanies these activities, connecting the way we teach with the way we evaluate (Camp and Levine).

This popularity of portfolios in the classroom setting has mushroomed into a wide range of uses outside the classroom as well. Portfolios have been used for placement, competency, and as part of accountability programs in school districts and in state mandated programs of educational reform. As portfolios begin to be used outside of the classroom, they will most certainly be subjected to the rigors of reliability and validity, two issues I will cover later on. For now, it's important to note that validity, or the purpose for which portfolios might be used, is an issue that needs to be addressed if we are to insure the most effective implementation of portfolios for a variety of assessment needs. The initial euphoria accompanying the advocacy of portfolio use has yet to consider purpose, and as I will detail later on, an understanding of validity can help direct our efforts to provide the best writing assessment possible.

The development of portfolios as a feasible assessment procedure has grown at an astonishing rate. Portfolios are probably the most popular form of writing assessment ever developed. In the last year alone three anthologies and an entire conference have been devoted to them, with more volumes, articles, and conferences on the way. This rash of activity is especially impressive in the context that there have only been four or so books on the entire subject of writing assessment in the last decade. The National Testing Network in Writing had its last conference two years ago, and none is scheduled in the near future. On the other hand, the proposal form for the 1993 Conference on College Composition and Communication lists portfolios as a separate and distinct area of study. At the 1992 Conference, Ed White called portfolios the future of writing assessment in composition. This popularity is especially striking considering that portfolios are more expensive and cumbersome to work with than conventional direct writing assessment, which is often tagged by the measurement community as an expensive alternative to indirect tests of grammar, usage and mechanics.

In spite of all the activity involving portfolios, a quick review of the present literature on portfolios shows that our knowledge about this popular form of assessment is sparse at best. Most of the work done with portfolios up to this time has been, to use terminology coined by Chris Anson to describe Writing Across the Curriculum literature, anecdotal or testimonial, what I call show and tell. While narratives of portfolio use are important, it is also important that we begin to explore systematically how portfolios work and what effect they can have. While an increasing number of teachers, school districts, institutions of higher learning and even state departments of education rush to try portfolios in different assessment contexts, we know little about how they work outside of the classroom and within the larger scope of assessing student writing ability.

Part of my goal in this chapter is to advocate that we stop, take stock and begin to ask some hard questions. What do we really know about the use of portfolios to assess student writing? What do we need to know? Are portfolios just another fad? Will our quest to find ways for assessing student writing that match our theories and practices for teaching but still allow us to be accountable to administrative pressures be too much for portfolios? It's impossible in one essay to answer all the questions I raise or perhaps impossible for us as a discipline to answer all such questions. For now, the answers might be less important than the necessity of beginning a line of inquiry that allows us to understand not only how portfolios work, but how they can best be used to satisfy the complex demands of effective writing evaluation. Many of us haven't begun to think or talk about such issues because so far we have been struggling just to incorporate portfolios into what we teach and how we assess.

Before we can begin to really talk about portfolios and understand how they assist our struggle to develop the best possible procedures for assessing student writing, it's important to remember some things about where assessment practices came from in the first place. If we are to agree that portfolios are better, then we need to consider what they are better than, what it is we want to replace with portfolios. For these reasons I'd like to briefly summarize some important ideas from the development of writing assessment. Among these ideas, I would like to frame the use of portfolios within the larger context of writing assessment.

In the last twenty-five years, composition has made tremendous strides in writing evaluation. Assessing student writing ability outside of the classroom directly with actual writing samples is a fairly recent development. Up until the 1970s, the assessment of writing outside the classroom usually included no student writing of any kind. In fact, this evaluation of writing indirectly with tests of usage and mechanics is still widespread. For example, in a recent survey of the placement practices of colleges and universities across the country, about half of the eleven hundred or so respondents report that they still use indirect tests of grammar, mechanics, and usage to place incoming students into composition courses (Huot, "A Survey of College and University Writing Placement Practices"). These tests continue to be used because they are relatively inexpensive and for the most part correlate with tests using student writing (P. Cooper). The reason student writing was evaluated with these indirect tests in the first place was that tests involving the reading and scoring of actual student writing could not ensure consistency in scoring of the same papers by independent raters. The importance of scoring consistency, dubbed interrater reliability by the testing community, became the focal point in the development of direct scoring procedures. The classic example of this inconsistency in scoring comes from a 1961 study (Diederich, French, Carlton) in which fifty-three raters scored three hundred papers on a nine-point scale, and 94 percent of the papers received at least seven different scores. In 1966 testers finally devised techniques that guaranteed scoring consistency (Godshalk, Swineford, Coffman) with which raters could agree with each other around eight out of ten times, and during the decade of the 1970s direct writing assessment using student writing read and rated by English teachers became a viable option. The methods developed to ensure scoring reliability required that students write to the same topic and in controlled or test-type situations because these conditions were necessary for raters to agree with each other on a consistent basis.

About fifteen to twenty years ago writing assessment, which typically consisted of one paper written to a single topic in a twenty- to ninety-minute testing session, became available for a wide range of educational purposes.

Regardless of the purpose of the testing of writing ability, the techniques employed were pretty much the same. This one shot, hit-and-miss sample was used to infer a range of ability, anything from whether a student had learned the basics of writing in elementary and middle school, could write an effective essay on demand in high school, should be admitted to college, could write well enough to exit freshman composition, or should qualify as a college graduate. An important thing to remember is that writing assessment looked and continues to look the way it does because of the need to satisfy consistency in scoring.

Considering the conditions under which writing assessment was first developed, portfolios are a radical departure from some of the ideas that inform conventional assessment practices. Portfolio assessment rejects the assumption that writing ability can be inferred from a single piece composed in response to a common topic. Instead, portfolios contain multiple pieces of writing on different and often disparate topics, allowing the importance of using a full range of writing produced in multiple drafts through revision. This diversity and richness that gives portfolios the ability to describe more adequately a student's ability to write pushes against the need to maintain consistency in scoring.

The methods for scoring that require some uniformity of the writing prompts and control over conditions in which students write (the basis for most of the criticism leveled at writing assessment procedures) are now being adapted to the scoring of portfolios. At this time, those using portfolios outside of the classroom have been able to attain acceptable levels of interrater reliability (Condon and Hamp-Lyons, Personal Correspondence; Sommers, Black, Daiker, Stygall, "The Challenges of Rating Portfolios"). However, the difficulty in finding ways to achieve consensus among raters and preserve the integrity of portfolios should prove challenging to the future of how widespread portfolio assessment can be. The challenge revolves around the tension between portfolios' ability to include the context within which a writer works and the need for enough consistency in the written products to permit consensus in scoring between independent raters. The very methods used to score writing portfolios have been seen as undercutting the value of portfolios to provide a rich description of a particular writer, since only a consensus score counts in conventional writing assessment procedures (Broad), procedures that are still being used to score portfolios. On the other hand, portfolios are seen by some as appropriate pedagogical tools but difficult and impractical for assessment purposes (Blum; White, "Portfolios as an Assessment").

It would be a grave error on our part not to consider the use of portfolios beyond the classroom for a range of future assessment needs, since they offer a real breakthrough over more conventional assessment methods. Portfolios are unlike any other writing evaluation techniques developed up to this time because their initial use was in the classroom. Other forms of direct writing assessment were developed by testing agencies for specific use in large-scale evaluation situations, and for the most part these methods were employed exclusively to evaluate writing outside the classroom. This distinction is important. It is politically and theoretically significant that portfolios have been developed by and for teachers. One of the real drawbacks to single-sample conventional writing assessment is that it has little to do with the way we teach or work as writers. Because of the need to satisfy scoring consistency, initial direct writing assessment techniques dictated an unnatural context in which students had to write. Portfolios, on the other hand, are widely recognized as having intrinsic pedagogical value, since they allow composing over time and delay evaluation until a student is ready to choose and or revise her best work. It follows, then, that using portfolios to assess student writing furnishes an important link between the way we teach and the way we assess. As Peter Elbow notes, the problem is not with evaluation but with the way we evaluate ("Ranking, Evaluating, and Liking").

It is necessary that we recognize that portfolios contain the potential for real change, not only in the way students are evaluated in writing but in terms of how writing ability is conceived. Portfolios challenge the notion that the ability to write can be inferred from a single sample written on demand. In fact, the notion of writing as a testable skill is transformed into something that can only be described and at best measured through multiple and related samples of written work. This reconception of what it takes to measure a person's ability to write is probably one of the most valuable aspects of portfolio assessment. As Grant Wiggins tells us, "an authentic test not only reveals student achievement to the examiner, but also reveals to the test-taker the actual challenges and standards of the field" (704). With the portfolio as a gauge of writing quality, being able to write well implies the ability to compile a representative sample of work, which reflects not only the writer's ideas, goals and interests but also her knowledge and awareness of her readers' criteria and expectations. In other words, portfolios exemplify to students, teachers and testers that writing is an ongoing process visible only in multiple written samples produced over time. Like Elbow, Wiggins reminds us that the problem is not with testing but with the test. He sees nothing wrong with teaching to the test as long as we change the test so it contains real or authentic educational relevance and value. Portfolios have the potential to be such a test.

Because portfolios are written and collected for multiple purposes, assessment becomes but one function of a student's writing, reducing the importance, power and significance of the testing moment as a legitimate reason to write. Diminishing the relationship between writing and testing is one more way to bring our methods of evaluating writing more closely in line with our approaches to teaching. This move will require some significant changes from those in the testing community who are involved in writing assessment. This change in the testing community is already underway as testers and psychometricians have begun to question conventional approaches to measurement which ignore the importance of context in assessment (Camp; Moss). Regardless of the impending changes in testing theory, we must recognize that the strengths we find in portfolio assessment can be viewed as weaknesses by those whose primary concern is testing rather than teaching. While portfolios have many advantages for the teaching of writing, their status as a measurement procedure is less secure.

Reading portfolios for reasons outside of the classroom must contend with the dilemmas of consistency in scoring and the resultant problems of controlling topics and ensuring enough uniformity to guarantee that raters can score portfolios on a consistent basis. What will these methods do, though, to some of the real strengths of portfolio assessment? For example, how diverse can these portfolios be? How much control will the teacher, let alone the student, have over what will be included in the portfolio and how it will be evaluated? If portfolios written within the classroom as part of students' writing instruction are to be used for outside scoring purposes, who will choose what these portfolios will look like? The teachers themselves, school administrators who don't teach or an outside testing consultant hired to make sure that portfolios are scored consistently? The further away from the students and teachers these important decisions are made, the greater the possibility that procedures used to make portfolios workable outside the classroom may short-circuit their effectiveness within.

There is a real danger that satisfying the needs of assessment may water down much of the pedagogical value of portfolios or that they might be rejected altogether as useful for teaching but not very practical for assessment purposes. This movement to make portfolios more suitable for testing could not only reduce their pedagogical value but even allow testing procedures to dictate the way we teach and evaluate within our own classrooms. We should, then, guard against outside pressures dictating what these portfolios and our curriculum will look like in the future. We must resist against the corruption of portfolios for testing purposes, while at the same time insist upon their value as an authentic description of students' growth as writers.

One way of keeping portfolios within the assessment options we now have without watering down their pedagogical value is to consider for what assessment purposes portfolios might best be utilized. A useful concept for dealing with purpose in assessment is to borrow the term "validity" from the testing community. (See The American Psychological Association *Standards for Educational and Psychological Tests* for a full discussion of validity.) For our purposes a simple definition is enough. The validity of a measurement instrument or test refers to whether or not it does what it purports to do. Because tests can be used for many different purposes, there are different kinds of validity. Even in a strict testing sense, validity is a context-dependent term because it is defined and understood only within the context of a specific testing situation. For example, predictive validity involves using a test to predict how well someone will do in a particular setting or with a particular task. In writing assessment, placement exams predict student's suitability for a particular course. This type of validity is fairly straightforward and can be documented fairly easily. Testing for writing competency, however, involves construct validity in that whatever means used should be able to measure the construct of what it means to be a competent writer. This type of validity is hardly straightforward and very difficult to document.

To decide how portfolios might best be used outside of a classroom context, we should consider each assessment situation separately. Are they, for example, especially useful for placement purposes? I'm sure we would all agree that it would be ideal to have high school students compile a record of their writing over a period of time and to have this record stand as the measure of their writing ability and the predictor of how well they would do in particular composition courses. This type of scheme would involve cooperation between school districts and postsecondary institutions and furnish a real pedagogical connection between the efforts of high school and college students and teachers. However, do we need a portfolio of student writing in order to decide what course an individual student should be placed into? Probably not. According to a recent national survey on writing placement, only 5 percent of schools using a writing sample reported being dissatisfied with their placement procedures (Huot, "A Survey of College and University Writing Placement Practices"). In a placement program I directed, we used a single sample to place nearly five thousand students per year and required a second sample written the first day of class to verify placement. Teacher dissatisfaction with placement was well under the 5 percent rate reported nationally. On the other hand, in a recent study on using portfolios for placement, teachers and students overwhelmingly preferred portfolios over single-samples (Sommers, Black, Daiker Stygall).[1] Clearly the evidence is not conclusive for either side, and decisions like these need to be made on a local basis. However, considering the extra time, effort and expense portfolios demand over single sample assessment, to use portfolios unnecessarily would be as logical as using a blow torch to kill a cockroach.

On the other hand, to go back to our examples about validity, can one writing sample produced in a timed testing situation measure the competency of a writer? Probably not. Writing competency is a complex, slippery concept resisting a simple definition. There are many manifestations of competency, just as there are many definitions and formats for successful communication across disciplines and discourse communities. The act of writing involves a range of personal, intellectual, social and academic influences for the writer. The reading given to any text depends upon the expectations of the reader based upon personal experience, academic background, and social and disciplinary boundaries too numerous to calculate out of context. Given this range of factors, it is extremely problematic to base any important and final judgments of writing ability upon a single sample of student writing. The multiple samples available in a portfolio written over time for a range of purposes and varying audiences, with the benefit of revision and even reflective or explanatory notes from the writer, provide a rich measurement of the complexities of writing competency. To use anything less than a portfolio to make profound, summative evaluations that have far ranging personal, social, economic, and pedagogical implications for a student misuses the evaluation options at our disposal.

Using the concept of validity to control and direct our decisions provides a useful way to look at writing assessment in general and portfolios in particular. Portfolios need to become part of a regular set of options from which teachers and testers can choose when deciding upon the most relevant and valid measure for a specific testing situation. Instead of asking which method of assessment is better or best, the question becomes what is it we want to know about a group of students' ability to write? Our knowledge about the importance of context to the linguistic and rhetorical decisions involved in writing ought to become the basis for making decisions about assessment. Instead of thinking in terms of portfolios, holistic scoring or other methods, we should begin to frame our assessment decisions in terms of why we are testing. Decisions about which method of writing assessment to use should revolve around the specific purpose for measuring students' ability to write. In this sense, portfolios cannot be the best evaluation option for every assessment purpose.

This need to consider the individual validity of portfolios for a specific testing situation is necessary to ensure the continued use of portfolios as an assessment instrument. If we overuse portfolios, convincing those who hold the purse strings to invest unnecessarily, we run the risk of having them branded as another educational fad. While experimenting with portfolios for a wide range of purposes is important and necessary, we should also realize that the overuse of portfolios can discredit much of the real value and advantages they hold over more conventional means of assessing writing.

Ultimately, the decision about which method of assessment is best in a given instance can only come from within an institution. A measurement instrument should have institutional validity in that it should be sensitive to the needs of particular students, teachers and educational programs that are part of the teaching and learning environment of a particular institution. We should guard against outside consultants and agencies making our assessment decisions as much as we would guard against allowing outsiders to make decisions about our classroom teaching. In the past, those of us who teach composition have often abdicated our authority over how our students were evaluated because we didn't want to be involved with the dirty job of assessment. One of the most important and promising features of portfolios as an assessment instrument is that it brings teachers and their concerns back into the assessment arena. Portfolios were first devised and used in the composition classroom because of their ability to diffuse the importance of grading and give students the opportunity to be evaluated for what they could do across a semester rather than within the week or two usually allotted for a writing assignment. It follows that the use of portfolios for assessment outside the classroom provides a significant link between the way we teach and the way we assess. The importance of portfolios as an assessment instrument should not be underestimated. Portfolios contain the possibility for the beginning of a new wave of assessment procedures that not only furnish the potential for giving evaluation back to the people who teach writing, but also provide new and more accurate ways to appreciate and describe our students' abilities as writers.

Notes

1. These data, while encouraging, come from an institution that is not representative of most placement systems (Huot, "A Survey of College and University Writing Placement Practices"), since the students are basically writing an exemption exam. Under this exemption scheme, students can receive either six English credits with no composition requirement, three English credits with one required composition course, or no English credits with the standard two-course sequence.

26

Portfolios in the Disciplines: Sharing Knowledge in the Contact Zone

Carl R. Lovitt
Art Young

The Ideology of Writing in the Disciplines

Nothing exposes the ideological tensions underlying writing across the curriculum as keenly as the attempt to develop a writing-intensive curriculum for a particular discipline. Although writing in the disciplines (WID) has traditionally been considered a logical and even necessary extension of writing across the curriculum (WAC), the two types of programs share only the most fundamental assumptions and goals.[1] In the first place, WAC programs typically appeal to those faculty members who, regardless of discipline, assign a high priority to teaching and student learning in their professional lives. In our experience, disciplinary differences at WAC workshops are most often eclipsed by participants' exuberant discovery of the interests they share with colleagues in other fields. Yet, as suggested by the fact that WAC programs seldom attract all members of any department, administrators of a WID program may have to contend with widely differing opinions about professional priorities. In the second place, whereas WAC programs emphasize generic strategies for using writing, WID poses the challenge of adapting writing to a specific academic context. Moreover, since WID targets students enrolled in major courses, these assignments must reflect the specialized content of courses in a way that WAC assignments need not.

Thus, for English faculty members, implementing a WID program represents an incursion into an unfamiliar and, insofar as the program aims to transform the host culture, possibly hostile realm. WID initiates a clash of

334

cultures: an encounter between two different ways of thinking, two different bodies of knowledge, two different sets of assumptions not only about what it is important to know but also about how to impart that knowledge. In her recent work on the "social spheres where cultures meet, clash, and grapple with each other" (34), Mary Louise Pratt has coined the useful concept of the "contact zone" to describe the locus and the moment in which the conflicting assumptions and beliefs of alien cultures collide. We propose to draw on this metaphor of the "contact zone" in describing the cultural intersection and cross-pollination that accompany the attempt to develop a WID program.

This essay will focus specifically on a project underway at Clemson University to develop a communication-intensive curriculum for the Department of Finance located in the College of Commerce and Industry, our business college. We will also discuss the impact and ramifications of our proposing a portfolio assessment system as the means of anchoring and organizing the project. Since we are only in the first year of a six-year project, our discussion will be about planning, problems, and possibilities. The conception and process of this unpredictable collaborative project across disciplines and academic departments continue to evolve. Our aim in describing the project is especially to highlight the ways in which we have confronted and negotiated, with varying successes, the ideological conflicts that invariably accompany any interdisciplinary collaboration.

Chris M. Anson and Robert L. Brown discuss how imperative it is that a group of interdisciplinary faculty, collaborating to develop a coherent approach to an educational problem—such as a university's integrated response to the development of students' written language abilities—reach consensus through the development of shared values. Yet, as William Condon and Liz Hamp-Lyons demonstrate in their study of composition courses at the University of Michigan, "shared knowledge" cannot be taken for granted even in a single discipline. Condon and Hamp-Lyons provide the instructive example of composition faculty assessing student portfolios for quality and structure of argument and, then, realizing that what the students wrote depended on what their different teachers taught as appropriate methods of argumentation; as they note in "Introducing a Portfolio-based Writing Assessment," "we have to learn to deal with the discrepancy between what the reader thought of as an argument and what the student had been taught about argumentation" (239). Their discussion brought home to us the impossibility of developing successful educational programs, pedagogies, and assessments without at least a baseline of shared knowledge and underlying principles.

Such a foundation of shared knowledge is also essential but perhaps even more difficult to achieve across departments and disciplines. As Lucille Parkinson McCarthy has shown, the lack of shared knowledge across disciplinary lines is especially dramatized by differing conceptions of writing. She likens her case-study student, Dave, to a "stranger in strange lands," who "believed that the writing he was doing [in each new class] was totally unlike anything he had ever done before" (234). However, in terms of the immediate concerns of this essay, it is not simply a case of the finance faculty's having assumptions about the writing process and about the role of writing in learning that differ from those of the English faculty. It is equally true that the English faculty have little knowledge of the discipline of finance—its history, its central organizing principles, its ways of thinking and arguing, and thus are just as prone to unwarranted assumptions about writing in finance. While it is comforting to think that ideological conflicts can be eased by reaching agreement about shared knowledge before undertaking an interdisciplinary collaboration, our experience confirms Anson's and Brown's intuition that such knowledge seldom occurs outside of specific incidents during the course of the project.

As we move now to a discussion of our collaboration with the Department of Finance, it is important to recall our opening remarks about the differences between WAC and WID programs. Our experience of administering a successful WAC program at Clemson did not prepare us for the challenges this new undertaking would present. By and large, our experience of working with groups in workshops or consulting one-on-one has convinced us that, beyond our disciplinary differences, we share as teachers many of the same assumptions, goals, and values; that we are generally receptive to new ideas that will help us become better teachers; and that we are committed above all to helping our students learn and become better learners. Moreover, we suspect that others who have been involved as we have in a bottom-up (as opposed to institutionally mandated) WAC program will bear out our perceptions of ideological compatibility. Owing largely to our inexperience with WID, the differences between the two types of initiative did not immediately become apparent.

Planning the Finance Project

In fall 1991, Rod Mabry, Head of the Department of Finance, approached us with the information that NCNB, an important bank in the region and a major employer of Clemson's finance graduates, might be interested in funding a project to improve finance students' communication skills. He requested our help in developing a proposal for such a project. We readily agreed and launched into what proved to be a remarkably smooth collaboration. After a couple of extended brainstorming sessions, during which we suggested some steps his department might take and he shared his own hopes for the project, he quickly drafted an impressive proposal, incorporating virtually every suggestion we had made, which the president of the university mailed to NCNB.

This entire process seemed to move with ease and confidence. In our experience, there was nothing remarkable about our discovery of shared values. Having attended one of our workshops, Rod had confidence in our experience with integrating communication in courses across the curriculum.

We didn't probe very deeply into our own possible ideological or even administrative conflicts (like how the money would be spent), and, at this proposal stage, we didn't thoroughly involve the rest of the finance and composition faculty on whose shoulders the success of the project would rest. We trusted in our own interpersonal collegiality, the goodwill of our colleagues and their concern for undergraduate students, the ideological assumption that at our university "money talks," and the belief that the best way to bring about change in departments and universities was to experiment with change. We believed we had enough shared values at the outset to undertake a large-scale project to improve the education of students and to carry us through negotiations over unacknowledged differences in our assumptions. In this process, we would develop an even stronger and deeper set of shared values.

We soon learned that our proposal had received a favorable preliminary review, and Art Young was invited to give a formal presentation to Joel Smith, President of NCNB in South Carolina. The highlights of the proposal were as follows:

- Develop finance courses that are communication intensive
- Develop a capstone course for seniors
- Develop leadership seminars for students
- Develop minors in professional communication for finance students
- Incorporate portfolio assessment throughout the finance curriculum
- Conduct formative assessment of all projects.

NCNB funded it for $500,000 over six years (1992–1998). Since NCNB has since merged with another financial institution, the project is now officially known as the NationsBank Communication Initiative.

Anticipating some of the conflicts that would arise, we must note that, even at this early stage, our thinking about the coherence of the project had evolved since the days of our brainstorming with Rod Mabry. We had not changed our ideas about what we would undertake, but we had begun to consider how portfolios could serve the pivotal function of anchoring and organizing the entire project. Rod had not objected when we originally recommended including portfolios in the project; to him, using portfolios was an interesting concept, but they were not a principal part of his agenda. We understood that his primary interest was to develop communication-intensive courses and to help finance faculty become more proficient at assigning and evaluating writing and speaking—an objective to which we were also firmly committed. We saw no reason then to be concerned with possible disagreements about what we perceived to be the most important aspect of the project.

When school ended in May 1992, the first payment from NCNB had still not arrived, but we proceeded to make plans to spend the money. The

Department of Finance hired a full-time project coordinator, Mary Dehner, who holds a master's degree in communication and had five years' experience in a similar position at another university. A certain amount of the budget was allocated for ongoing consulting services from faculty in English and speech. We also planned an off-campus workshop for August, which was to be attended by the entire finance faculty as well as by Susan Hilligoss, Carl Lovitt, and Art Young from English and Doreen Geddes from speech.

When Mary Dehner assumed her position on July 1, she met several times with us to share ideas about implementing the project and planning the August workshop. Having worked extensively with business faculty on developing communication assignments, Mary initially envisioned organizing this project much as she had the one at the other university. Accustomed to working on her own, she was not entirely clear about what role we were to play in this process. She assumed we had more of an interest in studying the undertaking for our own research purposes than in helping her carry it out. In this frame of mind, she wanted us to let her know what information we needed help in gathering, and she was eager to accommodate our needs. This is initially how she understood our insistence on the importance of instituting a portfolio system of assessment, a concept with which she was unfamiliar.

However, as soon as she understood that we envisioned using portfolios not only as a means of assessment but also—and primarily—as the basis for guiding the entire process of restructuring the finance curriculum, she voiced strong objections to the concept. The more we tried to explain and justify our rationale for such a guiding mechanism, the more resistance she revealed to a concept she considered an imprecise and unreliable measure of student abilities, an overly intrusive and prescriptive framework for developing assignments, and a potentially threatening tool for assessing how well she and the finance faculty were carrying out the project. It became apparent that our inability to reach agreement on the portfolio issue produced tensions that threatened to undermine the very possibility of a meaningful collaboration. If we couldn't work with Mary, we might as well forget about playing a decisive role in the finance project. However, at the point when we were privately resigned to abandon portfolio use, at least during the initial phase of the project, Mary agreed to proceed with that part of the plan. Despite her reservations, she believed that our attachment to the portfolio concept was motivated by sincere concerns for the integrity of the project, to which she was equally committed, and not by a desire to preempt her authority or to monitor her effectiveness. Although not wholeheartedly convinced about portfolio use, she decided to give us the benefit of the doubt, with the understanding that the concept would also have to be endorsed by the finance faculty at the upcoming workshop.

The satisfactory resolution of this conflict spared us from learning then what others who had experimented with portfolios had discovered long before—portfolios in their very nature are subversive. To encourage faculty to reach agreement about their course goals, the skills and knowledge they want their students to learn, and specific means of ensuring that students acquire and demonstrate those skills and knowledge, portfolios fundamentally challenge the way teachers customarily do business. Our disagreements with Mary were disagreements about pedagogy and power: how should courses be taught and who decides? Without realizing it at the time, we had our first taste of life in the contact zone.

Negotiating the Portfolio Concept

The workshop, which was held August 6–8 at an upscale conference center in north Georgia, Lake Lanier Islands, had several purposes; most were accomplished during the two-day retreat. Since most participating faculty members had not previously met, the workshop enabled members of the two parties to get to know one another and to decide on what terms the project would go forward. The workshop also served to introduce finance faculty to WAC concepts and to familiarize us with financial management (FM) as an academic discipline. To begin the process of developing communication-intensive courses, we collaborated on creating specific communication assignments and revising syllabi for the fall courses. We also decided which consultants would collaborate with which finance faculty members, and reached a decision about whether to proceed with the portfolios.

These outcomes resulted from a process that was anything but harmonious and that was threatened more than once by profound differences over our most basic professional assumptions and values. The workshop was a full-blown contact zone in which representatives from two alien cultures met for the first time to define a common ground for collaborative action. To illustrate our experience in this contact zone, we will focus on the fate of our portfolio proposal: how it was introduced and the way it was modified during the workshop.

Early in the workshop, we passed out a published article about a business college in a midwestern university that was implementing portfolios. This college's project did not match our expectations for portfolios, but we wanted Clemson's finance faculty to know that portfolios were attracting national attention as a powerful alternative to traditional modes of assessment and that their viability had been recognized by another business college. We wanted them to see the concept in print and in a context to which they could relate. What we didn't know—but which the Clemson finance faculty did know—is that the business college in question does not have a strong national reputation. "Who ever heard of X college?" one participant asked rhetorically, at which they all laughed. To them, the portfolio experiment at the college was a desperate attempt by a second-rate institution to disguise its lack of substance with glitzy window-dressing. The very fact that portfolios were adopted by this institution made our finance faculty suspicious of the concept—a conclusion diametrically opposed to the one we wanted.

Despite their unforseeable reaction, which made them leery of the very concept we wanted them to endorse, we proceeded with our initial plan to market portfolios as a central organizing principle of the Communications Initiative. We had faith in the inherent power of the model to secure the finance faculty's endorsement. We present below the main points of the logical but naive plan we invited the participants to approve:

The Magical Portfolio Plan

- Portfolios are the cornerstone of curricular and pedagogical reform in the finance department.
- Finance faculty agrees on what all FM majors should know and be able to do.
- Finance faculty decides what assignments (writing, speaking, computing) would allow students to demonstrate such knowledge and skills.
- Finance faculty identifies the courses in which students complete—and have the opportunity to revise—such assignments.
- Completed student assignments are kept in portfolios.
- Finance faculty and consultants will carefully read student portfolios at the end of each academic year and conduct formative assessments that lead to shared knowledge and ongoing transformation in curriculum and pedagogy.
- Students will construct separate portfolios, for which they select representative documents and compose reflective introductions, to present to potential employers and others.

The timing of our treatment of the portfolio concept did not allow for dissent. We depended on the finance faculty's consensus about key aspects of the concept to guide the subsequent discussion of specific assignments for the syllabi of the upcoming courses. Our initial experience with Mary Dehner, who was now a bemused observer, should have forewarned us of possible conflict, but we were totally unprepared for their outright rejection of our portfolio concept.

Foremost among the finance faculty's concerns was the potential for violating academic freedom. They uniformly objected to the suggestion that teachers might be required to include specific assignments in particular courses. They raised concerns about teachers having to implement measures they didn't believe in and then being evaluated for compliance with those standards. The fact that the teachers themselves were responsible for establishing requirements did not satisfy the objections. They also resisted the idea of developing standards for assessing student performance independent of specific course goals. To them, it was a small step from identifying student deficiencies to blaming faculty for failing to teach the requisite knowledge.

They also worried about the effect of increasing enrollment on assignments designed for courses with a specific course enrollment—especially since such enrollment increases were not uncommon in their department.

In short, our plan was scuttled. Fortunately, since our introduction to the portfolio concept had been cast as an open discussion, the lack of consensus did not result in a vote. While we struggled to formulate a more acceptable model for portfolios, Mary proceeded with the scheduled agenda of asking the faculty to identify the goals of the finance curriculum. Forming small groups to address this issue met with immediate success: the participants easily spelled out the objectives underlying their curriculum. Not that there was unanimity, but there was sufficient redundancy to define an acceptably coherent set of goals. However, problems arose when Mary proposed translating those goals into assignments for specific courses. The finance faculty objected that the same results could be achieved by teaching the same course with different approaches and that students could demonstrate mastery of the same finance content with a variety of different assignments. By denying that the department's goals could be converted into assignments that could, in turn, be tied to specific courses, the finance faculty had effectively repudiated the central premise of our original portfolio concept.

In response to the rejection of our original proposal and in consideration of what we had heard during Mary's session, we proposed the following alternative model:

Phase I (1992–93)

- Departmental portfolios are established for all juniors.
- Project team for the Communications Initiative establishes administrative procedures for portfolios respectful of privacy and academic freedom.
- On a voluntary basis, teachers who assign communication projects select one or more from each student for portfolio placement.
- Students submit two copies of these assignments to the teacher: one to be graded and returned and one to be placed unmarked in the student's departmental portfolio.
- Students are introduced to the Communications Initiative and to the portfolio requirement.
- Project team and finance faculty read and describe portfolios in summer 1993 and make recommendations.

Phase II (1993–94)

- Departmental portfolios are established for all juniors and continue for the now seniors.

- Recommendations from summer 1993 reading are implemented in the program.
- Senior students are invited to develop personal portfolios, for which they select and revise contents (which may include pieces from other curricula, co-op work, etc.) and to which they append resume and executive summary.
- Project director counsels students about portfolio development.
- Project team publicizes personal portfolios to recruiters.
- Faculty consider whether to award certificates for portfolio achievement.
- Selected student portfolios are photocopied (with permission) for publicity, research, and assessment purposes.
- Project team and finance faculty read and describe senior portfolios and make recommendations.

Admittedly, this hastily conceived alternative bears little resemblance to a concept predicated on correlating curricular goals with specific assignments. The plan does not require the finance faculty to come to any agreement about what is to be assigned or about which curricular goals the assignments fulfill. In fact, it does not *require* any writing at all. It simply calls for including in the portfolio samples of any writing that the faculty members choose to assign in finance courses. It also significantly changes the nature of the assessment process, which would now be confined to describing the contents of the portfolios and attempting to generalize about their strengths and weaknesses without reference to any external standard. The only undiluted feature of the original concept that is retained is the plan to have students develop personal portfolios, which we hoped they would support as a valuable medium for demonstrating their accomplishments and capabilities to potential employers.

The one undisputed advantage of this plan over the one we originally proposed is that it was unanimously approved by the finance faculty. Insofar as it was developed in response to what we learned at the workshop, it reflects the shared knowledge that we consider essential to any such collaboration. Only a plan such as this one, which is sensitive to the ideology of the finance department, had a chance of being accepted, so it seems fruitless to belabor its shortcomings as an ideal model.

Reaching agreement on the portfolio concept also had the felicitous effect of bringing the workshop to an unexpectedly productive and satisfactory resolution. Since there were to be no constraints on the kind of assignments that could be developed, every faculty member opted to include one or more communication assignments in his or her fall courses. As we discovered in a subsequent study, every finance syllabus had been altered to include writing assignments, oral presentations, or class discussion. We will undoubtedly have our hands full when it comes time to review the departmental portfolios in the summer.

Daily Life in the Contact Zone

The finance faculty's willingness to assign communication activities in all their courses meant that, from day one, the project was well on its way toward developing a communication-intensive curriculum. But this also meant that the project team would immediately have to immerse itself in an intricate collaboration, in an unfamiliar discipline, with colleagues we barely knew. To illustrate the kinds of problems that can arise in the course of a discipline-specific collaboration, we offer the two following stories.

Moments after the adjournment of the workshop, an English faculty member and a finance faculty member began a conversation in the hotel elevator about the finance member's plan to assign several short papers in her course. Learning that she intended to use the same kind of assignment for each of the papers, the English teacher asked if she had considered varying and sequencing the complexity of the assignments. Interested by his proposal, she asked if he could offer specific suggestions for varying the assignments. He mentioned a few ideas off the top of his head, which she seemed to like, so he promised to develop and send to her a list of assignments. He spent some time devising the assignments, which he dutifully forwarded. When he didn't hear from her within the week, he called to find out how she had responded to his suggestions. On the phone, she thanked him but told him that she had decided to stick with her original plan; she offered no explanation for rejecting his suggestions. Since her assignment involved summarizing articles in a popular business magazine, she wanted to know, however, if he had a list of guidelines for reading that might help the students complete the assignments. Although he had never developed such guidelines, he volunteered to work up some for her. He consulted several textbooks that stressed critical reading and sent to her a list that would help students identify an article's thesis, its argumentative strategies, the types of appeals it used, and its underlying assumptions. He never heard from her about his list. He was shocked to learn from the project coordinator, a week or so later, that the faculty member had decided not to work with him this semester because "his suggestions for the assignments had nothing to do with finance." The lack of shared knowledge between these two teachers was so pronounced that one party in the exchange saw no alternative to ending the conversation, like someone on the phone might hang up when she realized her interlocutor was speaking a language she didn't understand. When confronted with assumptions too foreign to assimilate to one's own, retreat is clearly one of the options in the contact zone.

The second story further illustrates the delicate nature of venturing into another's classroom, but it makes the point even more dramatically by showing how strongly teachers can resist any interference in the way they conduct their courses. If there was one pedagogical activity over which we expected finance faculty to relinquish control willingly, surely it would have been the grading of student papers. In fact, our greatest concern about the finance project was that the faculty would exploit the collaboration as an opportunity to have someone else grade their students' papers. Predictably, every finance teacher requested some assistance with evaluating student writing, to which we all agreed with the understanding that the papers would also be reviewed by the finance teachers. We would grade for English and they would grade for finance, even though we hoped they would eventually be convinced that separating the two was artificial and pedagogically unsound. We were frankly skeptical about how carefully they would read the papers after we had critiqued them. That they were willing to relegate what they considered a menial activity not only to English graduate students but also to Mary Dehner or the consultants (they didn't care who did it so long as they didn't have to) exposed what Mary Louise Pratt identifies as the historical outcome of most contact zone encounters: the domination of one culture by another. There was a serious risk that both the finance faculty and the consulting faculty might view the latter as the serving class in this collaborative project, one that exists to help the dominant class of finance professors fulfill its obligations in a secondary area of responsibility: teaching and assessing communication skills.

We were therefore completely unprepared for the call we received from a troubled finance teacher whose student papers had just been returned by his project team partner. The grades were much too high for his course; if students could do that well on their first writing assignment, what was the purpose of assigning writing? Besides, he had even found a few grammatical errors that his partner had overlooked. He saw no alternative to requesting that his partner henceforth confine herself to writing comments on the papers without assigning grades. As this experience has taught us, even those aspects of teaching that the faculty consider the most onerous and the least essential are nevertheless implicated in their teaching philosophy and, as such, cannot be surrendered to another without transforming the culture and compromising the autonomy of the classroom.

While these are by no means the only conflicts we have experienced, they typify the perils and pitfalls of operating in the contact zone—conflicts that we believe no WID-based collaboration can entirely avoid. But we do not wish our attention to the conflicts to eclipse the fact that we have already learned a lot about the step-by-step process of building shared knowledge, and through this shared knowledge to envision the possibility for meaningful changes in undergraduate education—changes that involve personal and political transformations at Clemson within individual classrooms and within the culture of the institution. We're learning a great deal from each other as we work as teacher-researcher partners, and even the occasional conflicts have contributed significantly to that process. We look forward to sitting down together next summer to read and discuss the portfolios because we know that will help us move toward a consensus on underlying principles based on mutual experience.

The finance faculty have begun this year cautiously optimistic; they think it is a good project and they are willing to invest some time in it. They hope it doesn't mean a lot of extra work, particularly extra work without reward.

They don't want their participation with English faculty in this joint project to work against their own interests, and we sympathize with those concerns, just as we recognize the need to ensure that our own interests are not compromised or neglected. In the concluding paragraph of her essay on the contact zone, Mary Louise Pratt issues a call: "We are looking for the pedagogical arts of the contact zone. These will include, we are sure, exercises in storytelling and in identifying with the ideas, interests, histories, and attitudes of others; experiments in transculturation and collaborative work . . . ." (40). And so, we would like to tell one final story, which not only illustrates how surreal life can sometimes be in the contact zone but also documents that, with adequate shared knowledge, mutually satisfying collaboration can occur:

A finance faculty member who was scheduled to explain a complex communication assignment to his students in their next class awoke one morning to find that he had lost the ability to speak above a whisper. Since the assignment involved an oral presentation, he invited (presumably in writing) Mary Dehner and Doreen Geddes, the speech teacher on the project team, to teach his class. The teacher gave Mary a copy of the written instructions he had given his students, but he did not have a chance to answer any questions about the intricacies of the assignment. Mary and Doreen devoted considerable time before class to plan their presentation. On the day of the class, Mary and Doreen were surprised to find the mute finance teacher waiting for them in the classroom. He seated himself in the front of the room and signaled them to begin their presentation to the students. But, no more than ten minutes into their lecture, which seemed to have started off quite well, the teacher tapped Mary on the shoulder and whispered that she was misleading students about his expectations. While the students sat silently watching, the finance teacher huddled with Mary and Doreen, who struggled not only to hear what he said but to comprehend his involved project. Suddenly, they both nodded: they understood what he wanted students to do. The finance teacher smiled and resumed his seat. He remained smiling for the rest of the hour, as Mary and Doreen explained the assignment to his satisfaction and gave the students valuable pointers about giving effective oral presentations. (The finance teacher's medical condition was not serious, and he was back to teaching his course the following week.)

Note

1. We are indebted to James F. Slevin and his colleagues Keith Fort and Patricia E. O'Connor for the useful distinction between writing across the curriculum and writing in the disciplines. They write:

> With regard to the teaching of writing, then, we distinguish between the concept of writing across the curriculum and the concept of writing within the disciplines. In the former, writing across the curriculum, we look for general

practices, common procedures for teaching that will work in all sorts of courses; so our attention here will be on generalization about the writing process, learning, and cognitive growth . . . Our notion of 'writing within a discipline' embraces both the student writing submitted and the writing studied by the student and teacher together . . . To master a particular discipline is in part to understand how statements of truth can genuinely inform one another or be made persuasive. How one effects comprehension, concern, and assent—that is, the study of writing and rhetoric—is thus a central question of all disciplines (11–12).

Bibliography

Alderman, Donald L. "Language Proficiency as a Moderator Variable in Testing Academic Aptitude." *Journal of Education Psychology* 74.4 (August, 1982): 580–87.

Anson, Chris M. Ed. *Writing and Response: Theory, Practice, and Research.* Urbana, IL: National Council of Teachers of English, 1989.

———. "Toward a Multidimensional Model of Writing in the Academic Disciplines." *Writing in the Academic Disciplines.* Ed. David Jolliffe. Norwood, NJ: Ablex, 1988.

Anson, Chris M., and Robert L. Brown, Jr. "Portfolio Assessment: Ideological Sensitivity and Institutional Change." *Portfolios: Process and Product.* Eds. Pat Belanoff and Marcia Dickson. Portsmouth, NH: Boynton/Cook, 1991. 248–269.

Anson, Chris M., Joan Graham, David A. Jolliffe, Nancy Shapiro, and Carolyn Smith. *Scenarios for Teaching Writing: Contexts for Discussion and Reflective Practice.* Urbana, IL: NCTE/Alliance for Undergraduate Education, 1993.

Austin, J.L. *How to Do Things With Words.* Cambridge, MA: Harvard University Press, 1962, 1975.

Baker, Nancy Westrich. "The Effects of Portfolio-Based Instruction on Composition Students' Final Examination Scores, Course Grades, and Attitudes Toward Writing." *Research in the Teaching of English* 27 (1993): 155–174.

Bakhtin, Mikhail Mikhailovich. *Speech Genres and Other Late Essays.* Tr. Vern W. McGee. Eds. Caryl Emerson and Michael Holquist. Austin: U of Texas P, 1986.

———. *Marxism and the Philosophy of Language.* ["By V.N. Volosinov"] Tr. Ladislav Matejka and I.R. Titunik. New York: Seminar Press-Harvard U P, 1973.

Ballard, Leslie. "Portfolios and Self-Assessment." *English Journal* 81.2 (February 1992): 46–48.

Barnes, Linda Laube. "Gender Bias in Teachers' Written Comments." *Gender in the Classroom: Power and Pedagogy.* Eds. Susan L. Gabriel and Isaiah Smithson. Urbana, IL: U of Illinois P, 1990.

Bartholomae, David. "Inventing the University." *When A Writer Can't Write: Research on Writer's Block and Other Composing-Process Problems.* Ed. Mike Rose. New York: Guilford, 1985. 134–65

Beach, Richard. "Showing Students How To Assess: Demonstrating Techniques for Response in the Writing Conference." *Writing and Response: Theory, Practice, and Research.* Chris M. Anson. Urbana, IL: National Council of Teachers of English, 1989. 127–148.

Beall, John. "Writing for Science." *Independent School* (Spring 1992): 43.

Beaven, Mary H. "Individualized Goal Setting, Self-Evaluation, and Peer Evaluation." *Evaluating Writing: Describing, Measuring, Judging.* Eds. Charles R. Cooper and Lee Odell. Urbana, IL: National Council of Teachers of English, 1977. 135–53.

Belanoff, Pat. "The Myths of Assessment." *Journal of Basic Writing.* 10.1 (1991): 54–66.

———. "Addendum." Ed. Pat Belanoff. *Portfolios: Process and Product.* Pat Belanoff and Marcia Dickson. Portsmouth, NH: Boynton/Cook, 1991. 30–36.

———. "Portfolios: Implications for Literacy." Miami University Conference on New Directions in Portfolio Assessment, Oxford, OH. October 1992.

Belanoff, Pat, and Marcia Dickson. Eds. *Portfolios: Process and Product.* Portsmouth, NH: Boynton/Cook, 1991.

Belanoff, Pat, and Peter Elbow. "Using Portfolios to Increase Collaboration and Community in a Writing Program." *WPA: Journal of Writing Program Administration* 9.3 (Spring 1986): 27–40.

Belenky, Mary Field, Blythe McVicker Clinchy, Nancy Rule Goldberger, and Jill Mattuck Tarule. *Women's Ways of Knowing: The Development of Self, Voice, and Mind.* New York: Basic Books, 1986.

Berkenkotter, Carol, Thomas N. Huckin, and Jon Ackerman. "The Legacy of Positivism in Empirical Composition Research." *Journal of Advanced Composition* 9 (1989): 69–82.

Berkenkotter, Carol, Thomas N. Huckin, and Jon Ackerman. "Conventions, Conversations, and the Writer: Case Study of a Student in a Rhetoric Ph.D. Program." *Research in the Teaching of English* 22.1 (February 1988): 9–44.

Berlin, James A. "Postmodernism, Politics, and Histories of Rhetoric." *PRETEXT* 11.3–4 (Fall/Winter 1990): 169–87.

———. "Poststructuralism, Cultural Studies, and the Composition Classroom: Postmodern Theory in Practice." *Rhetoric Review* 11.1 (Fall 1992): 16–33.

Bertsch, Debbie, Laurel Black, Don Daiker, and Edwina Helton. *The Best of Miami University's Portfolios 1992.* Oxford, OH: Miami University, 1992.

Bialostosky, Don. "Dialogic Criticism." *Contemporary Literary Theory,* Ed. G. Douglas Atkins and Laura Morrow. Amherst, MA: U of Massachusetts P, 1989. 214–228.

Bishop, Wendy. "Going up the Creek Without a Canoe: Using Portfolios to Train New Teachers of College Writing." *Portfolios: Process and Product.* Eds. Pat Belanoff and Marcia Dickson. Portsmouth, NH: Boynton/Cook, 1990.

———. "Revising the Technical Writing Class: Peer Critiques, Self-Evaluation and Portfolio Grading." Penn State Conference on Rhetoric and Composition, July 1987. State College, PA.

Bizzell, Patricia."Arguing About Literacy." *College English* 50 (Feb. 1988): 141–53.

———. "Cognition, Convention, and Certainty: What We Need to Know about Writing." *PRE/TEXT* 3 (Fall 1982): 213–43.

Black, Laurel, Donald A. Daiker, Jeffrey Sommers, and Gail Stygall. *Handbook of Writing Portfolio Assessment: A Program for College Placement*. Oxford, OH: Miami University Department of English, 1992.

Blitz, Michael, and C. Mark Hurlbert. "Cults of Culture." *Cultural Studies in the English Classroom*. Eds. James A. Berlin and Michael J. Vivion. Portsmouth, NH: Boynton/Cook, 1993.

Blum, Jack R. "Two Cheers for Portfolio Evaluation." CCCC Convention. Cincinnati, OH, March 1992.

Bohannon, Laura. "Shakespeare in the Bush." *Points of Departure*. Ed. James Moffett. New York: Mentor, 1985. 179–189.

Boyd, Richard, "Mechanical Correctness and Ritual in the Late Nineteenth-Century Composition Classroom." Unpublished paper.

Boyer, Ernest. *Scholarship Reconsidered: Priorities of the Professoriate*. Princeton, NJ: Princeton UP, 1990.

Brand, Alice. "A Director of Composition Talks to Students About College Writing Assignment." ERIC: ED340038, 1991.

Brandt, Deborah. "The Cognitive as the Social: An Ethnomethodological Approach to Writing Process Research." *Written Communication* 9.3 (July 1992): 315–55.

———. *Literacy as Involvement: The Acts of Writers, Readers, and Texts*. Carbondale: Southern Illinois UP, 1990.

Brannon, Lil. "Knowing Our Knowledge: A Case for Teacher Research." Keynote Address, Annual Summer Conference of the Council of Writing Program Administrators, July 1992. Breckenridge, CO.

Brannon, Lil, and C.H. Knoblauch. "On Students' Rights to their Own Texts: A Model of Teacher Response." *College Composition and Communication*, 33, 2 (1982): 157–66.

Britton, James. "The Composing Process and the Functions of Writing." *Research on Composing*. Eds. Charles Cooper and Lee Odell. Urbana, IL: NCTE, 1978. 13–28.

Broad, Robert L. "Portfolio Scoring: A Contradiction in Terms." Miami University Conference on New Directions in Portfolio Assessment, Oxford, OH. October 1992.

Brodkey, Linda. "Hard Cases for Law and Rhetoric." Conference on College Composition and Communication, March 1992, Cincinnati, OH.

———. "Opinion: Transvaluing Difference." *College English* 51 (1989): 597–601.

Brooke, Robert. *Writing and Sense of Self: Identity Negotiation in Writing Workshops*. Urbana: IL. National Council of Teachers of English, 1991.

Brown, Rexford. *Schools of Thought: How the Politics of Literacy Shape Thinking in the Classroom*. San Francisco: Jossey-Bass, 1991.

Bruffee, Kenneth A. "Collaborative Learning and the 'Conversation of Mankind.'" *College English* 46 (1984): 635–52.

Burke, Kenneth. *The Philosophy of Literary Form: Studies in Symbolic Action*. 3rd Edition. Berkeley: U of California P, 1973.

————. *A Grammar of Motives*. Berkeley: U of California P, 1969.

————. *Language as Symbolic Action*. Berkeley: U of California P, 1966.

Burnham, Christopher. "Portfolio Evaluation: Room to Breathe and Grow." *Training the New Teacher of College Composition*. Ed. Charles Bridge. Urbana, IL: National Council of Teachers of English, 1986.

Burroway, Janet. *Writing Fiction: A Guide to Narrative Craft,* 3rd Edition. New York: HarperCollins, 1992.

Butler, Johnnella E. "Toward a Pedagogy of Everywoman's Studies." *Gendered Subjects: The Dynamics of Feminist Teaching*. Eds. Margo Culley and Catherine Portuges. London: Routledge, 1985. 230–239.

Butler, Judith. *Gender Trouble: Feminism and the Subversion of Identity*. New York: Routledge, 1990.

CCCC Committee on Assessment. *Postsecondary Writing Assessment: An Update on Practices and Procedures*. Report to the Executive Committee of the Conference on College Composition and Communication. Spring 1988.

Calfee, Robert. "Assessment, Testing, Measurement: What's the Difference? An Editorial." *Educational Assessment* 1.1. In press, Spring 1993. MS pp 1–11.

Cambridge, Barbara. "Assessing the Assessors: Portfolios to Document Teaching." Miami University Conference on New Directions in Portfolio Assessment, Oxford, Ohio. October 1992.

Camp, Roberta. "Changing the Model for the Direct Assessment of Writing." *Validating Holistic Scoring for Writing Assessment: Theoretical and Empirical Foundations*. Eds. Michael M. Williamson and Brian Huot. Cresskill, NJ: Hampton, 1993. 45–78.

————. "Portfolio Reflections in Middle and Secondary Classrooms." *Portfolios in the Writing Classroom: An Introduction*. Ed. Kathleen Blake Yancey. Urbana, IL: National Council of Teachers of English, 1992.

Camp, Roberta, and Denise Levine. "Portfolios Evolving: Background and Variations in Sixth- Through Twelfth-Grade Classrooms." *Portfolios: Process and Product*. Eds. Pat Belanoff and Marcia Dickson. Portsmouth, NH: Boynton/Cook, 1991. 194–205.

Change, July-August 1993.

Charney, Davida. "The Validity of Using Holistic Scoring to Evaluate Writing: A Critical Overview." *Research in the Teaching of English* 18 (February 1984): 65–81.

Chodorow, Nancy. *The Reproduction of Mothering*. Berkeley: U of California P, 1978.

Clifford, John. "The Subject in Discourse." *Contending with Words: Composition and Rhetoric in a Postmodern Age*. Eds. Patricia Harkin and John Schilb. New York: MLA, 1991. 38–51.

Cohen, Miriam. *First Grade Takes a Test*. New York: Dell, 1980.

Cole, Michael. "Mind as a Cultural Achievement: Implication for IQ Testing." *Learning and Teaching the Ways of Knowing*. Ed. Elliot Eisner. *Eighty-fourth Yearbook of the National Society for the Study of Education,* Part II. Chicago: U of Chicago P, 1985.

Condon, William, and Liz Hamp-Lyons. "Introducing a Portfolio-based Writing Assessment: Progress through Problems." *Portfolios: Process and Product.* Eds. Pat Belanoff and Marcia Dickson. Portsmouth, NH: Boynton/Cook, 1991. 231–47.

————. Personal Correspondence.

Connor, Ulla, and Robert B. Kaplan. Eds. *Writing Across Languages: Analysis of L2 Text.* Reading, MA: Addison-Wesley, 1987.

Cooper, Charles R. "Holistic Evaluation of Writing." *Evaluating Writing: Describing, Measuring, Judging.* Eds. Charles R. Cooper and Lee Odell. Urbana, IL: National Council of Teachers of English, 1977. 3–31.

Cooper, Marilyn. "Unhappy Consciousness in First-Year English: How to Figure Things Out for Yourself." In *Writing as Social Action.* Marilyn M. Cooper and Michael Holzman. Portsmouth, NH: Boynton/Cook, 1989. 28–60.

Cooper, Peter. *The Assessment of Writing Ability: A Review of Research.* Princeton: ETS, 1984. GREB No. 82–15R.

Cooper, Winfield, and B.J. Brown. "Using Portfolios to Empower Student Writers." *English Journal* 81.2 (Feb. 1992): 40–44.

Daiker, Donald, Jeffrey Sommers, and Gail Stygall. "The Political and Pedagogical Implications of a College Placement Portfolio." *The Practices and Politics of Assessment in Writing.* Eds. Edward M. White, William Lutz, and Sandra Kamusikiri. Forthcoming from MLA.

D'Aoust, Catherine. "Portfolios: Process for Students and Teachers." *Portfolios in the Writing Classroom: An Introduction.* Ed. Kathleen Blake Yancey. Urbana, IL: National Council of Teachers of English, 1992.

Despain, LaRene, and Thomas L. Hilgers. "Readers' Responses to the Rating of Non-Uniform Portfolios: Are There Limits of Portfolios' Utility?" *WPA: Writing Program Administration* 16.1–2 (Fall/Winter 1992): 24–37.

Deyle, Donna. "Learning Failure: Tests as Gatekeepers and the Culturally Different Child." *Success or Failure? Learning and the Minority Student.* Ed. Henry Trueba. Cambridge: Newbury House, 1987. 85–108.

Diederich, Paul B., John W. French, and Sydell T. Carlton. *Factors in the Judgment of Writing Quality.* Princeton: Educational Testing Service, 1961. ETS RB No. 61–15.

Dixon, John. Writing Achievements Seminar for the Indiana Department of Education. Indianapolis: June 1992.

Durst, Russel K. "A Writer's Community: How Teachers can Form Writing Groups." *Teacher as Writer: Entering the Professional Conversation.* Ed. Karin L. Dahl. Urbana, IL: National Council of Teachers of English, 1992. 261–271.

Eagleton, Terry. *Literacy Theory: An Introduction.* Oxford: Blackwell, 1983.

Edgerton, Russell, Patricia Hutchings, and Kathleen Quinlan. *The Teaching Portfolio: Capturing the Scholarship in Teaching.* Washington, D.C.: American Association of Higher Education, 1991.

Elbow, Peter. "Assessing Writing in the 21st Century." In *Composition in the 21st Century: Crisis and Change*. Eds. Lynn Z. Bloom, Donald A. Daiker, and Edward M. White. Southern Illinois UP. In press.

―――. "Ranking, Evaluating, and Liking: Sorting Out Three Forms of Judgment." *College English* 55/2 (Feb. 1993): 187–206.

―――. "The Uses of Binary Thinking." *Journal of Advanced Composition* 12.1 (Winter 1993): 51–78.

―――. "Reflections on Academic Discourse." *College English* 53 (1991): 135–55.

―――. "Foreword." *Portfolios: Process and Product*. Eds. Pat Belanoff and Marcia Dickson. Portsmouth, NH: Boynton/Cook, 1991.

―――. *What is English?* New York and Urbana, IL: MLA and NCTE, 1990.

―――. "Portfolio Assessment." Workshop delivered at The National Testing Network, Montreal, 1989.

―――. *Embracing Contraries*. New York: Oxford UP, 1986.

Elbow, Peter, and Pat Belanoff. "State University of New York at Stony Brook Portfolio-Based Evaluation Program." *Portfolios: Process and Product*. Eds. Pat Belanoff and Marcia Dickson. Portsmouth, NH: Boynton/Cook, 1991. 3–16.

―――. "Using Portfolios to Increase Collaboration and Community in a Writing Program." *Portfolios: Process and Products*. Eds. Pat Belanoff and Marcia Dickson. Portsmouth, NH: Boynton Cook, 1991. 17–30.

―――. *A Community of Writers*. New York: Random House, 1989.

―――. "State U of New York: Portfolio-Based Evaluation Program." *New Methods in College Writing Programs: Theory into Practice*. Eds. Paul Connolly and Teresa Vilardi. NY: MLA, 1986. 95–105.

Faery, Rebecca B. "Teachers *and* Writers: The Faculty Writing Workshop and Writing Across the Curriculum." Midwest Modern Language Association. November 1992. St. Louis, MO.

Faigley, Lester. *Fragments of Rationality: Postmodernity and the Subject of Composition*. Pittsburgh: U of Pittsburgh P, 1992

―――. "Judging Writing, Judging Selves." *College Composition and Communication* 40 (Dec. 1989): 395–412.

Farrell, Thomas. "The Male and Female Modes of Rhetoric." *College English* 40 (1979): 909–921.

Fichtner, Dan, Faye Peitzman, and Linda Sasser. "What's Fair? Assessing Subject Matter Knowledge of LEP Students in Sheltered Classrooms." *With Different Eyes: Insights into Teaching Language Minority Students Across the Disciplines*. Eds. Faye Peitzman and George Gadda. Los Angeles: UCLA Publishing, 1991. 143–154.

Figueroa, Richard. "Test Bias and Hispanic Children." *Journal of Special Education*. 74.4 (1983): 431–440.

Fish, Stanley. *Is There a Text in This Class?* Cambridge: Harvard UP, 1980.

Flynn, Elizabeth. "Composing as a Woman." *College Composition and Communication* 39 (1988): 423–435.

They also worried about the effect of increasing enrollment on assignments designed for courses with a specific course enrollment—especially since such enrollment increases were not uncommon in their department.

In short, our plan was scuttled. Fortunately, since our introduction to the portfolio concept had been cast as an open discussion, the lack of consensus did not result in a vote. While we struggled to formulate a more acceptable model for portfolios, Mary proceeded with the scheduled agenda of asking the faculty to identify the goals of the finance curriculum. Forming small groups to address this issue met with immediate success: the participants easily spelled out the objectives underlying their curriculum. Not that there was unanimity, but there was sufficient redundancy to define an acceptably coherent set of goals. However, problems arose when Mary proposed translating those goals into assignments for specific courses. The finance faculty objected that the same results could be achieved by teaching the same course with different approaches and that students could demonstrate mastery of the same finance content with a variety of different assignments. By denying that the department's goals could be converted into assignments that could, in turn, be tied to specific courses, the finance faculty had effectively repudiated the central premise of our original portfolio concept.

In response to the rejection of our original proposal and in consideration of what we had heard during Mary's session, we proposed the following alternative model:

Phase I (1992–93)

- Departmental portfolios are established for all juniors.
- Project team for the Communications Initiative establishes administrative procedures for portfolios respectful of privacy and academic freedom.
- On a voluntary basis, teachers who assign communication projects select one or more from each student for portfolio placement.
- Students submit two copies of these assignments to the teacher: one to be graded and returned and one to be placed unmarked in the student's departmental portfolio.
- Students are introduced to the Communications Initiative and to the portfolio requirement.
- Project team and finance faculty read and describe portfolios in summer 1993 and make recommendations.

Phase II (1993–94)

- Departmental portfolios are established for all juniors and continue for the now seniors.

Bibliography

Foucault, Michel. Ed. *Herculine Barbin, Being the Recently Discovered Memoirs of a Nineteenth Century Hermaphrodite*. Trans. Richard McDongall. New York: Colophon, 1980.

Freedman, Sarah Warshauer. *Evaluating Writing: Linking Large Scale Testing and Classroom Assessment*. Occasional Paper No. 27. Berkeley, CA: Center for the Study of Writing, 1991.

Fu, Dan Ling. "One Bilingual Child Talks About His Portfolio." *Portfolio Portraits*. Eds. Donald H. Graves and Bonnie Sunstein. Portsmouth, NH: Heinemann, 1992.

Gadda, George. "Writing and Language Socialization Across Cultures: Some Implications for the Classroom." *With Different Eyes: Insights into Teaching Language Minority Students Across the Disciplines*. Eds. Faye Pietzman and George Gadda. Los Angeles: UCLA Publishing, 1991.

Garcia, Georgia E. "Factors Influencing the English Reading Test Performance of Spanish-English Bilingual Children." Diss. University of Illinois at Urbana-Champaign, 1988.

Garcia, Georgia E., and P. David Pearson. "The Role of Assessment in a Diverse Society." *Technical Report*. Urbana: Center for the Study of Reading, 1990. [A ...sion of this report also appears in *Literacy in a Diverse Society: Perspectives, ...es, and Policies*. Ed. Elfreida Hiebert. New York: Teachers College Press,

...*Multiple Intelligences: The Theory in Practice*. New York: Basic

...f School." *Literacy: An Overview by 14 Experts*. Ed. ...York: Noonday Press, 1991, 85–114.

...*Notes on Craft for Young Writers*. New York:

...aching a Biology-Linked Basic Writing ...s. Eds. Pat Belanoff and Marcia Dick-

...dians of college preparatory students, Mentor ...iami University Conference on New Directions ...OH. October, 1992.

...*Voice*: ...Harvard UP, 1982.

...*the Self: A Study of Language Competence*. New York: ...91.

...ances Swineford, and William E. Coffman. *The Measurement of ...y*. New York: College Entrance Examination Board, 1966.

...ok Press, 1973.

...*The Presentation of Self in Everyday Life*. Woodstock, NY: The

...e Ellen. "Increasing Student Autonomy through Portfolios." *Portfolios in the ...riting Classroom*. Ed. Kathleen Blake Yancey. Urbana, IL: National Council of Teachers of English, 1992.

Bibliography

Gould, Stephen Jay. *The Mismeasure of Man.* New York: Norton, 1981.

Graff, Harvey J. *The Literacy Myth: Cultural Integration and Social Structure in the Nineteenth Century.* New Brunswick: Transaction Publishers, 1991.

Graham, Barbara. "Assessing the Assessors: Portfolios to Document Teaching." *New Directions in Portfolio Assessment.*

Graves, Donald H., and Bonnie Sunstein. Eds. *Portfolio Portraits.* Portsmouth, NH: Heinemann, 1992.

Green, Bert F. Ed. "Issues in Testing: Coaching, Disclosure, and Ethnic Bias." *New Directions for Testing and Measurement.* San Francisco: Jossey-Bass, 1981.

Greenberg, Karen. "Validity and Reliability: Issues in the Direct Assessment of Writing." *WPA: Writing Program Administration* 16.1–2 (Fall/Winter 1992): 7–22.

Greenberg, Karen, Harvey Wiener, and Richard Donovan. "Preface." *Writing Assessment: Issues and Strategies.* Eds. Karen Greenberg, Harvey Wiener, and Richard Donovan. NY: Longman, 1986. xi–xvii.

Grego, Rhonda, and Nancy Thompson. "Writing Studio." Unpublished manuscript. Columbia, SC: Department of English, U of South Carolina.

Gumperz, John. *Discourse Strategies.* Cambridge: Cambridge UP, 1982.

———. *Language and Social Identity.* Cambridge: Cambridge UP, 1982.

Hain, Bonnie. "Portfolios and the M.A. in English." *Portfolios: Process and Product.* Eds. Pat Belanoff and Marcia Dickson. Portsmouth, NH: Boynton/Cook, 1991. 93–98.

Hairston, Maxine C. "Comment and Response." *College English* 52 (1990): 694–96.

Hamp-Lyons, Liz, and William Condon. "Questioning Assumptions About Portfolio-Based Assessment." *College Composition and Communication* 44.2 (May 1993): 176–90.

Harris, Joseph. "The Idea of Community in the Study of Writing." *College Composition and Communication* 40 (1989): 11–22.

Harrison, Susan. "Valuing Writing: Students and their Portfolios." Conference on College Composition and Communication, Boston, March 1991.

Hayes, Mary F., and Donald A. Daiker. "Using Protocol Analysis in Evaluating Responses to Student Writing." *Freshman English News.* 13.2 (Fall 1984): 1–4, 10.

Healy, Mary K. "Writing Communities: One Historical Perspective." *Teacher as Writer: Entering the Professional Conversation.* Ed. Karin L. Dahl. Urbana, IL: National Council of Teachers of English, 1992. 253–260.

Herter, Roberta J. "Writing Portfolios: Alternatives to Testing." *English Journal* 80.1 (Jan. 1991): 90.

Hilgers, Thomas. "Improving Placement Exam Equitability, Validity, and Reliability." Conference on College Composition and Communication, March 1992. Cincinnati, OH.

———. "How Children Change as Critical Evaluators of Writing: Four Three-Year Case Studies." *Research in the Teaching of English.* 20.1 (February, 1986): 36–55.

- Recommendations from summer 1993 reading are implemented in the program.
- Senior students are invited to develop personal portfolios, for which they select and revise contents (which may include pieces from other curricula, co-op work, etc.) and to which they append resume and executive summary.
- Project director counsels students about portfolio development.
- Project team publicizes personal portfolios to recruiters.
- Faculty consider whether to award certificates for portfolio achievement.
- Selected student portfolios are photocopied (with permission) for publicity, research, and assessment purposes.
- Project team and finance faculty read and describe senior portfolios and make recommendations.

Admittedly, this hastily conceived alternative bears little resemblance to a concept predicated on correlating curricular goals with specific assignments. The plan does not require the finance faculty to come to any agreement about what is to be assigned or about which curricular goals the assignments fulfill. In fact, it does not *require* any writing at all. It simply calls for including in the portfolio samples of any writing that the faculty members choose to assign in finance courses. It also significantly changes the nature of the assessment process, which would now be confined to describing the contents of the portfolios and attempting to generalize about their strengths and weaknesses without reference to any external standard. The only undisputed feature of the portfolios, which we hoped they would support as a valuable medium for demonstrating their accomplishments and capabilities to potential employers.

The one undisputed advantage of this plan over the one we originally proposed is that it was unanimously approved by the finance faculty. Insofar as it was developed in response to what we learned at the workshop, it reflects shared knowledge that we consider essential to any such collaboration.

plan such as this one, which is sensitive to the ideology of the finance ... had a chance of being accepted, so it seems fruitless to belabor its ... 's an ideal model.

...ement on the portfolio concept also had the felicitous effect ...shop to an unexpectedly productive and satisfactory ...ere to be no constraints on the kind of assignments ...ty faculty member opted to include one or more ...is or her fall courses. As we discovered in a ...labus had been altered to include writing ...ss discussion. We will undoubtedly ...eview the departmental portfolios

Hillocks, George Jr. *Research on Written Composition: New Directions for Teaching*. Urbana, IL: National Council of Teachers of English, 1986.

Hirsch, Bette. *Languages of Thought*. New York: College Entrance Examination Board, 1989.

Hoffa, Harlan. "Preparing High School Students for Admission to College Art Departments." *Art Education* 40 (1): 16–22, 1987.

Holt, Dennis, and Nancy Westrich Baker. "Portfolios as a Follow-up Option in a Proficiency-Testing Program." *Portfolios: Process and Product*. Eds. Pat Belanoff and Marcia Dickson. Portsmouth, NH: Boynton-Cook, 1991. 37–45.

Hunt, Russell A. "A Horse Named Hans, a Boy Named Shawn: The Herr von Osten Theory of Response to Writing." *Writing and Response: Theory, Practice, and Research*. Ed. Chris M. Anson. Urbana, IL: National Council of Teachers of English. 1989. 80–100.

———. "Speech Genres, Writing Genres, School Genres and Computer Genres." *Genres in Education*. Eds. Aviva Freedman and Peter Medway. Portsmouth, NH: Boynton/Cook, in press.

Huot, Brian. "A Survey of College and University Writing Placement Practices." *Writing Program Administration,* in press.

———. "Reliability, Validity, and Holistic Scoring: What We Know and What We Need to Know." *College Composition and Communication* 41.2 (May 1990): 201–13.

———. "The Literature of Direct Writing Assessment: Major Concerns and Prevailing Trends." *Review of Educational Research* 60.2 (1990): 237–263.

Huot, Brian, and Kim Lovejoy. "Revision and Portfolios: The Effects on Students' Attitudes, Process and Products." Miami University Conference on New Directions in Portfolio Assessment, Oxford, OH. October 1992.

Ingalls, Bob, and Joyce Jones. "There's a Lot of Things You Can Learn in English That You Can't Really See." *Quarterly of the National Writing Project and the Center for the Study of Writing and Literacy* 14.1 (Winter 1992): 1–4.

Johnston, Brian. *Assessing English: Helping Students to Reflect on Their Work*. Philadelphia: Open Court Press, 1983.

Joos, Martin. *The Five Clocks*. New York, Harcourt, 1961.

Keroes, Jo. "But What Do They Say? Gender and the Content of Student Writing." *Discourse Processes* 13 (1990): 243–257.

Kingston, Maxine Hong. *The Woman Warrior: Memoirs of a Girlhood Among Ghosts*. New York: Vintage, 1976.

Kirby, Dan, and Carol Kuykendall. *Mind Matters: Teaching for Thinking*. Portsmouth: Boynton/Cook, 1988.

Kirsch, Gesa. "Methodology of Pluralism: Epistemological Issues." *Method and Methodology in Composition Research*. Eds. Gesa Kirsch and Patricia Sullivan. Carbondale, IL. Southern Illinois UP, 1992. 247–269.

Kochman, Thomas. "Toward an Ethnography of Black American Speech Behavior." *Afro-American Anthropology: Contemporary Perspectives*. Eds. Norman E. Whitten, Jr. and John F. Szwed. New York: Free Press, 1970.

Kohlberg, Lawrence. "Stage and Sequence: The Cognitive-Developmental Approach to Socialization." *Handbook of Socialization Theory and Research.* Ed. D.A. Goslin. Chicago: Rand McNally, 1969. 347–480.

Lakoff, Robin. *Language and Women's Place.* New York: Harper, 1975.

Larsen, Elizabeth. "The Progress of Literacy." *Rhetoric Review* 11 (Fall 1991). 159–71.

Lawson, Bruce, Susan Sterr Ryan, and W. Ross Winterowd. *Encountering Student Texts: Interpretive Issues in Reading Student Writing.* Urbana: National Council of Teachers of English, 1989.

Lederman, Marie Jean, Susan Ryzewic, and Michael Ribaudo. *Assessment and Improvement of the Academic Skills of Entering Freshman: A National Survey.* NY: CUNY Instructional Resource Center, 1983.

Lucas, Catherine. "Introduction: Writing Portfolios—Changes and Challenges." *Portfolios in the Writing Classroom: An Introduction.* Ed. Kathleen Blake Yancey. Urbana: National Council of Teachers of English, 1992.

Lunsford, Andrea, Helen Moglen, and James Slevin. Eds. *The Future of Doctoral Studies in English.* New York: MLA, 1989.

Lunsford, Andrea A. "The Past—and Future—of Writing Assessment." *Writing Assessment: Issues and Strategies.* Eds. Karen Greenberg, Harvey Wiener, and Richard Donovan. NY: Longman, 1986. 1–12.

Lyons, Nona. "Two Perspectives: On Self, Relations, and Morality." *Harvard Educational Review* 2 (1983): 125–145.

McCarthy, Lucille Parkinson. "A Stranger in Strange Lands: A College Student Writing Across the Curriculum." *Research in the Teaching of English* 21, 3 (1987): 233–65.

McClelland, Kathy. "Portfolios: Solution to a Problem." *Portfolios: Process and Products.* Eds. Pat Belanoff and Marcia Dickson. Portsmouth, NH: Boynton/ Cook, 1991. 165–173.

Madaus, George. "The History of Testing in American Schools." Presentation to the Institute on New Modes of Assessment. Harvard University, July 8–13, 1990. [cited in Wolf, Dennie P., Janet Bixby, John Glen III and Howard Gardner. "To Use Their Minds Well: Investigating New Forms of Students Assessment." *Review of Research in Education* 17. Washington, D.C.: American Educational Research Association (1991):55.]

Mestre, J. "The Problem With Problems: Hispanic Students and Math." *Bilingual Journal* 32 (1984): 15–19.

Miller, Emily, and Stephen RiCharde. "The Relationship between the Portfolio Methods of Teaching Writing and Measures of Personality and Motivation." Conference on College Composition and Communication, Boston, March 1991.

Miller, Susan. *Textual Carnivals: The Politics of Composition.* Carbondale, IL: Southern Illinois UP, 1992.

Moss, Pamela A. "Shifting Conceptions of Validity in Educational Measurement: Implications for Performative Assessment." *Review of Educational Research* 62 (Fall 1992): 229–258.

Murphy, Sandra, and Mary Ann Smith. "Looking into Portfolios." *Portfolios in the Writing Classroom: An Introduction*. Urbana, IL: National Council of Teachers of English, 1992.

———. *Writing Portfolios: A Bridge from Teaching to Assessment*. Markham, Ontario, Canada: Pippin Publishing Limited, 1991.

New World Dictionary. Ed. David B. Guralnik. 2nd College Edition. New York: Simon and Schuster, 1980.

The New York Review of Books, September 24, 1992.

Newkirk, Thomas. "Looking for Trouble: A Way to Unmask Our Readings." *College English* 46 (Dec. 1984): 755–66.

North, Stephen. *The Making of Knowledge in Composition: Portrait of an Emerging Field*. Portsmouth, NH: Boynton/Cook, 1987.

Odell, Lee, and Dixie Goswami. "Writing in a Non-Academic Setting." *Research in the Teaching of English* 16.3 (1982): 201–224.

Padilla, Amado M. "Cultural Considerations: Hispanic-American." *Testing, Teaching and Learning*. Report of a conference on research on testing. Eds. Ralph W. Tyler and Sheldon H. White. Washington, D.C.: National Institute of Education, (1979): 219–43.

Paulson, F. Leon, Pearl R. Paulson, and Carol A. Meyer. "What Makes a Portfolio a Portfolio?" *Educational Leadership* 48.5 (Feb. 1991): 60–63.

Pearson, P. David. "How Can Literacy Best Be Assessed?" Keynote address. California Reading Association Summer Institute: Research in Reading-Language: Implications and Applications, June 1992. Lake Arrowhead, Ca.

Perry, William. *Forms of Intellectual and Ethical Development in the College Years*. New York: Holt, Rinehart, and Winston, 1970.

Phelps, Louis Wetherbee. "Images of Student Writing: The Deep Structure of Teacher Response." *Writing and Response: Theory, Practice, and Research*. Ed. Chris M. Anson. Urbana, IL: National Council of Teachers of English, 1989. 37–67.

Pratt, Mary Louise. "Arts of the Contact Zone." *Profession* 91: 33–40.

Purves, Alan C. Ed. *International Comparisons and Educational Reform*. Alexandra, VA: Association for Supervision and Curriculum Development, 1989.

———. "The Teacher as Reader: An Anatomy." *College English*. 46.3 (March 1984): 259–65.

Purves, Alan, and Sauli Takala. Eds. *An International Perspective on the Evaluation of Written Communication*. Evaluation in Education: An International Review Series, Vol. 5, no. 3. New York: Pergamon Press, 1982.

Reither, James A. "The Writing *Student* as Researcher: Learning From Our Students." *The Writing Teacher as Researcher: Essays in the Theory and Practice of Class-Based Research:* Eds. Donald A. Daiker and Max Morenberg. Portsmouth, NH: Boynton/Cook, 1991. 247–255.

Rief, Linda. *Seeking Diversity*. Portsmouth, NH: Heinemann, 1991.

Rincon, Edward T. "Test Speededness, Test Anxiety, and Test Performance: A Comparison of Mexican American and Anglo American High School Juniors." Diss.

University of Texas at Austin, 1979. [Dissertation Abstracts International, 40, 5772A]

Rodriguez, Richard. *Hunger of Memory.* New York: David R. Godine, 1981.

Roemer, Marjorie, Lucille M. Schultz, and Russel K. Durst. "Portfolios and the Process of Change." *College Composition and Communication.* 42.4 (December 1991): 455–469.

Romano, Tom. "A Time for Immersion, A Time for Reflection: The Multigenre Research Project and Portfolio Assessment." NCTE Annual Spring Conference, March 1991. Indianapolis.

Rubin, Donald L., and Kathryn Greene. "Gender-Typical Style in Written Language." *Research in the Teaching of English* 26 (1992): 7–40.

Said, Edward W. *The World, the Text, and the Critic.* Cambridge: Harvard UP, 1983.

Samuda, Ronald J. *Psychological Testing of American Minorities: Issues and Consequences.* New York: Dodd, 1975.

Schell, Eileen E. "Teaching Under Unusual Conditions: Graduate Teaching Assistants and the CCCC's 'Progress Report'." *College Composition and Communication* 43.2 (May 1992): 164–67.

Scholes, Robert. "Contemporary Composition Theory: Brilliant and/or Counterproductive." Conference on Composition and Communication, March 1990. Chicago.

Schön, Donald A. *Educating the Reflective Practitioner: Toward a New Design for Teaching and Learning in the Professions.* San Francisco: Jossey-Bass, 1987.

———. *The Reflective Practitioner: How Professionals Think in Action.* New York: Basic Books, 1983.

Schubert, William H. "Teacher Lore: A Basis for Understanding Praxis." *Stories Lives Tell: Narrative and Dialogue in Education.* Eds. Carol Witherell and Ned Noddings. New York: Teachers College Press, 1991. 207–233.

Scribner, Sylvia. "Literacy in Three Metaphors." *American Journal of Education* 93 (Nov. 1984). 6–21.

Shor, Ira. "Libertory Education." Canadian Council of Teachers of English Annual Conference, April 1991. Montreal.

———. *Critical Teaching and Everyday Life.* Chicago: U of Chicago P, 1987.

Shulman, Lee. "Paradigms and Research Programs in the Study of Teaching: A Contemporary Perspective." *Handbook of Research on Teaching.* Ed. Merlin C. Whitrock. New York: Macmillan, 1986. 3–36.

Sirc, Geoffrey. "Gender and 'Writing Formulations' in First-Year Narratives." *Freshman English News* 18.1 (1989): 4–11.

Slevin, James F., Keith Fort, and Patricia E. O'Connor. "Georgetown University." *Programs That Work: Models and Methods for Writing Across the Curriculum.* Eds. Toby Fulwiler and Art Young. Portsmouth, NH: Boynton/Cook, 1990. 9–28.

Smith, Barbara Herrnstein. *Contingencies of Value: Alternative Perspectives for Critical Theory.* Cambridge: Harvard UP, 1988.

———. "Contingencies of Value." *Canons.* Ed. Robert von Hallberg. Chicago: U of Chicago P, 1984. 5–39.

Smith, Mary-Ann, and Sandra Murphy. "Could You Please Come and Do Portfolio Assessment for Us?" *Quarterly of the National Writing Project and the Center for the Study of Writing and Literacy* 14.1 (Winter 1992): 14–17.

Sommers, Jeffrey. "Bringing Practice in line with Theory: Using Portfolio Grading in the Composition Classroom." *Portfolios: Process and Product.* Eds. Pat Belanoff and Marcia Dickson. Portsmouth, NH: Boynton/Cook, 1991. 153–164.

———. "The Writer's Memo: Collaboration, Response, and Development." *Writing and Response: Theory, Practice, and Research.* Ed. Chris M. Anson. Urbana, IL: National Council of Teachers of English, 1989. 174–186.

Sommers, Jeffrey, Laurel Black, Donald A. Daiker and Gail Stygall. "The Challenges of Rating Portfolios: What WPAs Can Expect." *WPA* 17. 1–2 (1993): 7–29.

Sommers, Nancy. "Responding to Student Writing." *College Composition and Communication* 33 (1982): 148–56.

Spender, Dale. *Man Made Language.* London: Routledge, 1980.

Stager, Elizabeth. Student Portfolio included in *The Best of Miami's Portfolios.* Eds. Donald A. Daiker, Jeffrey Sommers, Gail Stygall, and Laurel Black. Oxford, OH: Miami University Department of English, 1990.

Standards for Educational and Psychological Tests. Washington: American Psychological Association, 1985.

"Standards for English: Project Now Under Way." *The Council Chronicle* 2.1 (September 1992): 1–2.

Stern, Caroline. "Writing Portfolios: A Resource for Teaching and Assessment." Conference on College Composition and Communication, March 1991. Boston, MA.

Stock, Patricia Lambert. "The Teaching Portfolio: Documenting the Scholarship of Teaching." New Directions in Portfolio Assessment: Miami University, October 1992. Oxford, OH.

Stotsky, S. "From the Editor." *Research in the Teaching of English* 26.3 (October 1992): 245–48.

Sullivan, Patricia A. "Writing in the Graduate Curriculum: Literary Criticism as Composition." *Journal of Advanced Composition* 11:2 (Fall 1991): 283–99.

Tchudi, Stephen. *Teaching Writing in the Content Areas: College Level.* Washington, D.C.: National Education Association, 1986.

Trimbur, John. "Consensus and Difference in Collaborative Learning." *College English* 51 (October 1989): 601–16.

———. "Cultural Studies and Teaching Writing." *Focuses* 1:2 (Fall 1988): 5–18.

Tsang, Chui Lim. "Informal Assessment of Asian Americans: A Cultural and Linguistic Mismatch?" *Test Policy and Test Performance: Education, Language and Culture.* Ed. Bernard R. Gifford. Boston: Kluwer Academic Publishers, 1989.

United States. Cong. House Select Committee on Children, Youth, and Families. *College Education: Paying More and Getting Less.* 102nd Cong. Washington: GPO, 1992.

Valencia, Sheila, William McGinley, and P. David Pearson. *Assessing Reading and Writing: Building A More Complete Picture for Middle School Assessment.*

Technical Report No. 500. Urbana, IL: Illinois U Center for the Study of Reading, 1990.

Vidal, Jane. "Teacher Preparation in a Multicultural Society." *Liberal Studies News-letter*. San Diego: San Diego State U, University Advising Center (January, 1990): 1–2.

Vitanza, Victor. "An Open Letter to My 'Colligs': On Paraethics, Pararhetorics, and the Hysterical Turn." *PRETEXT* 11.3–4 (1990): 237–87.

Watkins, Evan. *Work Time: English Departments and the Circulation of Value*. Stanford: Stanford UP, 1989.

Weinbaum, Kerry, "Portfolios as a Vehicle for Student Empowerment and Teacher Change." *Portfolios: Process and Product*. Eds. Pat Belanoff and Marcia Dickson. Portsmouth, NH: Boynton/Cook, 1991. 206–214.

Weiser, I. "Portfolio Practice and Assessment for Collegiate Basic Writers." *Portfolios in the Writing Classroom: An Introduction*. Ed. Kathleen Blake Yancey. Urbana, IL: National Council of Teachers of English, 1992. 89–102.

White, Edward M. Rev. of *Portfolios: Process and Product*, Ed. Pat Belanoff and Marcia Dickson. *College Composition and Communication* 43.4 (December 1992): 537–39.

———. *Assigning, Responding, Evaluating*. 2nd Ed. New York: St. Martin's, 1992.

———. "Language and Reality in Writing Assessment." *College Composition and Communication* 41 (1990): 187–200.

———. *Teaching and Assessing Writing*. San Francisco: Jossey-Bass, 1985.

———. "Teaching and Assessing Writing in the Future." Conference on College Composition and Communication, March 1992. Cincinnati, OH.

———. "Portfolios as an Assessment Concept." Miami University Conference on New Directions in Portfolio Assessment, Oxford Ohio. October 1992.

———. "The Practices and Politics of Holistic Essay Scoring: The Past as a Guide to the Future." Conference on College Composition and Communication, March 1991.

White, Edward, and L. Thomas. "Racial Minorities and Writing Skills: Assessment in the California State University and Colleges." *College English* 42 (1981): 276–283.

Wiggins, Grant. "A True Test: Toward More Authentic and Equitable Assessment." *Phi Delta Kappan* 70 (May 1989): 703–713.

Williamson, Michael M. "An Introduction to Holistic Scoring: The Social, Historical, and Theoretical Context for Writing Assessment." *Validating Holistic Scoring for Writing Assessment*. Eds. Michael M. Williamson and Brian Huot. Cresskill, NJ: Hampton, 1993.

Wiseman, Stephen. "Symposium: The Use of Essays on Selection of 11+." *British Journal of Educational Psychology* 26 (March 1956): 172–179.

Witte, Stephen P., Mary Trachsel, and Keith Walters. "Literacy and the Direct Assessment of Writing: A Diachronic Perspective." *Writing Assessment: Issues and Strategies*. Eds. Karen Greenberg, Harvey Wiener, and Richard Donovan. NY: Longman, 1986. 13–34.

Witherell, Carol, and Ned Noddings. Eds. *Stories Lives Tell: Narrative and Dialogue in Education*. New York: Teachers College Press, 1991.

Wolf, Kenneth P. "The Schoolteacher's Portfolio: Practical Issues in Design, Implementation and Evaluation." *Phi Delta Kappan,* October, 1991. 129–136.

———. *Teaching Portfolios: Synthesis of Research and Annotated Bibliography*. San Francisco: Far West Laboratory for Educational Research and Development, 1991.

Wolkomir, Richard. "The Quiet Revolution in 'Hand Talk.' " *Smithsonian* 23.4 (July 1991). 30–41.

Yancey, Kathleen Blake. "Preface" and "Portfolios in the Writing Classroom" in *Portfolios in the Writing Classroom: An Introduction*. Ed. Kathleen Blake Yancey. Urbana, IL: National Council of Teachers of English, 1992. vii, 102–116.

———. "Still Hopeful After All These Years: Teachers as Agents of Change." *Michigan Journal of Language Arts* 81 (Spring 1992): 84–90.

Contributors

Chris M. Anson is Associate Professor of English and Director of Composition at the University of Minnesota. Among his books are *Writing in Context* (Holt, Rinehart, & Winston, 1988), *Writing and Response: Theory, Practice and Research* (NCTE, 1989), *A Field Guide to Writing* (HarperCollins, 1991), *Writing Across the Curriculum* (Greenwood, 1993), and *Scenarios for Teaching Writing: Contexts for Discussion and Reflective Practice* (NCTE, 1993). Anson's articles have appeared in numerous journals and edited collections. His research interests include writing to learn, response to writing, and the nature of literacy in and out of schools.

John Beall is the English Department Chair at Collegiate School for Boys in Manhattan. A graduate of Miami University and Cornell University, he has taught in Dallas, Texas, and in Canterbury, England. Beall's previous publications include essays in *Independent School,* an essay on "Gauguin's Uncanny Nudes" in *The Rutgers Art Review,* and poems in various journals. He is currently working on an essay about the sculptural carvings on the facade of the cathedral at Orvieto designed by Lorenzo Maitani in the fourteenth century.

Pat Belanoff is Associate Professor of English and Director of Writing Programs at the State University of New York at Stony Brook. She is the co-author (with Peter Elbow) of *A Community of Writers* and of *The Right Handbook*. With Marcia Dickson she co-edited the first major collection of essays on portfolios, *Portfolios: Process and Product*. She holds a Ph.D. from New York University and writes intermittently on the women of Old English poetry.

James Berlin is Professor of English at Purdue University. He is a former elementary school teacher, former Director of Composition at the University of Cincinnati, and former director of the Kansas Writing Project. Berlin authored *Writing Instruction in Nineteenth-Century American Colleges* and *Rhetoric and Reality: Writing Instruction in American Colleges, 1900–1985*. He and Michael Vivion recently co-edited *Cultural Studies in the English Classroom*.

Laurel Black is an Assistant Professor of English at Saint John Fisher College in Rochester, New York. While a graduate student and research associate at Miami University, she was one of the co-directors of the Writing Portfolio Program. Black is interested in assessment, sociolinguistics, and the ways in which gender, race, and class are part of teaching, theory, and research.

Robert L. Broad is currently completing his Ph.D. in Composition and Rhetoric at Miami University in Oxford, Ohio. His dissertation is entitled *Working in the City: Building Community and Negotiating Difference in a Portfolio Assessment Program*. In his efforts to integrate theory and research into teachers' everyday work, he has presented talks and workshops to NCTE, CCCC, the American Association of Higher Education, and National Writing Project sites in Washington, D.C. and Ohio. Broad's work has also appeared in *Works and Days, African American Review,* and other journals.

Agnes A. Cardoni, a doctoral candidate in English at Lehigh University, is on the faculty of the Wilkes-Barre (PA) Area School District. She is the author of articles and poetry published by the *Pennsylvania Writing Project Newsletter* and the *Northeast Pennsylvania Writing Council Newsletter.* Cardoni is at work on her dissertation, a study of ethical coming-of-age in the fiction of Margaret Atwood, Gail Godwin, Alice Munro, and Tillie Olsen.

William Condon is the Associate Director for Instruction at the University of Michigan's English Composition Board, where he pursues interests extending the usefulness of portfolio assessment, using computers in teaching writing, and developing software to support writing across the curriculum. He and Liz Hamp-Lyons are currently writing a book about portfolio assessment.

Glenda Conway is a doctoral candidate in rhetoric and composition at the University of Louisville, where she also teaches courses in the writing program. Her primary research interest includes issues related to reader and writer ethics. She is currently working on a dissertation that focuses on judicial writing.

Donald A. Daiker teaches courses in composition, American literature, the short story, and the teaching of writing at Miami University. He is a co-founder of the Miami University Center for the Study of Writing and the Miami University Portfolio Writing Program, which he directs. With his colleague Max Morenberg, he is co-editor of *The Writing Teacher as Researcher* and of *Sentence Combining: A Rhetorical Perspective.*

Russel K. Durst is Associate Professor at the University of Cincinnati. His publications include *Exploring Texts: The Role of Discussion and Writing in the Teaching and Learning of Literature* (edited with George Newell, 1992), as well as articles and reviews on composition theory and research in *CCC, English Education, Research in the Teaching of English, Review of Educational Research, Writing Project Quarterly, Written Communication,* and other publications. Winner of the NCTE Promising Researcher Award in 1987, his current research focuses on the development of students' analytic writing abilities.

Peter Elbow is Professor of English at the University of Massachusetts at Amherst. He has taught at M.I.T., Franconia College, Evergreen State College, and SUNY Stony Brook—where for five years he directed the Writing Program. He is author of *Oppositions in Chaucer, Writing Without Teachers, Writing With Power, Embracing Contraries, What is English?,* and a textbook (with Pat Belanoff), *A Community of Writers.*

Cheryl Forbes began to teach writing at Calvin College in Grand Rapids, Michigan, after seventeen years in publishing as editor and executive. In March 1992, she received her Ph.D. from Michigan State University and is now Assistant Professor of Writing and Rhetoric at Hobart and William Smith Colleges in Geneva, New York. Her latest book of essays, *Notes of a Reluctant Pilgrim,* was published in 1992. Her recent articles include "Eighty Years on Main Street," a study of the L.L. Bean anniversary catalogue, and "African American Women: Voices of Literacy and Literate Voices."

Rebecca Fraser is the Coordinator of the Writing Center at Nassau Community College, where she also teaches writing classes. Fraser received her Ph.D. in English Education from New York University in 1991. Particularly interested in teacher education through reflection and study of practice, she works closely with a staff of twenty-five professional Writing Consultants at NCC to examine the complex issues in student/consultant learning, teaching, writing, and language.

Sharon J. Hamilton (formerly Hamilton-Wieler) is Associate Professor of English and Adjunct Professor in the School of Education at Indiana University at Indianapolis (IUPUI). She has published several articles on writing across the curriculum, collaborative learning, and the development of voice in journals in the United States, Canada, and England. Hamilton is currently working on a case study exploring the role of literacy in leading an abused child from a dismal, self-destructive existence to a productive life as an English educator.

Liz Hamp-Lyons is Associate Professor of English at the University of Colorado at Denver, where she directs the Composition Program and coordinates the MA in Applied Language. Her research interests include composition theory and pedagogy, and language testing, with a particular focus on second language writing pedagogy and assessment.

Brian Huot teaches graduate and undergraduate courses in the English Department at the University of Louisville. His work on writing assessment has appeared in *College Composition and Communication, Review of Educational Research,* and other journals. He has recently co-edited *Validating Holistic Scoring for Writing Assessment: Theoretical and Empirical Foundations.*

Carl R. Lovitt is Associate Professor of English at Clemson University and Director of the Pearce Center for Professional Communication, an endowed center that oversees a wide range of interdisciplinary and outreach program to improve students' communication skills. His recent research focuses on approaches to assessing cross-curricular communication programs. He is also preparing a book-length study of narrative strategies in confessional fiction; several of his essays on this subject have recently been published in professional journals and books.

Sandra Murphy is an Associate Professor in the Division of Education at the University of California, Davis and Director of the Center for Cooperative Research and Extension Services for Schools. She has written several articles on writing assessment, and two books: *Writing Portfolios: A Bridge from Teaching to Assessment,* co-authored with Mary Ann Smith, and *Designing Writing Tasks for the Assessment of Writing,* co-authored with Leo Ruth. She consults with teachers, schools, and K-12 school districts on the design of portfolio assessment programs.

James A. Reither and **Russell A. Hunt** teach in the English Department at St. Thomas University, where they have been arguing about teaching, learning, language, and literature, and collaborating on projects, presentations, and publications since the late sixties. Both have delivered papers and seminars, conducted workshops on these topics, and published in a wide range of journals and edited collections. They are joint founders of the Canadian Association for the Study of Writing and Reading and its annual Inkshed Working Conference.

Nedra Reynolds is an Assistant Professor at the University of Rhode Island, where she teaches courses in writing, composition studies, and rhetorical theory. Reynolds also serves on a number of graduate students' committees. Her work on rhetorical ethos appears in recent issues of *Rhetoric Review* and *Ethos: New Essays in Rhetorical and Critical Theory*. In addition to serving as a rater and chief reader in holistic evaluation sessions, she has written about assessment practices in *Writing Program Administration* and *Journal of Advanced Composition*.

Marjorie Roemer is Associate Professor at Rhode Island College. Her articles on literary theory, composition, portfolio assessment, postmoderism, and the work of John Barth appear in such journals as *College English, The Harvard Educational Review, CCC, English Education, Journal of Teaching Writing,* and *Twentieth Century Literature*. Her most current work concerns critical pedagogy and a reception-theory of the classroom.

Tom Romano teaches courses in creative writing and English Education at Utah State University. Before coming to USU, he taught high school for seventeen years in Ohio. His book, *Clearing the Way: Working With Teenage Writers* (Heinemann), is based upon that experience. Tom has also written articles, book chapters, and poetry about teaching writing and learning to write.

Lucille M. Schultz is Associate Professor at the University of Cincinnati. In journals including *CCC, Written Communication,* and *The Journal of Teaching Writing,* she has written essays on the history and dynamics of school-college collaboration, on writing assessment, and on literacy acquisition. She has also published studies of individual works by Hugh Henry Brackenridge, William Styron, and Mark Twain. Schultz is currently studying early nineteenth-century figures in composition, especially John Frost and other authors of little known textbooks.

Charles I. Schuster is Professor of English and Comparative Literature at the University of Wisonsin-Milwaukee, where he directed the writing program from 1985–1993. Vice-President/President-Elect of the Council of Writing Program Administrators, he has published on Bakhtin, rhetorical theory, and nonfictional prose, particularly the writings of Richard Selzer and John McPhee. He is co-editor of *The Politics of Writing Instruction: Post-secondary* (Boynton/Cook) and *Speculations: Readings in Culture, Identity, and Values* (Blair).

David W. Smit is Associate Professor and Director of the Freshman Writing Program at Kansas State University. His articles on stylistics, collaborative writing, and rhetorical theory have appeared in the *Henry James Review, Style,* the *Journal of Advanced Composition,* and *Rhetoric Review*. Smit has also published two other pieces on the portfolio system at Kansas State: one in *WPA: Writing Program Administration;* the other, co-authored with Patricia Kolonosky and Katheryn Seltzer, in Belanoff and Dickson's *Portfolios: Process and Product.*

Jeffrey Sommers, Professor of English at Miami University-Middletown, has published essays on assessment and responding to student writing in Belanoff and Dickson's *Portfolios: Process and Product,* Anson's *Writing and Response, CCC, Freshman English News,* and *Teaching English in the Two-Year College.* He is the author of *Model Voices,* co-author of *The Writer's Options,* 5th ed., and co-author of the forthcoming textbook, *The Two-Year College Reader* (St. Martin's Press).

Janet Wright Starner is currently working on a Ph.D. in English at Lehigh University, where she teaches Freshman Composition and Literature. She has a particular interest in the collage form, offering it to her students, along with collaborative activities, as a new way to envision the art of composing. She and her husband Jed Starner live in Kutztown, Pennsylvania, with their daughters.

Gail Stygall is Assistant Professor of English Language and Rhetoric in the Department of English, University of Washington, where she teaches courses in writing, English language, discourse analysis, and rhetoric of the disciplines. Her work on legal discourse, *Trial Language,* is forthcoming from John Benjamins and her essays have appeared in the *Journal of Basic Writing,* the *Journal of Teaching Writing,* and as a chapter in *Textual Dynamics of the Professions.*

William H. Thelin is teaching at Indiana University of Pennsylvania while he completes his Ph.D. in Rhetoric and Linguistics. His main interests are in the politics of pedagogy and its relationship to English Departments, especially in the teaching of writing. Thelin has previously been published in *College Composition and Communication* and in the ERIC data base. He hopes to resume fiction writing once he earns his degree.

Irwin Weiser is Associate Professor of English and Director of Composition at Purdue University, where he regularly teaches the practicum for new teaching assistants. He has published most recently in *Composition Studies, WPA,* and *The Journal of Teaching Writing.*

Edward M. White is Professor of English at California State University, San Bernardino, where he has served prolonged periods as department chair and Coordinator of the Upper-Division University Writing Program. For five years he has directed the Consultant/Evaluator service of the Council of Writing Program Administrators. White's books include *Teaching and Assessing Writing* (1984; rev. ed. 1994), *Developing Successful College Writing Programs* (1989), and *Assigning, Responding, and Evaluating* (1992).

Kathleen Blake Yancey is Assistant Professor of English and Co-Director of the Writing Project at the University of North Carolina at Charlotte. She teaches courses in writing, teacher preparation, and writing assessment, and she works with teachers across the country to design model portfolio programs. Editor of *Portfolios in the Classroom: An Introduction,* she also co-edits *Portfolio Newsletter* and is currently working on a linked set of three anthologies on portfolios, *Portfolios in Practice: Voices from the Fields.*

Art Young is Campbell Chair in Technical Communication and Professor of English and Professor of Engineering at Clemson University. He coordinates the communication-across-the-curriculum program at Clemson and frequently conducts interdisciplinary faculty workshops for colleges and universities. He co-edited, with Toby Fulwiler, three books on writing across the curriculum at the college level and, with Pamela B. Farrell and Anne Ruggles Gere, a forthcoming book (Boynton/Cook) on writing across the curriculum at the secondary level.

Also available from Heinemann-Boynton/Cook . . .

Portfolios
Process and Product
Edited by **Pat Belanoff & Marcia Dickson**
Foreword by **Peter Elbow**

This book, the first to focus exclusively on portfolio assessment, is both practical and theoretical, broad in scope, offering places to start rather than claiming to be definitive. The articles, all by teachers with considerable experience in using portfolio grading, are free of jargon, making sound composition and assessment theory available to every reader, regardless of what level of writing is taught. Because the book covers the most recent developments, readers can expect a thorough introduction to portfolio practice and many suggestions for implementing a portfolio program. The diversity of projects described will allow readers to compose a system that is ideally suited to their own situation.

Portfolios will be particularly useful for college-level teachers, English departments developing exit or proficiency examinations, writing project directors, and high school personnel responsible for assessment programs.

Boynton/Cook / 0-86709-275-0 / 1991 / 352pp / Paper

Portfolio Portraits
Edited by **Donald H. Graves & Bonnie S. Sunstein**

"Portfolio Portraits *is the best book I have seen on portfolios."*
 —The Whole Language Advocate, Feb/Mar. 1993

At professional conferences, educational experts recommend portfolios as
alternatives to grading. Professional journals recognize portfolios as new
systems for evaluating teacher and student performance. Several states are
using portfolio assessments for entire school populations.

Portfolio Portraits allows portfolios some breathing space before they are
frozen into a definition or mandate. The book offers unique portraits of
portfolio keepers — from first graders to university sophomores and
graduate students, from teachers in graduate classes to administrators in
public schools — as they learn how to use portfolios, and the reader views
that learning process. The book is divided into three sections. The first
offers portraits of classrooms working with portfolios. The second makes
some broader observations of portfolio keeping itself — as an established
collecting practice in other fields, as a large-scale assessment technique for
entire school systems, and as a teacher's means of instruction and evaluation. The third portrays four very different portfolio keepers: a superintendent, a college senior, and two second-grade boys.

Portfolio Portraits invites readers to join the twelve contributors and the
writers they portray, to experiment with them as they work with portfolios.
Keeping a portfolio is a long and disciplined process, but for those teachers
and students who are willing to make decisions for themselves, portfolios
can be intimate records of personal literacy histories. The reward is worth
the struggle as portfolios not only catalogue successes and instructive
failures but become inextricably tied to the very definition of literacy.

Heinemann / 0-435-08727-4 / 1992 / 212pp / Paper